LEGAL DEVELOPMENT AND CONSTITUTIONAL CHANGE IN SIERRA LEONE
(1787-1971)

by

W. S. Marcus Jones
Ph.D. (Lond.), J.S.D. (Yale)
of the Honourable Society
of Gray's Inn.

Barrister and Solicitor
of the Supreme Court
of Sierra Leone

Associate Professor of Law,
Fourah Bay College,
University of Sierra Leone.

September, 1981

ARTHUR H. STOCKWELL LTD.
Elms Court   Ilfracombe
Devon

© W. S. Marcus Jones, 1988
First published in Great Britain, 1988

All rights reserved.
No part of this publication may be reproduced or transmitted in any form or by any means, electronic or mechanical, including photocopy, recording, or any information storage and retrieval system, without permission in writing from the copyright holder.

This book is dedicated in grateful appreciation to the memory of my parents
EDWIN MARCUS JONES and
HENRIETTA JOKO JOHNSON JONES

ISBN 0 7223 2210-0
Printed in Great Britain by
Arthur H. Stockwell Ltd.
Elms Court   Ilfracombe
Devon

PREFACE

This book is a revision for publication of my thesis submitted to London University for the award of a Ph.D Degree in Law. The primary purpose of this book is to record the legal and constitutional history of Sierra Leone from the founding of the Settlement in 1787 to the birth of the Republic in 1971. The justification for its publication is twofold. Firstly, there is no comprehensive publication of the legal or constitutional history of Sierra Leone. This book therefore breaks new ground in the published literature on Sierra Leone. Secondly, I have been teaching at Fourah Bay College, the University of Sierra Leone since 1961. Much of the material required for the Courses on Sierra Leone Constitutional Law and the Sierra Leone Legal System can only be obtained from original sources, such as the archives at the University, the Records of the Public Records Office in London or other private collections. A lot of relevant material is now brought together in one book for the first time and it should prove invaluable for future students, teachers and legal practitioners.

Over the years, I spent much of my vacations and my own personal funds in collecting the material and writing out the thesis. In spite of my teaching and professional commitments I found time to do the typing myself. My family were very understanding and supportive throughout, and it is to them, my wife Anne, and my daughters, Linda, Alison and Kim that I wish to express my profound gratitude and appreciation for their tolerance and co-operation at all times. Sierra Leoneans are a peaceful and law-abiding people. It is my profound hope and prayer that the publication of this book will lead to a more helpful understanding of the country and its peoples and the forces and events which culminated in the Independent Republic which exists today.

W.S.M.J.
Freetown
December — 1987

CONTENTS

		Page
1.	Introduction	7
2.	Plans for the Establishment of the Province of Freedom	15
3.	The Common Law in Sierra Leone and the Nationality of Settlers	28
4.	From Independence to Colonial Rule	33
5.	The Government of the Settlement 1791-1807	46
6.	The Government of Sierra Leone 1808-1896	94
7.	The 1924 Constitution	131
8.	Constitutional Changes 1951-1956	180
9.	From Independence to Republicanism 1961-1971	197
10.	The Republican Constitution 1971	227
11.	A Brief History of the Legal Profession	246
	Bibliography	250
	Index of Statutes	253
	Appendices I — XI	256

FOREWORD

I am very glad to have the opportunity of writing a foreword to Marcus Jones' account of legal development and constitutional change in Sierra Leone from 1787-1971. I have known Marcus since the late 1950s when I was a young lecturer and he a slightly less young student at the University of Birmingham. It was clear then that he had the capacity to make a major contribution to the legal life of his country. Much has changed since in the succeeding 30 years both in British universities and in West Africa, but it is pleasing to note that the quality of Marcus's work is not among the changes.

George Eliot said that "the happiest women, like the happiest nations, have no history". It is clear from the reading of this book that Sierra Leone has a history, but it is one that is deplorably little known, at least outside Sierra Leone. The pre-independence constitutional history is both complex and unique; the post-independence development no less so. It deserves to be widely known. This book will make it so.

BRISTOL.
March 1988. *Michael Furmston*

CHAPTER I

LEGAL DEVELOPMENT AND CONSTITUTIONAL CHANGE IN SIERRA LEONE FROM 1787-1971

INTRODUCTION
After about a century and a half of direct British rule, Sierra Leone became an Independent Country within the British Commonwealth on the 27th April, 1961. In 1971, it transformed itself into a Republic within the Commonwealth. Prior to these historic events, the country had experienced various forms of government. At its inception in 1787 it was an independent State. Thereafter it was ruled by a Company of Merchants and finally it became a multiple dependency — a Colony and Protectorate — of the United Kingdom of Great Britain and Ireland. It now forms a single constitutional unit within the world community of States.

The establishment of its political and legal Institutions antedates those of many of the former British possessions and certainly all of those in West Africa. Sierra Leone's history and the development of its constitutions is unique in many respects. It is largely unparalleled in British Colonial history. In the early nineteenth century, Sierra Leone became the centre of Government for all the British possessions on the West Coast of Africa.

The rich and colourful history of Sierra Leone's legal and constitutional developments has not as yet been recorded. This work will therefore attempt to set in its true perspective and against the history of the country, the important legal and constitutional changes which have taken place since the establishment of the territory as a home for the liberated blacks who found sanctuary in the United Kingdom in the eighteenth century. An attempt will be made to demonstrate that Sierra Leone is a classic example of the theoretical assumption that a country's constitution is usually the product of its past history and should be reflective of its primary objectives and future aspirations.

Sierra Leone's history can be traced back to the time of Hanno the Cartharginian, that is to say, around 500 to 450 BC. Some records exist of the country's contacts with Norman traders from Rouen and Dieppe in the period 1364-65. It is reported that Pedro da Cintra, the famed explorer, called there in 1462.[1] Sierra Leone's association with Great Britain was, in any case, firmly established by reason of trade relationships which had been formed through the Royal African Company from the year 1672. "SIERRA LEONA" as the territory was then known, achieved notoriety as a rendezvous for pirates and it was also well known as a slave trading centre from the sixteenth to the eighteenth centuries. Sir John Hawkins, the notorious explorer and infamous slave dealer visited the shores of Sierra Leone and exported Africans therefrom in 1562 and later years during which he was avidly engaged in that most inhuman of practices, the trafficking in slaves. In Sierra Leone at that time there were in existence a number of tribal governments, but there are no reliable records how these respective governments were organised. However, from available material, it is undisputed that a tribal system was in existence with the chief at the head of the administration supported by his subordinates who fulfilled specific functions.[2] Since the commerce in slaves would not have thrived without the express sanction and approval of the chiefs, it is fair to say that they approved of the trafficking in human beings. In fact there was prevalent at that time a form of domestic slavery among the inhabitants of the territory and so with or without the express sanction of the chiefs and tribal authorities, the local people ensured that slavery was an acceptable feature of commerce in Sierra Leone.

The cause celebre which took place in London and which led to the founding of the Settlement of Sierra Leone was the case of Somerset-v-Stewart.[3] That case raised the open question — for it had not by then been decided by English law, although it had been discussed before in Strong's case — whether a person could, in England, be held in servitude by another as his slave, or as his property, a mere chattel. The facts arose in this way. Jonathan Strong, a slave owned by one David Lisle, had been subjected to much brutality and then abandoned sick, hungry and destitute in the streets of London. Granville Sharpe found him and rescued him, sent him to hospital and nursed him back to health. About two years afterwards, David Lisle found him and claimed him as his property. He recaptured him and sold him again into slavery. He was purchased by a Jamaican slave dealer named John Kerr.[4] Upon discovering what had happened, Sharpe was most distressed. He fiercely resisted David Lisle's claim to ownership of Strong and resolved to institute legal proceedings, if need be, to ensure Strong's freedom. He consulted his legal advisers, notably, Sir James Eyre, Recorder of London. The legal opinion was far from reassuring. The lawyers thought it would be a hopeless and futile endeavour to bring the matter before the courts. They hesitated to do so. Sharpe remained undaunted. He was the son of a clergyman and had had no legal training. Yet he began to make a

1 See KUP, A. P. — *History of Sierra Leone 1462-1787.*
2 This matter is discussed in the next Chapter at p.21-2
3 (1772) 20 St. T. p.1.
4 The facts are given in detail in Averil Mackenzie Grieve's *"The last of the English Slave Trade"*, pp.37-9.

Introduction

detailed study of the law. In the end, he published a paper entitled "The Injustice and dangerous tendency of tolerating Slavery in England", which argued against the institution of slavery and sought to show that it was legally unjustified in England. Sharpe resolved to do everything possible to secure Strong's freedom. He instituted legal proceedings and also made strong representations to the Lord Mayor of London, Sir Robert Kite, who heard the case. On the 18th September, 1767, the court discharged Strong, granting him his freedom and restraining Kerr, the owner, from further imprisoning Strong.

This success was a source of great encouragement to Sharpe. He was elated that he had proved the lawyers wrong and had demonstrated that the law would indeed safeguard and defend the rights of slaves and ensure their liberty and freedom. The battle was by no means over and he needed another forum to drive the point home. The opportunity came with the case of Somerset-v-Knowles, better known as Somerset-v-Stewart. The circumstances were somewhat similar to those in Strong's case. Somerset was a Negro slave owned by Stewart who had brought him to England from the United States.[5] While in England, Somerset escaped but was recaptured and restored to his master's custody. Stewart then arranged for him to be transported to the West Indies in a vessel under the command of Captain Knowles. At this point Sharpe intervened and caused a Writ of Habeas Corpus to be issued directed to the Captain who then had Somerset under his custody, for the detention of the slave to be justified. The application came up for hearing before a Court presided over by the Chief Justice Lord Mansfield, and comprising Justices Ashton, Wells and Ashurst. Formidable arguments were canvassed on both sides. Sergeant Davy, opening the case for Somerset, put the matter eloquently and convincingly. His words are worthy of repetition. He said, inter alia:[6]

> There is the case of Cartwright who brought a slave from Russia and would scour him. For this he was questioned — and it was resolved that England was too pure an air for slaves to breathe in. That was in the eleventh of Queen Elizabeth. I hope, My Lords, the air does not blow worse since. I hope they will never breathe here. For this is my assertion; 'the moment they put their feet on English ground, that moment they become free.' They are subject to the laws and they are entitled to the protection of the laws of this country; and so are their master, thank God.

Other Counsel assisted,[7] all of them devoted to their cause and singularly devoted to the achievement of their objectives. They rendered their professional services without remuneration. Between them, they successfully disposed of the cardinal and crucial question whether,

(a) By English law, any one could be the property of another:
(b) Persons entering Britain became subject to the laws of Britain:

---

5   Virginia.
6   See HOARE: *Memoirs of Granville Sharpe.*
7   e.g. Mr Sergeant Glynn, Mr Mansfield: Mr R. Hargrave and Mr Alleyne.

(c) Such persons, in any event, brought with them odious practices permitted in other countries but not specifically proscribed by the laws of England.

They argued inter alia:

> Either this man remains upon his arrival in England in the condition he was in abroad in Virginia, or not. If he does so remain, the master's power remains as before. If the laws, having attached upon him abroad, are at all to affect him here, he brings them all; either all the laws of Virginia are to attach upon him or none.

This masterly and forceful exposition disclosed the utter fallacy and futility of attempting to import into a 'foreign' system the laws and practices of another for the purpose of achieving a favourable result in one particular case. Counsel went on to argue that Virginia was still a Colony and that Colonial laws were not per se applicable in the Home country. He asked:[8]

> Have the laws of Virginia any more influence, power or authority in this country than the laws of Japan? The king makes laws for Virginia alone if he pleases.

The case of Somerset-v-Stewart, contrary to what was then common belief, did not provide the first opportunity for a legal opinion to be canvassed in the English Courts about the validity of the institution of slavery. Chief Justice Holt, a courageous and fearless Judge, had, during the reign of William and Anne in the case of Smith-v-Brown and Cooper[9] expressed the opinion that "a Negro becomes free as soon as he sets foot in England". The learned Judge also said that "One may be a villain in England, but *not a slave*".[10]

It would not appear, however, that this opinion was cited to the Court in Stewart's case; nor does it appear that the attention of the Court was called to the opinion of the Solicitor-General and Attorney-General who, in 1729, at the request of the West Indian Planters, had opined that:[11]

> A slave by coming from the West Indies to Great Britain or Ireland either with or without his master does not become free and his master's property or right in him, is not thereby determined or varied; nor doth baptism bestow freedom on him, or make him any alteration in his temporal condition in these kingdoms.

It is not clear whether these principal law officers were in fact aware of the opinion of CJ Holt in the case of Smith-v-Brown and Cooper. If they did know of it then the only conclusion to be derived from their opinion is that they disagreed with the view of the learned Chief Justice with whose opinion theirs was at variance. The view of the law as expounded by the law officers was one that had remained virtually unchallenged for

---

8 See HOARE: *Memoirs of Granville Sharpe,* infra.
9 & 10 Ld. Raymond 1274 (See Vol. 2 *Salkeld's Reports,* p.666, Vol. II).
10 Emphasis are mine.
11 P. York and C. Talbot respectively. (York later became Lord Hardwicke).

Introduction

several years, although it "did not prevent a favourable verdict on behalf of two Negroes about the years 1732 and 1739."[12]

But, was it the law of England, as it then stood, that a slave could, by merely reaching the shores of England, acquire his freedom? In the Scottish Court of Session in the eighteenth century, a bold attempt was made by the distinguished Dr Johnson, to get a favourable judicial ruling on the status of slavery. He formulated his argument thus:[13]

> No man is by nature the property of another. The defendant is, therefore, by nature free. The rights of nature must be some way forfeited before they can be justly taken away; that the defendant has by any act forfeited the rights of nature we require to be proved; and if no proof of such forfeiture can be given, we doubt not but the justice of the court will declare him free.

Unfortunately, that case did not proceed to judgment because of the untimely death of the slave while the proceedings were still pending. This robbed the Court of a good opportunity of settling a troublesome point of law.

Lord Mansfield, however, lost no time in declaring what has been described as the "Charter of Emancipation". His judgment was an outstanding example of clarity and brevity. It was also an acute perception and analysis of the issues involved. The Lord Chief Justice recited the Return to the Writ of Habeas Corpus in which it was said that the Laws of Virginia and of Jamaica had authorised trade in slaves as goods and chattels. He continued:[14]

> The only question before us is whether the cause on the Return is sufficient. If it is, the Negro must be remanded: if it is not, he must be discharged .... The power of a Master over his slave has been extremely different in different countries. The state of slavery is of such a nature that it is incapable of being introduced on any reason moral or political, but only by positive law .... It is so odious that nothing can be suffered to support it but positive law. Whether inconveniences, therefore, may follow from the decision, I cannot say this case is allowed or approved by the law of England; therefore the Black must be discharged.

Analysis of the Judgment:
Lord MANSFIELD'S approach to the problem was pragmatic. He gave direct and unequivocal support to earlier judicial opinions, particularly that of CJ Holt, to the effect that slavery was unknown to the law of England. He affirmed the view that as soon as a slave sets foot on English soil, he becomes free. As far as Lord Mansfield was concerned, the legal issues were short and uncontroversial. Was there any positive legal enactment authorising slavery? If none, then the claims of the Master must fail. It was a simple, practical, down to earth

12 HOARE: *Memoirs of Granville Sharpe* — Vol. 1 p.8.
13 SIMON: "*Slavery*", p.227.
14 Somerset-v-Stewart, (1772) 20 St. T. p.5.

approach, devoid of legal technicalities and altogether faultless in its reasoning.

The immediate result of Lord Mansfield's decision was that thousands of slaves ran off to England. They mutinied on board ship and they did everything to reach the land of liberty. The exodus to England brought a number of problems, for many freed slaves were left destitute in the streets of London. Public concern for their welfare grew steadily and this gave rise to the creation of a Committee known as 'The Black Poor Committee'.[15] The need to repatriate the blacks from England to a home of their own led to the establishment of the territory known as the "Settlement of Sierra Leone".

Before proceeding to deal with the legal and constitutional developments of Sierra Leone in greater detail, it is essential to describe briefly the territory with which we are primarily concerned.

THE TERRITORY OF SIERRA LEONE:

The original territory of what was formerly "The Settlement of Sierra Leone", was only a piece or parcel of land just about twenty miles square lying on the West Coast of Africa, being the piece or parcel of land bought by the settlers from a local ruler named King Tom and his "other Kings, Chiefs and Potentates". This same territory was later sold to the settlers by a more powerful native ruler, King Naimbana who purported to sell the same by and with the authority of his "other Kings, Chiefs and Potentates".[16] Today the boundaries of the territory are well settled.[17]

Sierra Leone is situated on the West Coast of Africa roughly between 6 and 10 degrees North Latitude, and between 10 and 13 degrees West Longitude. It is bounded on the north and north-east by the Republic of

---

15 This committee was set up by a number of Abolitionists who were concerned about the deplorable conditions under which the liberated Africans lived in England. The words 'Black Poor' are a misnomer, in so far as they are used to describe the first settlers in Sierra Leone. Those who elected to go there to establish the Independent Settlement were by no means all Black; nor were they taken exclusively from the ranks of the poor.

16 The two Treaties are discussed infra at p.23.

17 Republican Sierra Leone today comprises the two portions of the territory formerly administered as a Colony and a Protectorate. The boundaries of the Colony comprised the original settlement and accretions thereto by conquest and treaties concluded with the local rulers. The boundaries of the Protectorate were finally settled between the British and the French following a Convention signed in 1882 settling the borders of the territories claimed by both powers. At the Treaty of Berlin, usually described as the Berlin Conference in 1885, these boundaries were formalised. Notwithstanding this, there were several border skirmishes and loss of territory to the French which led to the visit of a Sierra Leone delegation to the British Secretary of State in 1891. The delegation included the Mayor of Freetown, Mr Cornelius May who was the owner and proprietor of the *Weekly News,* and the Rev James Johnson. Boundary Commisioners were appointed and a further treaty signed in Paris in 1895. See J. D. HARGREAVES: *Prelude to the Partition of West Africa.* (Lond. 1965). ALSO The Archives of the Methodist Missionary Society (Lond.). Also Agreement between Great Britain and France fixing the boundaries between the British and the French possessions North and East of Sierra Leone (Paris 21st January, 1895) RS 966.4 G 798.

Guinea, on the west by the Atlantic Ocean and on the east by the Republic of Liberia. It is about 28,000 square miles in size.[18]

Lying as it is in the tropical belt, Sierra Leone has two seasons in the year. The rainy season which lasts roughly from May to October, and the dry season which runs from November to April. In the coastal region the vegetation is thick and there are dense forests but as the land runs inland the vegetation becomes sparse. Rainfall is heavy during the rainy season.[19] The temperature is fairly constant throughout the year and ranges from 70 to 90 degrees Farenheit.

Population:
The population of the country is about two and a half million people. There are approximately ten language groups in Sierra Leone. The lingua franca which is spoken widely throughout the country is 'Krio' which is the language of the Creoles, the descendants of the original Settlers and the Liberated Africans. Indigenous tribal languages include the Mende, Temne, Limba, Loko, Susu, Kuranko, Kono and Madingo which are the dominant tribal languages spoken by tribes throughout the country.[20]

Religion:
The settlement was originally founded as a Christian country. Apart from Christians, there are Moslems and animists or pagans. Islam has infiltrated substantially into the country and is now the religion of a dominant tribe, the Temnes. There is also a strong Moslem tradition among the Aku Mohamedans in Freetown, the capital. With the exception of this group, the Creoles are exclusively Christian.

Government:
Sierra Leone has a unicameral legislature consisting of a President, two Vice-Presidents and Members of Parliament elected from single member constituencies. In addition there are twelve privileged seats reserved for Paramount Chiefs from the hinterland who are elected from the twelve Provincial Districts. There are also under the 1971 Constitution, three nominated members, appointed to Parliament by the President. Two of them sit as members of the cabinet.[21]

Economy:
The Unit of currency is the Leone.[22] The economy is basically agricultural and mining. The staple food is rice which is cultivated

18 Roughly the size of England and Wales.
19 Around the coast it often reached 180 inches.
20 All the tribes, with the possible exception of the Limbas and Sherbros, were immigrants AD 1350 to 1400. *See* M. McCulloch: *Peoples of the Sierra Leone Protectorate.* (London: International African Institute, 1950).
21 Since 1978, Sierra Leone has become a One-Party State (Act. No. 12 of 1978). The number of appointed members has now increased to 10.
22 The Leone was, at Independence in 1961, backed by sterling. It has now been removed from the sterling area and put on the S.D.R. (Special Drawing Rights).

extensively but not in sufficient quantities for domestic consumption. Rice is therefore imported in large quantities. Cash crops include, piassava, coffee and cocoa, palm kernels, ground-nuts and a variety of fruits. There are also valuable mineral deposits and diamond mining is currently a mainstay of the economy. Gold, rutile, iron ore, bauxite and platinum are also mined in large quantities.

CHAPTER II

PLANS FOR THE ESTABLISHMENT OF THE PROVINCE OF FREEDOM

THE SMEATHMAN PLAN:
The earliest plan for the creation of a settlement for the liberated Africans and those who wished to emigrate from Great Britain, was that of Dr Smeathman, who designed a "Specific Plan for Colonising Africa with a view to civilisation".[1] Smeathman was a Botanist who had spent some time in Sierra Leone catching butterflies in the Banana Islands, just off the peninsular around Freetown. He considered the area an excellent one for locating a brand new settlement. He published his plan in 1786 the title of which was:[2]

> Substance of a Plan of Settlement to be made near Sierra Leona on the Grain Coast of Africa, Intended more particularly for the service and happy establishment of Blacks and People of Colour, to be shipped as Freemen under the direction of the Committee for Relieving the Black Poor, and under the protection of the British Government.

Interesting features of the plan were the following:
(a) It was based on the dual objective of philanthropy and profit.
(b) There was to be a contractual arrangement between the intending settlers and the Committee of the Black Poor, whereby each intending immigrant was to pay £5 and in return be provided with free transport and subsistence during the voyage to Sierra Leone and for some period of time after arrival. (See Art. 2).
(c) The committee was to acquire territory which would be communal property owned jointly by the settlers. Each settler was to be allocated as much land as he could cultivate.
(d) The settlement was to be free and independent, but under the protection of Great Britain, the colonists enjoying "both civil and religious liberty as in Great Britain".
(e) In keeping with the independent status of the settlement, the settlers were to promulgate their own laws based on the laws of England but without reference or recourse to Great Britain.

---
1 See J. C. Wadstrom — *Essay on Colonization*, 1794
2 This Plan is set out in full in Appendix I for ease of reference.

Provided that "disputes relative to property, or offences committed among themselves, will be settled according to the laws, by their own peers in a town meeting".

Smeathman died before his plan could be implemented. Notwithstanding his death, the plan proved to be a most useful precedent and a fruitful source of material for Granville Sharpe and his dedicated band of abolitionists who subsequently intensified their proposals for the establishment of a new home for the liberated Africans who were stranded in England and whose numbers were daily increasing.

EVALUATION OF THE SMEATHMAN PLAN:
The plan envisaged the purchase of territory for the establishment of a new country for the settlers. The land was to be "joint property". Clearly this was in keeping with the traditions of land holding on the African Continent. Simplistic though the idea appeared on paper, it was nevertheless a workable one. It aimed at encouraging the development of agriculture for it promised more land to those whose success at cultivation justified further allocations of land.

With regard to trade, Smeathman was enthusiastic about its benefits for the settlers. His assessment of the territory was that it was rich in natural resources. He therefore spoke eloquently of the benefits of agriculture, the abundance of "dyeing woods of various kinds, ivory, wax, tortoise shell, gold and other merchandise". He said that there was an abundance of "pleasant fruits and spices from which may be made oils, marmalades, wines, perfumes and other valuable articles". When these were sold, Smeathman thought that all the needs of the settlement by way of commerce would be met. He wanted them to trade with Great Britain and other countries, not forgetting the "natives" whom he described as of a "peaceable temper".

The provisions for the government of the settlement were modest, but interesting. He did not visualise an Independent Settlement. There would be an Agent and Conductor of the Settlement. There were no provisions indicating how he would be elected. Smeathman provided that "the settlers, being under the protection of the British Government, will consequently enjoy both civil and religious liberty, as in Great Britain". The absence of detailed provisions for the government of the territory would appear to suggest that he contemplated government by Great Britain through its administrator whom he described as "Agent".

Judicial administration was similarly to be in the hands of the settlers, but the laws were to be promulgated locally "according to the custom of the country, which is invariably fair and equitable". In this matter, clearly Smeathman imagined that the settlers would base their laws on English law and that the Agent would ensure the fair and impartial administration of justice.

The plan also made provision for the spiritual, educational and physical welfare of the settlers. It mentioned the sending out of a clergyman "in order to promote Christian knowledge"; a schoolmaster and mistress "that those who have children may have them instructed"; and a physician "who has had for four years practice on the coast of Africa and as many in the West Indies." He was to be "accompanied by skilful assistants in surgery, midwifery, chemistry and other medical arts". Thus every conceivable need of the settlement was catered for.

This plan was carefully thought out and although Dr Smeathman did not live to see it put into operation, the fact that it formed the basis of a later plan which was eventually brought into action and which thrived and developed, is ample testimony of the skill, foresight and imagination which characterised it.

SHARPE'S PLAN FOR "THE PROVINCE OF FREEDOM":
One of the most determined and consistent fighters for the cause of the disadvantaged blacks in England following Lord Mansfield's famous dictum, was Granville Sharpe. He was not a member of parliament but he had friends who were. He initiated and maintained activities in and out of parliament aimed at supporting his pleas for something to be done to mitigate the plight of the liberated Africans. At his instance, William Wilberforce led the fight in the British Parliament for governmental support of the project he was supporting. This was to establish a settlement for the liberated Africans in Africa. In this endeavour, he evoked the sympathy and support of William Pitt.

Sharpe's ideas were similar to Smeathman's. In fact, he had seen Smeathman's plan while trying to get the British Government interested in his proposals. He drafted a Code of Regulations which he thought might serve well as the Constitution of the Government of the new settlement. He conceived of this new government as an independent one and the settlement as something more than a home for unwanted vagrants.

His primary objectives were two fold:[3]
(a) To impart Christianity and Western civilization to the whole of Africa:
(b) To form a company to carry on an honourable trade with the Coast of Africa.

He envisaged a politically independent black settlement where there would be complete racial equality, freedom of thought and expression and, where the settlers would promulgate their own laws. He wished, however, that they should be guided by English law which he had studied and believed was very fair. He named the proposed settlement "The Province of Freedom". The constitution which he designed was published by him under the title of *"A Short Sketch of Temporary Regulations (until better shall be proposed) for the Intended Settlement in the Grain Coast of Africa, near Sierra Leone".*[4] The principal features of these regulations were the following:
(a) The Preface, which stated that the regulations were to be

3 See HOARE: *Memoirs of Granville Sharpe* op cit.
4 See Appendix II

B

temporary expedients and could be entirely set aside, rejected in part or altered in accordance with the wishes of the majority of the settlers "after mature deliberation in their Common Council". Alterations of the constitution, however, were not to be inconsistent with the fundamental principles of the common law of England.
(b) The proposal that the English system of frankpledge was to be adopted and put into operation in the Settlement "for securing peace, right and mutual protection".
(c) All the land comprising the Settlement was to be owned in common by all the settlers. Everybody over the age of sixteen should be entitled to an allocation of land.
(d) The institution of slavery to be abolished and not tolerated in the Settlement.

These temporary regulations were promulgated around 3rd July, 1786. As is well known, because of difficulties in setting up the expedition, the first settlers did not arrive in the territory until almost a year afterwards. In the meantime, Sharpe devised "Additional Regulations" which made detailed provisions for law and order.[5] These later regulations covered matters such as the acquisition of a proper knowledge of the common law; the tenure of office of holders of magisterial appointments; the holding of weekly courts and of county courts for the settlement of disputes.

Cumulatively therefore, these regulations envisaged an orderly community — a political community of free and independent persons — governed by a Common Council[6] where national matters would be debated and adopted. The proposed system of FRANKPLEDGE would ensure that matters relating to local government and internal security would be dealt with by community leaders who would also handle judicial matters, that is to say, adjudication and settlement of disputes.

Interestingly enough, by providing that all unappropriated land should be deemed "common", Sharpe reflected in his proposals the 'African' concept of "common ownership" of land and foreshadowed the later decision of the Privy Council in the case of Amadu Tijani-v-the Secretary to the Government of South Nigeria[7] which decided, almost a century and a half later, that "land belongs to the community, the village or the family, never to the individual".

Eventually, Sharpe and his small band of abolitionists succeeded in getting some parliamentary support for the scheme for the establishment of the settlement in Sierra Leone[8] although a substantial part of the funds raised to support the project had to be raised from private sources.

---

5   See Appendix III
6   In today's terminology, that would be the Parliament of the Province of Freedom. The idea of a 'Council' survived not only the Company administration but the Colonial era as well.
7   (1921) A.C. 399 at p.404.
8   There had been proposals for resettling the blacks in other locations, e.g. The USA, Nova Scotia, the West Indies etc.

Sharpe himself spent a considerable portion of his personal money to support the settlement and he was, in the process, almost reduced to penury. In spite of that, Sharpe was overburdened with joy and considerable relief when the initial expedition finally set sail for Sierra Leone. Before they left, Sharpe handed to each settler a copy of the proposed regulations and each agreed to be governed by them for the time being. They agreed, in effect,
(a) That they were going to a territory which was to become theirs in perpetuity:
(b) That they were to form an independent political community in which they would appoint their own leaders and govern themselves without any reference to or interference from any foreign power:
(c) That they had freedom to amend the regulations and promulgate their own laws, but they were to be guided by the principles of English law.
(d) They were to form a Christian community and promote western civilization.
(e) Slavery was proscribed and instead of trafficking in slaves, they were to strive to develop honourable trade with Britain and other countries.

EVALUATION OF SHARPE'S PLAN:
Sharpe's plan, though based on Smeathman's, was a distinct improvement on the latter. The basis of government was the system of frankpledge. Yet, Sharpe was flexible enough and had the foresight to see the need for variations as the circumstances demanded. In his temporary regulations, he commented as follows:
> The community of free American settlers, however, have already adopted (as I am informed) a small variation from the old English model of numerical divisions, by forming themselves into divisions of dozens instead of tithings or tens; but as this little change is by no means inconsistent with the true principles and intention of our legal English frankpledge, I am at liberty to acknowledge a most hearty approbation of it, as being an arrangement far more convenient and effectual for securing perfect subordination, peace and good government....

This flexibility and foresight was an outstanding feature of Sharpe's plan and it enabled the settlers to establish their government and carry out their activities without the crippling effects of a too rigid adherence to formal rules and regulations.

Although designed for conditions which existed at the time, that is, the latter half of the eighteenth century, yet the plan was so comprehensive and precise that it could have provided a model for any present day democracy. The Governor, again described as an Agent, was to be elected by popular franchise. There were to be no nominated members on the council. All the officials were to be elected by the people. Slavery was to be outlawed and abolished. Labour was communal, but not forced and landholding was to be common and allocated to settlers. It was a workable plan.

Equally interesting and full of imagination was the further constitutional document Sharpe termed "Additional Regulations". An interesting provision here was the requirement that certain offices should be "Honorary" because "it might be dangerous to the new settlement to permit men to hold offices of considerable profit without annual re-election, if they were permitted at the same time to obtain and hold offices of power."[9] Sharpe's keen foresight enabled him to appreciate one of the crucial problems of government in modern times, namely, the taming of power.

Finally, it can be said that the temporary regulations for the government of the Settlement of Sierra Leone, initiated, conceived of and put into effect by Granville Sharpe, provided the minimum standards necessary for the establishment of a democratic government; provided the settlers with a home and a sense of belonging; and in a practical way, offered many individuals, an opportunity for service in their own country and helped restore the confidence of a large number of people who had been subjected to a most degrading status. The establishment of a new country enabled these settlers to mould themselves into a nation with a unique identity unparalleled anywhere in the world.

THE PROVINCE OF FREEDOM 1786-1791

(A) KING TOM'S TREATY

In February, 1787, the first batch of settlers left Britain under the command of Captain Bouldon Thompson aboard the *'Nautilus'* for Sierra Leone. They were armed with Sharpe's great and worthy ideals for the founding of a free and independent settlement for blacks. They arrived in Sierra Leone on the 10th day of May, 1787. There were about four hundred settlers in all, black and white. Contrary to what the history books recount, they were not all of them liberated Africans. Nor were they 'the Black Poor'. Among this number, were whites from England. Again, contrary to what some history books maliciously report, they were not a handful of prostitutes. The British Government could not have hoped to solve its problems of women of the streets by sending them off as kept mates for the settlers. Nor would the abolitionists who were men of high ideals and Christian commitment, have tolerated that. The fact is that numbered among the first group of settlers were blacks from America who welcomed the chance of a new life in a new country and whites who were also motivated by the desire and need for adventure.

In accordance with his instructions, Captain Thompson went ashore the next day after his arrival to negotiate with the local rulers for a piece

[9] Sharpe to Lettson.

Plans for the Establishment of the Province of Freedom

of land on which to establish the settlement. Obviously, before the expedition set sail, they must have know that such land was available for sale to the abolitionists on behalf of the settlers. The person Captain Thompson met on his arrival in the town, was King Tom, who was obviously a Sub-Chief of the Temnes. He purported to negotiate on behalf of the Koya people.[10] After the usual formalities had been gone through, a treaty was signed between King Tom and Others on the one part and Captain Bouldon Thompson and Others on the other part. This treaty was executed on the 11th June, 1787.[11] It granted:

> All the land, wood and water which is contained from the Bay commonly called Frenchman's Bay, coastways up the River Sierra Leone to Gambia Island and Southerly or inland, twenty miles.

The King, in the treaty, undertook to bear allegiance to His Majesty George III "and protect the said free settlers to the utmost of my power against the insurrections and attacks of all nations and people whatever." The settlement was thus founded on "a fine track of mountainous country covered with beautiful trees of all kinds."[12]

History books record that this treaty was repudiated and superceded by a later one which was executed by King Naimbana and his associates, the following year. It therefore becomes essential to evaluate the legality of the Tom/Thompson Treaty.

The first obvious question is who were the parties to the treaty and what, if any, was their authority to negotiate it? The contracting parties were named in the instrument. They were the local chief and his subordinates on the one hand and the free community of settlers on the other. The treaty itself had the following recital:

> I, King Tom, Chief of Sierra Leone on the Grain Coast of Africa, by and with the consent of the other Kings, Chiefs and Potentates subscribing thereto, in consideration of these presents now made me by Captain Bouldon Thompson . . . . on and behalf of and for the sole benefit of the free community of settlers their heirs and successors now lately arrived from England and under the protection of the British Government . . . .

and the persons who signed on behalf of the Vendors of the land were the following:

King Tom
Chief Pa Bongee } These were Sub-Chiefs.
Queen Yammacouba

Now, in Temne customary law as it was practised among the Koya people at that period of time, the government of the tribe centred around the Bai or Paramount Ruler. Hence the Paramount Chief.[13] However, the Paramount Ruler could not act alone in respect of state functions. He

---

10 The same man has also been described as 'Prince Tom'. It was he who ceded the French Gambia Island in 1785.
11 The treaty is set out in Appendix IV.
12 See, Sharpe to Lettson (Letter op. cit.)
13 The Title Paramount Chief was introduced by the British over a century later. The local rulers were described as Kings and Queens.

was supported by a number of Sub-Chiefs who had sacred or ceremonial duties and acted as district overseers. The Paramount Ruler ruled his Chiefdom or State by and with the advice of the subordinates particularly the ceremonial ones. These would include, for example, the Naimbana, Pa Kappra, Naimsogo and three Mammy Queens[14] in order of seniority. Prior consultation was essential to the validity of decisions taken by the Paramount Ruler in respect of important Chiefdom or State matters. If he died or was absent from the territory, the next person in succession was the Regent who performed all his duties and acted for him in as ample a manner as if he had been personally present.

It would appear from all available records that King Tom was a Regent. There was a Naimbana, but he was, at that crucial time, absent from the locality. He was living further up the river. King Tom was therefore the person in effective control of the government of the tribe. The signatures of the subordinates, indicate that King Tom had acted with the advice and consent of his Tribal Council at the time he executed the treaty. These signatories also suggest that the tribal administration approved of the treaty in principle and in the form and manner in which it was executed.

It has been suggested, and it is submitted, erroneously, that in customary law, land could not be alienated or sold to outsiders. This is an assertion which is not backed by experience and it is a proposition which is of doubtful validity. In international law, territory can be acquired by accretion, by cession, by occupation or by prescription. The tribe, Thompson met, were the owners of their land and territory. There is nothing to suggest that they were without capacity to annex or cede any portion of their territory. Moreover, there are numerous treaties signed between the local rulers and the British or French which give the lie to the misconception that land cannot be sold outright or ceded to a non-native as customary law forbids this. The customary rule about appropiation of land, as far as my researches go, has always been that land can be sold, even to an individual when once title thereto has been acquired and established, usually by farming thereon for a long period of time. In this case, there was actual transfer of ownership by the local rulers of twenty miles of land as described in the treaty, to a group of settlers who proceeded to occupy the land they had bought. They made roads, built houses and settled there and effectively occupied the territory henceforth to be theirs in perpetuity. The acquisition was complete and henceforth the local inhabitants had no right or title to the land which had passed from their possession and ownership to that of the purchasers who were now the legal and de facto owners thereof.

In further analysing the legality of this sale, one has to take account of the fact that the land was exchanged for value. There was consideration for the sale, for the amount specified in the treaty.[15] Again, many commentators have unkindly and very ungraciously viewed the amount

14 The Bome Poseh: Bome Warah and Bome Rufah.
15 £59. 1s. 5d. See Appendix IV.

of the purchase price as ludicrously small. Of course, consideration need not be adequate. But who are we to say that the amount paid was inadequate? Whose standards are to be applied? It may well be that the local rulers thought they had got a good bargain. If not, why did they sell? On the other hand, it may well have been that they too, were aware of the plight of the liberated Africans and had a genuine desire to help in the circumstances. In any event, judged by the standards then prevailing £59 for a mere twenty mile stretch of undeveloped land did not seem such a bad bargain after all. That amount was considerable in those days.

The next point was with regard to the purchaser. Who was the real purchaser of the territory? Was it the British Government, the abolitionists, or the settlers? Captain Bouldon Thompson was not a settler himself. He was an Agent. He had instructions from the abolitionists to negotiate the purchase. He signed on behalf of the settlers. He paid from funds provided by Sharpe and others. The settlers did not contribute anything. In these circumstances, can it be said that the settlers were the purchasers of the land? It has to be admitted that one can be a beneficiary without providing any part of the purchase money. This was, in effect, the true position of the settlers. The abolitionists intended the settlement to be theirs. When they provided money to purchase the land therefore, they intended the land to be owned by the settlers. It was a gift to them. The settlers accepted the offer and did not repudiate Thompson's agency. Nor did they reject any part of the Sharpe Plan for their settlement in Sierra Leone. Therefore, as between the settlers and Captain Thompson there was identity of interest. Thompson paid the purchase price for and on behalf of the settlers who thus became the owners. But the matter does not rest there. Did King Tom and his countrymen think they were negotiating with the British Government? Clearly not. He admitted in writing that he had received the presents from Thompson for and on behalf of the settlers who were under the protection of the British Crown. He knew Thompson was no emissary from the British Government.

Consequently, all the elements of the contract had been established and there had been a valid and effective sale of the land by the owners to the free community of settlers and their successors and the treaty was a valid and effectual one both domestically and internationally. The settlers went into possession and set up their flag which was planted on the site of the present State House. They named their town "Granville Town" fittingly, after Granville Sharpe, the man who, single-handedly, had done so much to bring what seemed a distant dream into the realm of reality.

(B) KING NAIMBANA'S TREATY

Preliminary:
After the settlers had planted their flag and established their Province of Freedom along the lines of frankpledge as envisaged by Sharpe, they elected their Hundredors and Tythingmen and divided the town into

houses of ten. They thus laid the foundations for legislative and judicial functions. Moreover this was in keeping with the spirit of the regulations formally adopted by all the settlers when they agreed to set sail for Sierra Leone.[16] A system of trial by jury was established during the first year of the life of the settlement and a Chief Justice was appointed. The settlers thus made a serious attempt to set up an organised form of government.

The Province of Freedom was, however, subjected to considerable harassment and attacks from the neighbouring tribesmen and, ironically, from King Tom himself who went so far as to sell two of the settlers into slavery. Unfortunately, the province was ill-equipped for self-defence and was unable to withstand sustained external aggression. Another unfortunate circumstance which the abolitionists had not reckoned with was the inclement weather. The rainy season[17] of 1787 took its toll of the settlers and many of them succumbed to the vagaries of the climate. Arriving in May, they did not have much time to build themselves suitable houses to protect them from the heavy rains and cold. They suffered much hardship and privation. Nevertheless, the government survived. The first Governor, Weaver,[18] had been elected and so in law, as well as in fact, a new State had been brought into existence. It had defined territory, a settled population, a popularly elected government and above all, ability to conduct international affairs with other foreign states.

In 1788, five settlers robbed a store at Bance Island. The owner of the store, Captain Bowie, then threatened to seize every settler he could lay hands on. The threat was taken seriously by the Governor who ordered that the offenders should be surrendered to Captain Bowie. They were tried and found guilty by a jury of seven traders and five settlers. Their sentence was banishment. The Governor at that time was John Lucas and the Chief Justice, Charles Stoddard. Following this incident, King Naimbana, a more powerful king than Tom, who appeared to be the principal ruler of the area bought from King Tom, informed the Governor that he would not be responsible for the safety of the settlers and so he gave them notice to quit. It will, of course, be recalled that, in the treaty signed by Tom, the natives had undertaken to protect the free community of settlers from all attacks and insurrections whatsoever. Naimbana, therefore, having disclaimed his duty of protection, followed that up by purporting to repudiate the treaty between Thompson and Tom.

---

16 See Sharpe's letter to a correspondent in New York, dated 12th January, 1788. Also: PETERSON. *Province of Freedom*. Peterson states that the settlers made a serious attempt to follow Sharpe's regulations.
17 The rainy season lasts from May to October and is most intense between July and September.
18 He was popularly elected. He fell ill and was succeeded by James Reid. Weaver later on recovered and promptly accused Reid of stealing from the stores. He was reinstated as governor and stayed in office until he was replaced in an election by John Lucas.

THE TREATY OF 1788.

In August of 1788, another vessel, *The Myro,* under the command of Captain Taylor, arrived in the settlement with another batch of settlers. This was fortuitous as the few survivors of the original settlers could not have withstood any aggression from Naimbana and his tribesmen. When Taylor came ashore, Naimbana agreed to enter into treaty relations with him.

Unlike Thompson, Taylor had no authority to negotiate or enter into treaties. All he had to do was to bring the settlers to join the settlement. Taylor was not in government service. He was a private businessman and the owner of the brig *Myro.* On the 22nd August, 1788[19], with the concurrence of the government of the Province of Freedom, he signed another treaty with King Naimbana. This was done on the 22nd day of August 1788, a date which has often, but erroneously, been referred to by historians as 'the legal beginning' of the Settlement of Sierra Leone.

The treaty[20] provided, inter alia, that in consideration of the presents[21] made by Taylor "in behalf of and for the sole benefit of the free community of settlers, their heirs and successors", the king granted and quit claim to a certain piece of land twenty miles square.[22] Like King Tom the year before, he promised allegiance to His Majesty King George III and protection for the settlers. Again, he purported to act by and with the consent of "the other Kings, Princes, Chiefs and Potentates, subscribing hereto". The subscribers to the treaty on behalf of the king and his retinue, were the king himself, James Dowder, whom Fyfe says might have been King Tom's successor, better known as King Jimmy or Jemmy; Pa Bongee, Dick Robbin and Abrah Elliott Griffith, Secretary to the king.[23] On the part of the settlers, the Captain, Taylor was a signatory. So was the first Governor, Richard Weaver. The others were Thomas Peall and Benjamin Elliott.[24]

The Naimbana Treaty contains a certificate or endorsement subjoined to it, declaring that the purchase of the land . . . . made by Captain Thompson "was not (to our certain knowledge) valid, it having been purchased from people who had no authority to sell the same".

The Taylor Treaty was ostensibly executed in substitution for the Thompson Treaty. The ground for this was uncertainty as to the authority of King Tom "to sell". But what was this authority that King Tom needed? Unfortunately, there is no indication of what should have

---

19 This was the date on which the second expedition arrived. It must be taken for granted that King Naimbana was either in the settlement or close near by.
20 The treaty is set out in Appendix V.
21 Taylor paid the sum of £59.1.5d. in trade goods, making a total of £144.3.0d. for the land.
22 The land, the subject matter of the treaty with King Naimbana was the same land which had been sold by King Tom.
23 Griffith was apparently a witness. He was interpreter for the king who spoke hardly any English at all. See: FYFE: *History of Sierra Leone.*
24 Peall was a Doctor of Medicine who came out on *The Myro* with Taylor, but later returned to England. Elliott was one of the first settlers who were under threat by King Naimbana and who welcomed the arrival of the new set of settlers to augment their dwindling numbers.

been done by Tom. Conjecture has it, that he should have sought the permission of his superior chief, King Naimbana before concluding the treaty. This would have ensured that the payment for the land went to the hands of King Naimbana and not to Tom.

It is, however, most revealing that, King Naimbana was not complaining that under customary law, land could not be sold. Far from it. He did not deny the validity of an outright sale of native land to a non-native. He also, in fact, intended the settlers to have the land. All he said was that they should have paid him and no one else. Both treaties which were almost identical in form, showed the vendors as the local chiefs and the settlers as the purchasers. Both identified the land to be sold; both showed that the alienation of the land was for valuable consideration; both promised protection to the settlers who had gone into occupation of the land. In effect, there was no uncertainty about the nature or effect of the transaction. The Temne rulers, in accordance with native law and custom had effectively sold the land to the settlers and the fee simple had become vested in the latter. With this second treaty, confirming, as it were, the first, the Province of Freedom, with its capital Granville Town had now taken off from its very insecure beginnings.

CONCLUSIONS.
The Independent Settlement was, undoubtedly, a tiny one. Nevertheless, it was a viable one. It had all the essentials of a state. Its governor was elected. He might have been dubbed "President". There was a Common Council, which could have been named "Parliament". It was composed of elected persons, the Hundredors and Tythingmen. They made rules. These might have been called "laws" for the order and good government of the territory. In substance, there was an independent political community of free and independent black men.

The Province of Freedom was subjected to constant attacks and harassment from the Temnes. They defended themselves admirably from this 'external aggression' which was the greatest hazard facing them. In addition, they had to contend with another major hazard — that of attacks from captains of various ships anchoring to water in the bay. In December 1789, King Jimmy[25] burnt the Independent Settlement to the ground in retaliation for the burning of one of his villages by a sailor from a British warship. Many of the settlers fled to the nearby villages and set up their homes there. Those who stayed behind made a valiant and admirable effort to rebuild the settlement.

The slave traffic continued in the meantime and Sharpe decided to interest other people in his plans for augmenting the settlement's numbers by fresh settlers mainly from the West Indies and Nova Scotia. He succeeded in getting the interest of several private individuals but failed to secure governmental support. He then decided to form a private company to trade with the West Coast of Africa and to maintain a steady flow of supplies to the Province of Freedom. He secured the agreement

---

25 He was Tom's successor. See Fyfe: *History etc.* op cit.

Plans for the Establishment of the Province of Freedom

of thirty-eight persons whom he induced to become shareholders in the St. George's Bay Company, and then petitioned parliament for a Charter of Incorporation.[26] By the time the petition actually reached parliament the number had risen to one hundred.[27]

By a fortuitous coincidence, one Thomas Peters travelled from Nova Scotia to Great Britain to protest about the condition of freed slaves in Nova Scotia. He got in touch with Sharpe and the company became interested in his project. The outcome of his discussions was that in January 1792, one thousand two hundred Blacks left Nova Scotia to settle in Sierra Leone.

---

26 At this period of time, companies could only be incorporated by an Act of Parliament. Harrell-Bond, Howard and Skinner in their book '*Community Leadership and the Transformation of Freetown (1801-1976)*' think the company was in existence and governed Sierra Leone from 1787. This in erroneous. See footnote at p.2.

27 That was in April, 1791.

CHAPTER III

THE COMMON LAW IN SIERRA LEONE AND THE NATIONALITY OF THE SETTLERS

The original settlers who sailed from Britain on the *Nautilus*[1] pledged themselves before they left, to follow the laws of Britain. Each settler was handed a copy of Sharpe's Temporary Regulations before he left the United Kingdom and he was enjoined that it should form the basis of the system of government to be established in the Province of Freedom. Thus, all the settlers had prior notice of, and agreed to be bound by, the legal system to be introduced in their new homeland.[2] Each settler who accepted the proposed constitution, that is to say, Sharpe's Temporary Regulations, solemnly agreed that it "could be freely altered and amended" by the Common Council, but not in any way "at all inconsistent with the fundamental principles of the Common law of England". Also that the old English system of FRANKPLEDGE "which in the English book is called MAXIMA SECURITAS — the greatest security" should be adopted; and that each would bind and oblige "himself or herself to the other settlers for the protection and preservation of their common freedom". Thus, in the words of Fyfe, they accepted a "social contract rooted in history, in the institutions of the Anglo-Saxon Monarchy, and of Israel under the Judges".[3]

A great many historians have assumed that the first group of settlers in Sierra Leone were British subjects. This is not surprising as many approaches were made to the British Government for support and assistance in the project which was then under consideration. However, to determine the validity of this assumption, it is necessary to consider what the status of these "British Subjects" was in English law at the time they set sail for Sierra Leone. Were they regarded as British subjects or aliens? Was British citizenship expressly conferred upon them?

1. See page 20.
2. New Zealand had a similar history as Sierra Leone. When the settlers were about to leave, before the first ship sailed, the passengers signed an agreement accepting a defined form of government. This was done under the influence of the New Zealand Company. When they arrived at Port Nicholson in March 1840, they got a written declaration from the native chiefs that the agreement was binding and effective. The New Zealanders had learnt from the Sierra Leone experiment.
3. Fyfe: *History etc.* op. cit. p.16.

The Common Law in Sierra Leone and the Nationality of Settlers

Between the sixteenth and the seventeenth centuries, English law did not make a strict distinction between subjects and aliens. According to Parry:[4]

> The common law has never recognised any classification of individuals from the point of view of national status save the mutually exclusive categories of subjects and aliens.

But by 1730 when the British Nationality Act of that year[5] was passed, it had become well established that natural born subjects of Great Britain were nationals of that country. Later, the British Nationality Act of 1772[6] extended British nationality to foreign born children whose fathers were entitled to the rights and privileges of natural born children or subjects of Great Britain. So that by the second half of the eighteenth century one could claim British nationality either by birth or parentage. Much earlier on, by the statute of Anne[7] provisions had been made for the easy naturalisation of Protestant refugees from the Principality of Orange. Very few persons, however, took advantage of this measure and so it was repealed shortly afterwards.

From the time of the middle ages, the principle was well established that the status of nationality by naturalisation could only be obtained from parliament. After the conferment of that status, an alien could then by operation of law become a natural born subject of the king. There was an act passed in 1663[8] which provided that if foreigners engaged in hemp and flax-dressing, net-making and tapestry-weaving, bonafide for three years, they would be entitled to all the rights and privileges of natural born subjects of Great Britain. In spite of this provision, no significant naturalisation statute was passed before the Aliens Act of 1844.[9]

From this analysis, at the time when the settlers of Sierra Leone departed from the shores of Great Britain, it is submitted they could claim to be British subjects under the then existing legislation, only if:

(a) They had been born in Britain; or
(b) They were born abroad of British fathers, or
(c) They were naturalised either by statute or by operation of law.

There is no evidence that the liberated Africans fell into any of the above categories. They could not therefore claim to be British subjects and any assertion that they were is not supported by documentary evidence.

The next question for discussion is whether they could, in the circumstances, have taken along British law with them to Sierra Leone, as natural born British subjects could competently do. Having established that the liberated Africans were not British subjects, the answer seems inevitable that they could not carry a foreign system of law with them since English law was not the personal law of the settlers. Yet,

4 Parry: British Nationality.
5 British Nationality Act 1730.
6 British Nationality Act 1772.
7 Statute 1708.
8 (1663)
9 The Aliens Act 1844.

the obvious answer seems to be that the general principles of English law and the common law came to be introduced into Sierra Leone (The Province of Freedom), not because subjects of His Majesty the King had taken the British legal system along with them, but because the common law was the deliberate choice of the abolitionists. It was approved and adopted by the people themselves who agreed that it should be made applicable to them. Indeed, Sharpe had made it clear that they were free to choose their own legal system if they so wished. He said they could pass laws freely without interruption from any source and wholly without any sort of external control or direction. When the settlers therefore, adhered to the temporary regulations and divided their country into Tithings and Hundreds in accordance with the English system of frankpledge, they were exercising their own free and deliberate judgment in what they considered was the appropriate system of law for them. Statute law was not adopted as such, but the reason for this is not far to seek. English statute law was designed for conditions prevailing in Britain and these could not readily or easily be transplanted and transported to a foreign land and a foreign people without major revisions and adjustments.

It is therefore fair to say that the common law was introduced into Sierra Leone because the abolitions and the settlers, both clearly desired it to be the governing system of law in operation in the new territory and so voluntarily adopted it as the basis of their jurisprudence. The settlers reserved to themselves the right to make such refinements, additions, amendments, and alterations of the common law as they thought desirable and suited to their particular needs.

What is the COMMON LAW?

Did Sharpe and the others understand the phrase 'the common law' as it is understood today? Meanings of words and phrases change over the centuries but though ideas of what the common law is have been expressed in many ways, the effect of this rich variety of descriptions is to create misunderstanding about an important concept of law. To the layman, the common law typifies certain standards of excellence in judicial procedures; to some it is illustrative of the fair and impartial administration of justice; to others it is a term of emotive significance and represents safeguards for individual rights and liberties. To the lawyer, the term is one of art. It means quite simply the whole body of law determined and laid down by the courts. It is usually differentiated from statute law by describing it as judge-made law. In this respect, the common law is peculiar, when compared with other systems of law, in that most of the important principles which have been established and which affect the liberites of individuals, particularly in those instances when the claims of individual liberty conflict with the interests of the state, have been handed down and developed by judges and not by the legislature. The common law proclaims the supremacy of the law and, in this respect, asserts the subjection of all classes of persons within the state to the law and its discipline.

The history of the development of the common law is a distinguished and colourful one. The common law tradition can be traced back to the Decrees of King Ethelbert during the lifetime of Augustine, when, it is said, that English law was first handed down. Since then, the common law has made a formidable contribution to the development of English jurisprudence. It has reflected the teachings of Christianity about the fundamental equality of all men at a time when slavery was an institution fully recognised and accepted in Anglo-Saxon England.

By the twelfth century, the common law had laid down the principle of the free and lawful man,[10] and, significantly for Sierra Leone, by the middle of the eighteenth century, the common law had abolished the institution of slavery.[11]

THE COMMON LAW IN SIERRA LEONE.
Following the decision in the case of Somerset and Stewart[12] and the birth of the Province of Freedom, it became necessary for the settlers to have a system of law by which they could be governed. They came from a heterogeneous background, though many of them were liberated Africans who were uncertain of their countries of origin and had lost whatever nationality they originally had. Before they settled in the Province of Freedom, they were resident in England. A handful of them were Englishmen, but the vast majority were not. It was these first settlers that brought English law — the Common Law — into Sierra Leone with them. They succeeded in doing that partly because of the regulations to which reference has already been made, but also partly because of the principle of law decided in the old case of Campbell-v-Hall[13] in which the Master of the Rolls said inter alia:

> If there be a new and uninhabited country found out by English subjects, as the law is the birthright of every subject, so wherever they go, they carry their law with them, and therefore such new found country is to be governed by the laws of England.

The settlers of the Province of Freedom had undoubtedly left England for a 'new and uninhabited country' and they were taking their law along with them. Unfortunately they were not all Englishmen. Many of them did not know what their personal laws were. They found hope and consolation in a well tried system of law and adopted it. They took the common law with them as a matter of deliberate choice and so the common law was thereafter firmly established and entrenched in the territory of Sierra Leone and remains so to this day.

10   In its Latin connotation *"Liber et legalis homo"*.
11   In the case of Somerset-v-Stewart, Lord Mansfield said 'By the common law of England, no man may hold property in another . . . . . They (the slaves) are subject to the laws and they are entitled to the protection of the law of this country; and so are their master, thank God . . . .'.
12   Cited supra.
13   (1722) It should be remembered that the Black population of settlers, there were numerous different tribes and language groups, a motley collection of humanity. They were not nationals of any identifiable state and could not have taken their personal laws with them, whatever these may have been.

THE LEGISLATIVE POWERS OF THE SETTLERS.

At its inception, the Settlement of Sierra Leone was not a "Settled Colony". Many historians think it was. Sierra Leone was originally a fully independent country. Had it been a settled colony in the accepted connotation of that phrase, that is, settled by the British Crown, then it would undoubtedly have been given a legisature by Act of the British Parliament, with defined powers and with all the trappings of a colonial legislature, including the reserved powers of the Crown. It would have had a Governor, appointed by the British Government, responsible to it. The Legislature and the Executive would have owed their respective existence to the exercise of the Royal Prerogative.[14] But this was not so in the case of the first settlement of Sierra Leone. The founding of the settlement was unique and peculiar to the territory and the inhabitants who formed the first settled population of the territory. Instead of a colonial legislature, the settlement had a Common Council formed from among the Hundredors and Tythingmen who were elected. In their Common Council, the settlers exercised legislative powers with absolute freedom, unfettered by any interference or direction from anywhere else.. The council was one of unlimited powers.[15]

The Independent Government of the Province of Freedom was short lived. It lasted a bare four years, from 1787 to 1791. During this time, the leaders of the country in their Common Council, freely promulgated their own laws, as idealistically conceived of by Sharpe, but based on the common law. By the time the government came to an end, the citizens had, uniquely, become the citizens of a new state. Small though their numbers were, they effectively handled their administrative and judicial duties and did so with a skill and admiration suitably expressed in the words of a contemporary writer, Martin Wight who commented:[16]

> The early constitution of Sierra Leone .... was the first instance in modern history of a self-governing .... community of non-Europeans where .... Negro freemen were allowed the political and civil rights of Europeans ....
> The Black settlers of Sierra Leone had fulfilled administrative duties .... and had shown a judgement and intelligence that won the praise of Europeans.

---

14   The Settlement of Sierra Leone may be compared with "unauthorised settlements" of which British Honduras is a good example. That country had formal legislative machinery in existence for over a century prior to 1862 when it acquired its colonial status. Another example is Tristan da Cunha which had formal authority only in 1938. See. Sir K. Roberts-Wray: *British and Colonial Law*, pp.151 & 154.
15   The only limitation, if any, lay in the requirement that laws passed by the legislature should not be inconsistent with the laws of England. There is no question about the capacity of the settlers to legislate for themselves. There was a problem about this later on when company rule was established. New Zealand had a similar history.
16   See MARTIN WIGHT: *The Development of the Legislative Council*.

CHAPTER IV

FROM INDEPENDENCE TO COLONIAL RULE

COMPANY RULE 1791-1808

Introduction.
The period from 1787 to 1790 was one of great difficulty for the settlement. It was plagued by attacks from external sources and money was hard to come by. There were financial difficulties. The abolitionists in London therefore decided that it was opportune to form a trading company to help the settlement grow and develop into a thriving and prosperous country. They formed the St. George's Bay Company[1] primarily for the purpose of trade and also for taking over control of the Province of Freedom. They petitioned parliament to have the company incorporated. The bill was introduced in the House of Commons in April 1791 as the Sierra Leone Company Bill. It became law on the 6th June 1791 and the company became incorporated on the 1st July, 1791. With the passing of the Sierra Leone Company Act,[2] the Independent Province of Freedom came to an end. In its place, was set up a Government, colonial in form and content, controlled by Directors of a Company of Merchants resident in England. The passage of the bill was not without its opponents as there were many influential people who were opposed to the idea of transferring the government of the settlement to a company of merchants. However, it must be recalled that this was an era of great economic expansion and there had been a precedent in British India[3] for the government and administration of territory being in the hands of a Board of Directors of a Company Incorporated in England and resident in England.

COMPANY RULE — THE SIERRA LEONE COMPANY ACT.
The preamble of the act, as passed by parliament, was as follows:
    An act for establishing a company for carrying on trade between the kingdom of Great Britain and the coasts, harbours and

---
1 For the objects of the company see HARLOW & MARSDEN: *British Colonial Developments, 1774-1835,* Oxford (1953) p.460.
2 supra. Stat. 31 Geo. III C. 55.
3 The East India Company.

countries of Africa and for enabling the said company to hold by grant from His Majesty, his heirs and successors and from the natural princes of Africa, a certain district of land commonly called the Peninsula of Sierra Leone now vested in His Majesty or belonging to the said princes, for the better enabling the said company to carry on the said trade.

In the light of the immediate past history of the territory, this long title was remarkable and somewhat inexplicable. It indicated that the company was being formed for trade purposes and the purposes of the enactment could be summarised as follows:

(a) To establish a company to carry on trade between Great Britain and Africa:
(b) To enable the company to hold by grant from His Majesty AND the natural princes of Africa, the Peninsula of Sierra Leone "now vested in His Majesty or belonging to the said princes":
(c) To enable the said company to carry on the said trade.

The second of these principal objects is strange and its inaccuracy is indefensible. It is a historical fact that the land had been sold to the free community of settlers. It had not been conveyed to the British Monarch, nor had the British Government taken over the territory by conquest or otherwise. His Majesty exercised no jurisdiction over it; nor was the territory held by the settlers or the abolitionists in the name of His Majesty. Nor had the land been ceded to the Crown. How then could the Act describe the Peninsula of Sierra Leone as "now vested" in His Majesty? This was clearly a misunderstanding of the legal and constitutional position of the country.

Similarly, if the land was now owned by the Crown who had no right or power to exercise any authority over it, how then could it possibly give by grant to another, that is the new company, something that did not belong to it? The land was in point of fact vested in the settlers and could not be taken away from them without their consent. It would seem that parliament was itself unsure of the position, hence the use of the word 'or', in relation to the proposition that the land belonged to the "princes".

It is submitted that this preamble and the whole Act itself indicates brilliantly the omnipotence of the British Parliament. Only the parliament at Westminster could legislate to give to a company property which it did not own. That Britain contributed to the expenses of the settlement is not open to dispute. Sharpe and others, as we have seen before made constant appeals for help. There was sympathy and response, but Britain was unequivocal about its attitude to the project and its policy thereto. She did not want to be lumbered with the responsibility of a colony. It therefore resisted all overtures in that direction. As far as parliament was concerned, all it was doing was responding to the request of the company for its incorporation. Parliament could not therefore be blamed for what appeared legislative uncertainty about the status of the settlement.

Parliament also seemed uncertain whether the land belonged to the rulers in Africa or to the settlers. It described the settlement as "either vested in His Majesty or belonging to the native rulers". There was no basis for this and one begins to wonder who drafted the bill and what information the person had who did so. The abolitionists, or perhaps, the majority of them, had wanted the British Government to take over the settlement and worked hard at achieving this. They felt the British Government had the right kind of resources to take over the responsibility of a fledgling state. However, the Attorney-General of the day and other members of the government were opposed to this. There were strong views expressed in parliament opposing the taking over by Britain of any other colony by reason of the fact that they felt there were enough colonies already and any additional ones would merely add to the expense of the government and become burdensome.

There are other reasons which could be advanced to explain why the British Parliament seemed not to be aware of the status of the settlement. There was constant hostility between France and England at that time and it became necessary for the British Crown in response to the strong abolitionist lobby to do something to ensure the safety of the settlers and their defence against attacks from foreign vessels.

A third possible reason for this uncertainty is the fact that the maintenance of the settlement was beyond the financial ability of the settlers. Members of Parliament may have been under the impression that the local rulers were therefore still in control of the area of the settlement.

Fourthly, at this period of time, companies could only be incorporated by Act of Parliament as this was the great era of chartered companies which derived their authority and legitimacy from the Crown through Parliament. Logically therefore, it may have been deduced that since the Crown gave permission to any group of persons to trade and to hold property, the grant carried with it the right of the Crown to occupation and control of such property.

Fifthly, as has been pointed out before, the abolitionists thought that they were the owners of the land and the only persons who could claim right of ownership. This is understandable as they were the ones who had financed the whole project including the cost of the expeditions. It was they who provided the funds for the purchase, twice, of the land on which the settlement was built. The settlers were the beneficiaries of their bounty. In the circumstances when the time came for them to appeal to the Crown for help, it is reasonable to say that they may have suggested that in return for assistance from the British Government they would surrender their property to it.

Finally, in terms of free and independent governments, this was the great age of the democratization of governments and there was prevalent the idea that men were inherently free to form associations and to govern themselves. It was the time of the great revolutions in Europe and America which saw the development of new concepts of the 'Rights of Man'. Those who had gone to distant countries, according to the then prevailing legal concept of citizenship and nationality, took their personal law with them. All that was required from one's country, was protection. So, there developed certain concepts peculiarly colonial, among the main colonising powers, Britain, France, Portugal and Germany that overseas possessions were extensions of the home countries. Thus, if Britain were passing an enactment regarding the government and administration of a 'colonial' territory, it must be 'owned' by the Crown and the property vested in His Majesty.

OTHER PROVISIONS OF THE ACT.
Leaving the long title and looking at the other provisions of the enactment, Sec. 48 stipulated that the life of the Sierra Leone Company should be thirty one (31) years with effect from 1st July, 1791. This provision reflected the wish of the company that the rule by the directors would be a temporary expedient and that the government would be returned to the settlers after the territory had become strong economically and militarily: as later events showed, this hope was not realised.

Most of the other provisions of the Act were intended for the internal management and administration of the company. The Act authorised the appointment of thirteen directors. They were resident in England. The company was empowered by Section 29 to make "bye-laws, ordinances, rules, orders or directions for the good government of the company.[4]

The Act empowered the company to hold by grant from the Crown, the land originally the subject of the treaties with Kings Tom and Naimbana.

In keeping with the fine ideals of the promoters of the settlement since its inception, letters patent under the act foreshadowed complete equality between the races. This was also proclaimed in a statement issued by the company on the 2nd day of August, 1791.[5] The letters patent required the company's directors to legislate and form a government which would give "to the Black as well as to the White settlers the same voice" in deciding local matters. On the 19th October 1791,[6] the company made a Declaration which proscribed dealing in slaves and precluded anyone from being ill treated. The company further declared that it would punish criminal conduct but assured the settlers that both Black and White would be equally governed.

4 Section 33 of the Act was interesting. It empowered the company to make its own "reasonable laws and ordinances from time to time, for, touching or concerning the trade of the said company, and for making dividends of the profits arising from their capital joint stock, and for the good government of all, or any other affairs or business of the said company and for the good government of all the officers servants and others concerned in the same, and to inflict reasonable penalties and forfeitures for any breach or breaches thereof, so that the same be not repugnant to the laws of England."

The emphasis on the company in the Act, rather than on the settlement can be explained by the fact that the statute was setting out then what today would be in the articles of association which are the rules governing the internal administration of the company. The bye-laws enabled the company to legislate for the settlement.

5 The statement is set out in Appendix VI.
6 See the Report of the Sierra Leone Company, 19th October 1791, pp. 23-4 & 33.

THE LEGAL STATUS OF THE SIERRA LEONE COMPANY.

Our analysis of the Sierra Leone Company Act, particularly the preamble, suggested that the wording of some of the provisions was unfortunate.

One important and fundamental question which remained unanswered after the passing of the Act of Incorporation was, what was the legal status of the company, vis-à-vis the settlers. Was the company a sovereign entity, or a mere delegee of the British Crown? The Act, laid considerable emphasis on the control by the company over its officers. Questions were raised in and out of parliament about the extent of the powers of the company and the limits of those powers. The settlers challenged the company's authority to govern them and foreign captains of vessels also refused to acknowledge the company's authority in the settlement. It is therefore necessary to look a little closer at the Act and see to what extent the company was entirely autonomous and had power and authority to take over the Government of the Province of Freedom.

Reference has been made before to the parallel situation in India where the East India Company had a charter from the British Parliament which gave it both legislative and judicial powers not only over the company's servants, but also over all those within the possessions of the company. A case arose which led to a determination of this point. It was the case of Secretary of State-v-Kamachee Boyee Sahiba[7] in which Lord Kingsdown said that the East India Company was merely a delegee of the British Government and not a sovereign entity. Could it, by analogy therefore, be said that the Sierra Leone Company in the exercise of its powers over the settlement was a mere delegee of the British Goverment? The question can only be answered (a) objectively by looking at the circumstances which existed in the settlement and also in Britain at the time the Act of Incorporation was passed, and (b) by construing the Act of Incorporation of 1791.

Viewed from the point of view of the conditions in existence at the time, it is clear that when the Act was passed, the Province of Freedom was a free and independent state. The settlers had their own government and nowhere is there any assertion that the request for company rule emanated from the government of that state. Viewed realistically from the point of view of the abolitionists, there was such a desire on the part of the promoters of the company who felt that they still had some measure of responsibility for seeing that the settlement emerged as a viable state. But the abolitionists did not succeed in getting the British Government to take over their baby. So the company was not an agent of the British Government and the latter did not view the relationship in that light. The survival or failure of the project, as far as the Crown was concerned was entirely a matter for the promoters of the company. The Crown was clearly reluctant to get involved in the administration of the settlement.

With regard to the Act of Incorporation, it seems to be the inevitable

---

7 M.I.A. 476.

conclusion that the intention of parliament was to vest the lands forming the settlement in the company and for the company to be responsible for the government of the country. These objectives were clear from the words of the Act. The company was given all the powers it required over its own officials. Then these powers were extended to cover all. The manuscript orders showed that the company understood its role in the territory primarily as that of an independent administrator. The company were to appoint their superintendent who was responsible to the board of directors in England. There was nothing in the Act suggesting that the company had to refer to the British Government for anything, or account to it in respect of its activities in the settlement.

Historians have also concluded that by enacting the Act of Incorporation, the British Government acquired jurisdiction over the Settlement of Sierra Leone. This is an erroneous conclusion and it is also legally unsound. The Act did not reserve to the British Monarchy any powers nor did it authorise the British Parliament or the British Government to legislate or govern the country. In fact there was no express exercise of British jurisdiction in Sierra Leone. Indeed, if there was any semblance of the exercise of any such jurisdiction it was in respect of specific requests made from time to time by British traders who were committed to the protection and financial support of the peoples of that new territory. Finally, the British Government never at any time appointed any official to act for it in the settlement. The powers and authorities of the company conferred on it by the Crown were absolute. Appeals, for example, lay to the directors in England from the courts of the settlement unlike in the West Indies where appeals lay to the Privy Council. The conclusion therefore is that unlike what had happened in India, the Sierra Leone experiment was deeply rooted and founded on philanthropy and independence, not on colonial rule. The Sierra Leone Company, consequently, in the exercise of its powers, was not an agent or delegee of the British Government and it was a sovereign and independent entity responsible to no one for the manner in which it administered the settlement.

MANUSCRIPT ORDERS AND REGULATIONS.
Following its incorporation, the Sierra Leone Company, in 1791, promulgated "Manuscript Orders and Regulations from the Directors to the Superintendent and Council in Freetown." These orders and regulations made numerous provisions for the settlement, but those which are of interest and importance in the present context are those relating to the government and administration of the territory, including the administration of justice. When closely examined, these provisions show a marked improvement on English law as it then was. They provided the requisite authority which the company required to enable it to govern the settlement effectively.

From a constitutional point of view, the establishment of company rule in Sierra Leone and the promulgation of the manuscript orders and regulations were a retrograde step. The independence of the settlers was

From Independence to Colonial Rule

lost and the company took over control and government of the settlement. The important provisions dealing with the administration and justice will now be examined.

PROVISIONS RELATING TO THE ADMINISTRATION.
These can be summarised as follows:
(1) All offices in the settlement were elective, but supreme power resided in the hands of the directors in England.
(2) The Chief Administrative Officer was to be the Superintendent. He was to be appointed by the directors in England. He was the First Officer in the settlement and was to be assisted by a Council of eight. (This number was reduced to three in the year 1792-3 at the instance of Governor Clarkson).
(3) The Superintendent and Council were to form the Government of the Settlement and each member of the Council was to be a Justice of the Peace.
(4) The first town was to be named 'Freetown'.

PROVISIONS RELATING TO
THE ADMINISTRATION OF JUSTICE.
(1) The Superintendent and Council were to be responsible for the administration of justice both civil and criminal.
(2) Criminal trials were to follow committal within a fortnight where possible.
(3) Captial punishment was abolished even in cases of murder, except in those cases where the Council were of the opinion that it was desirable to send the accused to England for trial.
(4) One-half of the jury should be of the same race as the accused.
(5) There was a right of appeal to the directors in England.
(6) A Court of Session was to be established sitting every three months and presided over by two or three justices with a jury. It had both civil and criminal jurisdiction.
(7) Fines were substituted for corporal punishment.
(8) Imprisonment for debt was limited to debts over £10 and imprisonment for not more than three years.
(9) A court of Summary Jurisdiction was established to try offences triable summarily by English law.
(10) Jurisdiction was conferred on a Justice of the Peace sitting alone to try cases of debts under £2.
(11) Civil suits were to be tried by a jury according to the laws of England.
(12) Two marshalls were appointed. One each for Granville Town and Freetown to summon juries.
(13) Land was available for execution if personal property was inadequate.

Taken together, the Act and the regulations could properly be described as a constitution for the Settlement of Sierra Leone. For they prescribed the powers and duties of the principal functionaries and organs of the state and also formalised the machinery of justice.

The regulations set up a government under the company which was headed by the superintendent, assisted by a council. Originally, the council was one of eight. It had limited powers of government. Its powers were limited to internal affairs. The regulations also spelt out the powers of the superintendent and his council. Briefly, these were as follows:
(1) That the Superintendent and Council were invested with the Government of the Peninsula of Sierra Leone in all matters civil, military, political and commercial:
(2) They were to hold the same under the authority which the Company itself possessed until a new Constitution was promulgated:
(3) They were to act in accordance with orders from the Company:
(4) In the absence of specific orders, they were to look to the general principles of English law and the scope of the general instructions:
(5) They were to be responsible to the Company for the manner in which they exercised their powers and discretions:
(6) All acts and orders of the Council were to be in the name of the Superintendent and Council of Sierra Leone even though the Superintendent may not have been present or may have been outvoted.

Similarly, the same regulations set out the duties of the superintendent and council.[8] They provided as follows:
(1) To form general regulations for the good order and prosperity of the Colony.
(2) To make provision for general means of defence.
(3) To provide suitable machinery for the administration of justice:
(4) To make suitable provision for the prevention and correction of abuses of every kind:
(5) To undertake the chief care and control of trade, cultivation, building and all other concerns, "conformably to the orders which by this and any other further letters they receive from the Court of Directors."

The superintendent himself was given certain specific directions and his powers were spelt out in some detail. Inter alia, he was to :—
(a) Have precedence in the Colony.[9]
(b) Be the representative of the Company with the native Chiefs:
(c) Be the Head of the military and command the forts:
(d) Preside at the Council where he had a casting vote:
(e) Introduce such questions for discussion as he thought proper:
(f) Correspond with the Court of Directors without communicating his letters to the Council (which no other members of the Council

---

8 See Section 20 of the Manuscript Orders.
9 These orders described the territory as a "Colony" which strictly it was not. This term was used interchangeably with the word "Settlement".

From Independence to Colonial Rule 41

could do officially):
- (g) Act in accordance with the decisions of the majority and see that decisions of the Council were implemented:
- (h) Summon meetings of the Council at least twice a week.

The regulations also provided for the Governor (Superintendent) and Council to encourage the local members of the population to participate in its deliberations. For example, it was provided in clause 31[10] that the Directors

> "considered it a fundamental principle which the company ought at all times to proceed and in the highest degree essential to the welfare and comfort of the resident members of the settlement to ensure to them a share in its internal legislation."

It also affirmed that it was hoped before long to be able to institute a plan for that purpose adapted to the needs of the infant state of the colony and capable of being extended by degrees in proportion to the growing population and prosperity.

SUMMARY:
With the advent of company rule and the extensive constitutional provisions discussed above, certain conclusions can be drawn:

First: The Independent Province of Freedom was no longer free. It had lost its independence unwillingly. In place of the elected government which was a distinct feature of the original settlement, there was now imposed on the people against their will, a superintendent and council, both nominated by the Court of Directors of the Sierra Leone Company in England. The citizens of the new state could no longer participate in the choice of their leaders. Nor could they take part in discussions affecting their interest. Here was the beginning of colonial rule, albeit through a company incorporated in England expressly for promoting trade and commerce.

Second: The superintendent and council were a government of limited powers although on the face of it they seemed autonomous. They had exclusive control of internal matters but were nevertheless accountable, not to the settlers whom they governed, but to the directors of the company in England. This provision was the forerunner of the power of disallowance of colonial legislation which was a distinct feature of government under the Crown.

Thirdly: Although the superintendent and council had wide powers to initiate and pass legislation as the circumstances warranted, it was provided that laws passed by the council should not be inconsistent with or repugnant to the general principles of English law. This provision

---

10 This clause of the Manuscript Orders and Regulations dealt with the principle of internal legislation. See: Evans: *An Early Constitution for Sierra Leone* (Sierra Leone Studies, N.S.) 1932.

ensured that the laws of an advanced and developed country whose legal system was well tried, were available to a developing country which badly needed an impartial judiciary and a fair and just administration of the law. It badly needed reasonable laws and regulations to guide it in its march towards modern developments.

Fourthly: The company conducted the foreign affairs of the state and in this respect it delegated its powers of negotiating with foreign states to the governor/superintendent. The superintendent entered into all necessary discussions with the local rulers of the neighbouring hinterland. He also had authority to settle any disputes with captains of vessels calling at the capital for watering. As yet, the international community had not fully accepted that the settlement was free and independent and fully capable of entering into international obligations with other states.

Fifthly: The superintendent had power to initiate legislation, but this power was not exclusively reserved to him. The council also could do that, but with this important proviso, namely, that measures by the superintendent took precedence to those of the council in any event.

Sixthly: The council exercised both legislative and executive functions. They also had some judicial functions.

Thus, Sierra Leone now had a "Constitution" with all the makings of a colonial legislature. Later colonial constitutions had many features which were found in the company's pattern of government. For example, instructions to the company's servants could be compared with the Royal Instructions of the later colonial constitutions. The powers of the governor were almost identical under both systems. By virtue of his appointment as superintendent the person so appointed had sovereignty over the whole of the territory under his command. His powers and authority were absolute, except in so far as there were express limitations imposed by the company.

With regard to the legislature, in spite of its undoubted competence to pass laws for the order and good government of the territory, it could not pass any measures which were repugnant to or inconsistent with the laws of England. This parallels the 'non-repugnancy' clause of colonial constitutions, which usually provided that the measure passed by the subordinate legislature would be void to the extent of such repugnancy or inconsistency.

The governor/superintendent, was the chief executive; but the legislature was not an elected one. It was wholly nominated. There was no responsible form of government; so the executive could initiate legislation without the concurrence of the council at Freetown. Similarly, it could pass laws without the necessity of referring them back to the directors in England for approval. There were, however, certain measures which could not be enforced without the prior consent of the directors in England. This procedure was reflective of the colonial practice of reservation of bills.[11]

Consequently, it could be concluded that to a very substantial extent, the company's constitution was colonial both in form and content; the government was under the autocratic rule of the governor who was in fact, the government of the country. He could, with ease, impose his authority and his own brand of personal rule on the country. Hence, like the chancellors of old, the kind of government the country enjoyed varied with the length of the governor's boot.

ADMINISTRATION OF JUSTICE

Section 32 of the Manuscript Orders and Regulations, provided for the administration of justice in the territory. It provided, inter alia, that:

1. Each member of the Council should possess and exercise the functions of a Justice of the Peace.
2. The violation of any law of England (not inapplicable to the settlement) would be met by apprehension and detention on a warrant of arrest issued by such a justice.
3. Trial of cases by the justices on whose warrant a person was apprehended should be expeditious; if practicable, within fourteen (14) days by a jury summoned for that purpose.
4. Trials should proceed in accordance with the laws of England.
5. In jury trials, one-half of the jury should be of the same race as the accused person:
6. The Council were to be responsible for summoning juries and to sit as judges but without any power to inflict the death penalty and substituting fines for corporal punishment as far as possible. Punishment was to be of a kind recognised by the law of England.
7. The majority of the Council could exercise power to mitigate the punishment or grant a free pardon. They were to record their decisions as well as the reasons for such decisions.
8. In cases of conviction for murder, the Council could punish the accused on the spot or send the convict to England for trial provided witnesses were also willing to go over there; they would be indemnified for their expenses.
9. Civil suits were triable by jury according to the laws of England.
10. A Justice of the Peace sitting alone could try certain minor cases notably those where the debt or claim was not in excess of £2.

Following the promulgation of these manuscript orders and regulations, a hierarchy of courts was set up. Those in existence at the time when the company took over the administration and developed its own system of jurisprudence, were the following:

1. *The Courts of the Justices:*
   In these courts, the justices could sit either alone or in pairs. These courts were the equivalent of today's Magistrate's Courts. The justices exercised jurisdiction in summary matters both civil and criminal. The justices sat without a jury.

11 See Sir Kenneth Roberts-Wray:

2. *The Court of Quarter Sessions:*
   This was a criminal court which met at three-monthly intervals for the trial of offenders. It was presided over by two or three justices who sat with a jury.
3. *The Court of the Council:*
   This court was composed of members of the council who sat with a jury both in civil and criminal cases. It was the highest resident court. The governor often sat in this court and presided whenever he did.
4. *The Court of the Directors:*
   The members of this court were the directors resident in England. It was purely a Court of Appeal from the Court of the Council in Freetown. It had jurisdiction in criminal capital cases but this jurisdiction fell into desuetude.

The manner in which this jurisdiction was exercised is interesting as the following instances and facts reveal:

(a) Thomas Matthews,[12] a private was brought before the council, having been confined for drunkenness, disobedience of orders, insolent behaviour to Mr Cook a member of council,[13] and parting with some of his accoutrements. He confessed his crime and declared his sorrow and contrition.
The council severely reprimanded him and remitted his punishment. The prisoner was discharged.

(b) Daniel Prophet-v-James Othello. The charge being one of assault. Othello was sentenced to be tied up by his hands to a post for the space of two hours and then discharged with threats of severe punishment when next found guilty of an offence.[14]

(c) Thomas Matthews: He was brought in to answer the following charges:—

i. Drunkenness, disobedience and neglect of duty; for which he was confined.

ii. Breaking loose on March 10th from his confinement, breaking open the chests of James Pearson and Thomas Burton his fellow soldiers, and robbing them of monies.

iii. Deserting to King Jemmy[15] with the view of going to the Banana Islands.
The prisoner acknowledged the justice of the severe charges, but pleaded temporary insanity owing to a wound on his head, and drunkenness.
Evidence was taken.
The prisoner was ordered to be withdrawn. Sentence given by secret votation according to a majority, that one hundred lashes

12 C.O. 270(2). Minutes of the meeting of 21/2/1792.
13 Jas Cook was on this date a member of the council presided over by Falconbridge. He was personally present when the case was heard.
14 C.O. 270(2). Minutes of 6/2/1792 at pp.7-8.
15 Now known as 'King Jimmy', a landing post for small vessels across the bay from the other side of the capital, Freetown.

From Independence to Colonial Rule 45

be inflicted on him.

On this, the prisoner was brought in again and the sentence pronounced on him.[16]

(d) Thomas Matthews, a private soldier was again brought before the council on a charge of theft. The prisoner pleaded not guilty. Evidence was led. The prisoner was asked what he had to say for himself.

The prisoner ordered to be withdrawn.

SENTENCE: One hundred and fifty lashes on his bare back; that he be immediately discharged from the company's service, stripped with disgrace of his military clothing and accoutrements, and kept prisoner until such time that he may be sent back to England.

The prisoner was brought in to receive the sentence after which he was withdrawn.[17]

From the above extracts, certain conclusions can be drawn:

(1) The governor and council exercised both administrative and judicial functions simultaneously. Where a member of the council was involved personally in the matter in dispute, he could nevertheless sit in judgment over his own cause or matter.

(2) The governor and council also assumed jurisdiction in cases which could appropriately be described as military offences, properly punishable by a court martial.

(3) Corporal punishment was a recognised method of dealing with adult offenders. Similarly, other forms of punishment which would, today, be regarded as 'cruel and inhuman' were permissible.

(4) A persistent offender could be brought before the same tribunal several times and be dealt with in accordance with the law. Apparently, it did not matter that the court was seised of his previous offences.[18]

---

16 C.O. 270(2). Minutes of 20th March 1792.
17 C.O. 270(2). Minutes of 3rd April 1792.
18 This is borne out by the case of Thomas Matthews who appeared three times before the court. Each subsequent punishment was more severe than the previous one.

CHAPTER V

THE GOVERNMENT OF THE SETTLEMENT, 1791 to 1807

The first governor to be appointed by the company after the Act of Incorporation, was Governor John Clarkson. On the 10th March 1792[1] he took the following oath of office:
> I, John Clarkson, do swear that I will be true and faithful to the interest of the Sierra Leone Company and serve them in the capacity of Superintendent of the Colony of Sierra Leone to the best of my skill and power.
> So help me God.

This oath of allegiance, significantly, was to the company, not to the British Government. This is important as it again puts into perspective the constitutional status of the country. He swore and undertook to be true and faithful to the company, his employers, and to pursue its interest. His primary duty therefore was to the company which had appointed him, and not to the settlers whom he was to govern. Still less was it to the British Government who had no say in the matter. Yet, Clarkson turned out to be one of the greatest champions of the settlers and of their right to independence. More than any other governor or superintendent, he championed and advanced the interests of the settlers in practically all spheres of life. More particularly, he genuinely sought to give them an opportunity to participate in the deliberations of the council and to enable them to take over ultimate control of their own affairs. His performance in this respect was noble and unequalled by any other governor in the history of the settlement.

Under Clarkson's regime, the institution of Hundredors and Tythingmen developed rapidly and effectively. As a careful and able administrator, Clarkson discreetly made numerous concessions to the settlers towards achieving independent rule. He tried to get them to participate in the company's governmental activities so that in due course they would take over the responsibilities of the government themselves. For example, on the 12th December, 1792,[2] William Dawes proposed that for the proper dispensation of justice, inferior magistrates should be

---
1 C.O. 270(2). Minutes of 3rd April 1792.
2 See C.O. 270(2) p.38.

appointed from among the settlers. This was accepted by the council which, by its resolution dated 31st December, 1792, decided, in the presence of William Dawes and Zachary Macaulay, that:

> "In order, the more effectively to preserve the peace, it will be necessary to divide the town into Tithings, the ten heads of families in each Tithing to choose one of their number for Tithingman to act as Constable over those ten houses. The Tithingmen of ten contiguous tithings to cause among themselves a Hundredor to act as Head Constable over the same ten Tithings."

Following this resolution, regulations were drawn up for the Hundredors and Tythingmen, and on the 24th day of January 1793, a resolution was passed to the effect that the regulations or instructions drawn up for the Hundredors and Tythingmen should be communicated to them and explained to them and put immediately into force. On the 1st March, 1793,[3] the council resolved as follows:

> That John Cuthbert, one of the Hundredors of Freetown be created Marshall for the town and that James Reed, Hundredor of Granville Town, be appointed Marshall for the town and each to have for his trouble in discharging this office, a salary of £20 per annum. That it be given the Marshall in charge:
>
> 1st To summon the juries asking returns of the juries summoned to the Clerk of the Peace:
> 2nd To apprehend offenders:
> 3rd To execute writs for debts:
> 4th To levy the fees and fines ordered by the court:
> 5th To execute the sentences of the court whether they regard fine or imprisonment:
> 6th To overlook the prisoners and see that the inferior officers do their duty.
>
> That for any of the above purposes it may be lawful for them to command the assistance of any, or all, the Tythingmen in the colony.

It would appear that following this resolution, the Hundredors and Tythingmen began to play an important and significant role, not only in the administration of the government, but also in the administration of justice in the settlement where they claimed the right of adjudication and also succeeded in participating in the decision making process in so far as the adjudication and settlement of disputes was concerned. By the month of May 1793, they were already claiming the right to propose laws for enactment by the superintendent and council. Their right to do this appears to have been not only tacitly, but also expressly, recognised and accepted by the company's officials, for, on the 12th May 1793, the following notice was published under the authority of the council:

> NOTICE is hereby given that according to a law proposed by the Hundredors and Tythingmen of this town, and agreed to by Mr

---

3 See C.O. 270(2) p.38.

William Dawes, Acting Governor in the absence of Mr Clarkson. All persons possessed of hogs, goats or sheep are to keep them shut up so that they do no damage or trespass on the ground of any other persons and if in three days after this notice any hog, sheep or goat is found at large the owner of it will be fined in the sum of one dollar and pay for all damage done, which, if the person who owns the creature, refuses to pay to the Marshall, Mr John Cuthbert, on demand, he will be sued in the next court and will if he loses the cause have to pay all the costs and expenses of the prosecution.

This law is to continue in force for two months and no longer.

On the 4th June 1793, the following notice was published, with the "support and approbation" of the governor and council:

Notice is hereby given that by a law proposed by the Hundredors and Tythingmen of this town, and approved of by William Dawes Esquire, Acting Governor, no person whatever shall sell fresh beef for a greater price than 4d., nor goat and sheep, mutton, for a greater price than 6d., nor fresh pork for a greater price than 8d., under the penalty of forfeiting all such meat as the offender may have in his possession at the time of the information given.

In the following year, on the 1st day of May, 1794, the council passed a law regarding adultery. Before they did so, they consulted the Hundredors and Tythingmen. This is recorded in the minutes of the meeting of the council in the following terms:

Those who commit the crime of adultery should be punished. The following regulations which are agreeable to the laws of England . . . are passed:

1. It is lawful for a husband to prosecute any man who has committed adultery with his wife provided he prosecutes the wife at the same time.
2. If proved — fine of £5 on the man and damage to the husband. The offending woman shall be inflicted corporal punishment and confinement according to the gravity of the offence.
3. Lawful for the injured husband to apply for a divorce, but not unless the crime of adultery has been proved.
4. Ill conduct on the part of the husband ought to be considered by a jury as tending to lessen both damage and punishment on women.

***   ***   ***

7. Lawful for wife to prosecute husband together with offending woman. Punishment (corporal punishment) for woman. Fine of £5 on man and husband to afford his wife maintenance for life. Jury to fix the amount.

The Hundredors and Tythingmen signified their hearty approbation and acquiescence in the propriety of every part of it.

In the light of this kind of legislative activity, it is not at all surprising that the Hundredors and Tythingmen proved themselves quite a force to be reckoned with. They viewed their functions as both administrative and legislative. They did not regard themselves as merely 'Keepers of the Peace'. After all, they appeared to be painfully conscious of the fact that their country had once been completely independent. They did not take too kindly to company rules which meant a whittling down of their powers. That the company officials were now appointed and held positions in substitution for and in replacement of the settlers themselves, was unpalatable. It was not a matter of mere coincidence, that the majority of the persons elected Hundredors and Tythingmen were Nova Scotians who had been promised land before they embarked for Sierra Leone and who had been aware of the history of the establishment of the settlement. They discovered much to their dismay and disappointment that the promises held out to them remained largely unfulfilled.

Governor Clarkson was a superb administrator. With his keen perception and shrewd judgment he had visualised the breakers ahead. He therefore tried to rule by persuasion and consent. He went out of his way to seek the co-operation of the whole body of settlers through their representatives. Ironically, however, the institution of Hundredors and Tythingmen which the company had conceived of as a means of exercising more effective control of the settlers in fact gave them an organisation through which they, in turn, were able effectively to oppose and launch protests against the company's policies.

HUNDREDORS AND TYTHINGMEN-v-THE COMPANY:
One of the earliest occasions when the Hundredors and Tythingmen challenged the company over its administration of the settlement was over the question of land. The opportunity for this arose upon the departure of Governor Clarkson in 1793. Clarkson was succeeded by Dawes. The Hundredors and Tythingmen complained to Dawes that they had been offered ten acres of land for each adult settler at the time the settlement was established. Now they were being offered five. They alleged that this was a serious breach of confidence and so it was. They challenged Dawes about this. When they could not get any satisfaction from him, they petitioned the company and complained vigorously about Dawes' administration. The Hundredors and Tythingmen and the settlers generally had never trusted Dawes and sheer "distress and frustration continued to characterise relations between settler and company throughout 1793 and 1794".[4]

In the meantime, law suits were proliferating in the territory. The council were concerned. They passed a resolution on the 1st March 1793 to the effect that to discourage "frivolous and vexatious law suits", a fine of five shillings would be levied on the party losing the cause, to be added to the fund of fines for defraying the expenses of the jury, constables and other public charges.

On the 3rd August 1793, the governor and council passed another

---

4 See Peterson — *"Province of Freedom"* (Faber and Faber, London) p.31.

D

resolution making slander a criminal offence. They indicated that the need for such a law existed because they had taken into consideration the immense trouble which was caused to the court of sessions from the multiplication of trivial suits for slanderous words, such as 'whore, thief, robber, etc.' The council said that at that time, there existed no proper punishment for that malady and being apprised at the same time of a general desire expressed by the settlers of some regulations which might cure "this spirit and disposition leading to the use of such improper language", it was essential for the council to deal with the matter. They therefore resolved:

> That henceforth, on clear proof before a jury, that such words were used with a malicious intent, there be imposed on the offender a fine not exceeding twenty shillings together with costs of suit . . .
>
> That this regulation shall not exclude juries from their right of awarding damages where damages can be proved.

Thus, this measure, though passed by the council in exercise of its undoubted power of legislation, was passed as a result of the acquiescence or at the request of, the settlers through their representatives, the Hundredors and Tythingmen.

1793 was a fateful year in the history of Sierra Leone. It was also the year when the hostilities with France commenced. Early in that year, three European sailors from a ship which was watering in the harbour came ashore. They killed a duck belonging to a Nova Scotian. They were arrested and tried by Governor Macaulay, and a Nova Scotian jury. The verdict was one of guilty. One of them was sentenced to be publicly flogged and the others were subjected to fines and imprisonment. The captain of the vessel from which they came, complained to the captain of another vessel which was passing by. Together, they secured a copy of the Act of Incorporation, and having read it, concluded that the authority and powers of the company in respect of the government and administration of the settlement were ill defined. They challenged the authority of Macaulay and questioned his right to have treated the sailors in the way he did. They alleged that the company did not have any power conferred upon it by the Act of Incorporation to constitute, establish or operate courts of law. After giving due consideration to the views expressed by the captains, Macaulay released the sailors. He was concerned about what might happen if he did not relent. He concluded that the ships' captains had put forward an effective challenge to the jurisdiction of the courts of the settlement as well as to the authority of the company to try offenders within the settlement, particularly where those offenders were not settlers. Overall, they, the council at Freetown, felt that disturbing questions had arisen about the competence of the company, through its local representatives to govern the settlement and this called for new and express grants of powers.

Macaulay was in a quandary and this is understandable, because, the directors had themselves laid down a rule that runaway slaves could not be returned to their masters.[5] Serious doubts had therefore been expressed about the availability of competent jurisdiction in the company's officials to free slaves. As far as the Nova Scotians were concerned, this was a matter of tremendous importance to them, since many of them were Kurankos[6] who had been taken as slaves to Nova Scotia and had now returned 'home'. Fyfe gives illuminating accounts of how quite a fair number of slaves were reunited with their families by chance.[7]

On this issue of slavery, it is also worth recounting how the distinguished Thomas Peters, who had been very instrumental in getting the Nova Scotians back to Sierra Leone and to other parts of Africa, discovered his place of origin which was Cape Palmas, in Liberia.[8] It was therefore a matter of considerable importance to the settlers that the liberated slaves should not be returned to their masters after being reunited with their families or being offered an opportunity of a new existence in freedom and dignity.

It also appears that matters which were unquestionably within the exclusive competence of the company, were being referred to the Hundredors and Tythingmen from time to time for their support and approval. On the 29th October 1793,[9] Governor Dawes reported to the council that he had "opened to the chiefs on the Bullom Shore the design of forming a settlement on the district already sold by them to the company," and that "so far were the chiefs from stating any objection to the proposal that they seemed hearty to rejoice in the prospect of such a settlement." Dawes further reported that they were quite willing to treat for the purchase of more land. Similarly, on the 11th November, 1793,[10] the governor reported to the council that consequent upon a resolution of the council passed on the 8th November, 1793[11] he had traversed a fixed territory and settled the boundary with the chiefs, of a mile square of land already procured by the company on a perpetual lease in the

5 See the Report of the Directors, dated 27th March 1794.
6 Sierra Leone has a great many tribes of which the Kurankos are one. They claim to be one of the indigenous Sierra Leone tribes. See Harrell-Bond, Howard and Skinner: *Community Leadership and the Transformation of Freetown* (1801-1976) The Hague, 1978.
7 Fyfe: *A History of Sierra Leone* op. cit. Oxford University Press. Fyfe also mentions a striking coincidence when one returning slave discovered his mother who had been caught by, and was subjected to, servitude by a Temne chief. Another located and identified a Madinka trader who had sold him into slavery and offered his former "master" a present for unwittingly being the cause of his conversion to Christianity.
8 Liberia shares a common boundary with Sierra Leone on the east and has a similar history. The contribution of Peters towards raising the status and position of emancipated slaves is well known, but is merely of historical and not legal importance.
9 See C.O. 267(10) p.95.
10 See C.O. 267(10) p.96.
11 This was a Resolution empowering the governor to treat with the natives of the Bullom Shore which is on the other side of the Freetown Peninsular across the River Rokel. The company was interested in more land for extending the settlement. See C.O. 267(10).

presence of, and with the consent of the native chiefs. This action was also approved of by the Hundredors and Tythingmen.

Reference has already been made to the law relating to adultery which was passed on the 1st May 1794 after the resolution had been proposed by Mr Zachary Macaulay.[12] A feature of this enactment was the statement made by Mr Macaulay that it had been "laid before the Hundredors and Tythingmen" who had signified their hearty acquiescence in the propriety of every part of it. Thus, it seemed that the council was itself acknowledging that before exercising its legislative powers there was some need for prior consultation with, and approval of, the Hundredors and Tythingmen. This prerequisite seemed to be a general one and was not confined merely to legislation affecting the settlers in matters of personal law only. Amazing as it was, the fact is that the governor and council had virtually abdicated their legislative powers and subordinated them to the prior approval of the settlers' representatives. Although the directors in London had to give their approval to this measure before it became effective, the council in Freetown found it necessary to state explicitly that the law would become operative in the territory for the time being, and until the directors in London indicated what their pleasure was. In the circumstances, once the Hundredors and Tythingmen had agreed and the council had passed the measure, the law made adultery a criminal offence and to pin-point the position and make it clear beyond a shadow of a doubt, the governor, as it were, determined to stamp it out, ordered the whipping, at the August Quarter Sessions, of a woman who had been found guilty of the offence.

There were other measures of little significance but nevertheless reinforcing the point that the council had recognised the Hundredors and Tythingmen as a consultative body whose opinion should be sought before legislation was brought into effect. An example was the resolution of the 9th April 1793 which required that settlers be summoned to draw their town lots. The Hundredors and Tythingmen were consulted about this and they were the ones designated to supervise and control the drawing of lots. Similarly, another resolution which related to the administration of justice, required that a fine be imposed by the court on every witness summoned to appear and failing to do so. The amount was fixed at 10/-. In the case of a party losing a case, he was required to pay the witness attending court the sum of 1/6d.

In 1795, a Petty Debts Court was established in which the Hundredors and Tythingmen sat with justices to hear and determine petty cases. The court exercised a variety of powers and had jurisdiction of a very varied kind in relation to punishment. They had power, for example, to inflict whippings, to confine convicts to stocks and to fine.

Thus, the Hundredors and Tythingmen took an increasing share of the responsibility for carrying out the management and administration of the settlement's business. They fast became an integral and indispensable part of the administration of both law and government. Eventually, they

12 See p.48 infra.

drew up, with the concurrence of the council, their own rules and regulations. These covered a number of activities such as:
> Holding regular meetings.
> Freedom of Debate.
> Decisions to be taken by majority vote.
> Collective responsibility (for the preservation of order and for keeping watch for attacks from outside enemies).

On the 10th October 1795, the Hundredors held a joint meeting with the Tythingmen and they resolved inter alia:
> That any person found guilty of loose, indecent, disorderly or riotous behaviour should be apprehended and brought before the governor or a Justice of the Peace, and that such Justice of the Peace should send for one Tythingman, out of every hundred who would sit with the Justice of the Peace and form a court for the immediate trial of the offender. The punishment, if found guilty, was to sit in the stocks or be whipped. There should be no appeal.
>
> That any person selling spiritous liquor without a licence should be tried before a similar court. Fine to be eight dollars.
>
> That all male settlers over the age of sixty years were liable to be called up on six days a year to clean the streets and roads of the settlement.

The governor and council considered these regulations "to be highly proper and expedient" and that they should form part of the laws of the colony and be published as such.

From these randon examples of legislative activity on the part of the Hundredors and Tythingmen, it can be concluded that the governor and council had conceded to them the right to propose legislation to be introduced into the council and passed into law. Also, it is clear, that the governor and council now considered it an essential part of the legislative process that the Hundredors and Tythingmen were to be consulted and their approval secured, before any measure was passed into law. In view of the subsequent events which took place in the settlement during the last years of the final decade of the nineteenth century, these conclusions are of fundamental importance.

To return to the institution of Hundredors and Tythingmen, from 1796 onwards, elections to the office of Hundredor or Tythingman, were held anually. The meeting of the council held on December 13th 1796 ensured that this was followed, and the machinery for bringing it into effect set up. The minutes of the council for that date, record the following:
> An exact account having been obtained of the names of all the freeholders in the colony, preparatory to issuing writs for the election of Tythingmen for the ensuing year:
>
> RESOLVED: That writs containing the names of 10 to 12 freeholders . . . be issued addressed to the marshall ordering them to summon the said persons to assemble themselves on Tuesday next to choose from their number a person to act as a Tythingman and to represent them . . . .

Thirty persons were elected for the 1st to the 30th Tything.
In 1795, a serious revolt occurred among the Hundredors and Tythingmen in relation to their duties and functions vis-a-vis the administration. Mr Zachary Macaulay found it necessary to address them.[13] He bemoaned the fact that "there is now no law. The law books are destroyed". He continued:

> What is the sum total of law? It is that thou shalt do no wrong to anyone. And do you require volume upon volume to teach you this? Or do you require prisons, trouges, fetters and gallows to make you remember?

Macaulay then went into a flow of rhetoric, appealing, encouraging and pleading with the Hundredors and Tythingmen to submit themselves to the control and discipline of the government; reminding them that he loved them and that he was anxious that they should assume responsibility for their own affairs in due course. Eventually, a document setting forth the duties of Hundredors was read out to them and they subscribed their names thereto.

On the 27th January 1798, it was agreed that the Hundredors and Tythingmen should henceforth meet separately, but that two Hundredors should meet with four Tythingmen to form rules and regulations *for the use of the colony*. The governor (Macaulay) acquiesced in this request for what, in effect, was the formation of two legislative chambers of the settlers. A committee of six was then formed for the purpose of having consultations with the governor. This seemed to be in substance and fact an Executive Committee of the settlers, comprised of their own chosen representatives, but presided over by the governor. This committee took policy decisions regarding the government of the settlement. They initiated legislation to be subsequently passed by the governor and council. If this body lacked any legal validity, it made up for its defective legal status by the efficiency and effectiveness with which it discharged its de facto responsibilities.

The pattern of legislation in the mid seventeen nineties shows that there was no systematic plan, nor any specifically designed procedure laid down for passing laws. The directors of the Sierra Leone Company left the matter entirely in the hands of the governor or superintendent who had supreme authority in the territory. Measures were introduced in an ad hoc manner to meet particular situations and the governor and his council were not by any means the sole originators of legislation. The Hundredors and Tythingmen on several occasions would pass resolutions and these would then in turn be formally approved of by the governor and council and then formally registered in the statute books of the colony.[14]

One interesting feature of the meetings of the Hundredors and Tythingmen was the signature of a company official on their resolutions.

13 See C.O. 270(3) p.60, 7th March 1795.
14 Although in several communications, the settlement was described as a "Colony", it was not strictly speaking a colony, although it had all the attributes of one. The word in this context, is therefore not employed in its strict legal sense.

The following is an example of this:[15]
RESOLVED:
That no stranger shall be allowed to become a proprietor of land or houses within the Colony of Sierra Leone who has not first obtained the consent of the governor and council, expressed in writing to that effect, and who has not also subscribed an obligation to obey the established laws of the colony.

That no stranger shall be entitled to exercise the rights of freeholder, or voting for Tythingman, serving juries or other public functions till it shall have been made to appear that the title of such a stranger to a freehold has been entered in the public register of the colony for a year and a day.

Signed — James Jones — Chairman
Thomas Cooper — Hundredor
Richard Crankapone — Hundredor
Thomas Jackson — Hundredor

For the company, the last decade of the eighteenth century was a turbulent one. Both internally and externally, its administration was seething with problems of great magnitude. Externally, there was aggression from the Temnes who constantly attacked the settlement and made spurious claims to the land comprising the territory of Sierra Leone. Foreign vessels also which called at the harbour at the port of Freetown for watering, were more often than not, a nuisance to the government, challenging its authority on the slightest pretext. In 1794, the town was razed and burnt to the ground by the French. After that disaster, an urban plan was introduced. This covered the centre of the city of Freetown, which was beautifully divided into rectangles, a pattern which survives to this day. Three major avenues ran parallel to each other and they were intersected by several streets, all bearing distinctively English names. The major avenues, Westmoreland, Oxford and Water Streets, as they came to be called, retained their names for almost two hundred years until they were renamed in 1971.[16] This basic division was described as the Nova Scotian Allotments and it made it quite easy for various plots of land to be allocated by the company to the settlers.

Internally, the picture was even less rosy and the difficulties equally, if not more, severe. A fruitful source of controversy between the governor and the settlers was the issue of quit-rents. These were payments extracted from the owners of land. It was a kind of land tax which a landholder was required to pay annually. The company administration saw this as a purely revenue device, but to the settlers it was an unnecessary and unwelcome aggravation which struck at the very principle

---

15 See Resolution of 8th July 1796. C.O. 270(4) at p.44.
16 The major avenues were never described as "Avenues". They were called "Streets" all the time. Now they are named "Siaka Stevens Street, Lightfoot Boston Street and Wallace Johnson Street" respectively. Siaka Stevens was President of Sierra Leone from 1968 to 1985. Sir Henry Lightfoot Boston was Governor-General before independence and Wallace Johnson a politician during the Colonial era who never had an opportunity to serve in government.

of land tenure. The settlers complained that the company had been guilty of a breach of faith since they had failed to allocate to them all the land which had been promised and to which the settlers considered they were justly entitled. By asking them to pay quit-rents, the settlers saw that as a wicked and devious scheme by the company to deprive them of their land, for payment of rent for the land hit at the fundamental basis of their fee simple land holding and affected their titles to the land. The settlers therefore contended that as owners in fee simple of the land they could not acknowledge the right or title of anyone else thereto and so they declined to pay the rent demanded by the company. They argued that if they conceded and paid rent, it would amount to a tacit admission that their fee simple had been converted into a leasehold interest with the paramount title residing in the company to whom the rent was to be paid. So they protested and flatly refused to pay.

Unquestionably, the settlers were right. Their arguments were formidable. Individual ownership of land in the settlement was a cardinal principle of the land tenure system from the very beginning when the sponsors of the settlement undertook to grant to each settler twenty acres of land. The land belonged to them and the company was, at best, a trustee for the purposes of allocating and distributing it and no more. They were managers for and on behalf of the owners, the settlers. When once a grant had been made to a particular person, he became the absolute owner of the land and the company retained no interest therein. How then could the company turn around and claim rent for property which did not belong to it and in which it had no interest?

Another matter which strained the goodwill between the company and the settlers, ironically, was the institution of Hundredors and Tythingmen. This system had been introduced for the smooth running of the government of the settlement by the company and in keeping with the proposals of Granville Sharp and the abolitionists. Yet, its manner of operation and its very existence, tended to give the impression that it was a countervaling force and in opposition to the government set up by the company. Yet this was not so. On a close examination of the manner in which this institution operated, one could see that to a large extent, they were concerned with local, as opposed to national, affairs. It was the deliberate policy of the company which drew them closer and closer into the governmental machinery. By the second half of the seventeen nineties, the inescapable conclusion was that the governor and council had either surrendered or lacked effective power which was substantially in the hands of the Hundredors and Tythingmen. It was the voices of these people which sounded loud and clear in all matters of government.

We have discussed before the legislation relating to adultery. It illustrated a worrisome problem both for the company's administrators and the settlers themselves. There was a crucial shortage of women and this had a most unsettling effect on the life of the settlers as a whole. Adultery seemed almost the inevitable consequence of this unhappy social phenomenon, but the settlement had been established on very strict and, perhaps, puritanical traditions, which could not permit a

The Government of the Settlement 1791-1807

social evil of this kind to be overlooked. Certain marriages were called into question and their validity questioned. The government then declared that no further marriages were to be celebrated without the publication of banns. The governor (Macaulay), then drew up a set of bastardy rules which required the fathers of illegitimate children to maintain them.

These measures were hotly debated by the Hundredors and Tythingmen. Eventually, they gave tacit approval to the regulations, but they nevertheless found it necessary to challenge Macaulay's authority. This was done by John Garvin, a schoolmaster and a settler. He was, appropriately also, a local preacher. He easily generated popular support for a lively protest against these measures. Zachary Macaulay was obliged to make an impassioned plea for calm and peace in the settlement. His address was a masterpiece of oratory and persuasion. These talents, which he undoubtedly possessed, were used with consummate skill. He won some support for moderation, but Garvin countered by collecting a lot of signatures to a petition which he had drawn up in unfavourable terms about Macaulay and which was addressed to Horne in England. When Macaulay discovered this, he was livid with rage and set up an inquiry, the first in the history of the settlement. It was a public inquiry and he charged Garvin with defamation, incitement to riot and the forgery of a signature on the letter of protest. Evidence was taken at the hearing from both Macualay and Garvin.

The case of Macaulay-v-Garvin was not a court action. It was a public inquiry. Yet it illustrated quite clearly a favourite device of governments to eliminate their opponents from the political scene — the use of court procedures resulting in the conviction and punishment of the accused. The charges which Garvin had to face before the court of inquiry make interesting reading:

FIRST: That John Garvin was an enemy to the interests of the Sierra Leone Company:

SECOND: That he has disturbed the public peace of the colony and promoted disaffection towards the lawful government therein established.

THIRD: That he has greatly calumniated the character and conduct of Zachary Macaulay, Governor of this Colony. He has wilfully misrepresented the views and laboured to make Zachary Macaulay odious to the people of the colony.

FOURTH: That he has wilfully misrepresented the views of Rev. John Clark, Chaplain to the Colony, and circulated unfounded reports in order to alienate the affection of the people of the said colony from the said John Clark.

FIFTH: A charge by Zachary Macaulay that he has been an enemy to the interests of the company and a disturber of the public peace.

These charges, by today's standards would be tried by a court of law as treason. All of them were found proved by a twelve-man court of inquiry. It was resolved that Garvin should quit the colony by the first conveyance and that in the meantime he be given a bond for his good behaviour in the sum of ten pounds, and two sureties in the sum of five pounds each. Garvin was ultimately banished and given a free passage to America.[17]

There were further internal problems, not from the settlers, but, this time, from the local rulers. They continued to make devious and insubstantial claims to the land. On the 4th July 1797, King Tom called to see the governor. He was accompanied by "Signor Domingo his second king, Prince Tom and other natives to talk palaver[18] for the country". Prior to this meeting, the natives had been constantly harassing and attacking the settlement. So, the governor thought that the visit was a peace mission aimed at eliminating further conflicts and battles between the two sides. On the contrary, it turned out that the "palaver" King Tom and his retinue wished to discuss, was a further claim to ownership of the piece of land already sold to the settlers. He presented a paper to the governor which laid claim to the land comprising the Settlement of Sierra Leone. The document bore his signature as well as the signature of King Banna.

During the meeting the governor faced the native chiefs with the original documents relating to the sale of the land. These deeds of sale, produced by the governor, were signed by King Tom himself, King Naimbana and King Jamie. Another document produced at the 'palaver' contained the substance of an agreement made between Mr Clarkson on the one hand, and King Jamie on the other, fixing the boundaries of the territory. The governor pointed out to King Tom that Mr Domingo, King Naimbana and several members of the visiting entourage were present, including King Tom himself, and had assisted in the transaction which had been successfully completed and the rights of the settlers to the land successfully completed ratified and confirmed in the presence of Domingo, Prince Tom, King Firama and several others.

King Tom was embarrassed. The confrontation was salutary and the evidence overwhelming. He had to change his tune. He acknowledged that the sale of the land had been valid and perfected a long time ago. He acknowledged that he could not go back on the agreement and was most surprised that his signature had appeared on the document now being presented to the governor claiming the land again. He said that he could not be a party to the presentation of any such document to the governor, and had no desire to contest the validity of the sale of the land since he could not properly do so. As a face-saving device, he claimed that all he and his group wanted was a little money to be paid to them for the numerous services they had been rendering to the settlement from time to time.

The governor and council decided that they could no longer face the prospect of periodic and persistent claims for money from King Tom

---

17 See the proceedings reported in C.O. 270(4), pp.143, et seq.
18 'Palaver' connotes a dispute; a quarrel.

and/or his associates, and that the matter ought to be finally set at rest once and for all. There and then, he concluded an agreement with them in the following terms:—

1. The governor and council for the time being shall pay to King Tom or his successors the sum of one hundred dollars per year as a consideration for the trouble the king may have on account of the Sierra Leone Company and those under their government in settling palavers and adjusting differences with the natives.
2. The western boundary of the Sierra Leone Company's land shall begin at the mouth of the small brook on the east side of the bay known by the name of Frenchman's Bay being the first brook to the westward of the watering place, and shall run twenty miles directly south into the country.
3. The eastern boundary of the said company's land shall begin twenty chains eastward of the eastern extremity of the lot of land now belonging to Benjamin Elliott, and marked 3 in the register of Granville town lots and shall proceed thence northwards to the river and southwards in a direct line twenty miles.
4. The natives residing in the town formerly Pa Macquites in Fora Bay shall not be disturbed or obliged to remove thence, but there shall at the same time be free access for all belonging to the colony of Sierra Leone and for their boats or other vessels to the creek known by the name of Macquites Creek.
5. The Sierra Leone Company shall possess the land as above described according to the tenor of the former agreements *and shall not be liable to any further DEMANDS FOR PAYMENT ON ACCOUNT OF IT from King Tom or his successors or from any person or persons whatsoever.*
6. Governor Macaulay in the name of the Sierra Leone Company and King Tom in his own name and that of his chiefs and people do guarantee the performance of these articles of agreement.

Names of people at this transaction

Zachary Macaulay — Governor	King Tom
James Carr, Councillor, pro tem	King Banna
Alex Peterkin, Secretary	Prince Tom
Anthony Domingo, Clerk	Signior Domingo
Richard Crankapone, Marshall	Pa Toby
James Reid	Pa Dembo
George Clark	Will Tom
	Jas Macquite
	Banna
	Dua

With the signing of this agreement, all questions relating to the ownership of the land by the settlers became finally settled. The treaties of Kings Tom and Naimbana were again reaffirmed. If at all there was any doubt about the validity of the sale of the land in customary law, and it has been submitted there is no basis for such doubt, then this agreement put those doubts to rest. The matter was clearly and finally resolved. The land of the original settlement was no longer the property of the native kings, princes and rulers, or their successors. It was now owned by the settlers and their heirs who were to enlarge the boundaries of the original settlement by conquest.[19] For the settlers, the dominant principles on which they asserted their claims to individual ownership of plots of land since the inception of the settlement remained unaffected. In fact, they were impliedly reinforced. These principles could be reduced to two propositions, namely:

>FIRSTLY, that when land had been allocated to a settler, he became the undisputed fee simple owner thereof with rights of succession, and
>
>SECONDLY, that all unappropriated land was vested in the free community of settlers and held by the company in trust for them and their successors.

EVALUATION OF THE TREATIES OF SALE:

The frequency with which the local chiefs attempted to renege on their contract of sale of the land forming the settlement raised some pertinent questions for discussion. Was it a ruse to obtain more money from the company? Or did the chiefs feel that they had not been adequately compensated for the sale of the land? Or was it that they had some second thoughts about the legality or propriety of the transactions into which they had entered? More important still, were these treaties valid either in municipal or international law?

The price paid for the sale of the land.

It has been previously submitted that the treaties with Kings Tom and Naimbana cannot be avoided on the grounds of inadequacy of the consideration. There are just no legal grounds on which such a submission can be upheld. There was a bargain. Consideration was given and both parties were satisfied with the result. That the chiefs were well aware of this can be deduced from the fact that at no time did they ever attempt to allege that the scales were unevenly balanced and the settlers had got the better of them. This claim can therefore be dismissed without further discussion and entirely discounted.

Did the chiefs have full capacity and authority to sell and convey the land.

This aspect of the transaction has also been subjected to prior analysis. However, one or two matters call for further clarification. Under customary law, the chief is regarded as the residuary owner of the land. He is a trustee and, as such, exercises supervisory jurisdiction over

---

19 The extensions of the original twenty miles square were obtained largely by conquest as the local chiefs and tribesmen lost several battles with the settlers. Some of the accretions to the original settlement were settled by treaties. These are more fully discussed in the later pages.

The Government of the Settlement 1791-1807

the land and enjoys residuary rights thereon. He can deal with the land for the benefit of the whole community. In the exercise of his undoubted powers he can lease or alienate the land outright.[20] Therefore, the chief can enter into relationships with others in regard to the land, which would have the effect of disposing of it, subject to the concurrence of his advisers.

The view has been canvassed that if a native chief who is ignorant, affixes his mark to an agreement without understanding its legal implications, then such agreement is bereft of any legal validity and is not binding on the parties who are signatories to it.[21] In municipal law, the principle is well settled, that a party who executes a document without fully understanding or appreciating its contents, can in certain circumstances avail himself of the plea of *"non est factum"*. This plea, or concept, it is submitted has no application to international treaty obligations. States, with an international personality and possessed of a large body of advisers, must be presumed to know the nature and effect of contracts into which they are entering. However, if the scales are unevenly balanced, and this is unrealistic since all states in international law are equal in terms of their capacity to contract, then there may be some justification for seeking to abrogate a treaty entered into where the smaller and weaker state bows to the dictates of another more powerful state which completely dominates it so that its actions cannot be regarded as those of a free and independent entity.

But this highly speculative and hypothetical situation does not exist in the Sierra Leone situation. The kings of Sierra Leone at the material time, far from being ignorant of what they were doing, had full knowledge of the nature of the transactions. The documents, in this regard, speak for themselves. Moreover, they had interpreters and advisers who fully explained to them what the documents contained. They themselves entered into negotiations with the other parties with their eyes wide open and they fully knew and understood the nature of what they were doing. They put the settlers into occupation of the land and promised them protection. They knew the motives and the concern for the welfare of the liberated Africans which motivated the approach to them for a sanctuary for them. One would like to imagine that they also were equally public spirited and no less concerned for these victims of a cruel trade and undoubtedly must have felt proud and honoured to be associated with the venture and to be a part of the process of rehabilitating the Africans, some of whom, undoubtedly must have been their own kith and kin.

The participation of the chiefs in the discussions with the settlers and company officials was on a basis of complete equality. There was

---

20 See: ELIAS. *Nature of African Customary Law,* pp.164-5. Also, Elias: *Nigerian Law and Custom.*
Dr Elias quotes a Nigerian chief who, in giving evidence before a West African Lands Committee in 1912, said "I conceive that land belongs to a vast family of which many are dead, few are living and countless numbers are unborn".
21 LINDLEY: *The Acquisition of Backward Territories,* (1926) at p.173.

freedom and candour on both sides and a complete absence of any coercion or fraudulent representation. There was, indeed, no need for any. The transaction was fair and even handed. The treaties therefore could not be impugned on any pretended inability of the native rulers to understand its validity or effect. They had full authority to sell and the capacity to do so resided in those persons who exercised the right to do so.

Were the Treaties valid in International Law?
It has to be conceded that at the time the treaties were executed, international law had not developed the principles which today are well established as essential norms guiding the conduct of states inter se. Nevertheless, it cannot be denied that both sides were subjects of international law. The local rulers, then described as "Kings and Potentates" were rulers of independent states. They were not then subjected to the tutelage or dominion of any foreign power. No one conducted their international relations for them. On the contrary, the European powers which did business with them, dealt with them on the basis that they were independent states and monarchies. They conducted transactions directly with them and not through intermediaries. The fact that the territories were in some cases, quite small and militarily impotent, and somewhat economically weak, did not detract from their status as free and independent entities in the eyes of the international community.

The settlers at the time they conducted their negotiations with the local rulers, were not as yet nationals of any state. They did not have the same international personality as the native rulers. But it is submitted, that this did not affect the validity of the transactions entered into by both parties. It was not essential for the validity of the contract of sale that both parties should be states, subjects of international law. A state can and usually does enter into contracts with private bodies and these contracts are no less valid because one party is a state and other is not. Later on, the settlers did establish themselves as an international community and the later treaties were equally valid as the earlier ones.

THE HUNDREDORS AND TYTHINGMEN REVOLT.
On the 27th January 1798,[22] it was agreed that the Hundredors and Tythingmen who had previously held joint meetings, should henceforth meet separately, and that two Hundredors should meet with four Tythingmen to form rules and regulations *for the use of the colony.*[23] In 1799, they sent a petition to the company in which they proposed that they should have the right of electing and appointing two of their number as justices of the peace and one as a judge to sit at Quarter Sessions. The governor and council declined to accept this proposal and rejected the petition. The Hundredors and Tythingmen persisted in their request which by now had ripened into a demand, and in June 1799 they chose

22 See C.O. 270(4), p.188.
23 Italics are mine.

three persons as justices of the peace.[24] The governor then referred the matter to the Board of Directors in London. At that time, the directors had been plagued with problems regarding their powers and authority in the settlement and had been pleading with the Crown to grant to the company a new charter in order to remove all doubts about their powers to govern the settlement and to enable them to do so more effectively.[25] The Crown agreed to grant the charter and actually did so in July, 1799. It did not arrive in the settlement however, until 8th November 1800. In the meantime, the Hundredors and Tythingmen became more and more defiant of the company's authority and ceased to co-operate with the governor and council. On the 16th December 1799, the Governor, Ludlam, who had succeeded Macaulay, announced that the directors had refused the request of the petitioners for the appointment of justices of the peace and a judge, on the ground that this was wholly unprecedented. They said that all settlers were amenable to the laws of England and were subjects of the King of England.[26] That in any event justices were appointed and not elected and that that principle was well established both in England and the colonies.

The Hundredors and Tythingmen responded by appointing one of their number, Robertson, a judge. They also appointed another, Cuthbert, as a justice of the peace. Once again, the Governor, Ludlam, refused to acknowledge the correctness of what they had done and refused to recognise these appointments. He issued a statement which he personally read to them, explaining the constitutional position as he perceived it and denying the rights of anyone other than the company to make such appointments. At the end of his address, Robertson, the judge appointed by his colleagues, got up defiantly and announced that he was prohibiting the holding of any further quarter sessions until new laws were passed. The Hundredors and Tythingmen applauded this open challenge of the company's authority and then went further and issued regulations claiming the exclusive competence to make laws and decreeing that all foreigners should henceforth pay taxes.[27] This was rejected by the company.

On the 3rd September 1800, the Hundredors and Tythingmen published their own code of laws. These were comprehensively set out in a document which was in the form of a poster. It was stuck on the wall of the house of a prominent settler, Mr Abraham Smith. The code of laws was signed by James Robertson, Ansel Zizer, Isaac Anderson (all Hundredors) and Nathaniel Wansey (Chairman). It bore the following endorsement: "Signed this as a law in Sierra Leone".[28]

24 They were: Jordan, Anderson and Cuthbert.
25 The company's servants were merely mercantile agents. Kaye, describes them as "men of the slenderest legal attainment and the slightest judicial training. See KAYE: *History of the Administration of the East India Company*, p.321.
26 This claim was legally unsound since no UK statute had ever been passed conferring the status of 'British Subject' on the settlers en bloc. See Chapter III infra where this matter is fully discussed.
27 This was obviously aimed at the company's servants who were not settlers.
28 The Code is set out in Appendix VIII, p.321. See also C.O. 270(5) at p.58.

On the 10th September 1800, a settler named Bright, called on Mr Smith and remonstrated with him contending that the announcement was of an illegal and seditious nature. He tore the poster down. By this time however, a large number of settlers had become aware of the 'controversial' publication. On the 25th September, the poster was replaced. On the following morning a large number of settlers flocked to Mr Smith's house to see it and to hear it read out.[29]

At the venue, the Hundredors and Tythingmen took a firm stand against anyone who sided with the governor and council in opposition to the laws or who would refuse to obey them. They threatened such persons with both fine and banishment. The response of the governor was equally determined. He armed some of the company's employees and then summoned Robertson and Wansey to Thornton Hill[30] to explain why they had illegally assumed authority in the settlement. Both men treated the summons with contempt and refused to appear. A rebellion broke out. The governor issued warrants for their arrest as well as for the arrest of Zizer and Anderson, both of whom had also signed the code of laws. As the group of the company's agents proceeded down Gloucester Street to arrest the men, there was a lot of shouting and booing. Robertson was captured; Zizer surrendered; but Anderson and Wansey escaped. Later on the Maroons who had, fortuitously just arrived in the settlement from the West Indies, at the governor's behest, joined the government forces and together they were charged with the responsibility of putting down the rebellion. They attacked the settlers in full force on or about the 2nd October 1800. Attempts were made to capture as many settlers as possible. Large numbers of them escaped, including Anderson who was subsequently handed over to the governor and his soldiers by the Temne chief, Bai Farama, with whom he had sought refuge. Wansey got away altogether.

Because the charter of justice which the company had prayed the British Government to issue had not as yet arrived in the settlement, the Governor, Ludlam, concluded that he had no power or sufficient authority to try the 'insurgents' in a court of law. Instead of commencing legal proceedings against them, he therefore held an administrative inquiry. The team of commissioners included military and naval officers from *"The Asia"* which had brought in the Maroons.[31] The inquiry commenced on the 11th October 1800. It is instructive to examine the

---

29 The same day, "the Governor and Council having received certain intelligence of diverse meetings of a most seditious and dangerous nature held by the factious party among the Hundredors and Tythingmen and the justices and constables of their appointment, RESOLVED: That it was necessary to adopt without delay such measures of prevention as might most effectually defeat the designs of the party. That for this end, it would be expedient to call the well-affected settlers up the Hill, as well as the company's servants and Europeans for the purpose of forming a strong guard and assisting the civil power in the execution of its warrants". See C.O. 270(5) p.59.

30 This was the governor's residence. It was later called Fort Thornton. It is now called State House.

31 The officers included Lt. James Sheriff of HM's Navy, and Lt. Smith and Lt. Tolly of HM's 24th Regiment.

charges which the governor brought against James Robertson and others. They read as follows:—

1. The said James Robertson Sen., has shown himself hostile to the government established in the colony as well as to the interests of the Sierra Leone Company and in manifest contradiction to the obligations he entered into upon his being received into this colony as a settler.
2. The said James Robertson Sen., in opposition to the spirit as well as the letter of the Sierra Leone Declaration signed by him on the 11th of February last before he entered into his office as a Hundredor, and his allegiance as a British subject, did attempt to subvert the government of this colony by framing together with divers other settlers a code of laws in which the authority of the governor and council both in their legislative and executive capacities is totally annulled and every principle of English law as well as the bye-laws established in this colony are violated and set aside.
3. The said James Robertson Sen., is one of the persons directly concerned in forming a powerful combination among the settlers of this colony to reverse and engross the whole judicial power into their own hands and has adopted certain measures and been guilty of various overt acts on the prosecution of the said confederacy.
4. The consequence of this confederacy has been an open unprovoked rebellion against the government of this colony on which some lives have been lost, and divers persons wounded and some property destroyed.

(Sgd.) T. Ludlam — *Governor.*
R. O. Bright — *MC.*

These charges plainly alleged treason. However, in the light of the immediate past history of the country and the role played by the Hundredors and Tythingmen in the government of the settlement, it is questionable whether these charges could properly have been brought by the company against Robertson and others. The company undoubtedly had the legal and constitutional authority in the legislative, executive and judicial spheres of government. But over the last few years of the seventeen nineties, the government had gradually and deliberately led the settlers to believe that some of the powers of government had been passed on to them. They were considering themselves as part and parcel of the administration. Decisions of a policy nature were taken only with their concurrence. They were much involved in the legislative process. It is not unreasonable therefore that they took the stand they did.

The commissioners of the inquiry found them guilty of all the charges, and Robinson was banished to Goree Island for life. He was luckier than the others. The charter of justice arrived in Freetown on the 6th November 1800 and was "solemnly delivered to Thomas Ludlam Esquire, Governor, by L. Watts Esquire, Commander of the '*Ospney Sloop*'." The charter set up a system of courts and clearly set out their respective jurisdictions.[32] Isaac Anderson, John Stober and Joseph Waring were delivered up by King Firama to the governor and they were promptly sent for trial by the Court of Quarter Sessions. So were two others — Francis Patrick and James Harford. The sentences were severe. Isaac Anderson and Francis Patrick were sentenced to death for "Capital Felonies" and executed. John Stober was banished to the Bullom Shore for ten years. So was James Harford, whose period of banishment was reduced to five years. The indictment against Joseph Waring was thrown out by the Grand Jury. Thus, the company and its duly appointed officials in Sierra Leone triumphed over the settlers in what can appropriately be described as the first attempted coup d'etat in the history of Sierra Leone.

EVALUATION OF THE ROLE OF THE HUNDREDORS AND TYTHINGMEN.
The role of the Hundredors and Tythingmen in the administration and the circumstances which led to the open rebellion against the company deserve some close and critical examination.

When the company took over the administration of the settlement in 1791, the system of Hundredors and Tythingmen had already been firmly established. The settlers were, at that time, a self-governing class electing their own representatives. Company rule was superimposed on that system. It must be pointed out that Sharpe and his friends formed the St. George's Bay Association "for the purpose of opening and establishing a trade in the natural productions of Africa to the free settlement in St. George's harbour". The petition which was presented to the House of Commons in February 1791 said that the Joint Stock Company was being established for the purpose of promoting "a general trade and commerce from these kingdoms to and with the coasts of Africa, and from thence to and with the several interior kingdoms and countries of that continent". The primary objective was to promote commerce and not to govern. The settlers therefore were entitled to feel that they should have a share in the government of their country in co-operation with the company.

Initially, after company rule had become a reality, there was a council of eight. Clarkson reduced this to four. All of them were company officials. They had to seek the assistance and co-operation of the settlers. This might conceivably have been better achieved if some of the members of the council had been settlers since the governor had discovered that the Hundredors and Tythingmen were the appropriate representatives through whom they could carry out their objections and with whom they could deal. At first, the governor and council retained their powers of initiating legislation for the government of the settlement. This practice was contemplated by both the Act of Incorporation and the Manuscript Orders and Regulations. Without amending these instruments, however, the company changed the role of the Hundredors and Tythingmen and

---

32 See C.O. 270(5). Also Fyfe: *History etc.* op. cit.

consulted them before passing laws. Thus, although they were not members of the council, the settlers began to believe that their prior approval was an essential prerequisite to the passing of legislation.

Subsequently, the practice changed. Instead of consulting with the Hundredors and Tythingmen, the governor and council allowed them to *initiate* measures to be passed into law by the company's officials. The records are replete with measures in the second half of the last decade of the eighteenth century where the governor and council accepted measures sent to them by the Hundredors and Tythingmen as resolutions. These were received by the governor and council with pleasure and having signified their "hearty approbation" passed them into law. The Hundredors and Tythingmen therefore considered it their duty to determine what laws were to be passed by the governor and council. As far as they were concerned the governor and council were there only to rubber stamp their decisions and resolutions. They felt that their resolutions should be given formal validity by the council. In effect they saw themselves as the de facto government of the settlement and the governor and council as mere conduit pipes leading to the directors in England.

The Hundredors and Tythingmen kept watch and ward. They debated measures and passed resolutions which were effective. They performed municipal duties and they were an integral part of the judicial system although their activities were confined to the subordinate courts. Notwithstanding the absence of any formal constitutional provisions creating them either a legislative or an executive arm of government, they performed those functions with the tacit approval and encouragement of the company and its officials. The company realised too late that they had become very powerful and that their government was being slowly eroded and substituted by the Hundredors and Tythingmen.

The offending resolution was couched in the following terms:

> We the Hundredors and Tythingmen met and come to a resolution and found it necessary to choose James Robinson, Judge, John Cuthbert, Justice of the Peace; we the settlers do hereby take the above mentioned person to be a proper person fit to act and sit in judgment for us whenever quarter sessions commence.
>
> We do hereby choose Nathaniel Wansey, Chairman for the Tythingmen.
>
> We the Hundredors and Tythingmen desire an answer as quickly as possible.

This resolution appeared on the face of it innocuous. It was asking for approval, in keeping with the established practice. They wanted an answer to their resolution. They were not expecting any refusal. At the meeting with the governor they made two further points. First "That justice is not done to the settlers by our present judges" and second, "that a court of appeal is wanted". They complained about the trial of James Robinson Sen., in 1797 and of York's trial in 1798 following his quarrel with Captain Stott. Judges had not heard the cases and they saw this as a denial of justice. They argued: "It follows that if our laws are not to be changed according to the fancy or self-interest of a few men, they must be fixed and written. Our judges must be men who have leisure and ability to study them, as well as uprightness and firmness to execute them . . . . honesty and impartiality are qualities of the first importance".

The prerequisites of a judicial appointee described by the settlers two centuries ago are equally important today as they were then. In the light of their complaints and their petitions, it is unfortunate that the company deemed it necessary to impose the supreme penalty. The execution of some of the leaders of the settlers, did not detract one bit from the efficiency, dedication and public spiritedness shown by the Hundredors and Tythingmen, some of whom were illiterate and not at all trained in the complexities of government. Some of the proposals which emanated from their ranks, were admirable to say the least. They were well considered and cleverly designed to meet the exigencies of the situation which existed at the time.

The leaders of the settlers were elected. The purity of the elective process would put many electoral processes in Africa today to shame. Elections were not rigged; attempts were made to put the best men forward for public office. When elected, they had one overriding desire — the motive of unstinted and loyal service to the community without any hope of personal gain or reward.

At the turn of the 19th century, the Hundredors and Tythingmen of Sierra Leone had proved themselves to be fully capable of handling the reins of government. They demonstrated outstanding courage in the face of the military strength shown by the company backed by the hardiness of the Maroons.[33] Yet, ironically, when the charter arrived, their expectations were destroyed. Instead of creating an advanced constitution in which the power of government would be squarely put in the hands of the settlers, the charter did away completely with the institution of Hundredors and Tythingmen and put nothing in its place. Instead, it strengthened the hands of the company's officials and government was put squarely in the hands of the company. The dreams of self-government were thus put further away and an institution which had become very effective in the Settlement of Sierra Leone since its establishment in 1787 was eliminated.

THE CHARTER.
Some history books give the date of the charter as 1799. Others describe it as the Charter of 1800. The charter was granted in 1799 and so that ought to be the correct date in the absence of any specific provision describing it as the Charter of 1800. It arrived in the settlement in 1800

---

33 Following the bombardment of Freetown by the French, 500 Maroons were brought over to Sierra Leone. They had been transferred to Nova Scotia following an insurrection in Jamaica where they were considered a threat to the whites. To this day, the descendants of the Maroons in Sierra Leone are regarded as strong and tenacious.

and was put into operation on the 8th November, 1800. It substituted a new system of government for that which was in force in the settlement and made some significant changes in the administration as well as in the system of justice.

Central and Local Government changes.
The charter provided for a 'Governor' in place of the 'Superintendent'. The settlement was now officially described as a 'Colony'.[34] The governor was the head of the administration and chief representative of the company in the colony. He was to be assisted by a council of three. The lands which formed the settlement were now for the first time, formally vested in the company, Her Majesty "being desirous to afford all fitting encouragement to the Sierra Leone Company and to the Colony of Sierra Leone".[35] The lands which formed the settlement and which were now vested in the company appeared to be regarded as Crown property, for the company were asked to pay a minimal rent to the Crown. This was intended to be a way of eliminating the troublesome question of quit rents, but it was a substantial departure from the original method of land holding. The company was empowered by the charter and given authority to purchase, if necessary, additional land adjacent to the settlement.[36]

Although the governor and council constituted the legislative authority in the colony, the governor's position was strong. He had a veto and, contrary to what had been in force earlier on, his power was not limited to or made conditional upon his obtaining the concurrence of the council. However, neither he, nor his council, could pass any law which was repugnant to or inconsistent with the laws of England. The directors in England had the power of disallowance reserved to them. Thus to a very large extent, the governor was given effective control and management of the government of the territory independent of the council. He had a wide measure of discretion and, to that extent, he was also largely independent of the close control and supervision of the directors in England. This would have been necessary had the governor's authority not been so specifically delimited. In this respect the changes of 1800 were substantial and ushered in a type of constitution which was purely colonial in form and content.

LOCAL GOVERNMENT.
For the purposes of local government, the charter created Freetown a municipality with a mayor and three aldermen under the name and style of "The Mayor and Aldermen of Freetown". It was established as a 'Body Politic and Corporate' with perpetual succession capable of suing and of being sued in its corporate name. Thus Freetown became the first

---
34 In the words of the charter, the settlement was created "one independent colony by the name of Sierra Leone".
35 See the Report of the Directors for 1801.
36 This is further evidence that in Sierra Leone, land was freely alienable and could be purchased from the native rulers without infringing on any customary rule or law.

municipality on the continent of Africa. The first mayor and aldermen were to be nominated and appointed by the governor or, in his absence, by the senior in council within fourteen days. The first appointees were to hold office for life, but the mayor was to hold office for one year from the 29th day of September in every year. The mayors were to be elected annually from among the aldermen, and an incumbent was to be eligible for re-election. Any mayor or alderman absent for three months without reasonable cause was to lose his seat. The governor and council had power to remove the mayor and aldermen for reasonable cause.

In exercising the power of removal of either the mayor or aldermen, a complaint should first have been exhibited against such mayor or alderman in writing, and a reasonable time given to him to make a defence. On removal as aforesaid, the person involved had a right of appeal to the directors of the company in England upon giving security for costs. Any such appeal did not, however, operate as a stay of execution.

Pursuant to the provisions of the charter, the governor and council on the 8th November 1800, appointed Mr Thomas Cox as the first mayor of the municipality of Freetown. He was the company's storekeeper. Thomas Cooper, George Alex Smith and Peregrine Francis Thorne were appointed the first aldermen.

PROVISIONS FOR THE ADMINISTRATION OF JUSTICE.
The charter also made extensive provisions for the administration of justice. The various courts set up were as follows:

(a) *The Mayor's Court of Freetown:* This was a Court of Record, consisting of the Mayor and Aldermen for the time being of Freetown. The Mayor or Senior Alderman presided. The court was empowered and authorised to: try, hear and determine all civil suits, actions and pleas between party and party that should or might arise or happen, or that had already arisen or happened within the said Colony of Sierra Leone, or any of the factories, subject or subordinate thereto, except such suits or actions as should be between natives of Africa only not become settlers within the said colony or factories, in which said . . . . . the same should be determined among themselves unless both parties should by consent submit the same to the determination of the said Mayor's Court, and also except where the cause of action or suit should not exceed the value of 40/-.

The charter further decreed that if the mayor or any alderman should in any way be interested in the suit he should be precluded from sitting as judge in such suit or action; and that in any case where there was an equality of votes, the mayor, or in his absence, the senior alderman present "should have two voices".

Provision was made for the appointment of a sheriff by the governor, or in his absence by the senior member of council then residing in Sierra Leone, who should have power to summon juries, execute and make returns of all process of the said court and of any other court erected by the said charter. In the absence of the sheriff, the deputy or under-sheriff to be appointed by the sheriff, was required to make return of all processes and do all acts in the name of and by virtue of the authority of the sheriff.

(b) *The Court of the Governor and Council.*
Appeal lay from the Mayor's Court of Freetown to the Court of the Governor and Council. They were constituted a Court of Record for this purpose. They also had original jurisdiction in matters where the sum of money in dispute was upward of four hundred pounds. Where the amount was in excess of this amount, then appeal lay to the Privy Council in England.[37]

(c) *The Court of Requests for the Town of Freetown and the Factories and Settlements thereof.*
Another court set up by the charter was "The Court of Requests for the Town of Freetown and the Factories and Settlements thereof". The governor was empowered to appoint not more than twenty-four nor fewer than eight persons to be commissioners of requests to hear and determine suits in a summary manner. Rules and regulations governing the court were to be made and despatched from the directors in England to Freetown. Any three of the commissioners so appointed could form a quorum for a court sitting. Jurisdiction lay in cases not exceeding 10/-, and the commissioners were required to sit one day a week from 9 to 11 a.m. or longer if need be, or if the business of the court so required.

(d) *The Courts of the Justices.*
The fourth kind of court set up under the charter was the Court of the Justices of the Peace. For this purpose the governor and council were appointed justices of the peace for the town of Freetown and all the factories and settlements subordinate thereto. They had the same powers and authority as justices of the peace in England. Their courts were courts of summary jurisdiction.

(e) *Quarter Sessions.*
The charter required that the governor and council should hold Quarter Sessions of the peace four times a year. They were therefore constituted a Court of Record — the Court of Oyer and Terminer and general goal delivery for the purpose of trying and punishing all offenders and offences committed within the city of Freetown and elsewhere in the Colony of Sierra Leone. Indictments could be brought by the justices of the peace or the commissioners of Oyer and Terminer. They could summon a convenient number of the principal inhabitants to attend as grand

---

37 Appeals were originally to the directors. In the West Indies and other colonies, appeals were going direct to the privy council but this was because those territories were, strictly, colonies for which Britain had responsibility. This provision followed the colonial practice and the directors thus lost their appellate jurisdiction.

and petty juries. They had jurisdiction in respect of all offences except treason, and were a court of original, as well as, appellate jurisdiction, the latter in respect of petty offences tried by the justices.

(f) *The Mayor's Court for Probates & Administration.*
A new court introduced by the charter was the Mayor's Court. This was constituted a Court of Record. It was a Court of Probate for the purpose of granting probates and letters of administration of the estates of deceased persons.[38]

In summary therefore, the charter, at the turn of the century introduced a well organised judicial system designed to meet all contingencies. The method of trial by jury had been in force since the existence of the settlement in 1787, and it was preserved in the Mayor's Court for civil actions, Quarter Sessions, which was a criminal court, and the Court of the Governor and Council in some cases when exercising civil jurisdiction in an original capacity.

A Council of Government is set up.
The charter brought to an end the election of Hundredors and Tythingmen but did not substitute anything in its place. Consequently, the settlers who had played a formidable part in the administration of their territory for upwards of thirteen years and demonstrated their ability and courage and their acute perception of the problems of government, lost their opportunity of participating in the affairs of the central government. The establishment of a municipality, though laudable, was not quite the same. It did not fill the vacuum left in respect of settler participation in national politics.

On the 6th November 1800, a Council of Government was formed with Ludlam as Governor and Messrs S. Gray and R. Bright as first and second in council respectively. The Council of Government had its first meeting on the 7th Decemeber 1800. The Council of Government then proceeeded with the business of making all necessary appointments required by the charter. The council resolved that twelve be the number of commissioners to constitute the court of requests and that each commissioner be paid the sum of 2/6d. for each day's attendance. After nominating the first twelve commissioners of the court of requests, the council administered oaths of office to the new commissioners on the

---

38 It is not quite clear from the records what the practice was regarding the administration of estates. For example, when Thomas Cox, a former mayor died, the governor and council in a letter to Mr R. Bright signed by Mr A. Smith asked him to apply for a grant of letters of administration. These were granted on 26th April 1802. See C.O. 270(8) at p.85. It would thus appear that the right to a grant did not necessarily follow the right to a beneficial interest in property.

15th January 1801.[39]

EVALUATION OF THE CHARTER OF 1799.
The directors in their report in 1801,[40] expressed the view that the company had been given

> "a clear, formal, well-founded authority to maintain the peace of the settlement and to execute the laws within the company's territory."

With regard to the central government set up by the charter, it was unsuitable from the point of view of the settlers as they were not granted any right of representation. This was a retrograde step, taking into consideration the fact that the intention of the abolitionists was that the settlers should be self-governing and independent. At least some measure of elective representation should have been conceded to them. There was every justification for that since the Hundredors and Tythingmen had proved themselves to be efficient and effective in the governmental machinery when they had an opportunity of political service. This refusal to grant the people of Sierra Leone the right to choose their representatives marked the beginning of a sustained struggle between governors and governed which ran through the constitutional history of Sierra Leone until 1951.

With no African elected representatives in the Legislature, none could be expected to be in the Executive. None were in fact appointed: and so the company were denied the benefit of settler opinion in the policy making institutions of the country.

In the sphere of local government, the position was slightly better, since the charter established the first municipality on the African continent in Sierra Leone. Once again, the first mayor was not one of the settlers, but a company employee. Still, the settlement had been founded on the highest of ideals and the purest of motives. There was to be no racial discrimination and it mattered not whether the first mayor was white or black. The essential thing was that there was a competent person worthy of being appointed first citizen of the new state and new municipality. It would have been much better for elections to be held for such an appointee. Still, it was a progressive move and it filled to a small extent the lacuna which was created when the Hundredors and Tythingmen departed from the political scene.

With regard to the judicial arm of goverment, the improvements were laudable. The only criticism was the fact that the governor and council still exercised judicial powers. They were not men with legal training and

---

39 See C.O. 270(3) p.60. The first twelve were:
   James Carr   Michael Macmillan
   Hananiah Hermitage Thomas Fothergill
   Richard Crankapone David Edmonds
   David George Sen. Eli Akim
   Francis Warwick   Cato Burden
   Isaac James   George Clark
40 See the Report of the Directors 1801 at p.9.

besides they were involved in the administration and would have probably dealt administratively with legal matters and then had to handle the cases in a judicial capacity. With the best of intentions, this was clearly undesirable. As far as the other personnel of the courts were concerned, some legally trained persons had begun, at that time, to appear in the courts in Freetown. They were either settlers or employees of the company. As yet, there were no specific provisions regarding the minimum qualifications required for enrolment as a barrister or solicitor of the Superior Court of Judicature. That the governor and council members were themselves not legally trained persons would suggest that admission to the bar in England was not yet a prerequisite for appointment to the bench in Sierra Leone.[41]

Jury trial which was a feature of the system of justice from the very beginning was preserved. The qualifications for persons to serve as jurors were as follows:
- (a) He had to be in actual possession of freehold property in the colony or the legitimate son of a freeholder: or
- (b) He should have been appointed to serve the company by the Court of Directors: or
- (c) He should be a householder.

There were disqualifications as well. They were:
- (a) Conviction of wilful, corrupt perjury or of felony with or without benefit of clergy.
- (b) Dealing or having dealt with slaves at any period subsequent to the person's becoming a colonist.
- (c) Under the age of 21 years.
- (d) Refusing to take the oath of allegiance.
- (e) Not having signed the declaration of submission to the laws and government of the colony, with the exception of those who had been specifically received as colonists.

Certain categories of persons were exempted from jury service. They were
- (a) Persons in holy orders.
- (b) Those sick or diseased at the time of holding the court.
- (c) Those past 70 years of age.

The charter preserved the principle that the laws of England were ipso facto applicable in Sierra Leone.[42] Thus, the first court of Oyer and Terminer which tried the insurgents in 1800, imposed the death sentence for (a) sending the governor a threatening letter and (b) stealing a gun. Both of these offences were punishable in England at that period of time and carried the death penalty. They were therefore applicable in Sierra Leone.

---

41 Later on, there will be a discussion on the legal profession in Sierra Leone and it will be seen how the idea of representation through professionally trained persons developed in Sierra Leone.

42 The reception date of English law in Sierra Leone has erroneously been put at later dates by various writers. e.g. Elias: *Constitutional Laws of the Commonwealth* (Sierra Leone & Ghana) puts it at 1862. Also: Joko Smart.

On the 14th January 1801, the council appointed a magistrate with the powers of a justice of the peace, resident at Granville Town. The powers of a justice of the peace were also delegated to Mr George Ross, the Superintendent,[43] who was also authorised to appoint any one of the Maroons as High Constable of Granville Town. The same day the governor and council passed a resolution authorising the erection of a gaol and the fixing of stocks at Granville Town.[44]

Undoubtedly, the charter brought with it for the first time in the history of the Settlement of Sierra Leone a constitution that could accurately be described as purely 'colonial'. This was very far removed from the independent status the settlement had once enjoyed. For the first time, there was clearly reserved to the directors in London the power of disallowance of legislation passed in Freetown. Professor Andrews has classified the reasons for the principle of disallowance of colonial laws in the following manner and his reasons can be aptly applied to the Sierra Leone situation.[45]

(a) Unconstitutionality; and especially encroachment on the prerogative.
(b) Interference with the imperial economic policy.
(c) Interference with the rights of individuals or property rights.
(d) General expediency.

In the Sierra Leone situation, the Crown, as a colonial power, had no interest in the government of the colony at that stage. It was the company that exercised all the powers and authorities of the Crown normally applied in colonial territories. Curiously, the main thrust of the provisions still related to the matters of discipline by the company over its officials on the spot. The charter seemed to be concerned about whether or not those acting for the company in the colony were acting properly or oppressively or in the general interests of the local populations committed to their charge.

The charter brought to an end a short-lived, but unique experiment in the history of colonial rule. It was the first time black men anywhere in the world had enjoyed the privilege of self-government. It was the first occasion when a black community enjoyed complete equality with white men all over the world. Indeed, "the innovation of allowing Negroes to exercise political functions is of particular interest as marking a fresh but unrecognised departure in the government of dependencies".[46]

The Charter of 1799 has been described by at least one historian as "the legal beginning of the colony".[47] Theoretically, Crown Colony Government did not arrive in Sierra Leone until 1808, but the pattern of

---

43 He was superintendent of the liberated Africans. This office had always been in existence since the company took over the administration of the settlement.
44 See C.O. 270(6) p.28.
45 See ANDREWS: *The Royal Disallowance* (Printed originally in "the proceedings of the American Antiquarian Society", October 1914. See also: E. B. Russell, *Review of American Colonial Legislation*.
46 See *The Cambridge History of the British Empire*.
47 Fyfe: *History etc.* op. cit.

government set up by the charter was indeed purely colonial in form and character. All the elements of colonial rule were present. The only difference was, as has been pointed out before, that instead of government by the Crown, government by the company was in vogue. The manuscript orders and regulations promulgated by the Sierra Leone Company, interestingly enough, visualised "the formation of a colony in a country already peopled".[48] The charter completed and legally formalised this process. It enabled the company to rule effectively through its agents and appointed officials without any reference to or assistance from the British Government. It also effectively destroyed the sanguine hopes and aspirations of the settlers who were always expecting a return to the spirit of the concern which motivated the establishment of the settlement by abolitionists who could not by the wildest stretch of the imagination be described as pro-colonial. The charter was a clear departure from the aims and objectives of the early philanthropists. To this extent its promulgation was unfortunate. In spite of that, the early settlers had left a niche which had been admired and recognised by all who were aware of their activities. One writer commented:[49]

"The early constitution of Sierra Leone was a peculiarity rather than a precedent in British Colonial Government. But it has its importance as the first instance in modern history of a self-governing colonial community of non-European population where colour was no disqualification and Negro freeman were allowed the political and civil rights of Europeans. As Hundredors and Tythingmen the black settlers of Sierra Leone had fulfilled administrative duties that had developed into legislative powers; as jurymen, they had shown a judgment and intelligence that won the praise of Europeans. Thus, although the French Revolution was to abolish slavery forty years in advance of the British Parliament, Africans were exercising the rights of Englishmen in the British Empire a few years earlier than they were granted the rights of man by the French Convention: and though in the first case . . . the Negroes were few in number, yet the rights were actual, while in the later case, in conditions of insurrection and civil law, they were more than theoretical.

At the time of the promulgation of the charter, Britain had absolutely no responsibility for the colony of Sierra Leone. But concurrently with the granting of the charter, the British Parliament voted the sum of four thousand pounds for "defraying the charge of the civil establishment in Sierra Leone". This was because many of the abolitionists had friends in parliament and constantly appealed to them for Britain's financial help to the company for the purposes of administering the colony. In 1802, the first annual grant to the colony commenced. By 1807, parliament after being regularly approached by the company, had made a total grant in aid of £67,000. That the company found itself utterly unable to run the colony as a financial success is indicative of the failure of the

48 George: *A History of Sierra Leone.*
49 Martin Wight: *The Development of the Legislative Council,* p.43.

administration of the chartered government.

COMPANY RULE 1800 to 1807.

The post-charter era of company rule was a colourless one. The administration was plagued with numerous problems, principally internal conflicts with the Temnes, but more seriously, severe economic troubles.

The Settlers and the Temnes:

The Temnes never seemed to be quite content with what they had got and there were frequent skirmishes between the settlers and the Temnes. In February 1799, King Tom was involved in a dispute with a ship's captain who refused to pay anchorage dues to the king. When the Nova Scotians threatened to hand him over to King Tom if he did not pay, he promptly paid up. The Governor, Ludlam, was greatly angered over this incident and very disappointed. It led to strained relationships between the company and King Tom. On the 8th March 1800, King Tom and his headmen paid a visit to the governor to discuss 'a palaver'. It transpired that the palaver they wished to discuss was this incident involving the ship's captain. The king was struck by the governor's 'expostulations' and "exhibited manifest signs of confusion". The governor, at that time, was wanting to give up the governorship of the colony and this incident provided him the escape route he was seeking. He told King Tom plainly that he and his other officials were already fed up with their constant provocations and interference in the affairs of the colony. He said the company did not intend to pay him any more money. Shortly afterwards, he declined to continue in office as governor, although he still remained in Freetown. He was later on succeeded by Dawes. The skirmishes between Temnes and settlers continued in 1801. The numbers of the settlers however, was augmented by further arrivals, notably the Maroons. Encouraged by some dissident settlers, the Temnes attacked Fort Thornton.[50] About thirty people were killed including Mayor Thomas Cox, and Crankapone, a member of the Court of Requests. Governor Dawes was badly wounded. The Temnes were driven out and a fortnight later, King Tom's towns were burnt down and their farms destroyed in reprisal. Assaults continued on both sides until 1803 when King Tom was effectively defeated. The settlers pursued the Temnes towards the west and dislodged King Tom and his men from his towns. All the districts from King Tom to Cape Sierra Leone, including Ascension Town, Congo Town, Murray Town, Signal Hill and Aberdeen were depopulated and captured and burnt down. King Tom escaped to the Northern Rivers.[51] In July 1807[52] a treaty of peace and friendship

50 The official residence of the governor.
51 See George: *The Rise of British West Africa*, (Cass 1968) at pp.131-2. He gives the date of this conquest as 20th November 1801. All the areas identified in the text lie on the western area of Freetown and were not part of the original twenty miles square bought from the native rulers.
52 Treaty dated 10th July 1807. This treaty can be seen in *Montague's Ordinances* Vol. II pp.272-3. See also Fyfe's: *Sierra Leone Inheritance* p.127.

was signed between the governor and Kings Firama and Tom. Thus, in the words of Fyfe, "the colony's original right to the peninsula, was superseded by conquest.[53] That same year, the British Parliament, on the 25th March, passed an act forbidding and abolishing the slave trade with effect from the 1st May 1807.[54] On the 8th of August 1807, a bill which had been passed in parliament at the end of July 1807 to transfer the company's possessions to the Crown, became law.[55] This measure brought Crown Colony Government to Sierra Leone. Before considering its important provisions, some comment is pertinent about the conditions of law and the administration of the government from the date of the charter on to 1807.

Company Rule, 1800 to 1807:
>"A lawyer without history or literature is a mechanic, a mere working mason .... if he possesses some knowledge of these, he may venture to call himself an architect" ...
>Counsel Pleydell in *"Guy Mannering"*.

A legal historian must necessarily be concerned with the evolution and development of the legal system of the country with which he is dealing. In order to appreciate the growth and development of the Sierra Leone constitution therefore it is necessary to set out some of the ways in which the constitution and the laws developed so that the whole picture can be seen as one of organic growth, a living mechanism.

The first meeting of the "Council of Government" set up under the Charter of 1799 was held on the 7th December 1800. Present were the Acting Governor Mr S. Gray and Mr R. Bright, member of council. The meeting was formal. The next one at which real business was conducted took place on the 14th January 1801.[56] At that meeting, Governor Dawes presided and the two other members of the council were Mr S. Gray, 1st in council and Mr R. Bright, 2nd in council. The resolutions passed at that meeting, included the following:

(a) That a magistrate be appointed invested with powers of a JP, and resident in Granville Town.
(b) That the powers of a JP be delegated to Mr George Ross the Superintendent (of the Liberated Africans).
(c) That Mr Ross be authorised to appoint any one of the Maroons as High Constable of Granville Town.
(d) That a gaol be erected and stocks be fixed at Granville Town.

Later the same day,[57] the governor and council "think it expedient for the more effectual prevention of polygamy in time to come among the Maroons as well as for ascertaining the nature of the connexion by drawing a marked line of distinction between concubinage and

---
53 Fyfe: *History etc.,* op. cit. p.96.
54 The Abolition of Slave Trade Act, 1807. Statute 47 Geo. III c. 36.
55 The Sierra Leone Company Act, 1807. Statute 47 Geo. III Sess. 2 c. 44.
56 See C.O. 270(6) at p.28. Minutes of the Council for 14th January 1801.
57 Ibid: p.31.

matrimony"; resolved

"That every marriage henceforth be celebrated by the governor or senior member."

Thereafter the council debated the question of forming a police for the purpose of maintaining law and order within Granville Town.[58]

The power of the council was unlimited and later legislation passed by the council for example, dealt with the line of demarcation between the districts of Freetown and Granville Town and the delimitation of the territory subject to the jurisdiction of the mayor and aldermen of Freetown. The charter had prescribed the courts and their respective jurisdictions and so that aspect of the matter had already been settled. All that was left for the governor and council to do, was to pass effective laws to be implemented by the courts. Unfortunately, as will be mentioned at a later stage, the early courts of Sierra Leone were manned by persons without any legal qualifications. They were mainly traders and merchants, employees of the company and appointed by it. Thus the courts could not be divested from the influence of the executive.

The African Institution.
The abolitionists in London during the period 1791 to 1807, were preoccupied with the desire to get the British Government to assist financially with the running of the settlement as they were painfully aware that the cost of running and maintaining the settlement would be very much outside their competence. The constraints attendant upon the maintenance of the administration were innumerable and they needed the help of their friends and supporters in Britain. One of the methods they devised to achieve these objectives, was the setting up of the "African Institution". This body was formed in 1791.[59] The members included several of the directors of the Sierra Leone Company, peers, members of the House of Commons and other persons prominent in public life. The institution had the distinction of having a Royal Prince, the Duke of Gloucester as its patron and president. It was not organised for commerce or colonisation and the fact that some of its members included, at various periods, governors of Sierra Leone, led to the criticism that Sierra Leone was in reality a company colony.[60] It was also alleged, incorrectly, that the government of the colony had been transferred to the institution which was the governing authority therein.[61] The institution was finally dissolved in 1834 by which time it had played a most important part in getting the colony of Sierra Leone taken over as a British colony. The importance of the institution lies in

---

58 See JOHN, L. Levi: *Memorandum on the Evolution of the Legislative Council of Sierra Leone.* (7th Nov. 1924) S. L. Legislative Council,
59 It held its first meeting only on the 14th April 1807. See *The Edinburg Review* Vol. XXI pp.470-1.
60 See Schuyler, R. L. *Parliament and the British Empire,* p.120.
61 Claude George in *"The Rise of British West Africa"* comments that "although the company finally retired in 1808, the retirement was not real, as its very promoters were the organisers of the African Institution".

the fact that its existence and activities were almost inextricably intertwined with those of the government of the colony for the time being.

Legislative activity and other developments up to 1807.
It is not intended to catalogue the various kinds of laws passed by the governor and council during this period of time, but only to highlight some of the activities which took place and which illustrate the patterns of government and the problems the council had to face at this time. They will also indicate the reasons why the company eventually handed over the colony to the administration of the Crown.

On the 7th March 1801, a Register of Births and Deaths was set up.

In 1802, annual grants in aid from the British Government began. Same year, a charter was passed setting forth the jurisdiction of two courts, the Mayor's Court and the Court of Requests.

In 1804, the parliaments of Great Britain and Ireland were united and following that event, the British Parliament was enlarged by the addition of one hundred members of the House of Commons. The majority of these new members of parliament, were abolitionists. On the 30th March 1804, William Wilberforce sought and obtained leave to reintroduce his motion calling for the abolition of slavery. This was carried by a majority of 124 to 49 with the assistance of the new Irish members. The House of Lords followed the example of the House of Commons after three years.

In 1803, a Parliamentary Commission of Inquiry was set up which reported in 1804 and recommended inter alia that the object for which the settlement was established would be better accomplished if the civil and military authority of the Colony of Sierra Leone were transferred to the Crown. They also suggested that the proprietors of the Sierra Leone Company be invited to surrender their rights to the Crown. Following this 'adverse' report, the company decided to transfer its possessions and final authority in Sierra Leone to the Crown.

On the 18th April 1803, the governor and council passed a Resolution "that to avoid all further disputes on that subject (Quit Rents) and in consideration of the good conduct of all descriptions of persons during the present war, the lands both of Maroons and Nova Scotians shall be granted to them free of quit rents."[62]

In 1806, the council established the principle that divorces would be granted only by an Act of Parliament.[63] Same year, Pitt died in England, but by then his support for the abolitionists and the company who wanted to hand over the colony to the Crown had been firmly established. There was therefore no likelihood that the opponents of the surrender to the Crown would succeed. They had contended that instead of the Crown taking over the colony, the company should pay back to

---
62 C.O. 270(9) p.35.
63 The parties were Lazarus and Sylvia Jones and the act was granted on the ground of adultery.

the Crown all the money made to it by way of grants in aid. By that time, these sums had totalled well over £67,000.

Internal legislation was far from being vibrant but the indications were clear, namely that the company was increasingly finding the cost of maintaining the colony beyond their reach. On the 13th July 1807, the governor[64] signed a Treaty of Peace and Alliance with King Firama and King Tom and their princes and headmen.[65] The treaty decreed that henceforth there would be peace between the natives and the settlers. Secondly, King Firama and King Tom, with the consent of all the headmen,

> "at this time assembled, do hereby surrender to His Majesty the King of Great Britain, for the use and benefit of the Sierra Leone Company, all the right, power and possessions of every form and kind in the peninsular of Sierra Leone and its dependencies which they or either of them formerly had to the westward of the Colony of Sierra Leone or any part thereof".

This treaty also acknowledged the rights of the proprietors of Bance Island to the territory; it precluded the building of any native town nearer to the colony than Robis, and provided for the amicable settlement of any dispute between the parties "in a friendly way".

Here, again, the native chiefs confirmed their outright annexation of the land comprising part of the Colony of Sierra Leone; recognised the rights of the settlers therein and the trusteeship or guardianship of the company which was then about to hand over its trust to the government of the United Kingdom.

On the 8th August 1807, the British Parliament passed the Sierra Leone Company Act which became effective on the 1st January 1808.[66] The effect of the act was to transfer the rights and possessions of the Sierra Leone Company to the British Crown which immediately then assumed the management and government of the colony. The area of the new Crown Colony included the original settlement which had been bought from the local chiefs Tom and Naimbana as well as the accretions thereto which had been obtained by the settlers by conquest and thereafter settled by treaty. The act revoked the Letters Patent of the 5th July, made under the provisions of the Statute 41 Geo. III which had created the Independent Colony of Sierra Leone and the Municipality of Freetown. It divested the company of the lands and fortifications it had and vested them in His Majesty the King. It provided for the winding up of the company in seven years and prohibited trafficking in slaves. Its long title was "An Act for transferring to HM certain possessions and rights vested in the Sierra Leone Company and for shortening the

---

[64] Ludlam was governor in 1798 succeeding Macaulay. He resigned in 1801 and was succeeded by Dawes who was replaced by Day in 1803. Day retired to England and returned in 1805. He died the same year, the first governor to die in Office. He was succeeded by Ludlam who put down a military rebellion in 1806 and remained governor when the Crown took over.
[65] C.O. 267(24).
[66] 47 Geo. III Sess. 2 c. 44.

duration of the said company and for preventing any dealing or trafficking in the buying or selling of slaves within the Colony of Sierra Leone"

CONCLUSIONS.
No greater or better evaluation of the role of the company in forging the patters of government, education and progress in the territory of Sierra Leone can be given than the assessment which the company itself made in the official statement on the winding up of the company.[67] They said inter alia:

> However great may have been the Company's loss in a pecuniary view, the directors are unwilling to admit that there has been a total failure in their main objects or that their capital has been expended without success. It must afford sufficient satisfaction to reflect that the company should both have conceived and attempted to execute these plans of beneficence which led to the institution of the colony, and that they should have contrived to pursue them for so many years in the face of opposition, disappointment, and loss, in spite of severe calamities arising from European as well as African wars and much turbulence on the part of the colonists. The proprietors have the further satisfaction of knowing that the company have contributed to the abolition of the slave trade, by exposing its real nature before the views of a hesitating legislature and detecting the artifices and misrepresentations by which persons engaged in it laboured to delude the public.
> The Company have communicated the benefits flowing from a knowledge of letters and from Christian instruction to hundreds of Negroes on the coast of Africa, and, by a careful education in this country, they have elevated the character of several of the children of African chiefs and directed their minds to objects of the very first importance to their countrymen. They have ascertained that the cultivation of any valuable article of tropical export may be carried on in Africa, that Africans in a state of freedom are susceptible of the same motion of industry and laborious exertions which influence the nations of Europe, and that some African chiefs are sufficiently enlightened to comprehend and sufficiently patriotic to encourage schemes of development.
> They have demonstrated that Negroes may be governed by the same mild laws which are found consistent with the maintenance of national liberty even in this kingdom; and they may be safely

---

67 In setting out the positive report of the company, no attempt is being made to suggest that all was 'ideal' in the colony. There were numerous instances of alleged discrimination on the ground of race and personal animosity against those who had clandestine affairs with blacks of which the case of Dr Robson's flirtations with Anne Edmonds was the most famous.
   Similarly, the case of the five sailors who were tried by a black jury after killing a duck was full of racial overtones.

and advantageously entrusted with the administration of these laws not only as jurors but even as judicial assessors. They have in some measure retrieved the credit of the British — it may be added of the Christian name — on the continent of Africa and have convinced its inhabitants that there are Englishmen who are actuated by very different motives from those of self-interest and who desire nothing so much as their improvement and happiness. To conclude, they have established in the central part of Africa a colony which appears to be more provided with adequate means both of defence and subsistence, which, by the blessings of God, may become an emporium of commerce, a school of industry, and a source of knowledge, civilization, and religious improvement to the inhabitants of that continent and which may hereafter repay to Great Britain the benefits she shall have communicated by opening a continually increasing market for those manufacturers which are now no longer secured of their accustomed vent on the continent of Europe. The directors are persuaded that they only express the general feeling of the proprietors when they say that they cannot prevail upon themselves to consider these effects as an insignificant return for any pecuniary sacrifices which they have incurred for their attainment.[68]

Thus, in the words of the late Bishop T. S. Johnson, "it was not British power that founded the colony. Government can only be conceived to have stepped in to further the objects of the founders, that is, 'the benefit and interest of humanity as represented in the Negro race'."[69]

CROWN COLONY RULE, 1808

Under the Act of Incorporation, the British Government had the right of appointment of the governor of the colony. They also had the power to issue instructions about how the colony should be governed. Ironically, the act did not contain any statement as to what form the government should take. It merely provided that the governor and council[70] should make laws and ordinances for the good government of the colony. Temporary instructions were given to the governor to continue in all respects the administration of justice and the interior government of the colony according to the directions, powers and authorities of the charter as if the same were still in force. Consequently, the colony was administered in the initial stages of Crown colony Government, in much the same way as it had been under the company's rule. The one major exception was, that the settlers were now no longer consulted by the government in making local laws and regulations.

---

68 C.O. 270. Also Report of the Directors to the Company.
69 Johnson T. S. *The Story of a Mission*, p.18.
70 From 1801 to 1808, and indeed right on to 1818, the council was one of four, inclusive of the governor. See J. L. John — *Memorandum on the Evolution of the Legislative Council*, op. cit.

When the Crown took over the colony, they preserved the power exercised by the company's council of granting divorces by passing special enactments for that purpose to meet each individual case. This preserved a resolution of 1796 initiating that procedure. The Crown also retained the last governor under the company, Ludlam. He continued in office from January to July 1808 as 'Chief Administrator', in an interim capacity until the arrival of Mr Thomas Perronet Thompson, the first governor to be appointed by the Crown.[71] Laws passed by the council, which now included the Chief Justice and the Chief Secretary, had to be submitted within six months to the home government for approbation or disallowance. The governor and council were to have the same jurisdiction as the governor and council appointed by the company, unless otherwise provided.

There was no change in the format of local government. The mayor was to continue in office, as provided for under the 1799 Charter, until the first Monday in the next following month of September and the aldermen continued in office for life unless sooner removed. Thus the corporation of the municipality remained the same as it was constituted under the Charter of 1799.

With regard to the administration of justice, a Chief Justice was appointed by the Crown and he was to be Recorder of Freetown. Together with the mayor and aldermen or three of them at least, they constituted the Court of the Recorder of Freetown. That meant that the mayor and two or three aldermen, together with the Chief Justice formed the court. If the Chief Justice was interested in the matter in dispute, then the court would be constituted by the mayor and aldermen alone. In the case of death, absence or long incapacity of the Chief Justice, the Lt. governor or other commander was empowered to appoint a most proper and competent person within the colony to act as Chief Justice and recorder until a successor be appointed. Decisions of the court were to be taken by a majority vote, the Chief Justice and recorder having a casting vote in the event of an equality of votes. The Chief Justice took precedence over everybody except the governor. He was an ex-officio member of the council.

By an Order-in-Council dated 16th March 1808, a Vice-Admiralty Court was established in Freetown for the trial and adjudication of any captures of slaves taken as prize. The Chief Justice was Judge of the court of Vice Admiralty and Judge of Prize. All slave ships intercepted off the West Coast of Africa were brought to Freetown for adjudication by this court.

The 1st September 1808 was the date appointed by the charter for annually filling up the vacant offices in the Court of Judicature. It was therefore resolved:[72]

> That Mr Alderman Smith be appointed Mayor of Freetown for the ensuing year:

[71] Thompson took over from Ludlam on the 27th July, 1808.
[72] See C.O. 270(11) at p.11.

That George Rickard Esq. be appointed sheriff for the ensuing year:

That Messrs Hananiah Hermitage, Thomas Fothergill, Joseph Brown and Charles Chambers be appointed Commissioners of the Court of Requests in the room of the four oldest members who go out by rotation:

That Francis Leedam Esq., be appointed an Alderman of Freetown:

That Mr John Morgan be appointed to act as Clerk of the Crown for the time being.

A Charter of Justice was issued under Letters Patent on the 8th August 1809. This charter conferred limited powers of legislation and taxation upon the council.[73] This charter revised the earlier one of 1799 and made some refinements and alterations to suit the new status of the colony. For example, under it, the governor and council were empowered to hold quarter sessions for the disposal of criminal cases. It abolished the Mayor's Court and re-established it as the Court of Requests with the same jurisdiction. The Court of the Recorder of Freetown, whose jurisdiction has already been described,[74] was given the civil jurisdiction originally exercised by the governor and council. Appeals lay from the Court of the Recorder to the governor and council and from thence to the King-in-Council provided the amount in dispute was of the sum of £400 or upwards. The same year, 1809, the Government for the first time conferred freehold title to land on the settlers if such lands were under cultivation. Whether the Crown was justified in granting such extensive powers to its own appointees in a settled colony with no explicit authorisation to do so from Parliament, was a point not raised before 1820.

Another significant event which took place during this period was the court martial held on the 18th October 1809 at Bance Island, presided over by the Hon. J. Forbes of the Royal Artillery Corps and five others.[75] The accused were Adam and Others and they were charged by Samuel Walker, the agent at Bance Island for Messrs John and Alexander Anderson of London, with an insurrection and a conspiracy to take possession of the island and its dependencies. Governor Thompson appointed the court martial to try the matter because he was firmly of the opinion that the civil courts had no jurisdiction to try the accused persons. He said that the powers of a court martial to try offences not strictly military were powers arising solely from necessity and implied either that the operation of the civil power had become impossible or, that "as in the present instance" no civil power had ever existed which could take cognisance of the matter in question. The

---

73 C.O. 268(18) at p.33.
74 See page 84 infra.
75 These were Lt. Fyfe of the RAC and Lt. Col. Robertson, Capt. Leedam, Capt. Craie and Lt. Adjt. Macaulay all of the Sierra Leone Militia. The last named was judge advocate.

opinion of the court was that the prisoners were guilty of rebellion. Two of them, Banna and Morey, were sentenced to a hundred and fifty lashes, and all of them to be transported for life to any place which, to His Majesty, may seem fit. This exceptional exercise of power and invocation of military discipline by the governor against the civilian population was not challenged and probably could not have been challenged in the courts. It illustrated, once again, the total and unlimited authority which the colonial governor had over internal disputes.[76]

Commission of Inquiry:
Soon after the establishment of Crown Colony rule, the British Government decided to set up a Commission of Inquiry:[77]

> Into the state of the settlements and forts on the coast of Africa, whether belonging to Europeans or native powers, with a view to investigating the best means of carrying into effect the law for the abolition of the slave trade, of inducing the native chiefs to abandon that commerce and of preventing European companies from continuing and promoting it.

It would appear that the initiative for the inquiry was taken by Zachary Macaulay who, in a letter dated 8th May 1807 addressed to the Rt. Hon. Lord Castereagh observed inter alia:

> The British settlements in Africa form at present a very loose and disjointed whole, subjected to great diversity of management and pursuing ends which widely differ from each other; force is a military government immediately under the directions of His Majesty. Sierra Leone is at present governed by the Sierra Leone Company by the authority of a Charter of Justice obtained from the king. Bance Island, a fortified settlement in the same river, is the property of Messrs John and Alexander Anderson of London who hold it by virtue of an Act of Parliament and also have hitherto used it as a slave factory.[78]

Hence the rather comprehensive terms of reference of the Commission of Inquiry.

The nature and effect of Crown Colony Government.
With the introduction of Crown Colony Government, a completely new administration, colonial in form and substance, was set up. The governor was absolute ruler. He had power to appoint, suspend and dismiss his council, at will. The Home Government reserved to itself the power of disallowance of legislation. Largely because of the difficulty of communicating promptly with London, the governor had a large measure of autonomy and could initiate and effectively carry out his

---
76 C.O. 270(9).
77 C.O. 268(18). Castereagh to Ludlam 11th April, 1808. Note: it was this Commission that reported in 1811, sometimes described as the 1811 Commission of Inquiry.
78 C.O. 267(24).

The Government of the Settlement 1791-1807

policies before any contrary instructions reached him from London. Restriction was imposed on taxes and duties, "except such as may hereafter be found to be necessary for the making of roads, erecting and repairing public buildings or other purposes of local commerce and economy for the interior welfare of the said Colony".[79]

On the 11th November 1808, a bill to change the name of Freetown to Georgetown, and to name streets and to change the currency from dollars to United Kingdom pounds was passed by the council.[80]

In 1809, Governor Perronet Thompson was faced with a complex and tricky problem of a legal nature. One George Nicol sued the Mayor, Mr Walter Robertson in the Mayor's Court for the sum of five hundred pounds for failing to grant a writ of Habeas Corpus. The case was pursued by Nicol through his Attorney Daniel M. Hamilton, Esquire, whose bona fides in the matter was seriously brought into question by the governor. In a letter to Lord Viscount Castereagh dated October 2 1809, the Governor alleged inter alia, that

> Messrs Ludlam and Dawes[81] were both particularly active and an attorney of the name Hamilton, kept here we believe, for the express purpose of endeavouring to stir up the Negroes to insubordination, was sent to the mayor to demand a writ of Habeas Corpus. The mayor demurred and came to the governor, asked for the warrant, saw it and went away satisfied. Mr Hamilton then went to the aldermen severally.

In the end the governor held that the Mayor's Court alone had no right to grant the writ; that the aldermen were not even justices of the peace and that they did not have the powers of the chancellor. Therefore the claim was dismissed with costs.[82]

The degree of independence of the governor can be observed by examining the activities of two governors under the Crown, namely, T. Perronet Thompson and Columbine and their respective machinations in appointing members of council as well as their dispositions and attitudes towards the settlers.

Perronet Thompson was a very arrogant person. He was a military man who greatly personalised his rule. He disliked the traditional independence of the Nova Scotians; he tolerated the Maroons, but loved the liberated Africans. He distrusted the company's servants and was openly hostile to them alleging that they had supported the abolition of the slave trade only in name while they were themselves carrying it on ostensibly for the purposes of profitable trade. The company's servants who had variously been threatened with arrest and imprisonment by Thompson had an opportunity to get their own back at him at the time of his departure from the colony. They arrested him but Columbine, his

---

79 C.O. 270(11).
80 C.O. 270(11) at pp.32/3.
81 They were both employees of the Sierra Leone Company. It appears Thompson felt that the company's officials were not co-operating with the British Government.
82 See C.O. 267(25).

successor, released him on a writ of Habeas Corpus on the ground that Thompson was under instructions from the British Government to return home. Thompson's era of government was a colourful one. He released apprentices and declared that their apprenticeships were null and void. In this respect he acted generously since the practice was sanctioned by the Abolition Act. It was Thompson who developed and named the streets; he it was, who changed the name from Freetown to Georgetown, although this was reversed later on; he changed the currency from dollars to pounds in November 1808; he established rural communities; he set up a newspaper; established a postal and communications service and set up a number of public buildings, a court house, hospital, churches, etc. His period of government was one quite full of vitality and vigour.

As against the positive aspects of his tenure, Thompson certainly had some poor marks. His handling of the pregnancy of Anne Edmonds left him many critics in the colony. He was firmly of the opinion that there had been a complicity on the part of Ludlam and others to procure Anne Edmonds' abortion and in a letter to the Secretary of State, he reported "an instance of depravity far below ordinary savages, it is only to say that infant murder and the procuring of abortion, on the authority of the late governor, who appears to have been conscious of the fact with all coolness, were practices absolutely of ordinary occurrences among the class of the inhabitants who are held to have made the greatest attainment in religion and in civilisation".[83] Although Anne Edmonds had been tried and found 'Not Guilty' by a jury in 1807, after her marriage on the 11th February 1809 to John L. Morgan, the former clerk of Thompson,[84] the governor got her charged with murder and then proceeded to get a gallows erected at Fort Thornton. He then personally interrogated the girl and put her again on trial and secured a verdict of guilty with a sentence of death by hanging. He fixed the execution date for the 3rd April 1809 only five days after the beginning of her trial. Mercifully, he did not carry it out. He granted her a free pardon on condition she left forever, and avoided "all territories, countries and places" which were at any time subject to the control or in the possession of Great Britain.

It is therefore not surprising that eventually a Commission of Inquiry was set up by the Crown comprising his successor Columbine as chairman and two others, Dawes and Ludlam in 1810, with specific instructions to study, observe and report on Thompson's administration of the colony.[85] Ludlam, unfortunately died at sea before the work of the commission was completed. Columbine also died on his way home in May 1811. His successor, Maxwell arrived in the colony on July 1st 1811.

On the other hand, Columbine was a mild mannered person. He was fair and simplistic in his approach to many things. Thompson, the

---
[83] See C.O. 267(25).
[84] This clerk had been dismissed by Thompson and employed by Ludlam. Ludlam presided at the wedding banquet of Anne Edmonds.
[85] Thompson was a Cambridge undergraduate, very young and inexperienced (22 years old) at the time when he took over the administration of the colony.

firebrand had set his stamp on the administration and Columbine had little time to establish his own particular mode of government on the colony before his death. However, the colonial office had great faith in his judgment and integrity and he sought to placate the numerous persons whom Thompson had alienated by his brash and intemperate administration.

That a governor could take far-reaching and, on occasions, intemperate decisions and actions without any one being able to check his indiscretions is the sad conclusion that inevitably has to be drawn from the extensive powers and authorities conferred by a colonial system on one man on the spot.

The Royal Charter created the office of Chief Justice. Robert Thorpe an Irish barrister was officially appointed in 1808 as the first Chief Justice of Sierra Leone, but he remained in England for three years after his appointment before taking up office. The reason for the delay in assuming the functions of his office was because the charter was only drawn up in August 1809 and the Great Seal affixed to it a year afterwards in August, 1810. It was only formally handed over to the new chief justice in March 1811.[86]

After the Abolition Act and the setting up of the colony under the British Crown, Freetown was designated the seat of the Vice-Admiralty Court. Slave trading was prohibited within the colony. Captured slaves condemned in the Vice-Admiralty Court were forfeited to the Crown and had to be enlisted in the forces or apprenticed. The Vice-Admiralty Court, officially constituted with Thorpe, Chief Justice, as its head, sat during Thorpe's absence, with Alexander Smith presiding. Smith was a storekeeper of the company who had been appointed by Governor Columbine, without salary as acting judge. He collected court fees and on Thorpe's arrival and assumption of office, refused to pay in the court fees he had collected. Thorpe claimed they should be surrendered to him and demanded that they be refunded. When Smith declined, Thorpe promptly commenced proceedings against Smith in his own court obtaining judgment for £300 damages. Smith protested strongly to the governor, who was Charles William Macarthy. The governor presided over a council meeting on the 10th January 1814 at which Smith's petition and appeal were heard. The other members of the council present were Robert Purder and William Appleton. The petition was presented on Smith's behalf by his attorney Michael Macmillan. It was resolved "that as the parties are both in England and the appellant is in possession of true copies of the plea and record of proceedings of the Court of the Recorder in this action, cognizance of the cause of this court be remised and that Mr William Smith be and is hereby recommended to petition to be heard on appeal before the king in council in conformity with the opinion of counsel thereon in consequence of his having failed to lodge his appeal herein within the time required by the

---

[86] Thus Thorpe was receiving his salary for three years before he actually entered into his office in the colony as Chief Justice.

Royal Charter."[87] Smith finally appealed successfully and Thorpe was instructed to repay. Thorpe was livid with rage and he made strong representations to the Colonial Office about the matter. The conflict between himself and Governor Maxwell was long and bitter. It resulted in the revocation of Thorpe's appointment on the 23rd March 1815.

While Thorpe was in England, he received some representations from inhabitants of the colony complaining about the governor. These, he transmitted to Lord Bathurst and Maxwell in response, recommended Thorpe's dismissal. In 1817, Thorpe commenced proceedings in the king's bench in England against Maxwell. He set out 57 charges based on the information transmitted to him. The following constitute a representative collection of some of the charges and allegations levied against the former:

(a) giving false certificates to persons as having discharged offices which they never did:
(b) disregarding or refusing or failing to distribute land to settlers in accordance with his instructions:
(c) building an extensive house and offices for himself from public funds and selling the same:
(d) granting a free pardon to one William Tuft, a criminal, and exempting him from military duty:
(e) importing large quantities of merchandise from Britain for the African market which he sold and bartered.

It is not difficult to appreciate the seriousness of the allegations which, if substantiated, would have led to Maxwell's immediate recall. He was accused of almost every possible kind of irregularity in the conduct of his office. Maxwell had perforce to react effectively and quickly, if he were to save his own reputation and position. He was in the administrative arena and so Thorpe took the matter to a judicial forum. Unfortunately, he lost again.

However, an inquiry was set up to investigate the petition of the inhabitants who had complained about oppression by illegal sanctions and other arbitrary measures, encouragement to commit, and in some cases the actual commission of crimes of a heinous nature, and also about the activities of some subordinate officials, notably Kenneth Macaulay, the Collector of Customs and Robert Purdue the secretary, the surgeon and the acting judge.

Ironically, the inquiry was conducted by Maxwell. He was assisted by Kenneth Macaulay and Zachary Macaulay. No doubt it would have been a most noble gesture for the accused to render verdicts against themselves. They did not. They found the charges not proved and once again Thorpe was on the losing side.[88]

The Vice-Admiralty Court was kept rather busy. Naval and customs officers were empowered to bring in slaves who were being illegally transported into the territory to be adjudicated upon before the Vice-

---

87 See C.O. 270(14) pp.54-5.
88 See C.O. 267(88).

The Government of the Settlement 1791-1807

Admiralty Court. A register of slaves released by the court was kept. Instructions were given to send an annual return to London. The captors of these slaves were given a small allowance for the loss of their captives. Many of the freed slaves were apprenticed to families of the settlers.

Lt. Col. Maxwell was appointed governor on the first July 1811. His appointment was by commission, unlike the earlier ones. He was designated Captain General and Governor-in-Chief. He was also commissioned Vice-Admiral and was the senior member of the council.[89] The Chief Justice was the next senior, but in order to keep the functions of the judiciary separate and apart from those of the executive, it was decided that in the absence of the governor, the next senior person should act, instead of the Chief Justice. Maxwell further had instructions on an important issue which had plagued the settlement since 1792. That of land. He granted four-fifths of the allotments which had remained outstanding for nearly twenty years. The Royal Charter also empowered the governor to raise a militia. A local enactment was passed but the settlers misinterpreted the preamble and thought that they were being subjected to military control and discipline. They therefore refused to co-operate.

On the 14th May 1811, parliament passed another Abolition of Slave Trade Act[90] which made slave trading a felony rather than a misdemeanour which it was, before. It also made the offence punishable by transportation.

The settlers had bemoaned the fact that no provision had been made for them to participate in the government of the colony since the introduction of Crown Colony Government. They were therefore relieved when in 1811, royal instructions were despatched to the governor from the colonial office, authorising him to include in his council one unofficial member chosen by him "from among the most considerable of the Protestant inhabitants of the colony".[91] Thus, three years after the beginning of colonial rule proper, an attempt was made to introduce settler participation in the executive decisions of the colony. Unfortunately, this provision was not implemented until 1819. The term "Honourable" was first applied to members of the council in 1816.

External factors influencing
Constitutional Development and change.

THE ABOLITION ACT.

Ironically, one of the main reasons why the Abolition Act was passed, was the desire to obtain raw materials from Africa. The slave trade was

---

89 From the first meeting in 1801 until 1815, the governor was the only person whose official title was given in the minutes. The other members were styled "First in Council", "Second in Council" etc.
90 51 Geo. III c. 23. See C.O. 267(43).
91 See the Royal Instructions of 1811 constituting the first council under the Crown in CROOKS: *History of the Colony of Sierra Leone* (1908) Dublin p.86.

becoming more and more unprofitable and in addition, there was a movement concurrently taking place on the African continent for the total abolition of slavery. Denmark had abolished slavery in 1805, but this did not foreshadow a European continental movement for its abolition. In fact, it was a source of great annoyance and embarrassment to the British that after having renounced the spoils of slavery and its financial attractions, the plum, speaking figuratively, fell squarely on the laps of the other European powers, notably France and Portugal who took full advantage of acquiring the abandoned commercial profits. It is natural therefore that the British Government should take an active and foremost part in the conference in Paris in 1814 which sought to secure widespread continental agreement for the aboliton of slavery. Several European countries ultimately took steps for abolishing slavery although in some instances the effective measures came only after a number of decades.[92]

For Sierra Leone, the Abolition Act represented the ultimate in the sustained and concerted efforts of the abolitionists to erase from the globe the sad blemish which had shocked the conscience of sincere and upright men throughout the world and debased humanity itself. It was the zenith of their endeavour; the apotheosis of success. In the same year that the new colonial regime was taking over, the Vice-Admiralty Court was being set up to enforce the Abolition Act.[93] The Vice-Admiralty Court sat in Freetown for many years.

THE AFRICAN INSTITUTION.
A further reference to the African Institution is appropriate at this juncture for the purpose of setting out its objectives:
> To promote the civilization and happiness of the natives of Africa; to cultivate friendly relations with them; to enlighten them with respect to their true interests and the means whereby they might substitute a beneficial commerce for the slave trade; to introduce among them the useful arts of Europe; to acquire a knowledge of the principal languages of Africa and reduce them to writing;[94] and to encourage and reward individual enterprise in promoting any of the purposes of the institution.

The institution[95] urged the introduction in parliament of a proposal for

---

92 The US abolished slavery in 1807; Sweden in 1813; Netherlands 1814; France 1818; Brazil 1825. Between 1825 and 1865 nearly 1,800,000 slaves were exported from West Africa alone. During the same period, British naval patrols intercepted about 130,000 slaves, only 7.2 per cent of the total exported.
93 See J. D. Fage: *An introduction to the History of West Africa.*
94 The Vai script in Sierra Leone is regarded as the first African dialect ever put into writing; See CONTON: *West Africa in History,* Vol. II.
95 See Report of the Committee of the African Institution read to the general meeting on the 15th July 1807, together with the rules and regulations which were then adopted for the *Govt. of the Society* (London 1807) pp.68-71. Reproduced in SCHUYLER *"Parliament and the Br. Empire"* (N.Y. Columbia Press 1929) p.120. Also: Gilbert Mathieson: *A short British Review of the reports of the African Institution,* London, 1816. pp. 14-16.

the registration of all slaves in order to defeat any attempted invasion of the territory or any evasion of the provisions of the Act. It suggested that slave dealers should compulsorily furnish extensive and detailed descriptions of slaves in their custody. In its opinion the existence of such records would effectively prevent the substitution of one slave for another who had either died or disappeared. This proposal was severely opposed by West Indian slave owners who had powerful and vocal representatives and sympathisers in parliament. They succeeded in getting the bill withdrawn.[96]

THE MIXED COURT OF JUSTICE —
Sierra Leone's first International Court.

In June 1819, one of the earliest international tribunals was set up in Sierra Leone. It was the Mixed Court of Justice, better known as the Mixed Commission Court.[97] Its name arose from the presence on the bench of representatives from several nations. At first, the court's membership was made up of Britain, Portugal and Spain. Later on, it included the Argentine Republic, Bolivia, Chile, Uruguay, Brazil and the USA. The Governor of Sierra Leone had power to adjudicate or arbitrate over difficult cases. The court attracted to Sierra Leone many able lawyers from Britain and the United States both black and white and it remained in existence for about forty years. Each signatory government sent two commissioners to the court, one of whom sat with a British commissioner, in cases where his own national was involved. Its first judge was Thomas Gregory. The court had no jurisdiction over persons, only over slave ships which had been intercepted. To prevent technicalities arising during its hearings a set form of questions was asked of witnesses. On the recommendation of a Select Committee of the House of Commons[98] it was proposed that the court be transferred from Sierra Leone to Fernando Po, but the Spanish Government did not cooperate, and in 1832, the idea was dropped.

The Foreign Office had charge of the court. Gradually, with Spain, Brazil and other countries sending their personnel to other places and diverting them from the court, much of the work passed on to the Chief Justice of Sierra Leone who sat as Vice-Admiralty Judge. The court exercised its final jurisdiction on or about the 26th December 1864.

---

96 The African Institution published a pamphlet in 1915 entitled "Reasons for establishing a Registry for slaves".
97 The Court was established under the Statute 58 Geo. III c. 35 and 36.
98 13th July, 1830. See *Parliamentary Papers 1830* 661 Vol. X pp.3-4.

CHAPTER VI

THE GOVERNMENT OF SIERRA LEONE 1808-1896

Reference has already been made to events immediately following the establishment of Crown Colony rule with effect from the 1st day of January 1808. One of the first measures of importance taken by the governor and council was the passing of the Police Act. This was done on the 11th November 1808. The act provided for the division of Freetown into wards and the appointment of constables.[1] No attempt will be made to recapitulate the ground already covered regarding the administration of the territory under Governor Thompson. However, in 1811, H. E. Charles William Maxwell was appointed Governor of Sierra Leone and on the 1st July, he took the oath of office.[2] He succeeded Columbine. He introduced into the council the first Absconding and Distant Debtors Bill which was passed into law in July 1811.[3] On the 20th November, 1811 he passed into law, a measure relating to the militia[4] the long title of which was "An act for amending and reducing into one statute, the laws relating to the militia, for the better defence of this colony". Section 2 provided as follows:

> Every male person becoming a resident of this colony, for the purposes of trade, or any other purpose whatsoever, shall within three months, after such residence, enrol himself in the aforesaid militia and take the said oath, unless entitled to be excused by the exemptions aforesaid; and if he does not so enrol himself, and take the said oath, he shall from that time, be out of the protection of the laws.

The intention of this enactment was to provide for compulsory military service by all the male residents of the colony. This was considered necessary in the light of the existing conditions at the time.

The Report of the Commissioners of African Inquiry in 1811 greatly strengthened the hands of the governor vis-a-vis the council. The

---

1 This measure remained in the law books until 1857 when it was repealed.
2 See C.O. 270(13) at p.8. Same day, Robert Thorpe took oath as Chief Justice and as Judge of the Vice Admiralty Court. He delivered to the governor the Charter of Justice of the Colony.
3 See C.O. 270(13) pp.15-21.
4 Act No. 3 of 1811 passed on 20th Nov. 1811.

commissioners commented as follows:[5]
> The peculiar circumstances of Sierra Leone require much prompitude and vigour in the government; and it is evident, that neither of these points can be obtained, if the council have the power (as they no doubt will occasionally have the inclination) to thwart the governor, or impede his views by tedious and trifling discussions on every subject, and any oppositions made chiefly to display their own weight. To avoid these inconveniences, it is proposed that the power of council should be limited to their voting, when any new law is to be enacted, or an old one repealed; to sitting with the governor to hear appeals; and as judges at the Court of Quarter Sessions, in the absence of a professional judge.
>
> A point of law respecting the governor and council should be finally settled. The governor and council when they act, do not vote as two separate authorities, but together. It is therefore contended that all those acts which the law requires to be done by the governor and council, may in the event of the death or absence of every member of council, be legally performed by the governor alone, he being then the only representative of the collective body; and that his act, on this point of view, is to be taken as the act of the governor and council.

The commissioners therefore recommended that the governor should unquestionably be the sole authority in the colony and be able to perform his duties independent of the actions of the rest of his council. In short, while he could have measures debated and also seek the opinion of the council he was not to be impeded by the council in his work and the ultimate decisions were to be his alone.

On the 26th September 1812, the governor established the new Court of Requests and Police.[6] Under this enactment, there were to be twelve commissioners appointed and nominated by the governor in council. The court was required to hear and determine in a summary manner all actions of debt or damage in which the amount involved did not exceed £5. Appeal lay to the recorder in cases involving an amount in excess of 40/-. Interestingly enough, the court had power to "commit to the 'House of Correction' for hard labour for one month or to the stocks for 12 hours, or order to be ducked (giving three dips only in deep water)". One would have thought that these kinds of punishments would not be permissible under the Crown, but they were.

Governor Charles Macarthy, succeeded Governor Maxwell in 1814. He remained governor for ten years. He was a brilliant administrator and many important constitutional events took place during his tenure of office. He settled the discharged officers of the West India Regiment and the Royal African Corps at Waterloo and Hastings, following the

---
5 Parliamentary Papers 1816 (506) Vol. vii B p.127. Appendix to Report of Select Committee on African Forts, 1816.

6 Act No. 6 of 1812 — "An Act for Establishing a Court of Requests and Police with certain powers and under certain regulations".

Convention of 1819.[7] He was governor at the time of the Mixed Commission Court's establishment in Sierra Leone. He tidied up internal legislation.[8] But by far his biggest responsibility came with the legislative changes of 1821. In that year, the British Parliament passed the West Africa Act[9] which provided, inter alia, that all the possessions and territories of Great Britain in West Africa, between latitudes 20 degrees north and 20 degrees south should be annexed to and or made Dependencies of the Colony of Sierra Leone. They were also to be made subject to its laws. This meant that the Gold Coast, Lagos and the Gambia automatically became dependencies of Sierra Leone and subject to the laws of Sierra Leone. They were governed from Freetown which was the seat of the administration and also the administrative capital of British West Africa. The Governor, Sir Charles Macarthy, thus had control of the government of territories scattered over a vast area of land of over one thousand five hundred miles, on the West Coast of Africa.

On the 17th October 1821, the charter was again revised following the West Africa Act and the enlarged jurisdiction of the territory under the command of the Governor of Sierra Leone. The Royal African Company had also been disbanded and its possessions transferred to the Crown. The charter, as revised, made far-reaching alterations both in the administration of the government and of the courts. It is not correct, as has been alleged that it made only slight changes in the existing provisions.[10] The changes may not have been fundamental, but they were far from minimal.

The charter provided for nine or more councillors[11] advising and assisting the governor, five of them to form a quorum. In the making and passing of laws the governor or commander-in-chief for the time being had a negative voice;[12] in certain cases, the governor had power to suspend councillors and, when the number fell below nine, to appoint others, subject to His Majesty's approval.

The increased number of nine took account of two members of the council to be stationed and resident in the Gold Coast.

The mayor and aldermen now forfeited their judicial powers. The Court of Requests was abolished: but the governor was directed to appoint justices and commissioners for particular districts. The jurisdiction was limited to cases under 40/-. The Freetown Court of the

---

7 Macarthy signed three important treaties ceding territory to the Crown: 6.7.1819 with the Chief of Bago Country ceding the Isle de Los (which was ceded to France by the Anglo-French Convention of 1904) 25/5/1819 — Waterloo and Hastings and 21/7/1820, the Banana Islands.
8 e.g. Acts Nos. 4 of 1816 — Debtors Act and No. 29 of 1822 — Speedy recovery of small debts.
9 Stat: 1 & 2 Geo. IV c. 28. 7th May 1821 pp.241-4.
10 See Fyfe — *History* op. cit.
11 This was an increase from the original three (exclusive of the governor) so that other territories would have some form of representation. By now the governor had begun to implement the 1811 Instructions which provided for one of the settlers to be nominated by him to serve on the council.
12 This was a veto.

Recorder was reconstituted and granted jurisdiction to hear and determine cases from all the dependencies except where the cause or matter did not exceed forty shillings.[14] The Chief Justice presided over the court which was duly constituted with two other members of the council sitting with him as assistant judges. All three or any two, including the Chief Justice, could form a quorum. The Chief Justice had a casting vote. The governor was appointed chancellor to hear chancery cases.[15] His status was thus raised. In chancery, two members of the council again sat with the Chief Justice as additional judges. The governor, whenever he sat, presided over the court.

It will be recalled that the commissioners of African inquiry in 1811, had pointed out the deficiencies of the system whereby it was possible for members of council to obstruct or delay legislative measures introduced by the governor. The amended charter therefore sought to do away with this uncertainty over the extent of the governor's powers and functions in the legislative arena. It therefore sought to prescribe as fully as possible the role and functions of the governor in relation to the other members of his council. It made the governor the sole person in command of the government both in law and in fact.

The governor used his powers to the fullest advantage. He was very keen on extending territory and developing trade world-wide and also improving the standard of local institutions to make them more effective. On the 6th February 1822, he signed the convention with Pa London, commonly called Pa Conko, and his chieftains by which the Banana Islands, situated near and opposite to Cape Shilling, were ceded to the British Crown.[16]

On the 24th September 1825, a treaty[17] was signed between Governor Turner and the King of Sherbro and Queen Ya Comba which asserted full British sovereignty over the greater part of the south eastern coastal zone from the Bumpeh River down the coast to a point opposite Camalay on the Kittam River. Governor Turner negotiated the treaty. The circumstances under which the treaty came to be signed were as follows. Turner went to the Sherbro with a force of men to suppress the slave trade. While there, in September 1825, he discussed with the Caulkers the ceding of Plaintain Island. They agreed and a treaty was

---

14 By Act of 20th October 1825, Governor Turner who succeeded Macarthy, increased this jurisdiction to £10. Appeal was allowed to the Court of the Recorder. Section 14 prohibited the appearance before the Court of Attorneys, unless they swore that they had neither received, nor expected to receive any reward for their services.

A similar provision remained in the Statute Books, the Legal Practitioners Act, but the requirement was that laymen who prepared legal documents should make the endorsement on the document. The provision was repealed — 1983.

15 See the Royal Instructions of 1821.

16 Reference has been made at p.96 (Footnote 7) to this treaty. See. C.O. 270(16). The same day, a convention was tabled between His Honour Capt. Alexander Grant, Ag. Governor on behalf of the Crown and Thomas Caulker and Others, giving "full, entire, free and unlimited possession and sovereignty of the Islands of Bananas" and lands in their immediate vicinity.

17 This treaty was not ratified but was revived in 1861.

signed to effect this agreement. In the following year, he took another expedition there and the coast was then accurately surveyed by Captain W. F. Owen. It was named Turner's Peninsular. The extent of the territory was some one hundred miles long. In return for this massive cession of territory which included the Sherbro Island and over half of Turner's Peninsular, the treaty extended to the aboriginal inhabitants, British protection and "the rights and privileges of British subjects".[18] Britain did not want to extend territory any further and so did not ratify this treaty. It remained dormant until it was again revived in 1861. By order in council of the 26th April 1862, the Island of Sherbro was declared part of the Colony of Sierra Leone.

No fewer than fourteen treaties were negotiated between the various governors and the local rulers between 25th May 1819 and 24th June 1827.[19] After Turner signed a treaty with the chiefs of the Bacco Loco territories on the 12th December 1825, Lord Bathurst wrote to him as follows:[20]

> I cannot too strongly impress on you the necessity of avoiding entering into any treaty with a view to the acquisition of territory or rights of sovereignty.

It would thus appear that British policy at this time was not to obtain any further extensions of territory, having obtained the colony and its extensions and additions, including the Sherbro Islands.

In 1827, by an amendment to the charter, the united government was abolished with the removal of the Gambia and the Gold Coast from the jurisdiction of Sierra Leone. The power of legislation was however retained. At this time, the following were the courts in existence having jurisdiction in Sierra Leone:

1. The Privy Council (Resident in England).
2. The Governor and Council.
3. The Court of Royal Commissions:
   Governor,
   Chief Justice,
   Commissary Judge of Mixed Court,
   King's Advocate,
   Colonial Secretary and
   Others specified in the Commission.
   Three were to form a quorum. Any one of the first four could preside.
   Their jurisdiction was extra-territorial and covered all crimes where no local British jurisdiction existed.

18 See C.3597: 26-28 (Treaty with King of Sherbro and Queen Ya Comba. Not ratified).
19 See Hertslet: *British and Foreign State Papers*. The area of the colony was increased gradually from time to time as a result of further cessions of territory. Outstanding examples, other than those discussed here, were the treaties of 10th July 1807 by which Kings Firama and Tom ceded all the land they possessed in the peninsular west of the colony and that of 1861 from Bai Conteh, King of Kwara of land measuring 10 miles wide and 16 miles long from the River Sierra Leone to the River Ribbi.
20 See C.O. 267(66).

4. Vice-Admiralty Court (Chief Justice, Judge).
5. Court of the Recorder of Freetown. Now constituted by Chief Justice as Recorder, Presiding. Two assistant judges appointed by the governor from his council.
   This court resembled "most closely the Court of Common Pleas in England". It sat once a month. The Chief Justice had a casting vote. It had jurisdiction in all civil suits within the colony or any of the forts, settlements, islands or territories subject or subordinate thereto. The revised Charter of 1821 gave this court power over *all* Africans born in the colony.[21]
6. Courts of Quarter Sessions, Oyer and Terminer. Sessions of the Court were held in March, June, September and December. It was presided over by the Chief Justice and members of the council. Proceedings were initiated by indictment or by such other ways and means as are used in England as nearly as the condition and circumstances of the colony and the inhabitants could permit.
   Judges issued warrants and precepts to the sheriff to summon juries, both grand and petty. The Charter of 1821 abolished the Court of Requests and replaced it with district justices or commissioners.
7. District Justices or Commissioners.
   By Act of the 21st September 1822, No. 29/1822, Intituled "An Act for the Speedy and easy recovery of small debts and for regulating the proceedings thereon". Jurisdiction was extended to suits where the debt, duty or matter in dispute did not exceed £10. The recital read:
   Whereas Letters Patent dated 7/8/22 of the 2nd year of Geo. IV decreed that authority of the Court of Requests for small debts should cease and be abolished; and required the governor to appoint justices or other commissioners for particular districts for debts under 40/-.
   Justices have power to hear and determine in a summary way . . . matters in dispute . . . shall not exceed £10.
   The court sat once a week as a "Court for the recovery of small debts" from 10 a.m. to 1 p.m. No jurisdiction existed in the court to hear matters relating to titles to land, nor assault and battery, nor slander.
8. Police Court of Freetown.
   Two magistrates sat twice a month. One of the magistrates was a member of the council and he presided. Together, they formed a Petty Session.

Further Imperial Legislation during this period had a profound effect on constitutional change and progress in Sierra Leone. The most important ones were three in number. They were:

---

21 See Newbury, C.W.: *British Policy towards Africa*. Select Documents 1786-1874. Clarendon Press, 1965 p.539.

(a) The British Settlements Act[22]
(b) The Status of Liberated Africans Act[23]
(c) The Foreign Jurisdiction Act[24]

The British Settlements Act, 1843.
An order in council under the British Settlements Act, 1843, made provision for the establishment of laws, institutions and ordinances for the peace order and good government of Her Majesty's subjects and others within the settlements on the African Coast. This enactment paved the way for the establishment of regular courts, similar to those which existed in England before the Judicature Acts, and also for the eventual separation of the Gold Coast from Sierra Leone. This latter event was achieved in 1850 when a Legislative Council and an Executive Council were established for the "Gold Coast Colony".

The Status of Liberated Africans Act, 1852.
The Status of Liberated Africans Act was of fundamental importance to the settlers of Sierra Leone. The act was passed in order to remove doubts about the legality of Sierra Leone courts trying liberated Africans for offences committed outside Sierra Leone. Its necessity was dictated by the Abolition of Slavery Act, 1833.[25] "Liberated African" was defined in Section 4 of the act as:

> All persons dealt with or detained as slaves who heretofore have been or hereafter may be seized or taken, under any of the acts for the abolition or suppression of the slave trade by Her Majesty's ships of war or otherwise, and liberated or delivered to the officers appointed to protect, receive, or provide for such persons, and all other persons who, as having been dealt with, carried, kept or detained as slaves, may have been taken and liberated or received, protected, or provided for, under any of the said acts.

Sierra Leone courts had already received a greatly extended jurisdiction to deal with a large body of offences and offenders, but there had arisen the somewhat unusual practice of sending accused persons to England to be tried for serious offences, a relic of the days of company rule. There was strictly no necessity for this since a system of trial by jury was in operation in the colony. Further, the Sierra Leone courts were dispensing British justice according to the laws of England with only slight variations and alterations designed to meet the local situation, as the governor thought fit. But it was the extra-territorial jurisdiction of the Sierra Leone courts which was questioned; and the act was conceived

---

22 6 and 7 Vic. c. 13 — 1843.
23 16 and 17 Vic. c. 86 — 1852/3.
24 6 and 7 Vic. c. 94 — 1843.
25 3 and 4 Vic. c. 73. See also 6 & 7 Vic. c. 98. The act for the extension of acts for suppression of slavery to all British subjects wherever residing and the ultimate effects of that enactment.

of and passed to meet these uncertainties and to put the authority and competence of the judicial system beyond any doubt.

The act in fact went a great deal further, in its provisions, than a mere question of jurisdiction. It purported, inter alia, to grant the power of testamentary disposition to the liberated Africans and to British subjects within the jurisdiction of the Sierra Leone Government. This was the first time in history that such powers had been conferred on a colonial people. The measure was framed as follows:

> ALL liberated Africans domiciled or resident in the Colony of Sierra Leone or its dependencies shall be deemed to be and to have been natural born subjects of Her Majesty and .... to be capable of taking or transmitting or devising .... any estate real or personal within the said colony or its dependencies.

The Foreign Jurisdiction Act, 1843.

Ironically, one of the reasons which led to the passing of this measure concerned certain events which were occurring in Sierra Leone. Disgruntled settlers had caused trouble and moved from Freetown to the hinterland. The governor could not get them back since the neighbouring territory was an independent foreign country. He therefore went to his council, initiated and passed into law an ordinance to enable him to recapture fugitive settlers. The colonial office viewed the governor's action with alarm and disapproval since it authorised a trespass on foreign country without the consent or approval of the native rulers thereof. The matter was put before parliament which then proceeded to do exactly the same thing. It passed the Foreign Jurisdiction Act, 1843, "to remove doubts as to the exercise of powers and jurisdiction by Her Majesty within divers countries and places out of Her Majesty's Dominions and to render the same more effectual".[26]

Prior to this, there had also been considerable dissatisfaction among the local chiefs over the fact that the governor was unable to deal with settlers who went into their territories and committed offences. They were not amenable to native law and custom and the courts in the colony could not try them for offences committed outside their jurisdiction. So, in February 1842, Governor Jeremie signed a treaty which provided that British offenders in Temne country should be extradited and "tried according to the English law and shall be punished if found guilty". Of the Koya chiefs, only Mohammadu Bundu of Foredugu signed this agreement. It was significant that he did, since the son of the colonial schoolmaster had stabbed a man at Foredugu and then gone away scot-free as neither the local chiefs nor the colony courts could try and punish him.[27]

---

26 See Sir Kenneth Roberts-Wray: *Commonwealth and Colonial Law,* pp.101-2, where he discusses the problems of the prerogative and the opinion of Mr Hope Scott QC, on the matter.

27 See Fyfe: *History* op. cit.
   Also, ELIAS, T.O.: *Nigerian Legal System,* p.43.
   He expresses the view that the effect of the Foreign Jurisdiction Act was that the settlements were assimilated to the position of Crown Colonies.

To revert to 1827, the united government was dissolved, but the power of legislation retained. With the removal of both the Gambia and the Gold Coast from the United West African Settlements and from the control of the Sierra Leone courts, the settlers began to urge, and to demand, greater participation by them in the conduct of their own affairs. That same year, a Commission of Inquiry which had been sent out in 1825, and made up of Henry Wellington and Major James Rowan, reported to Parliament its findings on the Liberated African Department. The report was unfavourable.

In 1843, the Gambia was separated finally from Sierra Leone and granted its own Legislative and Executive Councils, but the constitution of Sierra Leone remained substantially unaltered from what it was in 1821.

LOCAL LEGISLATION.
Some significant measures 1847-63.
Immediately prior to the constitutional changes which emerged in 1863, the governor and council embarked on a number of important legislative measures of which the following were, perhaps, the most significant.

(a) Ordinance No. 28 of 1847, following Letters Patent dated 17th February 1846. The measure established the Court of the Ordinary. The Chief Justice was created Judge of Probate, called "Judge of the Court of Ordinary". He was given power to grant Letters of Administration and Probates of the estates of deceased persons. With the passing of this measure,[28] the power of granting probates or letters of administration formerly exercised by the governor and council as a matter of administrative discretion was formalised and discontinued.

(b) In 1848, the colony was divided into five districts, each under the control of a manager or magistrate with a salary of £250 per annum . . . . Two of these officials were Africans. Their decisions were subject to appeal to the governor.[29]

(c) On the 31st October 1849, the governor and council passed Ordinance No. 32 which was an ordinance for defining the jurisdiction and regulating the practice of the Court of the Recorder of Freetown. This ordinance provided that the court would have the same jurisdiction as Her Majesty's Court of Queen's Bench, Common Pleas and Exchequer in the United Kingdom. It was to be held before the chief justice and one assistant judge. The Chief Justice, in the event of an equality of votes had a casting vote. Section 3 of the ordinance empowered the governor to appoint any two members of the council to be assistant judges of the court, each to hold office for one year. Section 8 provided that no member of the council was to be disqualified to sit and act as a judge upon any appeal from a

---
28 This Court fell into desuetude in 1858.
29 See Forbes: *Six months service in the African blockade from April to October 1848.*

decision of the said court to the governor and council, except such as shall have sat as assistant judges when the judgment, decree, sentence or order appealed against was actually pronounced or made. Section 13 preserved the English practice and laws as those of the court.[30]

(d) The Police Ordinance No. 40 of 1851. This enactment is usually regarded as the first police ordinance of Sierra Leone. This view, however, is not historically sound. Apart from the role of the Hundredors and Tythingmen in the earlier years of the settlement, Ordinance No. 14 of 1808 divided Freetown into wards[31] and appointed constables for the city. Also, Ordinance No. 9 of 1814 was a police ordinance which in fact set up the police force as a national one, specifying its functions, duties and powers.

(e) Ordinance No. 50 of 1853 provided that the Chief Justice should be appointed vice-chancellor. This measure has been discussed.

(f) Ordinance No. 59 was a law relating to jurors and juries. It was an amending measure and prescribed the procedure for trial by jury in criminal cases. It abolished the procedure whereby Grand Juries were utilised for the purpose of indicting criminals and sending them for trial. Section 4 provided that if, in any trial, the jury could not agree after twelve hours, the court could discharge the jury without requiring them to deliver a verdict.

(g) Ordinance No. 7 of 1857 empowered the supreme court to grant divorces. It thus took away this important jurisdiction from the governor and council who had to pass special laws each time a divorce was sought. The matter had become one of considerable anxiety and concern and in 1830, the Under Secretary of State, Sir James Stephen, had pronounced his considered opinion that the governor and council had no right to grant divorces. The ordinance regularised the position.

Significant Imperial Legislation affecting Sierra Leone.
At this period of time, there were some measures emanating from the British Government which were of both historical and constitutional importance for Sierra Leone. Among these, were the following:

(a) The Admiralty Offences (Colonial) Act of 1849 which provided for the prosecution and trial of offences in the colonies committed upon the high seas. This was of major importance to Sierra Leone which had a long history of punishing those who were engaged in acts of slavery on the high seas. It gave the courts

---

30 This Ordinance was repealed by Ord. No. 10 of 1858, Sec. 44. NOTE: Both Elias and Joko Smart are in error in saying that the first formal reception of English law into Sierra Leone came respectively in 1862 and 1857. See: Allott: *Judicial and Legal Systems in Africa.*
31 See p.94 infra.

in the colony just the kind of authority it needed to deal with this kind of situation:

(b) The Sierra Leone Offences Act[32] of 1861 was peculiarly relevant to the needs of the colony. It provided for the punishment of offences committed in territories adjacent to the Colony of Sierra Leone by Her Majesty's subjects within the colony.

(c) The Colonial Letters Patent Act, 1863, provided that no Letters Patent were to take effect in any colony unless and until they were published by proclamation or public notice. It was during this period that a Registry for Instruments was established in Freetown and so the provision in the UK legislation was timely.[33]

The period from 1821 to 1863 was one of excitement both in the law and in the administration. At this time, the settlers had proved themselves extremely capable and responsible and it is only right to observe that only British colonial policy which left no room for local populations to conduct the government, precluded them from achieving independent nationhood. There was considerable legal development during this period and the courts were carrying out their duties with credit. It was at this period of time that the country, under colonial rule, had its first African Chief Justice, Mr Justice John Carr.[34] He held office for twenty-five years and sat as a member of the Executive Council, ex virtuti officii. It was the time of the great case of John Langley v the manager of the school at Kent. This case raised squarely for the first time for judicial determination, the question, which was as yet undetermined judicially, whether a recaptive had the right to bring proceedings in the Sierra Leone courts.[35] It was also the period when the trial took place of the prisoners of the Cobolo War.[36]

*BRITISH COLONIAL POLICY PRIOR TO THE
CONSTITUTIONAL CHANGES OF 1863.*
Before dealing with the events which led to the Constitution of 1863, a short discussion of British colonial policy at this time, would put the discussion in perspective. First, the area of the colony was small. Settlers had already established trade relationships with the people in the hinterland and several occasions had arisen when the colonial power found it essential to exercise jurisdiction in respect of matters arising in the hinterland or in respect of settlers who had gone there. Moreover, the governors had tried to establish good relationships with the chiefs and their people. But the British policy was one of very cautious extension of jurisdiction into the hinterland. When Sherbro Island was to be annexed

---

32 24 and 25 Vic. c. 31.
33 The first Registration Ordinance was in 1857.
34 His appointment was as from the 19th August, 1841. Prior to that, he had been Queen's Advocate for two years.
35 The Judgment of the Court, (1829) was that he had a right to do so.
36 For details of this, see Sibthorpe's *History of Sierra Leone.*

in 1825, Lord Russell wrote to the Governor of Sierra Leone in the following terms:[37]

> You are to consider yourself absolutely prohibited from concluding any treaty which should have the effect of binding (Great Britain) to give military aid to African chiefs or to assume any right of sovereignty or protection over any portion of the soil or waters of Africa.

Similarly, in 1846, Earl Grey in a communication addressed to Mr MacDonald who was then Governor of Sierra Leone instructed as follows:

> The settled policy of Her Majesty's Government is not to extend the limits of the colony.

It was therefore clear that Britain did not intend the governors to enter into any arrangements which would result in an extension of the area of the colony. It wished to rule Sierra Leone as a colony and it would appear that its primary objective was that the settler population would in due course take over the government of the colony and British practices and policies would be firmly entrenched therein. An African had been appointed to the post of a Chief Justice with a seat in the council. In 1844, this policy of "Africanisation" was taken one step further when the first black governor, William Fergusson, of Sierra Leone was appointed. He succeeded MacDonald. Fyfe comments that Fergusson's "even temper, medical skill, long experience, allied to a commanding military appearance, gave him a distinction many of his European predecessors and successors might have envied."[38]

In 1842, the Madden Commission, chaired by Sir Robert Madden, was sent out to report on the conditions of the British territories in West Africa. His instructions, inter alia, were to find out to what extent British merchants participated in the slave trade. His report was inaccurate in many respects and so a parliamentary committee was appointed afterwards to take evidence. At that period of time there was a powerful influence in parliament which wanted Britain to pull out from and abandon her West African possessions altogether. It had also become apparent that the experiment of a joint or federal form of government for the British West African territories was unworkable and, if pursued, would end in dismal failure. Efforts were therefore made to dissolve the union or what remained of it.

The decision not to pursue a federation in West Africa, was an unfortunate one. It deprived West Africa of a marvellous opportunity of developing joint institutions of both an economic and political kind. It also prevented the rapid development of the resources of the region and the raising of the standard of living of the peoples therein. Communications were not developed, and these remained at a painfully inefficient level for several decades. As the reasons for the dismantling of the proposed federation were not purely legal any further inquiry into all

---

37 C.O. 268.
38 See Fyfe: *History* etc. infra. op. cit.

the causes for its failure would be strictly inappropriate. However, governing four distant territories from Britain with all the delays and difficulties of communication in those days was not a very efficient way of running a proposed federation. Had there been a greater participation in legal and political matters by the indigenous populations of these territories then a union of West African states might have been born over a century ago and would most probably have been a strong, viable, economic unit today.

Events leading to the Constitutional changes of 1863.
Internally, the settlers in Sierra Leone were becoming increasingly anxious and determined to have further legal and constitutional change. In 1853, they formed a "Committee of Correspondence" which was a powerful group of business men. It was a small, vocal body interested in securing for the settlers the right of political representation. This committee was later expanded and superseded by "The Mercantile Association" which became far more influential. It was a larger group and included both black and white settlers and others who controlled a substantial part of the economy. Some professionals also joined the association.

In 1858, the committee of merchants petitioned against abuses over taxes and duties and asked for a new constitution for Sierra Leone. They asked that an elected assembly should be provided.[39] By this date, Sierra Leone had been overtaken in its constitutional development by the other British West African countries under British colonial rule which had obtained "advanced" constitutions providing for legislative and executive councils. In England, the Aborigines Protection Society and the Anti-Slavery Society took an interest in the matter. Through their activities, a question was asked in the British House of Lords regarding alleged maladministration in Sierra Leone. In spite of all these, when the new constitution was devised and announced, it turned out to be one for governing the country more firmly and effectively as a British colony than a concession to demands for settler participation in their own affairs.

In the hinterland, wars were going on between the Temnes and the Mendes and between the Temnes and the Lokkos and various governors were busy establishing treaties of peace. In 1853, the British Government sent a consul named Augustus Hanson to the Sherbro. He had earlier been in Monrovia in 1848. He established his post at Victoria in Sherbro Island and asked for military assistance to bring the remnants of the slave trade to an end. This request was refused. Undeterred Hanson parleyed with the local chiefs and obtained the sympathy of the Governor of Sierra Leone, Governor Hill. His relationship with Caulker, one of the chiefs of the Sherbro, became strained and in 1857, when a French gunboat landed at Bendu, it demolished Caulker's stockade and prohibited its being rebuilt until Caulker had signed a treaty promising to

39 C.O. 267: 260.

protect French traders and only with French permission. The next year, Bendu was bombarded and Caulker signed the treaty agreeing to protect French interests and traders. Caulker was expelled and Hanson put a new king in his place. Caulker demanded compensation from him for his losses but Hanson reacted sharply by charging Caulker with extortion and deporting him to Freetown. On his release, he declined to return to Bendu and retired instead to Shenge. While there, he suggested that Britain should annexe the Sherbro as another French trader had asked his permission to settle at Bendu. Caulker refused to grant the permission and turned to Governor Hill for assistance. He responded. Hanson was sacked by the Foreign Office and in November 1861, Hill signed the formal treaty twenty years later, the Caulkers formally executed the treaty, and so settled once and for all this long standing matter of the annexation of the Sherbro.

In the colony, legislation was being passed to prepare the ground for the formal introduction of the proposed new constitution for Sierra Leone. Among the measures introduced were the Registration Ordinance of 9th February 1857 which was passed "to provide the means for a complete Register of Titles to Lands, Births, Deaths, Baptisms, Burials, Marriages and other matters of Her Majesty's subjects in the Colony of Sierra Leone whereby evidence of title to property may be more easily obtained and statistical information afforded for purposes of public interest and utility and whereby also crime may be more readily discovered and more effectively suppressed".

In 1860, parliament passed the British Settlements Act, 1860[40] which conferred on the Crown the requisite power to provide for the administration of justice in the new settlements. The purpose of the act was to extend the Act of 1843 to settlements in which no government had been "established by the authority of Her Majesty". It extended the provisions of the 1843 Act to all British possessions not acquired by cession or conquest and not being within the jurisdiction of the legislative authority of a British possession. Section 2 of the act provided for the trial of cases arising in a British settlement by courts in other possessions.[41]

Ordinance No. 1 of 1861 was passed to enable the governor to appoint a permanent sheriff. In 1862, Ordinance No. 3 was passed, Intituled "An Ordinance to amend the law". This was an amending measure which sought to tidy up the various provisions of the law relating to the procedure and practice of the courts. Ordinance No. 5 of 1862, vested all the estates and property in the colony of Sierra Leone occupied by or for the Naval Service of the United Kingdom of Great Britain and Ireland in the Lord High Admiral, or the Crown for executing the Office of the Lord High Admiral of the United Kingdom. Ordinance No. 1 of 1863 which was passed on the 5th day of February 1863, vested in the Chief

---

40 23 and 24 Vic. C. 121.
41 These provisions were reproduced in a revised form in Section 4 of the British Settlements Act, of 1887.

Justice of Sierra Leone certain jurisdictions vested in the vice-chancellors in England. Section 1 of this ordinance provided:

> That where under any act of parliament or order issued in pursuance thereof any jurisdiction, power, authority or duty is vested in, or is to be exercised or performed by the vice-chancellors in England or any of them whilst sitting in chambers or in open court, all such jurisdictions, powers, authority and duty, and the ministerial powers and authorities incident thereto or consequent thereupon, shall be vested in, had, exercised and performed by the Chief Justice or acting Chief Justice of the Supreme Court of the Colony of Sierra Leone.

THE CONSTITUTION OF 1863

Following internal pressures by the settlers for further constitutional advance and efforts by their supporters in Great Britain for their demands to be met, the British Government acceded to the demands for constitutional change and introduced a Charter dated 27th May, 1863 together with Royal Instructions dated 30th May 1863 providing a new "Constitution" for the Colony of Sierra Leone. The Governor, Major Samuel Wensley Blackhall on the 26th July, 1863, issued the following Proclamation:

> I do hereby publish and proclaim the said Charter of Justice to be in full force and effect from this date.

Both documents together revoked the Charter of 1799 and established two councils for Sierra Leone in place of the former Advisory Council, namely, a Legislative Council and an Executive Council.

The Legislative Council of 1863.
The Legislative Council was composed of the governor who now bore the official title of "Governor and Commander-in-Chief" in place of his former designation as "Captain-General and Governor-in-Chief", the Chief Justice, the Colonial Secretary, the Queen's Advocate, the Officer Commanding the Troops and "such other person or persons nominated and appointed to serve on the Council". No specific number of such nominated members was given, but it was the practice to nominate one African and one European member.[42] At various times, the numbers of such nominated members varied from two to seven during the 19th and 20th centuries. The nominated members were to be confirmed by the Secretary of State. In a draft despatch dated the 17th December 1869, the governor was required in making his selection to take into consideration "not only those who are most likely to support the government but those who will be taken to represent and will really inform you of the wishes of the more intelligent portion of the community". This followed the Duke of Buckingham's Circular Despatch of 1868 which had said:[43]

---

42 The circumstances are set out in the text at p.109.
43 See Martin Wight. *Development of the Legislative Council*, p.112.

You will naturally understand that holding his seat by nomination of the Crown, he has been selected for it in the expectation and in the confidence that he will co-operate with the Crown in its general policy, and not oppose the Crown on any important question without strong and substantial reasons.

Prior to these despatches, the governor had consulted the Mercantile Association in December 1863 to ask for their choice of the first member he wished to nominate for service in the new legislature. Two candidates were put up for election at the meeting of the association, John Ezzidio an African and John Levi a European. The voting was by secret ballot and John Ezzidio won by a substantial majority. His name was therefore sent to the governor for nomination to the Legislative Council. The governor formed the opinion that the election had taken place on racial lines and therefore decided to appoint a white man as well. However, Ezzidio was nominated and appointed as the first African nominated member of the Legislative Council.

The quorum of the Legislative Council was three. Decisions were to be taken by a simple majority. The governor was given an additional or casting vote. In practice, this was unnecessary, since all the official members were supposed to support government policy and could not freely dissent from the official government line. The governor also had complete charge and control of the public service.[44]

The Executive Council of 1863.

The Executive Council was composed entirely of the official members, that is to say, those forming the Legislative Council, without the governor's appointees. It should be noted that, apart from the official members specified by the charter as entitled to be members of the Legislative Council, the governor had nominated both the Collector of Customs, Mr J. T. Commissiong, and the Colonial Surgeon, Dr R. Bradshaw as members of the Legislative Council. Although they were officials of government, they were not "official" members. So they did not have a right to sit in the Executive Council. The members of the Executive Council therefore, were the following:

H. E. the Governor (Major S. W. Blackhall).
The Chief Justice (John Carr).
The Colonial Secretary (George Nicol).
The Queen's Advocate (H. J. Huggins).
The Officer Commanding Troops (Col. Hughes).

EVALUATION OF THE CHARTER OF 1863.
An imprisoned man upon will and pleasure is
    1. A Bondman.
    2. Worse than a Bondman.

---

44 This policy of appointing Africans to senior offices in the government continued until the end of the nineteenth century, when, following the declaration of a Protectorate over the hinterland it was suddenly changed.

3. Not so much as a man
for "mortus homo non est homo". A prisoner is a dead man.
(C. J. Coke in the case of the Five Knights or Darnel's Case.
Howell: 3 St. Trials (1816) at p.128.)

For over half a century, royal instructions had been the foundation of Sierra Leone's constitutional structure. Under and by virtue of the prerogative powers, the Crown delegated to the governor all its powers essential for the effective and autocratic government of the territory. The governor had the right to nominate and appoint whomsoever he pleased as members of the legislature. He could summon the council to meet, adjourn, prorogue or dissolve it at will. He had the power of veto; the right to dispense offices and to appoint judges and justices of the peace; he could grant pardons; impose taxes and regulate the same in respect of the government's financial needs. He was the undisputed ruler, subject only to directions from the Home Government.

The Constitution of 1863, introduced by charter, did not change any of this. The charter, as opposed to the royal instructions, was merely an enabling instrument exerciseable within the scope of the power of administration conferred upon the governor. Hitherto, the country had been governed by acts, charters, royal instructions and imperial legislation. Now, for the first time in the history of the country, Sierra Leone was to be governed by a "Constitution". Is a charter, significantly different from a constitution?

A charter government is in the nature of a civil corporation with power of making bye-laws for its own internal regulation, not contrary to the laws of England and with such rights and authorities as are specially given in the Charter of Incorporation.[45] While the territory was under company rule, the issue of a charter, from the point of view of the Crown, was unexceptionable. But from the point of view of the settlers their expectations were destroyed. They were seeking to secure basic human values but these were not allowed them. Assuming that the Sierra Leone company was never envisaged as an instrument of political power but a purely mercantile enterprise what was wrong or difficult about allowing the settlers the independence they sought to conduct their own affairs? They were clearly imprisoned by the circumstances in which they found themselves, needing financial and military assistance to justify their entitlement to live in peace and freedom without any control or supervision. Assuming, on the other hand, that there was the dire necessity for a period of tutelage, had not that period of apprenticeship come to an end by 1863? The records show that the black settlers of Sierra Leone by 1863 had held the highest offices in the state. There had been a black governor under the Crown, a black Chief Justice, black men in the medical field; black men in business, all of them extremely competent and capable. Why then did the British government not turn over the administration to them, particularly at a time when Britain itself was not terribly anxious to keep and maintain further colonies? In spite

[45] See B1. *Commentaries* Vol. 1. 108. Clarke op. cit. 17.

of the widely held view that "the history of the world proved that the black man was incapable of civilization",[46] a view which thrived in the southern parts of the African continent, Britain was convinced that black men could govern themselves and in fact was anxious that this should happen in all the West African territories, excepting Sierra Leone. The reason for holding the black settlers in bondage therefore was not political. It was humanitarian. It was also sentimental taking into account the peculiarity of the conditions leading up to the establishment of the settlement.

Now, the functions of a constitution can be said to be as follows:
(a) To erect a government.
(b) To confer rights.
(c) To impose liabilities.

It can and often is, a legal document containing the framework of the order of the state. Usually, the word is used in an abstract sense denoting the rules governing the working of the state. Dicey described the constitution as "a body of rules which directly or indirectly affect the distribution and exercise of sovereign power in the state".[47]

Messrs Wade and Phillips described the constitution as "a document having a special legal sanctity which sets out the framework and the principal functions of the organs of government of a state and declares the principles governing the operation of these organs".[48]

In all these definitions of the word "Constitution" there is one central theme recurring. They all envisage a document containing rules which concern the "order of the state"; or "the working of the state"; or "the exercise of sovereign power in the state". The terms "Law" and "State" have been satisfactorily defined but the crucial question in our analysis is whether the Constitution of 1863 foreshadowed a "State" in the international law sense of the word? The expression "the State" is often used legally to describe the whole community, i.e. and independent political society. In international law, there is a state when there is and exists,
(a) A defined territory.
(b) A permanent population.
(c) Capacity in that population to enter into relationships with other states.
(d) A government [49]

In this sense, the Sierra Leone Constitution of 1863 fulfilled all these prerequisites, save that the foreign relations were conducted by Great Britain. The Constitution of 1863 therefore could not be regarded as that of a territory soon to be independent. It did not foreshadow any independent political community.

46 Thompson: *The Unification of South Africa* p.216.
47 See Dicey: *The Law of the Constitution,* 10th ed.
48 See Wade and Phillips: *Constitutional Law,* 8th ed.
49 This is a provision of the Montevideo Convention of 1933. See Grieg: *International Law* and also Quincy Wright: *The Status of Germany and the Peace Proclamation 1952,* 46 A.J.I.L. 307 for further definition and discussions of this topic.

With regard to the vexed question of representation, there is no doubt that if the British Government were minded to allow the settlers to share in the government and administration of the country there would have been ample grounds to justify such a move. The settlers were already versed in the patterns of colonial government and quite accustomed to English constitutional practice. They were bitterly disappointed when the constitution failed to meet their expectations. In spite of this, it is to their credit that they attempted to operate within the framework of the constitution designed for the country. This singular devotion to regularity and their penchant for peace and good order, earned the settlers of Sierra Leone, for several decades the unflattering but fully descriptive title, "ancient and loyal".

Finally, the 1863 Constitution, was a true arch-type colonial measure. The governor did not share with anyone, his powers of appointment of members to the legislature or dismissal at pleasure. He was still exercising judicial functions and the Chief Justice sat with him in the Legislature and in the Executive. The courts could not by any means be described as fair and impartial. All the serious defects of the judicial system which existed prior to 1863 were preserved. Although there was some systematic and regular form of administration of justice, there were several instances where lay justices found it difficult to reach their decisions. The 1863 Constitution therefore lacked any distinctive or distinguished features and the chorus of praise suggesting that it was an advanced and welcome measure is unjustified.

POST 1863.

In 1865, a Select Committee of the House of Commons was appointed to investigate the state of the British settlements in West Africa and particularly whether or not they were worth keeping. The appointment of this committee was the result of the war in Ashanti which had taken place the previous year and which caused much loss of life and considerable financial expense to the British. Fyfe records that there was "an outcry in Parliament against West African wars and irresponsible governors" and that the July estimates were challenged on the ground that the colonies were useless and were neither suppressing the slave trade nor promoting "legitimate trade".[50] It was therefore proposed that the settlements should be reunited as they had been in 1821 under one governor "who in an age of steam transport would be able to control the subordinate governments".[51] So the Select Committee was sent out to find out whether the West African settlements were in fact advancing the objectives of British colonial policy in the area or hindering it. The committee submitted their report in June. The House of Commons adopted the resolutions of the committee which recommended inter alia:
 1. That it was not possible to withdraw the British government wholly or immediately from any settlement or engagements on the

50 Fyfe: *History* op. cit. at p.336.
51 Fyfe: *History* etc. op. cit. p.337.

West African Coast.
2. That further annexation of territory or the signing of new treaties offering protection to the native tribes would be inexpedient. But that a policy should be adopted of encouraging the natives to take over the administration of the government, with a view to British withdrawal from all, except, probably, Sierra Leone.
3. That the reasons for the separation of the settlements had ceased to exist and a central government should be re-established at Sierra Leone "with steam communication with each Lieutenant Governor."

This committee was dominated by its chairman, Mr C. B. Adderley, an anti-humanitarian. Under his influence, it questioned sceptically the supposed benefits of British rule. It recommended among others

Economy in colonial government.
Preparation of Africans for self-rule.
Eventual withdrawal from all of West Africa (except Sierra Leone).
An end to expansionism.
An end to domestic slavery in Lagos.[52]

The settlers of the colony were looking forward to some measure of self-rule. Regrettably, the Constitution of 1863 did not provide the required response to those demands. Instead, the two councils, the legislative and the executive were clear and formal instruments of British policy. The fact of the presence on the council of one African nominated member did not alter the position. The record, in fact shows that Governor Blackhall did not approve of a receptive being a member of the legislature, and he proposed that the other member John Levi, who had been trounced in a free election, but who was a European should also take his seat in the legislature. This proposal was rejected by the Colonial Office.

In 1865, Parliament passed the "Colonial Laws Validity Act" 1865,[53] which had some importance for the Sierra Leone judicial system. The immediate cause of the introduction of the measure was the concern felt in Britain about a series of judgments given by Mr Justice Boothby of the Supreme Court of South Australia. He cast grave doubts on the validity of colonial legislation which conflicted with English law. As far as the Colonial Office was concerned there was never any doubt that Britain could legislate for the colonies; but the question was whether the colonies could themselves pass any laws which were repugnant to or inconsistent with English Law.

52 See C. B. Adderley: *Review of "The Colonial Policy of Lord J. Russell's Administration" and of subsequent Colonial History*. (London, 1869). Also DIKE: *Trade and Politics,* p.166. Dike asserts that there was no abatement in British expansion and that the committee were creating confusion by over-simplified thinking; whereas occupation entailed expense, free trade was free. This was an over-simplification since free trade entailed expense and involvement.
See: House of Commons Sessional Papers 1865, V. Report from the Select Committee on Africa (Western Coast).
53 28 and 29 Vic. C. 63.

The act was therefore passed "to remove doubts as to the validity of colonial laws".

Section 1 provided the definition of the term "Colony". It was defined to include all Her Majesty's possessions abroad in which there shall exist a legislature. A legislature was defined as the authority other than the Imperial Parliament of the Queen-in-Council competent to make laws for the colony. Thus the act was made applicable to all colonies possessing legislatures.

The second section provided that any colonial law repugnant to any act of parliament extending to the colony, should be read subject to such act, order or regulation and to the extent of such repugnancy "shall be absolutely void," and inoperative.[54]

Section 3 provided that no colonial law should be void on the ground of repugnancy to the law of England unless it was repugnant to an act of parliament, order or regulation. This meant that colonial law could be inconsistent with the common law, but not statute law applicable to the colony. That was the most important provision of the act. Thereafter, a colonial legislature was free to depart from the common law as it wished and a governor could not be required to revoke his assent to colonial legislation.

Section 4 provided that a colonial law was not to be void for inconsistency with instructions to the governor and Section 5 provided that every colonial legislature had full power to establish courts of law, to abolish and reconstitute them and to alter the constitution thereof. If the legislature was a representative one, then it had power to make laws respecting its constitution, powers and procedure. A representative legislature was defined in section 1 as a legislative body with half the members elected. The act had no application to territories outside Her Majesty's jurisdiction.

Internally, the governor and his Legislative Council were proceeding with new laws. By Ordinance No. 5 of 1864 which was passed on the 8th April 1864, the Chief Justice was empowered to hear cases of up to £100 without a jury. In cases where he sat with assessors, he had power to revise the damages awarded if the jury was not unanimous.[55] At the same time the property qualifications of juries was raised and it was provided in Act No. 15 1864 that in capital cases, the jury were to be unanimous; in other cases a two-thirds majority verdict would suffice. Act No. 8 of 1864 altered the sittings of the Supreme Court and repealed the Act of 1858 dealing with the same matter. No. 9 of 1864 consolidated the law relating to jurors and juries. On the 5th December 1864, the procedure for appeals to Her Majesty in council was prescribed when Ordinance No. 16/64 was passed. The appellant was required to give security for

---

54 See R. V. Marais (1902) A.C. 51 at 54 where the court said that the purpose of the section was to preserve the power of the Imperial Parliament to legislate for a colony and to prevent the colony passing measures repugnant to English enactments.
55 Intituled "An Ordinance for Improving the Administration of Justice in Civil Cases." See C.O. 269 2.

costs of appeal only and the amount was to be determined by the Chief Justice when the appeal emanated from the Supreme Court and, by the governor and council when the appeal was from the governor and council sitting in their judicial capacity. In any event, the amount of security was not to exceed £500.

A Court of Requests was established by Ordinance No. 6 of 1865 to establish the speedy recovery of small debts in Freetown and the districts. The jurisdiction was set out in section 5 and was as follows:

For Freetown and the districts attached thereto — Up to £5.

For other districts — Up to £30.

Questions of title to land were not to be tried in the Court of Requests, nor cases of assault and battery, libel and slander. These were within the jurisdiction of a Judge of the Supreme Court. Appeal lay from the Court of Requests to the Supreme Court.

SUPREME COURT ORDINANCE.
By a constitution brought into effect in 1866, and dated 19th February 1866, the United West African Settlements was established. The Supreme Court of Sierra Leone was declared the Supreme Court of the various territories thus unified. A second judge was appointed because of the extended jurisdiction. Each territory had an administrator and the Governor of Sierra Leone was appointed Governor-in-Chief responsible to the Secretary of State for Sierra Leone, the Gambia, the Gold Coast and Lagos.

A new Supreme Court Ordinance, at the request of Governor Blackhall, was drafted by Judge Carr and hurriedly introduced into the Legislative Council. It was passed into law the same day.[56] The measure, Ordinance No. 4 of 1866, was intituled "An Ordinance to make further provisions for the administration of Justice within the Settlement of Sierra Leone and its Dependencies". The name of the court was changed from the Supreme Court of the Colony of Sierra Leone to "The Supreme Court of the Settlement of Sierra Leone". The jurisdiction of the court was expressed to be the same as that exercised by Judges of the King's Bench, Common Pleas and Exchequer at Westminster. It provided further that the court "shall be a Court of Equity and have the like powers and jurisdiction of the Lord High Chancellor of Great Britain and the Vice-Chancellors in England. The court shall have the like jurisdiction as the Court of Prize in England". The ordinance abolished trial by jury in civil cases thus limiting jury trial to criminal cases only. Thus this ordinance, foreshadowed the development which took place in England ten years afterwards when the Judicature Acts 1873-5 fused the administration of justice in England and made law and equity administrable in the same courts within the one Supreme Court of Judicature.

A storm of protest burst forth both in Sierra Leone and London in respect of the manner in which the ordinance was passed. The Secretary

56 It was passed on the 16th November 1866.

of State sought an explanation from Governor Blackhall before the measure was finally sanctioned and confirmed.[57]

In 1866, a House of Commons Select Committee was appointed to study the report of the Commission of Inquiry on the affairs of the British settlements on the West Coast of Africa. This led to the constitutional changes of 1866 linking Sierra Leone, Gambia, the Gold Coast and Nigeria again. The Constitution, dated 19th February 1866, established the "Unified West African Settlements". Blackhall, the Governor of Sierra Leone, was appointed Governor-in-Chief of the new territory. The Supreme Court was unified and a second judge appointed. The unification of these territories led to a number of legal and constitutional developments of which the following are the most significant:

(a) Ordinance No. 5 of 1866, an ordinance for establishing a Court of Summary Jurisdiction within the Settlement of Sierra Leone. This ordinance conferred jurisdiction in all matters where the amount in dispute did not exceed £100. It gave a right of appeal to the Supreme Court. The Judge of the Summary Court was given jurisdiction as a Commissioner of Escheat. The Court of Requests was abolished.

(b) Ordinance No. 4 of 1867. This ordinance was passed to extend to the settlement, the statutes in force in the County Courts in England. This UK legislation became available to the Courts of Summary Jurisdiction in the settlement.

(c) Ordinance No. 5 of 1867. This measure vested in the Judge of the Court of Summary jurisdiction the powers of the Commissioners of the Court commonly called "The Land Commission Court".

(d) Ordinance No. 6 of 1867. By this enactment the jurisdiction of the Court of Requests in the districts of Sherbro and Bulama which had not been affected by the Summary Jurisdiction Ordinance, was increased.

(e) By Order in Council dated 26th February 1867 made under the provisions of the Coast of Africa and Falkland Islands Act, 1843, the Supreme Court of the Settlement of Sierra Leone was constituted a Court of Record. The West African Court of Appeal was established and two judges were appointed who sat in Freetown. The Supreme Court of Sierra Leone was constituted a Court of Appellate Jurisdiction from courts of civil or criminal jurisdiction in the Gold Coast, Gambia and Lagos. Appeals could go direct to the privy council from the Supreme Court of Sierra Leone. In respect of the West African Court of Appeal, the judges were supposed to be unanimous in their decisions but if they were divided then the original decision would stand.

(f) Ordinance No. 3 of 1868 abolished appeals from the courts to the governor in council. Thus, for the first time since the inception of the settlement in 1787, the governor and council lost their judicial powers

[57] Allegations were made by the settlers that the action of the governor in passing the Supreme Court Ordinance in the manner in which he did, was malicious and done to meet the circumstances of a particular case.

which were now firmly in the hands of professional judges in the regular courts.

(g) Ordinance No. 7 of 1869 was passed "to remove doubts as to the verdicts of juries". This enactment permitted a two-thirds majority verdict, but stipulated that the jury were to be unanimous in cases involving a sentence of death.

(h) Ordinance No. 12 of 1869, the Personal Servitude Ordinance, declared legal sentences of personal servitude.

In November 1867, Blackhall was promoted Governor of Queensland and was succeeded by Sir Arthur Kennedy who had earlier on been a Governor of Sierra Leone. That same year, prior to his assumption of office, the Chief Justice, George French, had decided he would no longer sit in the Executive Council as his predecessor Judge Carr, had done, as he wanted to keep the functions of the judiciary separate and apart from that of the Executive.[58] However, he remained a member of the Legislature and sat there regularly. Kennedy was a popular governor, unlike Blackhall, and he immediately set about introducing some reforms. He allowed debates of the Legislative Council to take place in public; he published bills after the first reading; he appointed Africans to positions which he felt their ability and inclination merited and which he thought they could hold with credit and distinction; he introduced competitive examinations for entry into the civil service; he transferred officers from Sierra Leone to senior positions in the other territories forming the United West African Settlements; he improved conditions in the prison service and then increased the unofficial representation in the Legislative Council.

Further cessions of territory occurred during this period. By Treaty of 9.11.1861, Banoh Boom, King of Shey and his chiefs and headmen, ceded the East Sherbro to Her Majesty "to be annexed to and be a dependency of the Colony of Sierra Leone and be subject to the laws now in force and hereinafter to be in force in the colony." By Order of Council dated 26th April 1862, the Island of Sherbro was declared part of the Colony of Sierra Leone.

In 1871, proposals were made to review the court system in Sierra Leone. Prior to these proposals, a case had arisen in England between George Cooke[59] and Governor Charles Maxwell in which the plaintiff sued the governor in the British Courts for damages for assault, false imprisonment, seizure of goods and destruction of a factory in River Pongo. A verdict was given for the plaintiff for £20,000 on the ground that the governor had exceeded his authority. On the 15th February 1868, a circular letter was sent from Buckham & Chandos to Sir A. Kennedy, Governor of Sierra Leone in the following terms:[60]

A question has recently arisen whether the Imperial Treasury

---

58 See minute on the question by Sir French Rogers, Permanent Under Secretary in the Colonial Office, 1867.
59 He was a trader resident outside Sierra Leone. See (1871) 2 Starke 183.
60 See Montague: Vol. 4, p.103.

should defray the expense of defending an action brought against a colonial judge for acts done in the discharge of his duty; and it has appeared that precedents exist for taking this course, under some circumstances. Her Majesty's Government will not, in future, be guided by these precedents, but will consider the expense of defending any colonial judge or officer from an action at law which may be brought against him for acts done or purporting to be done in the performance of his duty to be properly chargeable on the officer himself, as is the rule in this country, unless there should be some very special reason for the interference of the colonial or the Imperial Government.

So the Colonial Office served notice on all its overseas officials that if they found themselves involved in litigation, the cost thereof would be charged to their personal accounts save in exceptional circumstances.

In spite of Governor Kennedy's wise and progressive administration, the unified settlement did not succeed and within five years, demands for its dismantling had begun to emerge. Meanwhile, the legislative process continued for Kennedy saw growth in the law as a living mechanism and wanted an organic development both in the administration and in the law. Ordinance No. 4 of 1870, the Larceny Amendment Ordinance, was passed to ensure that deviant members of companies or partnerships did not escape with stealing or embezzling property of the company or partnership but could be tried in the same way as someone not a member. Ordinance No. 4 of 1871 provided that the officer administering the government could appoint a Deputy Judge of the Court of Summary Jurisdiction.

On the 24th July 1874, a new charter was brought into effect. The provisions of the Royal Commission of 1866 were revoked in so far as they affected the Gold Coast and Lagos. This meant that the West African settlement was dissolved, leaving Sierra Leone and the Gambia still together. By Ordinance No. 4 of 1876, the number of Judges of the Sierra Leone Supreme Court was again reduced to one. Thus, the Supreme Court reverted to its previous position when it was manned exclusively by the Chief Justice. The ordinance abolished the Court of Summary Jurisdiction and conferred summary jurisdiction on the Supreme Court. It abolished the rules of the Summary Court.

1874 was a year which witnessed a host of political and constitutional changes. With the dissolution of the settlement changes and refinements were introduced in the area of local legislation. For example, in 1875, Ordinance No. 5 was passed which amended the law relating to married women. It provided, inter alia, that the earnings of a married woman should be "deemed and taken to be property held and settled to her separate use independent of any husband to whom she may be married". It also empowered a married woman to maintain an action in her own name. With the merger of the Gold Coast and Lagos, appeals were taken to the Supreme Court established in 1876 and thereafter to the Privy Council. Ordinance No. 4 of 1877 simplified appeals from Magistrates' Courts. On the 23rd October 1877, an order in council abolished the

West African Court of Appeal.

The union of Sierra Leone and the Gambia was short lived. In 1888, the West African Settlements comprising Sierra Leone and Gambia was dissolved. Letters Patent of the 28th November 1888, created Sierra Leone as an independent colony, with its own governor and commander-in-chief. Thus Sierra Leone gained its independent existence for the first time since 1821. The office of the Chief Justice of the West African Settlements was abolished. The Supreme Court Ordinance No. 9 of 1881 was passed which made statutes in force in England on the 1st day of January 1880, applicable in force in Sierra Leone. This ordinance prescribed rules of the Supreme Court which were attached to it. An order in council of the 6th April 1889, constituted the Supreme Court of Sierra Leone a Court of Appeal from all final decisions of the Supreme Court of the Gambia. This was amended by order in council dated 24th November, 1891.

We turn now to the next stage in the constitutional and legal history of Sierra Leone which was the establishment of the protectorate in 1896.

THE ESTABLISHMENT OF THE PROTECTORATE

The second half of the nineteenth century was an era of great expansion in West Africa and the period when the scramble for Africa reached its greatest intensity. The British, French, Portuguese and Germans were the chief protagonists of this new doctrine. Each of them had territorial ambitions on the African continent. They met in Berlin in 1885 and established the principle of "effective occupation" as the test for determining whether any particular European power was entitled to territory claimed by it.

As far as Britain was concerned, the necessary legislative machinery for this development had already been established. The Foreign Jurisdiction Act, 1843, in its preamble, recited that Her Majesty had power and jurisdiction in places outside Her Majesty's dominions by treaty, capitulation, grant, usage, sufferance and other lawful means. It also recited that there was some doubt about the exercise of power and jurisdiction under the common law and that such doubt ought to be removed. Consequently, it asserted the right of the Crown to the exercise of such power and jurisdiction in any country or place out of Her Majesty's Dominions. In 1890, the Foreign Jurisdiction Act was passed. It was a consolidating measure. It declared that Her Majesty could "hold, exercise and enjoy" jurisdiction within a foreign country in the same and as ample a manner as if Her Majesty had acquired that jurisdiction by the cession or conquest of territory. By Section 1, whenever Her Majesty exercised whatever jurisdiction she claimed to possess, that exercise of jurisdiction could not be questioned in any court.

The validity of this excessive acquisition of jurisdiction has not remained unchallenged. In the case of Sobhuza-v-Miller[61] the validity of

---
61 (1926) A.C. 518.

an order in council relating to Swaziland was challenged on the ground that it offended a convention by reason of which the country was governed. The Judicial Committee of the Privy Council held that an extension of jurisdiction "may be referred to an exercise of power by an Act of State, unchallengeable in any British Court, or it may be attributed to statutory powers given by the Foreign Jurisdiction Act, 1890."[62] As far as Section 1 of the Act is concerned, this dictum has been held to be slightly inaccurate in so far as that section does not confer jurisdiction. It merely provides for the exercise of jurisdiction.[63]

Thus, as far as imperial legislation was concerned, the combination of the Foreign Jurisdiction Acts, 1843 and 1890 and the British Settlements Act, 1887 which gave the Crown power to make laws for protectorate areas in West Africa, ensured that legally, the stage was already set for the acquisition of territorial sovereignty over the hinterland of Sierra Leone. However, some comment is apropos on the factors which finally led to the declaration of a protectorate and the manner in which it was done.

During the last two decades of the nineteenth century, there were several visits by the Governors of Sierra Leone into the hinterland. Several treaties of friendship were signed. Under the Governorship of Sir J. S. Hay, important treaties were signed in 1890 and 1891. Simultaneously, relationships were developing between the settlers in the colony and the peoples of the hinterland while there was fierce competition between Britain and France in the struggle for the partitioning of West Africa.

An insight into the wealth of the Creole merchants of this era can be guaged from the estate of the late Samuel Benjamin Thomas who died in 1901 leaving property worth over £70,000. He endowed the Agricultural College at Mabang. Similarly, J. J. Thomas endowed a library which is still operating in Freetown.[64] There were other property and business magnates such as J. H. Thomas, T. C. Bishop, Cornelius Crowther, the Hebrons, the Boyles, F. A. John and C. C. Nicols who were men of great wealth and who, from their considerable resources educated their children abroad, mainly in England, and contributed generously to charitable causes.

In 1885, the Sierra Leone Association was founded. Like the Mercantile Association thirty years or so earlier, it drew its membership largely from the business and professional class, both white and black. It had as one of its main objectives, the extension of trade into the hinterland and the development of business opportunities between the Creoles and the natives. Sir Samuel Lewis, the distinguished lawyer and first African to be knighted by the British from Sierra Leone, read a paper to them on the 8th August 1885 in which he advocated annexation

---

62 See Sir Kenneth Roberts-Wray op. cit. 186.
63 See S. of S.-v-Sardar Rustam Khan (1941) L.R. 68 I.A. 109 at pp.121-2. Also, see Sir Kenneth Roberts-Wray, "*Commonwealth and Colonial Law*" op. cit. at p.187.
64 See Fyfe: *History*. op. cit. pp.535-6.

by means of purchase, instead of the declaration of a protectorate. His views were sharply criticised by T. J. Shorunkeh-Sawyer, another lawyer, who opposed annexation and did not see what the people of the hinterland would gain by this. The debate raged in the colony and the views of Shorunkeh-Sawyer gained much support. Regrettably, as later events showed, Sir Samuel Lewis lost and instead of getting a unified country from the start, the hinterland developed as a foreign country.

On the 28th August 1895 an order in council was passed declaring that the Crown had acquired jurisdiction in territories adjacent to the Colony of Sierra Leone. This preceded the formal proclamation of a protectorate in Freetown. The proclamation was made by the Administrator of the Government of the Colony of Sierra Leone. It is short and is reproduced here:

PROCLAMATION
By His Excellency Lt. Col. Arden Lowndes Bayley, Officer Commanding the Troops on the West Coast of Africa, Administrator of the Government of the Colony of Sierra Leone etc.

A. L. Bayley
Administrator

WHEREAS HER MAJESTY has been advised that it is best for the interest of the people in the territories adjacent to the Colony of Sierra Leone and on the British side of the boundary between the British and French possessions to the North and East of the Colony aforesaid by an Agreement dated the 21st day of January in the Year One thousand Eight hundred and Ninety-five and made between Great Britain and France, that Her Majesty should assume the Protectorate over the said territories:

AND WHEREAS it is Her Majesty's pleasure that the said territories should come under the protection of Her Majesty:

AND WHEREAS Her Majesty has authorised me to take necessary steps for giving effect to Her pleasure in the matter:

NOW THEREFORE I do hereby proclaim declare and make known that the territories adjacent to the Colony of Sierra Leone and on the British side of the boundary between the British and French possessions to the North and East of the Colony aforesaid fixed by the Agreement dated the twenty-first day of January in the year One thousand Eight hundred and Ninety-five and made between Great Britain and France are now under the protection of Her Majesty.

Given under my hand and the public Seal of the Colony of Sierra Leone at Government House, Fort Thornton, in the City of Freetown in the Colony aforesaid this Thirty first day of August, in the year of Our Lord, One thousand Eight hundred and ninety

six, and of Her Majesty's reign, the sixtieth.
By His Excellency's Command,
W. J. P. Elliott.
Ag. Colonial Secretary.

GOD SAVE THE QUEEN

Following this proclamation, steps were taken to put into effect the provisions of the order in council which empowered the legislature of the colony to legislate for the protectorate in the same way as it did for the colony. Five frontier districts were set up for the protectorate, namely:

> Karene
> Ronietta
> Bandajuma
> Panguma
> Koinadugu

A district commissioner was appointed and stationed in each district. They all shared their powers and responsibilities with the "Paramount Chiefs" the new designation now adopted to replace the earlier titles of "Kings" and "Queens".

The Legislature Council of the colony then passed a local ordinance, the Protectorate Ordinance No. 20 of 1896, which made detailed provisions for the administration of the protectorate.

The System of Courts in the Protectorate.

Three separate courts were established for the administration of justice in the protectorate:
 (a) The Courts of the Native Chiefs.
 (b) The Court of the District Commissioner sitting with chiefs as native assessors.
 (c) The Court of the District Commissioner.

The District Commissioner's Court exercised jurisdiction "in all cases between persons not natives or between a person not a native and a native and all cases involving a question of title to land although arising exclusively between natives". It exercised jurisdiction in criminal matters regarded as inimical to modern developments and civilisation e.g. pretended witchcraft, slave dealing, murder, homicide, rape, cannibalism and ritual murder connected with secret societies, e.g. The Human Leopard Society, Alligator Society, dealing in slaves, or cases "arising out of factional or tribal fights .... and such other cases as the governor in council may from time to time deem expedient".

The criminal offences listed, if committed exclusively by natives, were also triable in the second type of courts, that of the District Commissioner sitting with native chiefs as assessors.[65] In the third type

---

65 Note that in the colony, trial by Assessors was introduced in criminal cases by Ordinance No. 89 of 1895. This method of trial was introduced after the case of R.-v-J.H. Spaine discussed infra.

The Government of Sierra Leone 1808-1896

of court, the Native Court, jurisdiction was exercised largely in those cases not within the jurisdiction of the other courts; the jurisdiction was thus, a sort of residuary one. The native court dealt with disputes arising exclusively between natives, including questions of family law.

The District Commissioner had to refer capital cases to the Supreme Court. He was guided by, but not bound to follow, English law and procedure.

A sentence which involved flogging or a heavy penalty had to be confirmed by the governor. Lawyers were not allowed to practise in the protectorate except by special permission.

"THE NATIVE ADMINISTRATION".

Before a protectorate was declared over the hinterland, the boundaries of the territory over which the Crown was to extend its "protection" had been delineated in various agreements, particularly, the Anglo-French Convention of the 28th June 1882, the Anglo-French Agreement of the 21st January 1895 and the Anglo-French Arrangement dated 10th August 1889. The boundary with Liberia was settled by the Anglo-Liberian Convention dated 11th November 1885. The intention was clearly for Britain to provide protection for the Protectorate at a time when there was tremendous interest by the other European powers in acquiring territories in Africa. Britain did not set out to govern and rule the protectorate. They regarded it as foreign territory. In fact the British Government were very reluctant to take on any further burdens of running and administering undeveloped territories in Africa which would have imposed further financial burdens on that country. Consequently they did not wish to take over completely the administration of the day to day running of the protectorate.

The protectorate ordinance provided machinery for the government of the protectorate. Control, both administrative and legal, was effectively exercised by the district commissioners personally, and through the chiefs and their tribal councils. Inevitably, some English law was introduced but its reception had its problems. Although no attempt was made to interfere with the personal law of the various tribes, yet matters which were formerly within the exclusive jurisdiction of the chiefs were now being handled by the district commissioners. There was conflict of jurisdiction and of substantive law. The people of the new protectorate could not understand this. They saw their natural leaders being subjected to English law and could not understand how their chiefs could be tried by the district commissioner, and in some cases subjected to punishment and imprisonment in Freetown. The imposition of taxes and attempts to enforce the tax laws placed an undue strain on the general administration of law and justice in the protectorate from the very start. Some chiefs at Bandajuma were imprisoned for failing to pay their taxes and, one of them, Francis Fawundu was deposed. As if seeking support and sympathy, the natives threatened the Creole merchants with death if they also paid the taxes imposed by the British administration. Governor Cardew, believed, erroneously, that the Creole merchants were advising the natives not to pay and were behind the resistance to the tax measures. So the Creoles found themselves caught in the middle of the dispute between the natives and the British administration. The result of this unfortunate impasse is well known. There was a rebellion by the natives against the hut tax measure which took a heavy toll of life and the Temne Chief, Bai Bureh, who spearheaded the revolt, emerged as the central figure in the hut tax rebellion. Although he was ultimately defeated, yet his defeat came only after several Creoles in the protectorate had met a violent and untimely death at the hands of the natives.

British administration was superimposed over a tribal system and it is therefore necessary to describe the political organisation of the tribes in the protectorate which existed at the time the protectorate was declared. The whole chiefdom represented the state. The chief and his chiefdom councillors, then called the Tribal Authority, controlled the land and its distribution. Each tribe had its own secret society which exercised subtle control on the community. The political life of the community centred around the family and the land. Decisions affecting the tribe were taken by the chief and his Tribal Authority which included persons who had sacred or ceremonial functions. Consultation was a central feature of the tribal administration, locally described as "hanging heads". No decision would be validly taken without "hanging heads" and arriving at a consensus. Any dissentient would accept the will of the majority. There was no room for open and sustained dissent when once the decision had been taken. The decision of the elders was final and bound everyone.

As far as the legal system was concerned, the chief and his elders were also the fons et origo of the law which was administered in the Chief's Court. There were informal methods of settling disputes but the Chief's Courts were the formal institutions for administering the law. Native, or customary, law, disclosed a marked absence of "criminal" law in the English sense. Rather the emphasis was on offences against the individual, not the community. Again, there was a marked absence of sanctions; on the contrary, emphasis was on restitution in various forms.[66] Offences against the individual which could take numerous forms, for example, stealing of crops or personal effects, livestock, kidnapping and so on, were settled by fines or restitution as there was a marked absence of jails. Offences against the community appeared to be offences against certain native "Institutions", like the secret societies. Customary law distinguished and recognised offences against the Poro, Sande, Wunde, Humoi and Yase cults, all of them religious or semi-religious.[67] This was clearly different in conceptual terms from the English concept of "community". Some of these institutions, notably the Poro were semi-political in character and provided a unifying force within the particular tribe. Finally, the tribe or clan, prior to 1896, and to a large extent today, is inalienably attached to the soil. Because of this identity

---

66 e.g. Pledging (Kpomba in Mende and A kotamu senke in Temne or selling the wrongdoer, from which arose domestic slavery or loss of status).
67 These were secret societies of various tribes.

of tribe with land, aliens could have no place in the tribe. Hence the ma-a-webu. Customary law considered that the introduction of foreigners into the tribe would destroy its social organisation and divorce the land from the people.

This was the kind of tribal set up on which the British superimposed their administration and system of justice. In order to avert any great or major upheaval, the British Government decided that they would not disturb the traditional patterns of life and government and the clear policy was to introduce British rule and British influence as far as possible through the assistance of the native authorities.[68] The paramountcy of English law was preserved, for wherever there was any conflict between English law and customary law, the former prevailed. Legislation was also passed to ensure that the courts would not give effect to any native law which was repugnant to or inconsistent with the principles of English law, equity and justice. British rule was secular, both in substance and in form and it posed a challenge to the chiefs. It produced understandably severe strains and stresses as it changed the social stratification of the society. Protectorate society was quite accustomed to the secret societies and their roles in native life and tribal administration. The British regarded them as barbarous and unsuitable for the needs of modern government. The new social grouping which emerged, had the district commissioner at its head, then the chiefs; the expatriates and Creoles in business or the professions, officials and other traders with the bulk of the natives at the bottom of the scale. So a new middle class developed and this had an important bearing on the pattern of life within the Protectorate. Another factor of great social, economic and political change was the introduction of English law which, by bringing in western values and norms caused fundamental changes in attitudes and behavioural patterns which perforce had to be responsive to its demands.[69]

It was not surprising, therefore, that a rebellion broke out over the imposition of a tax for huts by native owners of houses. They saw this as an attempt to take over their properties. The view here was not dissimilar to the objections raised by the settlers over quit rents. While the British saw it purely as a revenue matter, the natives viewed it as a diabolical and sinister device to rob them of their lands. The British Government held a post-mortem on the causes of the riots. They appointed Sir David Chalmers to hold an inquiry. He submitted a voluminous report.[70] He received great assistance from Governor Cardew who held strong views about the situation that had been created; and he was unrestrained in his comments and criticism of the native

---

68 See Margery Perham: *Native Administration*.
69 See Kenneth Little: *West African Urbanisation* (1965/6). Also; The Report by Her Majesty's Commissioners and correspondence on the subject of the insurrection, Sierra Leone Protectorate, 1898 Part II Evidence and Documents S. L. Archives p.241.
70 See Chalmers Report (1899) C. 9388 Vol. LX. Parliamentary Papers — Accounts and Papers (10).

systems of law and government. On the Native Courts, Cardew commented:[71]

> I question whether it is wrong for a civilised government to restrict the iniquities that often take place in the courts of the native chiefs where human beings are "betted" and pawned by either side in a case, the judgment being given in favour of the party who can produce the greatest number, where the ordeal or innocence may be the drinking of a poisoned concoction or the plunging of the hands in boiling oil, and the punishment may be death, mutilation, enslavement or absolute forfeiture of all property, even including wives and children.

He was equally scathing about the chiefs:[72]

> I think they are quite unfitted from their almost total want of civilization and other habits of slavery, which has been a curse to the Negro race.

Chalmers was more accommodating but still concluded that the protectorate was not yet ripe for the introduction of British rule. He said:[73]

> I admit all the defectiveness of a rule by the native chiefs, but I still hold to the opinion that the settlement is not in a position to replace it by any other; that such rule needs to be restrained in some things, encouraged in others, and to be influenced in all its notions; and it will probably gradually give place to something more perfect; but I am quite sure that the time has not yet come for the substitution . . . . for this rule of administration based on the principles of British law as it prevails in Freetown.

COMMENTS ON THE DECLARATION OF A PROTECTORATE OVER THE HINTERLAND OF SIERRA LEONE.

The sad fact is that at the time of the declaration of the protectorate over the hinterland, Sierra Leone's tribal groups were a mass of heterogeneous people all of whom, with the possible exception of the Limbas and the Sherbros were migrants[74] who had not developed any common traditions and who were living in backward and impoverished conditions. Even today, there has not yet emerged among the peoples of the protectorate a cohesive national consciousness which would have eased the transition from a peasant economy to a modern industrialised country. In 1896 this was even further away from reality and there were marked enclaves of ethnic minorities very much unlike the settlers in the colony who, after an exposure to the mechanics of modern government for over a hundred years were participating in law and government and fully aware of the needs of modern government.

71 Ibid — Report of the Commissioner at p.106.
72 Ibid. C. 9388 at p.105.
73 Chalmers Report op. cit. C. 9388 p.17 citing Sir Samuel Rowe.
74 See M. McCulloch: *Peoples of S.L. Protectorate* (London) International African Institute 1950.

It appeared to have been British policy to keep the Creoles of the colony and the natives of the protectorate distinctly apart. This conclusion is inevitable from the following, among other, facts and circumstances:

(a) Although the principles and practices of a more advanced legal system were being introduced into the protectorate, no lawyers from the colony were permitted to appear in the Courts of the Protectorate without special permission.

(b) No settlers in the colony were allowed to buy land in the protectorate.

(c) The Creoles were excluded from the government in the protectorate. Whereas, hitherto, Creoles had been appointed to top positions in government, after the declaration of the protectorate, these positions were gradually closed to them. All the district commissioners who were sent to the protectorate were British, and the vacancies created in the administration of posts held by Creoles were filled by British persons.

(d) No representation was allowed to the peoples of the protectorate in the Legislative Council of the colony which now made laws for the protectorate.

(e) The protectorate was still regarded as a foreign state and so there were no schemes for education, health, road development and so on. In fact treaties[75] were signed with the native chiefs right up to the time the foreign relations of the hinterland were conducted by the British.[76]

(f) Land in the protectorate remained vested in the chiefs and the tribal system preserved[77] whilst land in the colony was freehold and freely alienable.

(g) The jurisdiction of judges in the colony was not immediately extended to the protectorate where the district commissioners administered English Law in their own courts.

The manner in which the declaration of the protectorate was brought about, seemed to indicate that it was merely intended to serve the oligarchic and autocratic interests of the governing power than to advance democracy. It is true that the Governor (Cardew) had toured the Protectorate to inform the chiefs of Her Majesty's intention to declare the protectorate. It is also true that at least one chief had asked for British annexation of his territory rather than having French control exercised therein. Yet, it is also painfully true that the chiefs were not

---

75 See Ol Le Njogo-v-the A.G. (1913) E.A.L.R. 70 at 77 in which the East African Courts held that a native tribe over which a chief in council is the executive authority vis-a-vis other states, is a foreign country having capacity to conclude treaties. The question for determination was whether an agreement made between the chiefs of the Masai tribe and the Imperial Government in 1911 through His Majesty's Commissioner for the East African Protectorates was a valid treaty. HELD: It was.
Also in Ndibarama-v-The Enganzi (1960) E.A.L.R. the court held that the Ankole Agreement of 1901 was an Act of State.
76 See p.120 supra.
77 The distinction between British Subjects in the Colony and British protected persons in the protectorate, was also maintained.

offered a choice, nor were they consulted as to what they would rather have. They were faced with a fait accomplait as the proclamation itself clearly shows. "Whereas Her Majesty has been advised that it is best for the interest of the people . . . . and . . . it is Her . . . . pleasure that the said territories should come under the protection of Her Majesty . . . . I do hereby proclaim . . . . that the territories . . . . are now under the protection of Her Majesty". In fact, inherent in the relationship between the protectorate and the protecting power was the principle of non-interference with the internal affairs of the protectorate. Hence the application of the principle of indirect rule.[78]

If the establishment of the protectorate demonstrated anything, it was not so much the contrariness or caprice of different philosophies of government as the inherent perplexities of the law's adjustment to novel problems. It illustrated one of the most treacherous tendencies in legal doctrine, the attempted transfer of generalisations developed for one kind of situation to a seemingly analogous, but wholly different situation.

Constitutional and Legal Developments 1896 to 1924.
Just immediately prior to the establishment of the protectorate, Royal Instructions were issued in 1895 withdrawing the Chief Justice from membership of the Executive Council. This was short-lived as he was again restored to membership by Instructions of 1897.[79] He remained a member until he was finally removed from the council by Instructions dated 3rd April, 1913.

In 1903, the Legislative Council of the colony passed the Protectorate Courts Jurisdiction Ordinance[80] which modified the hierarchy of courts in the protectorate. It provided for:
 (a) The Circuit Court of the Supreme Court of the Colony.
 (b) The District Courts.
 (c) The Native Courts.
In 1905, the Native Law Ordinance recognised the Paramount Chief together with the principal men of the chiefdom as the Tribal Authority. It also recognised the elective principle of chieftaincy but required that the candidate should be from a ruling house.

These further legislative changes were occasioned by the early experiences of the Crown in the administration of the protectorate. In 1901, by Ordinance No. 14 of 1901, a system of revision of sentences imposed by district commissioners in their judicial capacities was introduced. This practice whereby the Chief Justice reviewed sentences in his administrative capacity had been tried with some success in India. So the Chief Justice of Sierra Leone, on receiving returns from the district commissioners would examine the sentences and alter them where appropriate. This was not a procedure of appeal, but strictly of review.

78 See Lugard: *Indirect Rule.*
79 See Additional Instructions dated 23rd Oct. 1897.
80 No. 6 of 1903.

However, it did not appear to work well in the protectorate. The Bar Association kept a close watch on the administration of justice in the protectorate and came to the conclusion that this was less than fair. In 1901, they sent a petition to the governor protesting about the "crude and peculiar" method of administration of the law being carried out by the district commissioners in the protectorate. As a result of this protest, the government decided to deprive the district commissioners of the Supreme Court jurisdiction they had hitherto exercised and so a Circuit Court of the protectorate was set up to deal with serious criminal matters, leaving the district commissioners with only their magisterial functions and juridiction.[81] Originally, the Circuit Court was an independent court over which the Chief Justice had no control. This position was subsequently reversed and the Chief Justice given overall control of the judiciary of both colony and protectorate.

The process of legislation continued and the colonial government sought to introduce into the protectorate by stages, the system of laws and courts already in existence in the colony and the legality and propriety of this was discussed in the press.[82]

By Ordinance No. 14 of 1904 the administration of law and equity was fused. It repealed the Supreme Court of the Colony of Sierra Leone Ordinance No. 10 of 1858 which had been amended in 1859 to change the name of the court from that of the Court of the Recorder. A Magistrate's Court Ordinance was passed in 1905 as Ordinance No. 29/1905 and in the same year, combined courts were instituted in the protectorate. The Court of Requests was abolished in 1906. Same year, two orders in council were passed establishing districts. The first, dated 27th March 1906, established the Northern Sherbro District and the second, dated 29th October 1906, established the Railway District and the Central District. By Ordinance No. 4 of 1907, the Supreme Court Ordinance, appeals were again allowed from the Supreme Court in its Summary Jurisdiction to the governor in council and then direct to the Privy Council. In 1909, an order in council was passed providing for appeals to

---

81 In 1895, a remarkable perversion of justice took place in the case of R.-v-J. H. Spaine. He was tried three times for embezzlement. In the first trial, the jury returned a verdict of 9 Guilty and 3 Not Guilty. At that time, a majority verdict was not available. Governor Cardew passed an ordinance to allow any official charged with an offence against public property to be tried by a judge and three or more assessors. Immediately after passing this new measure, he put Spaine on trial again, with a jury. The jury acquitted, but on a 8-4 majority. He then caused Spaine to be further tried by assessors before the same judge. Five defending counsel protested and refused to carry on. Spaine was convicted by a 4-1 majority. Five assessors were selected. Under the ordinance the judge was not bound to accept their opinions.

Section 37 of the Protectorate Courts Jurisdiction Ordinance prescribed the jurisdiction of the court. See the Judgment of Beoku-Betts J. in the case of Solomon-v-Solomon (1937-49) A.L.R. Sierra Leone series p.303. Also the Judgt. of the Full Court in Conteh-v-R. 1920-36 A.L.R. S.L. Series at p.53 in which it was held that the Circuit Court had no jurisdiction to issue a writ of Habeas Corpus.

82 T. J. Thompson on the Protectorate Court Jurisdiction Ordinance, Weekly News, May 16, 1903.

the Privy Council. This order provided that appeals could go as of right in cases involving the sum of three hundred pounds or more and secondly, by discretion of the court on matters of general public importance. There was no specific provision for criminal cases, but it was held that appeal lay as of right by Lord Goddard in the case of A.G. for Ceylon-v-Keemarasinghage Don John Percia.[83]

By Ordinance No. 14 of 1912, the Supreme Court Amendment Ordinance, the Chief Justice was appointed to preside over the "Full Court", which was an Appellate Court. The Full Court was now empowered to hear appeals from the Gambia by Order in Council dated 13th June 1913. This jurisdiction was formerly exercised by the Supreme Court. The Chief Justice continued to sit on appeal in cases in which he had sat as the trial judge. He was not removed from sitting in appeal over his own judgments until 1923 when an order in council was issued preventing him from doing so.[84] The Full Court was replaced by the West African Court of Appeal in November 1928. The Appeals to the Privy Council Order in Council 1909 provided for appeals from the Supreme Court of the Colony and Circuit Court of the Protectorate to the Privy Council.

With regard to the Protectorate, Sec. 5 of the Sierra Leone Protectorate Order in Council dated 7th March 1913, provided that:

> It shall be lawful for the Legislative Council for the time being of the Colony of Sierra Leone, by an ordinance or ordinances to exercise and provide for giving effect to all such power and jurisdiction which His Majesty at any time before or after the passing of this order has acquired or may acquire in the said territories or any of them.

With the passing of this order, the Legislative Council of the colony now had full authority to legislate on behalf of the Crown, for the protectorate. Finally, under the Protectorate (Amendment) Ordinance of 1918, No. 12/1918, the governor was empowered "to depose any chief who, in his opinion, is unfit for the position, and to appoint a person to be chief in his place".

---

83 (1953) A.C. 200.
84 See Supreme Court Amendment Ordinance No. 4 of 1923. Also Order in Council dated 16th December 1912 by which the name of the court was changed to "Full Court". In spite of the orders in council, it appears it was the practice also to pass local ordinances to give effect to the orders in council.

CHAPTER VII

THE 1924 CONSTITUTION

Prelude to the 1924 Constitution
The next important constitutional change in the history of Sierra Leone, took place in 1924 when a new, revised constitution was brought into effect. This new constitution was important in that for the first time, it brought into the legislature of Sierra Leone, representatives from the protectorate, a foreign state, who, though they were not British subjects, sat in and participated in the councils designed for a British settlement. The circumstances leading to the constitutional changes of 1924 will now be set forth.

In 1909, the first Ratepayers' Association was formed in the colony to contest elections to the Freetown City Council.[1] This association played a very effective role in local politics and though its primary objective was to ensure the effectiveness of settler representation in the municipal council, it was nevertheless very much concerned with national politics in which there was a vacuum. It provided the most vocal and effective pressure group in the colony against the colonial government. Other pressure groups and articulate organisations were the Civil Servants Association formed in 1907 and the Bar Association which had been in existence for several decades before.

In 1917, the National Congress of British West Africa was formed by Mr J. E. Caseley-Hayford, a Gold Coast lawyer and member of the Gold Coast Legislative Council. It was a West African organisation which drew its membership from the four British territories in West Africa.[2] It had as its primary objectives, the realisation of self-government for each of the territories; representation of African interests by elected representatives and the unification of certain governmental and other services in the four territories. It also demanded the setting up of a West African Court of Appeal.

1 It will be recalled that under the 1863 Constitution which was still in force, there was no elective principle, although the governor had increased his nominated members (Africans) to four, since 1900. See also: Lengar-Koroma — The Freetown City Council.
2 Nigeria, the Gold Coast, Sierra Leone and the Gambia.

Section 19 of the Congress' Constitution set forth its primary objectives as:

> To aid in the development of the political Institutions of British West Africa under the Union Jack so as eventually to take her place beside the sister nations of the Empire, and in time, to ensure within her borders the government of the people, by the people, for the people.

In Sierra Leone, there had been grave dissatisfaction over the new British policy of refusing to appoint qualified Africans to senior positions of responsibility, for, since the establishment of the protectorate in 1896, there was a deliberate shift in policy and progressively, Africans were being replaced by British civil servants in all the top positions in government.[3] For example, the press decried the policy of appointing British doctors of medicine rather than African doctors who were available in large numbers and who possessed exceptional skills and ability. Similarly, no Africans were being appointed to the Magisterial or Supreme Court Bench even though there were many able lawyers and some of them had held similar positions with great distinction and credit.[4]

The *Weekly News* commented:

> Is it not a very sad matter, then, that English rulers, in West Africa, should initiate a policy of repression among natives when they could find no cogent, no sufficient, no reasonable reason for this policy, except, perhaps, this utterly unworthy one, viz, that they alone as being masters, might enjoy the good things of the country which they never created . . . ?

The formation of the Congress as a regional organisation therefore, was most welcome in Sierra Leone and it provided not only a forum whereby the Sierra Leoneans could bring their grievances to the attention of the British Government, but also a means of making their needs and demands known to their counterparts in the other territories in West Africa. It was a unifying force against the British Colonial Government and provided pressure for constitutional change.

Soon after its formation, the Congress sent a petition to the Secretary

---

3 Fyfe at pp.301 et seq. sets out extracts from the *Weekly News* Editorials in 1910 and 1912 criticising the absence of African members in the Executive Councils in the British West African Territories.
The editorial of 5th March 1910, said:
We have often wondered how any one can be induced to believe that Europeans utterly ignorant of West African affairs are capable of tendering sound, useful and helpful advice to any governor anxious to secure the advantageous development of the resources of British West AFRICA . . . .
We have also wondered why a Government with the most benevolent intentions towards progress . . . . should . . . . not cordially invite the best elements among the educated Africans to co-operate with the European elements of Govt.

4 For example, Sir Samuel Lewis had acted as Queen's Advocate. In fact it was he who prosecuted Mr Spaine at the time he was convicted. It was his misfortune to do so, but he performed his task with candour, honesty and efficiency. In other areas as well there had been distinguished Sierra Leoneans in the principal professions.

of State for the Colonies and appointed a delegation composed of representatives from each of the four territories to present it in London. The Sierra Leone delegates were Dr H. C. Bankole-Bright and Mr E. Cummings. The Congress demanded inter alia:
> That a Legislative Council be established in each of the West African territories, one-half of the members to be elected Africans and the other half nominated.
> That a House of Assembly composed of members of the Legislative Council and six other financial representatives elected by the people be created to control taxation, revenue and expenditure.
> That Africans be appointed to judicial offices.
> That a West African University be established.

The Congress delegates went to England to present these modest demands in their petition to the Secretary of State. While they were away, the governors of the four territories were busy working on the local chiefs to dissociate themselves from the aims and aspirations of the Congress. Indeed, when the Congress delegation met Lord Milner, he declined to accede to their demands because "he had received from the Governors of Nigeria and the Gold Coast, information which shows that the Congress is in no way representative of the native communities on behalf of whom it purports to speak." There was, in fact, some opposition to the Congress from some of its opponents who allied themselves with the government. But the popular support for the Congress was never in doubt. Funds for the trip were raised from the public and generally, the people were in sympathy with the demands for further constitutional change.

Typical of the attitude of the Colonial Governors and their representatives, was the speech of Sir Hugh Clifford on the 25th September 1916 to the opening session of the Gold Coast Legislative Council in which he declared that there was no place in a Legislative Council for a Government and an Opposition. Constitutionally, he was quite correct, but this was a clear reflection of the view that the British did not wish to tolerate any opposition to its policies, nor give to the Africans any measure of self rule. Sir Hugh was an uncompromising exponent of pure colonialism and he did not concede the idea of popular elections under colonial rule. At the time of the Congress' visit to London, he was the Governor of Nigeria. In a speech to the Nigerian Legislative Council in 1920, he said that the members of the Congress were:
> A self-appointed and self-selected congregation of educational African gentlemen . . . . born and bred in British administered towns situated on the sea-shore who, in the safety of British protection have peacefully pursued their studies under British teachers, in British schools in order to enable them to become ministers of the Christian religion or learned in the laws of England, whose eyes are fixed, not upon African native history or tradition or policy, nor upon their own tribal obligations and

duties to their natural rulers which immemorable custom should impose on them, but upon political theories evolved by Europeans to fit a wholly different environment, for the government of peoples who have arrived at a wholly different stage of civilisation.

The governor's attack on the delegation and its intentions, was both virulent and pungent. His message was equally clear. It was an uncompromising rejection of all that Congress stood for. As far as Sierra Leone and the Gambia were concerned, the delegation had no "tribal obligations" to their "natural rulers". Sir Hugh, obviously, had no love lust for the Africans, nor did he dream that independence was within their reach. As far as he was concerned, such a goal was inconceivable and he thought it rather impudent for them to think of independence from Britain. He successfully deployed the old colonial technique of engineering a cleavage between the "intelligentsia" and the chiefs, in order to suppress the ambitions and demands for nationhood.

The Gold Coast delegation were intensely annoyed especially as it became apparent that their chiefs had fallen victim to the overtures from the governor. The chiefly opposition was led by Nana Sir Ofori Atta, a distinguished Chief of the Kibi in Ghana, who said that the delegation did not represent African opinion but had gone to England without the authority of the people and therefore represented only their own views and interests. This was the first time in Gold Coast history when there had been an open breach between the Gold Coast Chiefs and the professionals. A feud blew up between the chief and Mr Caseley-Hayford. It was openly fought out later in the Legislative Council of the Gold Coast where Caseley-Hayford severely criticised Nana Sir Ofori Atta for the views he had expressed. Caseley-Hayford contended that by making unauthorised statements and holding communications with the Head of the Colonial Government on issues not directly pertinent to his own domestic situation, and particularly taking into account his position as a chief, Nana Sir Ofori Atta had rendered himself open to impeachment under customary law. He concluded:[5]

> I regret I cannot impeach you before the bar of your own conscience; but in the silence of the night, in your beds, you and your supporters will acknowledge to yourselves that you have proved traitors to the cause of British West Africa.

Sierra Leone was in a much happier position than the Gold Coast since the chiefs/intelligentsia dichotomy was strikingly absent and there was popular opinion unquestionably in favour of the activities of the Congress. Dr Bankole-Bright and Mr Cummings returned to Freetown triumphantly and reported on the Congress' activities in London. Both in and out of the Legislative Council, pressures developed for an advanced constitution for Sierra Leone. The same demands were made simultaneously in all the other three territories.

5 See Debates of the Gold Coast Legislative Council for 25th April, 1921. Also: KIMBLE: *Political History of the Gold Coast*, (1963) p.394.

It is well known that the Congress returned to West Africa from Britain empty handed, but shortly afterwards, there were changes in the constitutions of all the British territories in British West Africa. In the Gold Coast, Nigeria and Sierra Leone, the elective principle was conceded, though not in the manner nor to the extent the Congress had demanded. This was the forerunner of movements for independence which emerged in the territories much later on.

Dr Bankole-Bright was not a nominated member of the legislature, but Mr E. H. Cummings was. However, there had been formed in Freetown in 1919, the African Progress Union composed of Creoles in the colony of which Bankole-Bright was a member. The union was dedicated to pressurising the government for further constitutional advance. In the protectorate, there was no political body as such, but the Committee of Educated Aborigines was formed ostensibly to present an address of welcome to Sir Ransford Slater who was appointed governor in 1921 in succession to Mr R. J. Wilkinson. This was the first time an organisation had been formed in the protectorate to reflect protectorate opinion in an organised form.[6]

During the 1922/3 Session of the Sierra Leone Legislative Council, Governor, Sir Ransford Slater, informed the council that the Duke of Devonshire had approved certain proposals for the "enlargement and reconstruction of the Legislative Council". In a policy speech in May 1923, he said that he had accepted proposals that there should be some protectorate representation in the Colony's Legislative Council, since the Legislative Council was legislating for the protectorate. The National Congress had agreed to this, but had suggested that this representation should be on an "elective franchise". The governor found himself unable to accede to that suggestion on the ground that:[7]

> If the principle of direct representation of the protectorate was to be conceded (as in my opinion it ought to be conceded) it necessarily followed, in my view, that the representatives must, at the present at least be Paramount Chiefs; under the tribal system no others would have adequate title to speak with authority.

It is a tribute to the colony politicians that in spite of the formidable legal objections to having representatives from a foreign state sitting in the colony legislature, they did not object to that, but rather magnanimously suggested that the protectorate representatives should be elected. Having thus got a concession for elected representatives to be in the legislature from both sections of the country, the question now arose as to how those representatives should be elected, and what their status in the legislature should be. In the colony, the principle of having elections for municipal councillors was well established and there was some way in which it could be determined how the electorate should choose their

---

6 See The *Weekly News* of 9th September, 1922 pp.8-9. Also: The Address of the Sierra Leone National Congress on the same occasion reported in the *Weekly News* of May 20, 1922.
7 Debates of the Legislative Council, 8th Nov. 1922.

representatives. However this was a problem in the protectorate but not an insoluble one. The colony opposed representation by and through chiefs on the grounds that:
   (a) The chiefs were not representatives of the people, consequently, nominating them, would be yet another shrewd device by the colonial power to maintain its grip on the country and its domination over the colony by ensuring that it secured support from black stooges from the protectorate:
   (b) That in any event, chiefs were not politicians but natural rulers and were not the nominees of their people whose interests they were to represent.
   (c) The status of the protectorate representatives should in any event be changed to avoid problems of representation on the basis that they were aliens and not within allegiance.

On the 21st May 1924, after the 1924 Constitution had been introduced[8] and the decision taken to nominate chiefs as the representatives of the protectorate, the Hon. A. J. Shorunkeh-Sawyer introduced a motion in the council in the following terms:[9]

That whereas under the pending reconstitution of this council, persons nominated thereto from the inhabitants of the territories described as the Protectorate of Sierra Leone in the Sierra Leone Protectorate Order in Council 1913, will, in the exercise of their rights and privileges as members thereof legislate inclusively for the colony, and that whereas doubts appear to exist as to whether or not such inhabitants are to all intents and purposes aliens, and it is expedient that such doubts should be disposed of, this council do present its dutiful petition to His Majesty the King, praying that such inhabitants be declared to be British subjects by an Order in Council to be made under the Foreign Jurisdiction Act, 1890 or otherwise.

This motion was opposed by government and after considerable private consultation and discussion with the Hon. Member, it was withdrawn before voting took place.[10]

The 1924 Constitution:

Following the Governor's Policy Speech to the Legislative Council, the 1924 Constitution was promulgated. It was contained in four instruments:
   (a) The Sierra Leone Legislative Council Order in Council of 16th January 1924.
   (b) Instructions to the governor under the Royal Sign Manual dated 28th January 1924:
   (c) Letters Patent dated 28th January 1924: and

---

8 Voting under the new constitution had not yet taken place and the old council was still in session.
9 Leg. Co. Debates. 1923-4 Session V. p.15.
10 He withdrew to avoid misunderstanding by the natives of the motives of the colony.

The 1924 Constitution

(d) The Sierra Leone Protectorate Order in Council dated 16th January 1924.

These instruments together made detailed provisions for the government and administration of both the colony and protectorate. The constitution for the first time conceded to the colony people the elective principle, but denied this to those in the protectorate. The first three documents mentioned above related to the colony and the fourth which was expressed to be made "by virtue and in exercise of the powers by the Foreign Jurisdiction Act, 1890, or otherwise in His Majesty vested", related exclusively to the protectorate. The 1863 Constitution was repealed. In its place, the 1924 constitutional instruments provided for a Legislative Council of twenty one members, exclusive of the governor who was the president, and an Executive Council composed of official members. The Legislative Council of eleven official and ten unofficial members was made up as follows:

Official Members:
  The Officer Commanding the Troops
  The Colonial Secretary
  The Attorney General
  The Colonial Treasurer
  The Principal Medical Officer
  Three Provincial Commissioners
  The Comptroller of Customs
  The Director of Public Works
  The Commissioner of Lands and Forests

Unofficial Members:
  3 Elected members from the Colony
  2 Colony Africans nominated by the Governor
  2 Europeans nominated by the Governor
  3 Paramount Chiefs from the Protectorate, one each for the three major Administrative divisions, nominated by the Governor.[11]

For the purpose of the election of members to serve on the council, two electoral districts were created:
  The Urban Electoral District and
  The Rural Electoral District.

The Urban Electoral District was to return two members and the Rural Electoral District, one.[12]

The first two colony Africans nominated by the governor to serve in the new council were the Mayor, Mr J. Claudius May who was a member of the former council and Mr Claude Emile Wright a barrister, whose father, before him, was also a distinguished lawyer and member of the Legislature, having served as a nominated member from 14th July 1903 to 1911 when he died. The two first European members were new-comers

---
11 Sections 6-7a required them to be literate in English.
12 Section 7(4) of the Leg. Co. Order in Council.

to the Legislature, Mr J. H. Phillips, a merchant and the Rev Dr G. W. Wright.[13] Bishop of Sierra Leone.

The result of the elections in Freetown showed that Mr E. S. Beoku-Betts, a lawyer and Dr H. C. Bankole-Bright, one of the two Sierra Leone congress delegates to London, had been returned as the first and second urban members respectively. Mr A. F. Tuboku-Metzger was returned as the rural member.

The first chiefs to enter the Legislature were Bai Kumpa, Bai Comber and Baki John Tucker, all of them nominated by the governor in accordance with the instruments forming the 1924 Constitution.

The Legislative Council, in passing laws for the protectorate, was required to respect native laws "by which the civil relations of the native chiefs, tribes, or populations under His Majesty's protection are now regulated" except "so far as the same may be incompatible with the due exercise of His Majesty's power or jurisdiction or clearly injurious to the welfare of the said natives."

The Sierra Leone Protectorate Order in Council, in Sections 5 and 6, provided that the Executive Council of the Colony:
> Shall be and be deemed to be the Executive Council of the Protectorate and that the persons who shall from time to time compose the Legislative Council of the Colony shall have full power and authority . . . . to establish such ordinances, and to constitute such courts and officers, and to make such provisions and regulations for the proceedings in such courts, and for the administration of justice, as may be necessary for the peace, order and good government of the protectorate.

The Executive Council was made up of the five senior members, namely:
> The Officer Commanding the Troops.
> The Colonial Secretary.
> The Attorney-General.
> The Colonial Treasurer.
> The Director of Medical Services

and such other persons as the governor should from time to time appoint.

Certain features of these constitutional instruments need identifying:
(a) The governor was empowered to make laws for the peace, order and good government of Sierra Leone, which now meant, the colony and protectorate together. In the exercise of his discretionary power, he could summon, adjourn, prorogue or dissolve the Legislative Council.
(b) All the prerogative powers of the Crown were delegated to the governor, hence he could
   (i) Nominate members to the council.

---

13 It is interesting to note that from 1924 until 1936 when he was replaced by an African member, the governor regularly appointed the Bishop of Sierra Leone to a seat in the Legislative Council. (See: BLYDEN: *Sierra Leone: The Pattern of Constitutional Change: 1924-1951.* PH. D. Thesis — Harvard. Unpublished).

(ii) Exercise the right of Veto which meant he had an additional or casting vote.
(iii) Appoint judges and justices of the peace.
(iv) Grant pardons.
(v) Regulate fees collected as general revenue.
(vi) Dispense offices.
(vii) Reserve bills for His Majesty's pleasure and refuse his assent to them.
(c) The Crown reserved to itself the power of dissallowance of the ordinances as well as the powers of legislation.

EVALUATION OF THE 1924 CONSTITUTION.
Before dealing with particular aspects of the 1924 Constitution, by way of general comment, one can say that it was clear that, by the joint administration of both parts of the country in 1924, the British had taken the first step in the attempted merger of the colony and protectorate. When the protectorate was declared, some Creole politicians argued fiercely that the protectorate should be annexed. The British Government resisted that and decided that both parts should be administered separately. With hindsight, they must have concluded that the original policy was erroneous. The government of the colony was provided for, and its administration conducted under the provisions of the British Settlements Acts; and the courts were established as contemplated by the Colonial Laws Validity Acts, 1865. The policy of the British Settlement Acts was to limit control by British settlers over the territories in which they resided. So these acts were designed to enable the Crown to legislate and control them as effectively as it thought fit and necessary to do.[14] On the other hand, in the case of the protectorate, the Foreign Jurisdiction Acts 1843-1890 made it quite clear that protection, rather than nationality, was the essence of the relationship between the British protected person and the United Kingdom. In the case of the Ionian ships, Dr Lushington made this abundantly clear. In discussing "Ionian Subjects", he said:[15]

> I am of the opinion that allegiance, in the proper sense of the term, undoubtedly they do not owe: because allegiance exists only between the sovereign and his subjects, properly so called, which they are not. A limited obedience, according to the treaty, they do owe and that .... as a sort of equivalent for protection.

The Ionian islands, under the Treaty of Paris, had become a British protectorate. Dr Lushington's judgment was quoted with approval by Kennedy L. J. in the case of R-v-Crewe ex p. Sekgome.[16] However, it is clear that whilst the British protected person is travelling abroad he owes some allegiance, not to his own ruler, but to the British Crown, because

---
14 See Sir Henry Jenkys: *British Rule and Jurisdiction Beyond the Seas.* (Oxford, 1902) Clarendon Press, at p.5.
15 (1855) 2 Ecc. and Adm. 212 at 226.
16 (1910) 2 K.B. 576.

the United Kingdom government is responsible for the protectorate's external affairs. Therefore a duty of allegiance follows that person in return for the right of protection which he claims.

Lord Justice Kennedy in an oft-quoted passage from Crewe's case, said:

> What the idea of a protectorate excludes and the idea of annexation includes, is that absolute ownership which was signified by the word "dominium" in Roman law and which, though perhaps not quite satisfactory, is sometimes described as territorial sovereignty. The protected country remains in regard to the protecting country a foreign state; and that being so, the inhabitants of a protectorate, whether natural born or immigrant settlers do not by virtue of the relationship between the protecting and the protected state become subjects of the protecting state.

Legally therefore, by having one Legislature for both parts of the territory, the British Government were creating a new system — for parliament cannot be said to act illegally. They were beginning to sow the seeds of integration between the colony and protectorate, a process which was to introduce into the territory considerable strains and stresses and create suspicion and mistrust for several decades thereafter.

The propriety of administering the oath of allegiance to chiefs whom the colonial goverment proposed to admit to the Legislative Council, was seriously challenged by the Hon. A. H. Shorunkeh-Sawyer in the Legislative Council immediately preceding the introduction of the constitution.[17] Governor Sir Ransford Slater, contended, on legal advice from London, that the chiefs could properly take the oath of allegiance to the King, their status of British protected persons, notwithstanding. Sir Samuel Lewis, who had read a paper on the same issue which had already been much debated had died in 1903 and so did not live to see the matter brought to a head. However, his views were already well known and there had been lively debates on the matter. The popular view, all along, had been that the protectorate should be annexed, rather than bringing its representatives to participate in the colony's legislature and so create technical problems of administration. Nevertheless, the governor went ahead with his proposals and superimposed on an African tribal system of government something altogether alien to it. For, in traditional societies, agreement was reached by consensus. The implications of this for the Sierra Leone legislature were the utter bankruptcy of ideas which emanated from the chiefs. They felt that they were members of the "government" and did not feel free to differ from decisions of the colonial government. Regularly, they sided with the colonial government, even in matters patently against their interests.

It would appear that the intention in 1924, was to create a protectorate elite and bring them in line with the colony elite, but if this was so, then

---

17 See Debates of the Legislative Council for the 20th November, 1922. See also, Fyfe's *Sierra Leone Inheritance, for the proceedings of the Sierra Leone Association,* pp.194-201.

the manner in which representation was provided for, did not help to achieve this. There was no opportunity for a large participation of Africans in the legislature and the restriction of membership to chiefs did not provide the necessary stimulus for this kind of development. Rather, it created a deep mistrust by the Creoles for the provincials and vice versa. The Creoles were limited to the colony, and the chiefs to the protectorate, so sectional interests developed in the legislature. Both the Creole representatives and the chiefs were conservative and this affected the character of the house. Outside, however, both sides were busy forming groups and associations to further their own individual interests. The Committee of Educated Aborigines began to oppose the colony politicians and the chiefs in the protectorate exploited the Creole businessmen at will. The Committee of Educated Aborigines, expressed the view that they wanted to be at par with the Creoles, educationally. They commented:

> When all these shall have been accomplished and the protectorate can literally march with the colony in every sphere of life, then, but not until then, will a new era dawn on Sierra Leone and . . . . Colonial Africans and protectorate aborignes will join heads and shoulders together to confer seriously on the question of elective franchise.[18]

In March 1925, a small number of those in the CEA joined Creoles to form the Sierra Leone Aborigines Society, but this was short lived. Their wish was "to promote the welfare of the aborigines". They had to contend with opposition from the colonial government which seemed bent as much as possible to keep the peoples of the colony and protectorate severely apart.

Finally, the 1924 Constitution was inappropriate to the needs of the country at the time it was promulgated. It was not responsive to the demands of the local populations and was singularly inappropriate to meet them. It preserved the autocratic nature of colonial rule and did not provide any opportunities for responsible or enlightened leadership by the peoples for whose government it was designed.

Post 1924.

In 1924, the League of Nations adopted a resolution in its 4th Assembly to inquire into the question of slavery. That lead to a despatch from the Secretary of State for the Colonies to the Governor of Sierra Leone, requesting particulars of slavery in Sierra Leone. The governor replied reviewing the history of slavery in the territory since the proclamation of the protectorate in 1896. The reply was surprising in its revelations that there was widespread slavery and slave dealing in the country and that attempts to render this trade illegal had caused considerable concern and distress to the chiefs who felt that it would seriously affect the political and social system of the tribes if it were eliminated. The governor

---

18 See Kilson M., *Political Change in a West African State* where he analyses from a political point of view the effects of the changes brought about in 1924.

expressed great surprise that in Sierra Leone "of all colonies, having regard to the history of the first settlers that there should still exist, even in the hinterland, an admitted form of slavery, certain release from which could only be obtained by the payment of redemption money". They found that domestic slavery existed on a large scale and that there were about 219,000 slaves in the protectorate, or 15.15 per cent of the population, excluding slaves of the fourth generation. A report was prepared which showed the percentage numbers of slaves in each of the tribes of the protectorate. The Madingo headed the list with 35 per cent: the Susu, 33 per cent: Vai, 30 per cent: Yalunka, 25 per cent: Temne, 20 per cent: Bullom, 20 per cent: Mende, 15 per cent: Foulah, 15 per cent: Kuranko, 10 per cent: Kono, 10 per cent: Loko, 5 per cent and Limba, 5 per cent.[19]

As a result of this, an ordinance was passed in 1927, No. 24 of 1927, which became effective on the 1st January 1928 and which abolished the legal status of slavery in the protectorate. This measure reversed the decision of the Full Court of Sierra Leone in the cases of Rex-v-Salla Silla and Rev-v-M'fa Nonko which held that it was legal for a master to use reasonable force to recapture his runaway slave.[20] By abolishing the status of slavery in the protectorate, all slaves were legally free and their masters could not claim any redemption fee for them. The protectorate was thus brought into line with the colony which had abolished slavery from its inception.

In 1925, the Protectorate Laws Ordinance was passed[21] which removed all matters involving Creoles or Europeans from the chief's judicial jurisdiction. This was essential since one of the theoretical-assumptions on which the judicial status of the protectorate was based, had been demolished, namely, the assumption that the native chiefs were free and the legal system was based on the assent of free men.

In 1926, there were riots in the colony arising out of a strike organised by the Railway Workers' Union. Governor, Sir A. R. Slater, sent a confidential dispatch to the Colonial Secretary on the matter.[22] He said he regarded the strike as serious in that "it revealed a widespread defiance of discipline and revolt against authority." The colony elite supported the strike to the chagrin of the governor and the colonial administration. The Colonial Secretary, Mr H. C. Luke, said that "as a mark of their displeasure with the unworthy behaviour in this crisis, of the entire Creole community, His Majesty's government should be asked to suspend for an indefinite period, that part of the constitution which provides for an elected element in the Legislative Council". The governor disagreed on the ground that this would be too harsh and dangerous.[23] What the governor decided was that he would proceed with

19 See Cmnd Paper No. 3020 of 1928. Correspondence relating to Domestic Slavery in the Sierra Leone Protectorate.
20 See Vol. 1, *The Sierra Leone Recorder*.
21 Cap. 169 of the Laws of Sierra Leone, 1924.
22 See Confidential Dispatch from the governor to the Rt. Hon. L. S. Amery dated 20th April, 1926. Sierra Leone Government Archives.
23 See Kilson — op. cit. at p.121 where he reproduces the Governor's Statement.

Africanisation at a much slower pace and that he would refuse any further constitutional development. "I have always made it absolutely clear", he said "that there can be no question for many years of conceding the smallest modicum of self-government".

In 1928, the West African Court of Appeal was established. This court now heard appeals from all the four British territories in West Africa.[24] It was an itinerant court and sat in all the territories. As far as Sierra Leone was concerned, appeals lay to the Court of Appeal from the decisions of the Supreme Court in both civil and criminal matters.[25]

POLITICAL AND LEGAL CHANGES, 1938-1951

The patterns of government created in 1924, survived basically unaltered until after the Second World War. The Colonial Government, however, had to contend with several demands for constitutional change and the government was subjected to considerable criticism from time to time, both in and out of the legislature.[26]

The West African Youth League.

In 1938, the West African Youth League, a radical political organisation, emerged on the scene. It was led by the late Isaac Theophilus Akunna Wallace-Johnson who, in the early nineteen twenties, was a clerk and typist in the Freetown City Council's offices. Wallace-Johnson then went abroad for several years during which time he was heard of in the Soviet Union, Great Britain and the Gold Coast. In the Gold Coast, he had been arrested and tried with Dr Nnamdi Azikiwe[28] on a charge of sedition, following the publication of an article entitled, "Has the African a God?" He and Azikiwe were convicted and sentenced to a term of imprisonment. They appealed to the West African Court of Appeal which quashed Azikiwe's conviction and sentence but upheld that of Wallace-Johnson who was the writer of the offending article. Wallace-Johnson appealed to the Privy Council and lost. He had to serve his term of one year's imprisonment.[29]

It was after this kind of record that Wallace-Johnson returned to

---

24 A conference was held in Accra under the aegis of the Secretary of State for the Colonies in October and November 1927 "with a view to the formation of definite proposals for the establishment of a single Court of Appeal for the Gold Coast, Sierra Leone and the Gambia. It was attended by judges and law officers. Nigeria at first refused to join. The Order in Council was issued on the 1st November 1928 and the court created for the three territories. The Chief Justice of the Gold Coast was President. Nigeria joined in 1933 and in 1934 the WACA (Further Amendment) Order in Council extended the jurisdiction of the Court to Appeals from the Supreme Court of Nigeria.
25 WACA (Civil Cases) Ord. No. 9/29: Criminal, No. 10/29.
26 The elected members of the Sierra Leone Legislative Council, were active participants in debates in the Leg. Co. and called the government's attention to a number of matters which required urgent and necessary reform. See Debates of the Leg. Co. 1924 to 1938.
27 See La Ray Denzer's doctoral dissertation on Wallace-Johnson.
28 Dr Azikiwe ultimately became President of Nigeria.
29 See R.-v-Wallace-Johnson (1940) 1 All.E.R. 242.

Sierra Leone in 1938. By that time, he had associated abroad with nationalist aspirants from other British territories, such as Azikiwe, Kwame Nkrumah and George Padmore. He had flirted with communist ideas and freely used Marxist-Leninist cliches in his speeches. He appealed to "the masses" in Sierra Leone and in a short time achieved considerable mass support. He formed the West African Youth League which he saw as a radical political movement aimed at causing considerable embarrassment to the British Government and some discomfort to the aristocracy in Sierra Leone. For the first time, the gap between the educated elite and the impoverished and illiterate majority in the protectorate was bridged and there was a common approach in both the colony and protectorate to demands for self-government.

The league obtained considerable sympathy and financial support from a number of influential Creoles and through the assistance of its General Secretary, Mr S. M. O. Boyle, secured premises at Trelawney Street in the centre of Freetown which it used as its offices. These premises were virtually donated by a leading Creole family who sold it at a vastly reduced price. The purchase price was paid from public subscriptions.[29a] It also bought a printing press from the Albert Academy[30] and then ran a weekly newspaper *"The African Standard"* which afforded it an opportunity of putting across its views on a number of important matters. Wallace-Johnson also organised numerous public meetings at which he severely criticised the government and made demands for political change.

Perhaps, not surprisingly, when one takes his background into account, he quickly tackled the Freetown City Council and the league succeeded in a short time in fielding its own candidates and winning the seats in free elections. This displeased the government not a little and caused alarm in Whitehall.

At first, the government approved of the provision for an African unofficial majority in the Standing Finance Committee of the Legislative Council. This was the first occasion in which the British Colonial Government had approved of an African majority in any colonial institution in Africa. Unfortunately, that was insufficient to stem the tide of opposition to the government which had been generated by the activities of the West African Youth League. The pressures for constitutional change proceeded unabated into 1939 when the Colonial Government countered by first taking action against Wallace-Johnson on a charge of criminal libel. On the 11th August 1939, Wallace-Johnson published an article in the *African Standard* intituled "Who killed Foni?" Wallace-Johnson wrote that "He", Foni, "was ordered by the district commissioner to be roped (according to the practice in that district to enforce payment of tax monies). The order was accordingly

---

[29a] The owner, the late Mrs Hebron, was not paid the full asking price for the premises. The league is now defunct and claims have been made to the property, first by Wallace-Johnson himself and later on by his successors.
[30] At that time a leading Secondary School in Freetown.

transmitted by the sectional chief to his messengers who did the necessary. Fonnie was accordingly tied with his elbows meeting each other at the back and a piece of stick set in between thus causing his chest to protrude forward. His legs were similarly bound. These acts were all done to the knowledge and in the presence of the district commissioner who, as reported, took great interest at the procedure of tying".[31]

The article further went on to make serious allegations about the complicity of the paramount chief of the district whom, it was alleged, had been convicted in the Supreme Court of Sierra Leone as an 'unfortunate dupe' while the 'real villain' behind the drama, the district commissioner, had been left unscathed and free.

The trial took place in November 1939 before the Supreme Court. The Chief Justice was assisted by assessors instead of a jury at the request of the Attorney-General who prosecuted in person and who had exercised his right to apply for trial with the aid of assessors whenever he was of the opinion that a more fair and impartial trial would be obtained with the aid of assessors rather than with a jury.[32] In spite of the objections of counsel for the defence,[33] the application was granted as 'of course'. Was the court right in granting the application of the Attorney-General?

Section 40 of the Jurors and Assessors Ordinance, which the attorney-general invoked, read as follows:

> The Attorney-General, whenever he is of opinion that a more fair and impartial trial of any person or persons charged with any criminal offence, who has or have been committed for trial, can be obtained by such person or persons being tried by the court with the aid of assessors instead of by a judge and jury, may make an application to the court for an order, which shall be made, as of course, that any such person or persons shall be tried by the court with the aid of assessors instead of by a judge and jury.

However, Section 14 of the Courts Act, had the following provision:

14(1) Any person charged with a criminal offence at any sessions of the Supreme Court held in the colony shall:
(a) if such criminal offence be punishable by death be tried by the court with a jury consisting of twelve men, and
(b) If such criminal offence is not punishable by death, be tried by the court with a jury consisting of twelve men unless:
(i) such person shall have elected to be tried by the court with the aid of assessors or:
(ii) the court shall have ordered such person to be tried by the court with the aid of assessors in accordance with the jurors and assessors ordinance . . .

---

31 See the *African Standard* for 11/8/1939.
32 Section 40 of the Jurors and Assessors Ordinance.
33 Leading Counsel for the Defence was the late C.D. Hotobah-During, a member of the league, who was once an elected member of the Legislative Council. He was assisted by several other barristers.

It would seem that the courts ordinance contemplates and in fact acknowledges the right of an accused person to trial by jury, unless he is deprived of that right on the sole ground that a "more fair and impartial trial" would be had with the aid of assessors. On the other hand, the jurors and assessors ordinance provides that the order "shall be made as of course", which suggests that, irrespective of the merits of the arguments which may be advanced by an accused person, the court has no alternative but to make the order when once the Attorney-General has applied for trial by assessors. In fact, this is precisely what the court held. The learned Chief Justice ruled that the court had no option to grant or refuse the application when once it had been made by the Attorney-General. But did the legislature intend that the Attorney-General, rather than the court, should exercise a discretion as to the mode of trial of an accused person? If so, it meant that the legislature was permitting the Attorney-General to deprive an accused person of his 'right' to a trial with the aid of a jury, which is a right specifically set out in an enactment.

Assuming that the Attorney-General was in fact given such extensive powers, which of the two enactments would prevail, since they were plainly inconsistent in their provisions. On general principles of statutory interpretation, it would seem to be the correct conclusion that since the later enactment was the jurors and assessors ordinance, its provisions must be taken to have impliedly repealed those of the courts ordinance inconsistent with it. The effect of these cumulative provisions therefore, was that the court could not assist an accused person who wanted to be tried with a jury, against the wishes of the Attorney-General. The court was bound to accept the subjective judgement of the Attorney-General that circumstances existed which rendered it likely that trial with the aid of assessors would be more fair and impartial than trial by jury. The disturbing part of this provision is that the Attorney-General was not required to disclose the basis of his information. Nor did the exercise of this privilege by the Attorney-General do anything to allay the very genuine fears of the accused that there must be some sort of collusion between prosecutor and judge. This was a common complaint in colonial territories where the firm view was always held that the judges were not as independent as they were in England and that colonial judges were servants of the Crown and therefore subject to the directions of the Crown. The withdrawal of counsel from Wallace-Johnson's case illustrated the concern the members of the legal profession felt about the futility of this exercise, even if it left the accused, as it must have done, in greater jeopardy.

Wallace-Johnson appealed from his conviction in the Supreme Court to the West African Court of Appeal. The judgment was delivered on the 19th June, 1940.[34] By that time, Wallace-Johnson had been detained under the emergency provisions.[35] Prior to this, there was a court martial

34 See 6 WACA 186.
35 The war commenced on 3rd September 1939 from which date the emergency began in Sierra Leone. The Defence Regulations No. 11 of 1939 empowered the governor to detain any person if he thought it fit to do so.

of gunners in the Royal West African Frontier Force who allegedly mutinied on the 29th January 1939. The allegation of the Crown, was that this mutiny was inspired by Wallace-Johnson and the activities of the Youth League. There were eleven of them[36] and the court martial lasted for seventeen days. They were convicted and sentenced to varying terms of imprisonment from 15 years penal servitude to 84 days for Joe Powder, whose sentence was the least. The sentences were confirmed on the 28th April 1939.[37] On the 5th May 1939, Wallace-Johnson published in the *African Standard* an article intituled "Rewarding the African's loyalty. A review of the result of the court martial trial and its after effect". The article was a scathing criticism of the colonial administration. In May 1939, the Legislative Council passed a number of measures[38] giving the governor extremely wide powers of control of citizens and particularly, to detain and deport British subjects. Wallace-Johnson, apart from the determined assault he mounted on this legislation, wrote an article entitled "If the governor thinks fit". The following extract from a communication sent by the Governor of Sierra Leone to Mr Dawes of the Colonial Office, illustrates the mood of the people and the concern felt by the administration at the time. He wrote:[39]

> The publication of the Sedition, Undesirable British Subjects Control and Deportation Bills, led as was to be expected to a considerable outcry in the press and at public meetings: but I personally was not prepared for the noisy demonstration on Tuesday 16th May. The mob collected outside Fort Thornton and the council chamber about an hour before I was due to drive to the chamber for the First reading of the bills. The din was terrific and they were saying in a very defiant way, a Negro spiritual with jargon something like
>
> 'we wont be slaves
> till we're in our graves'
>
> The 'mammies' (with children) by the thousands were placed in front.

Wallace-Johnson is detained.
Wallace-Johnson's penchant for publishing secret communications in the *African Standard* was a matter of grave concern to the government. They were anxious to know how he came by secret and confidential despatches. An inquiry was held in the Legislative Council Chamber. Wallace-Johnson was subpoenaed to give evidence. He refused. He was brought before the magistrate in Freetown on a criminal charge. Almost one-half of the total strength of the Sierra Leone bar turned up in his

---

36 The accused were Emmanuel Cole and others. See C.O. 267 671. No. 33216/1.
37 By Lord Russell.
38 These will be considered later.
39 See C.O. 267 673. Letter from Sir George Beresford-Stooke, Governor of Sierra Leone, dated 1. 6. 39 to Dawes.

defence. The Crown entered a Nolle Prosequi and he was released. The government were not any the wiser.

On the 3rd September 1939, the police conducted a detailed search of the headquarters of the Youth League. Prior to that, the Colonial Government in the United Kingdom had passed the Emergency Powers (Defence) Act, 1939[40] which provided in its Section 4 that His Majesty could, by order in council extend the regulations to the colonies. By the Emergency Powers (Colonial Defence) Order in Council, 1939, Section 3, the provisions of the act were extended to the colony and protectorate of Sierra Leone. Section 1 of the Act empowered His Majesty to make such regulations "as appear to him to be necessary or expedient for securing the public safety, the defence of the realm, the maintenance of public order and the efficient prosecution of any war". The Governor of Sierra Leone, acting as His Majesty's duly authorised and appointed representative, and 'being thereunto duly authorised', made the defence regulations[41] which, by Section 16, gave the Governor of Sierra Leone power to detain any person

> "if satisfied .... that with a view to preventing him acting in any manner prejudicial to public safety or defence, it is necessary to do so".

On the 6th September 1939, pursuant to these powers, the governor made an order for Wallace-Johnson's detention on the ground that he was engaged in subversive activities prejudicial to the public interest. A press release was published to that effect and it was promptly challenged by the Youth League which denied that Mr Wallace-Johnson had been involved in any activities inimical to the public interest. A corrected press statement was then issued by the government which said that "on the night of the 3rd September 1939 last, the premises of I. T. A. Wallace-Johnson was searched as a result of which His Excellency and his advisers were satisfied that this person was engaged in activities prejudicial to public safety and defence in Sierra Leone."

Exchanges between London and Freetown suggested that there was some disquiet about leaving Wallace-Johnson in Sierra Leone after his detention. Abott, the acting Attorney-General suggested that he should be deported to the Falkland Islands, St. Helena or Cyprus. Mr Hilary Blood, the colonial secretary, suggested the United Kingdom or such other part of the United Kingdom's empire as the secretary of state should think fit.[42] He was eventually banished to Bonthe, Sherbro.[43]

Objections were made to the Governor's Order of Detention and Deportation in compliance with the provisions of the Regulations and an Advisory Committee was set up to consider these objections. The committee reported on the 27th October 1939, the objector being Mr

---

40 2 and 3 Geo. VI.
41 No. 2 of 1939. This measure was later revoked and replaced by Regulation No. 11 of 1939.
42 C.O. 267 — 670. 1939 32210/2 Part 1.
43 In the south-eastern part of Sierra Leone. It is an island very far from the capital, Freetown.

Wallace-Johnson. The chairman was the Chief Justice Mr Justice C. A. G. Lane.[44] Counsel for the objector, raised the following points:
1. That the governor's order was ultra vires.
2. That the Advisory Committee had no jurisdiction:
3. That the detention of a British subject was a contravention of the inherent rights of the subject.
4. That in the case of a British subject where concrete evidence was necessary, more was required than in the case of an enemy subject.
5. That with regard to procedure, the internee should have been informed of the reasons for the order.

All the objections were overruled. The order for the deportation and detention of the objector was therefore unaffected and stood. Wallace-Johnson thereafter stood trial for the offence of criminal libel. He served his sentence after the Court of Appeal had upheld the conviction and then the prison sentence superceded the detention order. He was released from prison on the 13th March 1941 but then he reverted to the detention imposed by the governor in 1939. On the 19th March 1941, the detention order was revoked and a restriction order substituted which confined him to Bonthe, Sherbro until the 21st October 1944, when he was eventually released following persistent demands for his release from members of the British parliament and others in Britain and in Sierra Leone.

THE LEGISLATIVE MEASURES OF 1939.
The activities of the West African Youth League were anathema not only to the Colonial Government ensconsed in Freetown, but also to some of the elite Creole Politicians, notably, Dr H. C. Bankole-Bright. Dr Bankole-Bright was an uncompromising opponent of Wallace-Johnson and he felt insulted by the latter's style and brand of politics. He wrote articles, addressed public meetings and attacked the league in and out of the Legislative Council. The government, having secured an influential ally in its attempt to eliminate Wallace-Johnson from the political scene, now took steps to introduce certain legal measures to ensure the achievement of that objective. During the months of May and June 1939, the governor took the opportunity of introducing a number of bills, namely,

> The Sedition Bill.
> The Incitement to Disaffection Bill.
> The Aliens (Expulsion) Bill.
> The Undesirable British Subjects Control Bill.
> The Production of Telegrams Bill.
> The Undesirable Publications Bill.
> The Press Censorship Bill.
> The Trade Union Bill.

Those which met with the greatest public opprobrium and disapproval

---

44 The other members of the Advisory Committee were the Commissioner of the Northern Province Mr A. H. Stocks and the Rev I. E. C. Steady, a member of the Legislative Council.

were disdainfully described as "the Three Bills". They were published together. They were:
> The Sedition Bill.
> The Incitement to Disaffection Bill and
> The Undesirable British Subjects Control Bill.

Together, they conferred on the governor exceptionally wide powers of arrest and detention. In a colonial setting with the governor possessing absolute powers in any event, the necessity for these extreme measures seemed hard to justify, save on the rather inelegant and unnecessary ground that they served notice on the colony politicians that the government was not prepared to surrender or abdicate its power and was determined and willing to inflict heavy blows on its opponents.

Dr Bankole-Bright was a member of the Legislative Council at this time. He was the second urban member for Freetown and unquestionably belonged to the old Creole aristocracy.[45] He objected to and feared the mass appeal of the Youth League. He despised Wallace-Johnson who did not belong to the same class or brand of politicians who had previously entered the Legislative Council. Wallace-Johnson was no professional gentleman; nor did he emerge from the middle class. He was a grass roots trade unionist with some communist ideology and training. Dr Bankole-Bright saw him as a distinct threat to the aristocracy of Freetown. He resented Wallace-Johnson's brand of politics. Not only did he closely identify himself with the stand of the government on these measures, but he actively supported and sponsored the bills seconding both the Sedition and the Undesirable British Subjects Control Bills. He echoed the views of the governor expressed in the Legislative Council that there had "arisen up in our midst, organisations which are definitely subversive of law and order . . . . which obviously have as their main objectives the undermining of authority, the vilification of those in authority and the eventual frustration, if not downfall, of British rule in this country".[46] He continued:

> "I ask, would a governor like Sir Ransford Slater tolerate the impudence, the impertinence of that scurrilous crowd at the Wilberforce Memorial Hall which passes resolutions of such vile nature against the governor of this colony? We should be ashamed of ourselves; our heads should be bowed down with shame to think that Sierra Leone had deteriorated to that standard. I say it today for it to be passed on to them that I have no intention of representing as an elected member a community of such degenerate hooligans. I would rather sit at home than come here as their representative.
>
> . . . . This is not the Sierra Leone I knew when I first entered this council.
>
> . . . . A different Sierra Leone has now come into being."

---

45 See Blyden's Thesis — *Constitutional Change in Sierra Leone* — op. cit. Harvard University (Unpublished dissertation).
46 See Debates of the Leg. Co. 1939, p.72 et seq.

In comparing the Sierra Leone of 1924 with that of 1939, Dr Bankole-Bright was quite right that things had changed and that the conditions were not the same. The difference was startling. While he expected and wished the status quo to remain, a wind of change had blown over the country. New ideas had emerged and the colonial experience was being subjected to critical examination. The country no longer felt that the machinery for representation was adequate. The Sierra Leone of 1939 was no longer willing to tolerate the characteristic colonial mechanisms for governing an underdeveloped country. There had now grown within the rank and file an enlightened self-interest with optimistic assumptions about the patterns of government which they expected to emerge. The people now expected to see politics of accommodation and co-operation between the governors and the governed. The demands of the electorate were that the country should take an inward look and assume the major burdens of government and administration. Since Dr Bankole-Bright was clearly out of touch with these new concepts and expectations, it was also clear that he would no longer be acceptable to the people as their representative in council. He lost his seat at the next elections, thanks largely to the activities of the league which he so freely denigrated. Before this event occurred, however, the harm had been done. He had rendered an irreparable disservice to the bulk of the community he was called upon to serve. His hostility to the league had repercussions on the wider community, since his judgment often did not reflect what was good for the country as a whole. He seemed to be completely oblivious of the fact that the measures he was supporting were a serious threat to individual liberty and an attempt to suppress the democratic rights of the people. No doubt, he would in the end be judged largely by his performances covering a much larger period of time than that spanning the era of his conflict with the Youth League; but the judgment of history must be that he did a great disservice to the cause of freedom in Sierra Leone by his support for repressive measures aimed at the downfall of one man and the institution he founded.[47]

It is now desirable to examine the measures passed in 1939, mentioned above.

THE SEDITION ORDINANCE:

The Sedition Ordinance was passed in the Legislative Council on the 25th May 1939 and received the governor's assent on the 10th June 1939.[48] It followed very closely the Sedition Ordinance which had earlier on been introduced in the Gold Coast.[49] Section 4 made it an offence if anybody
> does or attempts to do, or makes any preparation to do or conspires with any person to do any act with a seditious intention;

---

47 For comments on Dr Bankole-Bright's performance and his role in Sierra Leone Politics, see: Blyden: op. cit. *La Ray Denzer:* and L. Spitzer: *I.T.A. Wallace-Johnson and the W.A. Youth League.* (International Jo. of Afr. Hist. Studies vi. 3 & 4 1973. A. J. Wyse — *Dr H. C. Bankole-Bright.* (Unpublished). Spitzer: *The Creoles of S.L.* etc.
48 Ordinance No. 7 of 1939.
49 See the Criminal Code Sec. 330 of 1936.

or utters any seditious words; or prints, publishes, sells, offers for sale, distributes or reproduces any seditious publication, unless he has reason to believe it is not seditious.

Thus, it created the offence of sedition, whether by words spoken or written, or by conduct. It defined a "seditious publication" as "a publication having a seditious intention". A "seditious intention" was further defined under five headings as follows:

(a) To bring into hatred or contempt or excite disaffection against the king, his successors or the government of the colony as by law established.
(b) To excite His Majesty's subjects to attempt to procure the alteration other than by lawful means, of any other matter in the colony as by law established.
(c) To bring into hatred or contempt or to excite disaffection against the administration of justice in the colony.
(d) To raise discontent or disaffection among His Majesty's subjects or inhabitants in the colony.
(e) To promote feelings of ill-will and hostility between different classes of the population of the colony.

But an act, speech or publication was not to be declared seditious by reason only of the intention to do any of the following:

(a) To show that His Majesty has been misled or mistaken in any of his measures: or
(b) To point out errors or defects in the government or constitution of the colony as by law established or in the legislation or in the administration of justice with a view of remedying the same: or
(c) To persuade His Majesty's subjects or inhabitants of the colony to attempt to procure by lawful means the alteration of any matter in the colony as by law established:
(d) To point out, with a view to their removal, any matters which are producing or have a tendency to produce feelings of ill-will and enmity between different classes of the population of the colony.

For the purpose of determining whether the intention with which any words were spoken or any document published is seditious, everybody was deemed to intend the consequences of his act.

There were two safeguards built into the sedition ordinance:

First, no prosecution could be commenced without the consent in writing of the Attorney-General:

Second, no prosecution could be commenced after the expiration of six months from the date of the commission of the offence.

Thus, the Sierra Leone Sedition Ordinance was similar in some respects to sedition in the United Kingdom[50] but with two significant differences:

(a) The mere possession of seditious material would not appear to be an offence in English law and (b) English law requires that to constitute

---

50 In the UK sedition is a misdemeanour indictable at common law and punished by fine and imprisonment. See Stroud's case 3 St. Tr. 235.

the offence, there must be an actual or threatened breach of the peace. This does not seem to be a requirement of the law of Sierra Leone.[51]

In England, the word "sedition" has not been satisfactorily defined. According to Archbold's Criminal Law and Practice,[52] it "embraces those breaches, whether by words, deed or writing, which fall short of high treason,[53] but directly lead or have for their object to excite discontent or disaffection to excite ill-will between different classes of the sovereign's subjects to create public disturbance, or to lead to civil war; to bring into hatred or contempt the sovereign or the government, the laws or constitution of the realm, and generally all endeavours to promote public disorder."

The word has been employed in the United Kingdom to embrace "seditious words", "seditious conspiracy" and "seditious libel" with which it appears to be synonymous. They are all misdemeanours of the same genus. Historically, the offence of sedition was an offshoot of treason and like that offence, was once punished by death. Today, however, it is regarded as of a lower level of opprobrium and is hardly ever charged.

Sedition, at best, is a troublesome offence and one that is difficult to describe. A Sierra Leonean who had the distinction of being one of the few people and the first ever to be charged under the ordinance with sedition, has described the offence as "speaking the truth to the inconvenience of government".[54] A leading American author says that there is a distinction between the noun "sedition" and the adjective 'seditious" when the latter is used to define the particular offence committed, e.g. seditious words, libels or conspiracies. When used as a noun, it is applied to "practices which tend to disturb internal tranquillity by deed, word or writing, but which do not amount to treason and are not accompanied by or conducive to open violence." When used as an adjective, "it signifies that the practices are accompanied by a seditious intent, the legal definition of which has changed however, with the development of toleration and political rights."[55]

Regrettably, the Sierra Leone courts did not contribute any learned judgments to help simplify the problems of definition of this offence.

THE INCITEMENT TO DISAFFECTION ORDINANCE:
This measure was passed into law on the 26th May 1939 and received the governor's assent on the 10th June 1939.[56] Its date of commencement was fixed for the 15th June 1939. Its long title was:

> To make better provision for the prevention and punishment of endeavours to seduce members of His Majesty's forces from their

---

51 Unlike Ghana and Nigeria, Sierra Leone never had a criminal code. Attempts to introduce one in Sierra Leone were always fiercely resisted and dropped.
52 35th Edition para. 3147 p.1217.
53 1 Hale: Pleas of the Crown 77.
54 Mr Sydney M. O. Boyle whose trial is described in the subsequent pages (p.159).
55 See CHAFFEE: *Free Speech in the United States* (1948), Harvard Univ. Press. p.497.
56 Ordinance No. 10 of 1939.

duty or allegiance.

Since its main purpose was to punish anyone who was guilty of "seducing" members of the forces, the ordinance provided that the seduction must have been done maliciously or advisedly. Section 3 of the ordinance made it an offence for anyone to have possession or control of a document of a nature such that "the dissemination of copies thereof among members of His Majesty's forces would constitute such an offence". There was a statutory requirement of 'mens rea' — the intention to commit the offence or to aid, counsel, abet or procure the commission of the offence. The police were empowered to search any premises with a warrant at any time and to arrest any person therein. The ordinance did not define "seduction".

THE ALIENS (EXPULSION) ORDINANCE:

This ordinance was passed on the 26th May 1939, received the governor's assent on the 10th June 1939 and became operative on the 15th June 1939.[57] This was not the first aliens expulsion ordinance in Sierra Leone.[58] There was one in 1924 providing for the deportation of aliens. The present enactment defined "alien" as someone not of British nationality. By this definition, "natives" of the protectorate, not being of British nationality, were aliens.

The ordinance provided that the governor could make an expulsion order against any alien (a) whenever he deemed it conducive to the public good or (b) on the recommendation of a court which had convicted an alien of any felony or misdemeanour, or of any offence punishable by imprisonment without the option of a fine. When such an order had been made against any alien, he could be detained in custody until his departure from the country.

In 1940, this ordinance was amended to provide that a native of the protectorate could not be expelled from the protectorate. By a further amendment in 1952, natives of the protectorate were wholly excluded from the provisions of the ordinance.[59]

THE UNDESIRABLE PUBLICATIONS ORDINANCE.

This ordinance was passed into law on the 25th May 1939, received the governor's assent on the 10th June and became operative on the 24th June 1939. Its object was "to prohibit the importation and publication of undesirable literature" in Sierra Leone. It gave an absolute discretion to the governor to prevent the importation of indecent, obscene, seditious, defamatory, scandalous or demoralising publications.[60] It also conferred on the governor the like powers in respect of "all or any other publications of the same publisher". The ordinance also made the mere

---

57 Ordinance No. 8 of 1939. It was repealed and replaced by the Expulsion Act No. 35 of 1963.
58 See the Laws of Sierra Leone, 1924.
59 See Ordinance No. 27 of 1952.
60 Section 3.

possession of such prohibited publication, without lawful excuse, an offence punishable by fine or imprisonment or both.

Power was conferred on three classes of persons to examine and detain any package which they considered might contain prohibited material. These were: any police officer not below the rank of inspector or assistant superintendent; any officer of the customs department not below the rank of collector and any other official authorised by the governor to do so. The phrase "public interest" was not defined.

THE UNDESIRABLE BRITISH SUBJECTS CONTROL ORDINANCE.

This was one of the "three bills" but its passage was delayed because of the stormy reception it received when it was first published as a bill. It was first introduced with the other bills and finally passed on the 22nd June 1939, almost a month later than the others.[61] It received the governor's assent on the 30th June and became operative on the 1st July 1939. Its primary objective was to "control the movements of undesirable British subjects and for similar purposes". It empowered the governor to make three kinds of orders:

>Deportation Order.
>Security Order.
>Restriction Order.

A deportation order removed a person from a particular district or from the country altogether to some place designated by the governor. While in force, it prevented his return on pain of imprisonment. A restriction order required the victim to live in a designated area and not to leave it without the permission of an authorised official. A security order required the person to whom it applied to give security by two or more solvent sureties in such amount and for the time specified therein, to keep the peace and to be of good behaviour, and to indemnify public funds for costs, charges and expenses which may be incurred on behalf of himself by the government. A failure to provide the required security resulted in the restriction or deportation of the person concerned.

These orders were applicable to "undesirable" British subjects, who were those conducting themselves in a manner dangerous to "peace, good order, good government or public morals". The persons against whom the orders could be made were further spelt out as follows:

DEPORTATION   An immigrant British subject who did not belong to Sierra Leone and who was a convicted person, an undesirable person, a destitute person or an undesirable immigrant.
RESTRICTION   A convicted person or an undesirable person.
SECURITY   A convicted person, an undesirable person or a destitute person.

In each case, before the order could be issued against a convicted

---

[61] No. 25 of 1939. Later Cap. 87 of the Laws of Sierra Leone 1960. It has now been repealed.

person, a recommendation should have been made by the court of conviction. In the absence of such an order, a single judge of the Supreme Court could make the order, but this jurisdiction did not apply in the former circumstance. The governor could make a recommendation in the latter situation if satisfied that the order could lawfully be made.

The ordinance further provided for certain procedural measures to be taken. Notice had to be served on the person concerned by the Attorney-General, or the commissioner of police, specifying the facts alleged and the grounds on which the order was sought. On receiving such notice the person named in the order could apply to a judge in chambers within a specified time to show cause why the order should not be made. A return date would then be fixed for the hearing after which the judge would send a report to the governor.

Under the ordinance, a person could be detained for twenty-eight days but in a case which was one referable to the secretary of state, this period could be extended. Proceedings could be instituted under the ordinance only with the written permission of the Attorney-General. If an affidavit of merit was presented to a judge, he could issue a warrant for the arrest of any "undesirable person". The governor had a right to direct any public officer, as he thought fit, to examine, withhold, or detain the personal papers and documents of any person. The ordinance also gave to the government wide powers to search the person or premises of "undesirable persons".

THE PRODUCTION OF TELEGRAMS ORDINANCE.
The main thrust of this ordinance was to compel the production of a telegram by a person named in a warrant issued by the governor in the public interest. Failure to comply with the order for production was a criminal offence punishable by fine and punishment. It was passed on the 25th May, received the governor's assent on the 19th June and came into force on the 24th June 1939.[62]

THE TRADE UNION ORDINANCE.
For the first time in the history of Sierra Leone, this ordinance required the compulsory registration of all trade unions in Sierra Leone. Any union which was unregistered and which was carrying on business as such, could be dissolved within three months of the coming into operation of the ordinance. The Master and Registrar of the High Court was designated the Registrar of Trade Unions. He was empowered to refuse the registration of any union, but could refer any question to the governor, whose decision in the matter was final. By an amendment in 1944, the registrar had absolute discretion to grant or refuse registration; where registration was refused, the union could itself refer the matter to the governor who, if he thought fit, could order an inquiry and thereafter decide for or against registration.

The Trade Union Ordinance was passed on the 23rd May 1939 and

62 No. 17 of 1939. Cap. 163 of the Laws of Sierra Leone.

received the governor's assent on the 20th June 1939. A complementary ordinance was passed later in 1939, the Trade Disputes Ordinance, No. 42 of 1939. It made provision for certain protections usually accorded to trade unions to be extended to unions in Sierra Leone. This did not affect the powers of the registrar in the substantive enactment to cancel any registration on the ground of mistake, fraud, the violation of some provision of the ordinance, or that the registration was void or that the union had ceased to exist. Registered unions were required to submit annual returns to the registrar of their "receipts, funds, effects and expenditure".

Evaluation of the 1939 Legislation.
Cumulatively, the legislation described above were a serious encroachment on fundamental liberties. They interfered with the freedom of the person; the right to free speech; freedom from arbitrary arrest and detention; freedom from arbitrary searches and seizures and freedom of movement. The measures were all clearly intended to suppress the West African Youth League and more particularly, Wallace-Johnson and his supporters. This is borne out by comments which were made in the Legislative Council when these measures were being debated. The Colonial Secretary, Mr H. R. R. Blood in moving the reading of the Undesirable British Subjects Control Ordinance, said, inter alia:[63]

> The council will have noted that this bill which appeared last in the order of the day last Tuesday has been promoted to the top of the list today. The reason is not far to seek. Of a considerable corpus of contentious legislation which the government has had to introduce at this sitting, the Deportation Bill has aroused most public interest. It has, also, I regret to say, been the subject of no little misrepresentation. And it is therefore obviously desirable that government should take the earliest opportunity of making its position transparently plain, of reducing what has just been described as the present hectic temperature, and of doing all it can to allay the fears of the genuine critics of the bill who are honestly and conscientiously concerned as to the need for and the scope of, the powers which government considers it is necessary to assume ....
> In the first place, council may be interested to learn something of the genesis of this legislation which is based on a model ordinance sent by the colonial secretary to all colonies ....
> There is international tension of which honourable members know from the wireless just as much as I do. There are military and naval works going on here of which Hon. members know much and I could tell them more if it were not impolitic for me to do so. It is this complete change in world affairs that is the first and most important reason for this bill. Government in present conditions

[63] See Leg. Co. Debates 1938-9 No. II, pp.34-9.

must have the power to regulate and restrict the activities of undesirable British subjects in the interests of national defence.

The second reason is best stated in Your Excellency's own words which have been broadcast and published: "There have arisen up in our midst, organisations whose methods are definitely subversive of law and order . . . . His Majesty's Government desires, and from the bottom of my heart, I desire that, associations, leagues, societies and so on, whose object is the attainment by constitutional means of the betterment of the conditions of life of the labouring classes, should be given all freedom and liberty to express their views at public meetings, to organise themselves on sound lines, and to make representations in the right quarter with a view of the fulfilment of their very laudable aims and objects. But His Majesty's Government must view in a different light associations which obviously have as their main objects, the undermining of authority, the vilification of those in authority, and the eventual frustration, if not, downfall, of British rule in this country. Such conduct, of course, cannot be tolerated indefinitely, and our first duty as a government is to maintain the safety of the realm".

Those sir, are the reasons for this bill at this stage in Sierra Leone's history. Heaven knows we do not want to pass oppressive legislation; we do not want to cast the slightest reflection on the loyalty of this country or on its love of liberty of peace and of order, or on its affection for the laws and usages of England to whom it owes everything. Why should we? We spring from the same country and are of the same race as Sharpe and Wilberforce and Clarkson and the giants of old . . . .

The colonial secretary's emotional appeal did not fall on deaf ears. The bill was postponed for a month. When eventually it was brought up again, it was passed. However, the nominated and elected members had comments on these measures. The rural member opposed the Undesirable British Subjects Control Bill as he considered the law "unnecessary, tyrannical; an infringement of freedom and one which affects the rights and liberties of British subjects; full of danger and cowardly and manifestly cruel and inhuman".

Dr H. C. Bankole-Bright was unswerving and unequivocal in his support for all the measures. The paramount chiefs supported the government. So did the nominated member, Hon. C. E. Wright. The second urban member, Mr T. E. Nelson-Williams described May 8 1939 as "a fateful day in the history of Sierra Leone". He agreed to the Sedition Bill but not to the others. It was clear therefore, that, contrary to what the colonial secretary had said, the international situation was not the primary cause, but a secondary one. The principal objective of the government was to put down the subversive organisations, as they saw it, which had emerged in the country.

The conclusion therefore, is that the 1939 legislation was anti-fundamental rights and liberties of the individual; it was autocratic; it was a direct attack on the rise of nationalism and a firm answer to demands for political independence.

R.-v-GEORGE THOMAS AND SYDNEY BOYLE.
FIRST SEDITION TRIAL AFTER 1939.

Shortly after the passing of the 1939 legislation which was aimed at curbing the activities of the West African Youth League, an opportunity arose for invoking the newly passed Sedition Ordinance. Wallace-Johnson had been tried and put in detention and during his absence from the scene, Mr Sydney M. O. Boyle, the General Secretary of the Youth League took over the editorship of the league's paper, the *African Standard*. Together, as editor and assistant editor, they published an article headed "Political Persecution of Wallace-Johnson". The writer of the article was "J. R. Johnson" an obvious nom-de-plume as the article was said to have been culled from *'The Socialist Appeal'* a black American newspaper. The article formed the basis of the prosecution of Thomas and Boyle in the Supreme Court of Sierra Leone for sedition. After their arrest and appearance before the magistrate, and while they were awaiting their trial, they published another article "Liberty or Death" which concluded in the following terms:

> Neither principalities nor powers could compel us to swerve from our purposes or to bow to the idol of hypocrisy, injustice and oppression and we know definitely that eventually we shall emerge victorious from the struggle for 'liberty or death', inasmuch as:
> 'Right is right since God is God,
> And right the day must win.'

This second article formed the subject of the second charge when both men appeared to take their trial before the Supreme Court. However, as in the case of Wallace-Johnson, before the trial began, both men were detained by the governor under the defence regulations. Like Wallace-Johnson before them, both men were also tried by the court with the aid of assessors, rather than with a jury. They did not have the assistance of counsel and the Attorney-General appeared to conduct the prosecution personally, on behalf of the Crown. In opening the case for the prosecution, the Attorney-General submitted that the issue resolved itself into determining only two questions:

(a) Did the accused publish the articles and:
(b) Were the articles seditious?

It will be recalled that when the Sedition Bill was before the Legislative Council, the colonial secretary who moved the reading said, inter alia:[64]

> In the case of the offences now under consideration, that of seditious acts and seditious libels, that government at present possesses the general powers at English common law by virtue of the Supreme Court Ordinance and the Imperial Criminal Libel Act is presumably a statute of general application. To a layman

---

64 See Debates of the Leg. Co. 1938-39 p.72.

like myself the former is a mystery and the latter not conveniently accessible; whereas the bill without in anyway widening the scope of the present law; I am informed it limits, rather than extends existing powers — is simple, self-contained and explicit . . .

Sierra Leone, as might be expected from its history and traditions, has been very free of this offence (sedition). That is all to the good and I hope it may remain so. But I have read in the past months various articles which have seemed to me on the verge of sedition.

Did the Sierra Leone Sedition Act, really limit, rather than extend the English law of sedition which then applied to Sierra Leone? One of the crucial problems in sedition is to provide an adequate definition of the offence. As a learned reviewer has commented:[65]

In the lay press, we read that the learned judge had not adequately charged the jury on the meaning of the word 'sedition'. We can well understand his difficulty. Even if he had his law library with him, he would have found it difficult to construct a definition which would have been consistent with all the changes and judgments — and there are many — on the true significance of this debatable term.

Under English law there is no unanimity among the judges as to the meaning of the offence or whether the question of sedition is one of fact or law. Mr Justice Littledale, in his charge to the jury in the case of R.-v-Collins[66] said that if the jury were satisfied that the defendant had published the paper with the intent as charged, then a seditious libel had been committed. Thus, the learned judge reduced the matter to one of law. The motive is usually irrelevant. It is usually sufficient to prove that the accused published the words and that he had the intent to produce the result which is usually set out in the indictment. In the case of R-v-Aldred,[67] Mr Justice Coleridge, as he then was, said that whosoever, by language incites or encourages others to use physical violence or force in some public matter connected with the state is guilty of publishing a seditious libel. He continued:

The man who is accused, may not plead the truth of the statements that he makes as a defence to the charge; nor may he plead innocence of his motive. That is not a defence to the charge. The test is not either the truth of the language or the innocence of the motive with which he published it. The test is this. Was the language used calculated, or was it not, to promote public disorder or physical force?

In the case of R.-v-Burns,[68] the intention was set out in the Indictment of a well-known leader who was charged with "seditiously contriving and intending" to disquiet and disturb the peace. The learned judge placed a great deal of importance on the intent with which the alleged

---

65 See Article on Sedition in Vol. 191 Law Times p.31.
66 3 St. Tr. (N.S.) 1149.
67 (1912) 22 Cox 1.
68 16 Cox 335.

offence was committed. He said:[69]

> If you think that these defendants, if you trace from the whole matter laid before you, that they had a seditious intention to incite the people to violence, or create public disturbances and disorder, then undoubtedly, you ought to find them guilty.

The learned Sierra Leone Attorney-General did not leave any room for lawful criticism for the English law of sedition does not prevent a full, free and fair discussion and criticism of public matters. This is clear from the course the trial took. There were five witnesses for the prosecution. The assistant commissioner of police was the first witness. He produced the Attorney-General's fiat to prosecute. The next witness was the deputy Registrar-General. He merely produced the registration particulars of the *African Standard*. Witness number three was a messenger in the Attorney-General's office who had been sent to buy a copy of the paper. The fourth witness was a civil servant from the office of the colonial treasurer who read the article and the final witness was the printer of the *African Standard*, Mr Bailey.

With the exception of the last two the whole of the evidence for the prosecution was merely formal. The printer actually helped the case for the defence when he testified that the accused had adopted a cautious policy in regard to the printing of articles. He mentioned that on one occasion, in spite of the shortage of print and the heavy financial loss to the press, they had abandoned printing after a run-off of 2,000 copies of the paper, because the editors were of the opinion that a particular article being carried in that issue might be offensive and considered defamatory. Equally thin, from the prosecution's point of view, was the evidence of the civil servant who could barely testify that there had been demonstrations and protests at the time the 1939 measures were being introduced into the Legislative Council. He told the court that he had seen more excited crowds than those assembled at public meetings following the introduction of the "three bills".

The Defence.
Thomas elected not to give any evidence on oath, but Boyle went into the witness-box to testify. He thus faced cross-examination by the Attorney-General. He said that the first article had been discussed between himself and Thomas and before deciding to publish, they cut off some parts of the article which "might give trouble". He contended that as published, he considered the article a fair comment on matters of public interest. "The same applies to 'Liberty or Death'," he concluded. He was extensively cross-examined by the Attorney-General during which he disclosed that the articles related to matters of considerable public interest and that the word "despatches" mentioned in one of the articles related in fact to confidential despatches between the governor and the

---

69 Ibid at p.174.

colonial office in respect of which an inquiry had been mounted.[70]

He was asked about the reference to "indiscriminate demolition" of houses in Bonthe. The medical officer in the Sherbro area had apparently reported that a number of houses in that district were sub-standard. Accordingly, he ordered their demolition. One of the houses so demolished was owned by Mrs Lucy Hamilton who challenged the demolition order with some success before the Chief Justice, Mr Justice Webb. As a result, the Legislative Council rushed through The Sherbro Judicial District Rules (Validation) Ordinance, No. 34 of 1938, which exempted and held indemnified the officers concerned with the demolition and who had acted under instructions received from the medical officer, against all actions and liabilities at law in connection therewith. The ordinance operated retrospectively.[71] Boyle was cross-examined on the point by the Attorney-General. His reply was that the article referred to this incident which was true and which was a matter of public interest.

There were several other questions asked regarding particular issues raised in the articles. The purpose of these extensive questions is not clear since, on the Attorney-General's submission, the law did not require proof of an evil intent. If the words were seditious and that question was one of law to be determined by the court, the judge should have ruled on the point without any reference to the defence put up by the accused. Reference can be made at this juncture to the decision of the West African Court of Appeal in the case of R.-v-Wallace-Johnson.[72] The Chief Justice of Nigeria, Kingdon, C. J. dealt briefly with the question of whether or not the words were seditious: "In this case", he said, "it is sufficient to say that the words complained of are obviously seditious". After referring to a possible wrongful admission of evidence which he dismissed as being of minor importance, he continued to justify the fact that the trial judge put the issues to the assessors. The real issue for him, was "the question of whether the article was seditious or not, namely, was it calculated to bring the Government of the Gold Coast into hatred?"

At that point of time, decisions of the West African Court of Appeal were binding on the Supreme Court of Sierra Leone. Was there,

---

70 The point here was that the governor in one of his despatches to the colonial secretary, had, so it was reported, mentioned that certain Africans were receiving pay of between £8 and £13 per month when in fact this was not so. Low as the reported figures were, they were allegedly grossly inflated and the misrepresentation was deliberate in order to conceal the appalling conditions which then existed in the colony. The article described this as 'wilful misrepresentation' and this annoyed the Colonial Government considerably.

71 See the Debates of the Leg. Co. 1939 p.105. The colonial secretary in moving the second reading of the bill said that as a result of the Supreme Court action, further legal actions could be instituted against district commissioners and medical officers. The bill would abate these actions. There was a free vote on the matter.

72 See 3 WACA 104. The court was composed of the Chief Justices of Nigeria, the Gold Coast and Sierra Leone but those who actually sat were CJ Kingdon, CJ Webber, (Sierra Leone) and J Yates.

consequently, a legal requirement that the articles forming the subject matter of the charges against Thomas and Boyle, should be calculated to bring the Government of Sierra Leone into hatred? It is submitted that the Privy Council decision in the Wallace-Johnson case put the legal issue in its proper context. The Privy Council said:

> The case presented by counsel for the appellant for their Lordships' consideration was that the prosecution could not succeed unless the words complained of were themselves of such a nature as to be likely to incite to violence, and unless there was positive extrinsic evidence of seditious intention. The foundation for these submissions was sought in the summing up by Cave J in R.-v-Burns, quoted at length in Russell on Crime 9th ed. pp.89-96. Reference was also made to a number of cases on the law of sedition in English and Scottish cases, which it was said, supported the statement of the law by Cave J. Their Lordships throw no doubt upon the authority of these decisions and, if this was a case arising in this country, they would feel it their duty to examine the decisions in order to test the submissions on behalf of the appellant. The present case, however, arose in the Gold Coast Colony and the law applicable is contained in the criminal code of that colony. It was contended that the intention of the code was to reproduce the Law of Sedition as expounded in the cases to which their Lordships' attention was called. Undoubtedly, the language of the section under which the appellant was charged lends some colour to this suggestion. There is a close correspondence at some points between the terms of the section in the code and the statement of the English law of sedition in *Stephen's Digest of Criminal Law* 7th Ed. Articles 123-126 quoted with approval by Cave J in his summing up in R.-v-Burns. The fact remains, however, that it is in the criminal code of the Gold Coast Colony and not in English or Scottish cases that the law of sedition for the colony is to be found. The code was no doubt designed to suit the circumstances of the people of the colony. The elaborate structure of Section 330 suggests that it was intended to contain as far as possible a full and complete statement of the law of sedition in the colony. It must, therefore, be construed in its application to the facts of this case, free from any glosses and interpolations derived from any expositions, however authoritative, of the law of England or of Scotland.

According to the Privy Council, the whole of the law of sedition should be found in the Sedition Ordinance of Sierra Leone. That is a sensible, common sense view. However, Sierra Leone law has to be interpreted in accordance with the provisions of the laws of Sierra Leone and its legal system. In Sierra Leone, English law has never been irrelevant for the purposes of constructing any statutory provision. On the contrary, English law is and forms the basis of the statutory construction and interpretation of the law. The Sierra Leone Courts will, in every possible instant, turn to the laws of England and Scotland for support even though each case would be decided "on its own facts and in its own setting of time and circumstance."[73]

The Privy Council decision did illustrate that there was difference between the law of sedition in England and the Sedition ordinance of Sierra Leone which was modelled after the Sedition Code in the Gold Coast. The Privy Council was in fact saying that the Colonial Government had introduced their own peculiar brand of sedition law suitable for the colonies which contained less safeguards for the individual than those available under English law. In the colonial brand of this offence, there was no place for the concept of "incitement to violence" nor did it require proof of "bad tendency", that is, a tendency to cause a breach of the peace. In Britain, prosecutions for sedition are, as a rule, never instituted unless there is proof of actual incitement to violence.[74] But in the case of Thomas and Boyle, there were a number of circumstances which led irresistibly to the conclusion that their trial was oppressive and unfair, apart from the Privy Council's view of the ingredients to be satisfied in law for the establishment of the offence. These could be succinctly summarised as follows:

(a) The conduct of the trial with the aid of assessors.
(b) The conduct of the prosecution by the Attorney-General in person and the unavailability of counsel for the defence:
(c) The grave suspicion of collusion between the executive and the judiciary.

These factors will now be examined.

TRIAL WITH THE AID OF ASSESSORS.
There were many defects in this mode of trial as compared with a jury trial. The assessors are hand-picked by the trial judge. In a jury trial, they are balloted for. The accused has no right to object to any of them. Selected, as they are by the court, a huge responsibility is cast upon them in returning their opinions. Unlike the jurors, each assessor is required to give his opinion individually in open court. It would take a very brave man in the Civil Service to give an honest opinion without fear or favour in cases where he knows the result expected by the colonial administration of which he is part.

In a jury trial, the judge is bound by the unanimous verdict of the jury and may accept a majority verdict. In a trial by assessors, the judge is not bound to accept the opinions of the assessors. The decision is his alone.

In the case of Thomas and Boyle, the judge chose three persons who, in a jury trial, would most certainly have been challenged peremptorily, if not for cause. The first assessor was Mr Hume-Dawson, one-time town clerk of the Freetown City Council and ex-member of the Youth League. Having been at odds with the league and resigned therefrom, not only by

---

73 See the Bank Nationalisation case. Commonwealth-v-Bank of New South Wales (1949) 79 C.L.R. 497 at 639.
74 See *Hood Phillips*: 4th Edition p.437; **474** et seq.
   Also: *The King b. Aldred* (1909) 22 Cox C.C. 1.
   Stephen: *History of the Criminal Law*, Vol II Ch. 24.

himself, but also withdrawing the membership of his wife and daughter, he had no business to sit in judgment over the officials of the league standing trial. In fact, he could not restrain himself and asked Boyle a number of questions when he was in the witness-box giving evidence. The following exchange is illuminating;
Dawson: Mr Boyle, you have mentioned in your paper that some members of parliament have been to prison before.
Boyle: Yes
Dawson: Is it by writing articles like these that they went to prison?
Boyle: Ask me another?
Dawson: I said, is it by writing articles like these that they went to prison?
Boyle: I said, ask me another, I do not know.
Chief Justice: Have you another question Mr Dawson?
Dawson: No Sir.
Chief Justice: (To Boyle): You may go down.

The second assessor was Mr Beckley who had been a member of the National Congress of British West Africa and was closely associated with Dr Bankole-Bright and his policies. Dr Bankole-Bright was a well-known and unrepentant enemy of the Youth League. For that reason, he too had no business being an assessor at the trial of officials of the league.

The third assessor was Mr J. T. Nottidge, a retired civil servant. He was of the old-school, having grown up at a time when government was all-powerful. He, like many of the Creole middle class families, resented the rise of the Youth League and their particular brand of politics. They saw the league as an "affront" to the government. Another assessor who had a less obvious dislike for the West African Youth League would have been a more discreet choice. Taking all the above factors into consideration, it is not surprising that the assessors returned verdicts of guilty. They were, one would like to think, men of the purest of motives, but their opinions were suspect.

THE ABSENCE OF COUNSEL FOR THE DEFENCE AND THE PERSONAL APPEARANCE OF THE ATTORNEY GENERAL.

Another unsatisfactory aspect of this case was the fact that these two accused persons were not defended by Counsel. The state did not provide any assistance for them in their defence. Justice Stephen, said this:[75]

> When a prisoner is undefended his position becomes often pitiable, even if he has a good case. An ignorant, uneducated man has the greatest difficulty in collecting his ideas and seeing the bearing of the facts alleged. He is utterly unaccustomed to sustain the attention of systematic thought, and it often appears as if the proceedings on a trial which to an experienced person appears plain and simple must pass before the eyes and mind of the prisoner like a dream which he cannot grasp.

If ever any case required the assistance of counsel, it was this one. It dealt

---

75 See Stephen: *A History of the Criminal Law of England.* Vol. I p.442 (1882).

with a highly technical subject matter on which lawyers and judges of great eminence have disagreed. It was most unfair to the accused that they should have had to face the prosecution without any knowledge of the legal ingredients of the offence of sedition or the defences open to them.

That the Attorney-General prosecuted in person was an indication of the importance the government placed on the action. The scales were unevenly matched and he exercised one of his privileges very harshly indeed. At the close of the case, he took full advantage of his right to the last word. He addressed the court and had the last word even though the accused were without legal representation. This was certainly not in the best traditions of the bar.

THE EXECUTIVE AND THE JUDICIARY.

All along, the accused persons were convinced that there was some collusion between the government and the judiciary. This was understandable as they saw the courts being used as the instrument for their political demise. However, it is curious that at the end of the trial, after the opinions of the assessors had been delivered, the Chief Justice did not deal with the accused there and then. He adjourned the court for a day for sentence, remarking that he could "not send these boys to prison". He was very disturbed. On the following morning, he addressed the accused. He referred to a case of counterfeiting coins which he had tried in another colony. The accused, according to him, were "the unfortunate dupes of the real perpetrators" of the crime. "It is you, and people like you", he continued, "who enable the makers of the base metal of sedition to put it in circulation among the people some of whom have not the intelligence to recognise the base metal for what it is and because of that it is my duty to punish you, so as to deter others from following your example".

Punishing people in order to deter others is one of the most unworthy reasons for punishment. Yet the Chief Justice boldly stated that as one of the main reasons why the accused were being punished. He wanted to set an example of them so that no other members of the league could take up the gauntlet and continue the struggle. In the end, he inflicted a mild enough sentence of imprisonment; three months and twelve days. He carefully calculated the months and days to the end of the year and wanted them released at the end of the year to "start afresh" in the New Year. He underestimated the resolve of the accused,[76] and failed to take into account prison regulations.

---

76 The accused were still under detention under the Emergency Regulations and it took much discussion between the Director of Prisons, the Governor and the Chief Justice before they were finally released. There was a problem over the remission they had earned under the prison rules for good conduct and the fixed sentence passed by the court. They both returned to their jobs at the *African Standard* when they eventually received their freedom.

CONSTITUTIONAL CHANGES, 1943 TO 1951.

Other political trials followed the case of R.-v-Thomas and Boyle[77] but, by 1943, with the detention and conviction of many of the leaders of the West African Youth League, there was relative quiet in the political scene in Sierra Leone. In any event, the Second World War was still on and there was unlikely to be any significant change in the constitution during the currency of hostilities with Germany. However, the colonial office was painfully aware of the need for change in all the West African countries and the need for this became very acute as the defeat of the Nazis was imminent. In November 1938, the government had taken the significant constitutional step of appointing a Standing Finance Committee of the Legislative Council. This committee comprised only two official members, the colonial secretary and the colonial treasurer. All the unofficial members were in it, that is to say, the seven African and three European members. This was the first organ to have an "unofficial" African majority in Sierra Leone.

In 1943, the governor announced that he was appointing two Africans to the Executive Council. The first two people he appointed were Mr J. Fowell Boston, a lawyer, and at the material time, editor of the *Daily Guardian*, and paramount chief A. George Caulker. The appointment of these two men to the policy-making body of the government was, undoubtedly, a significant constitutional break-through, but did this satisfy the demands for representation? Did it remove the tensions and anxieties which had built up and developed over the years when demands for constitutional change were being consistently frustrated? Was this an attempt to establish effective communication between the government and the people of both the colony and the protectorate? Were the governor's nominees the kind of people who could have fulfilled this role, assuming this was government's intention?

It cannot be said that the nomination by the governor of two Sierra Leoneans to serve on the Executive Council was a serious attempt to improve the country's constitutional position. Moreover, the manner of their selection and appointment did not suggest a genuine reflection of the British Government's wish to accede to popular demands for further constitutional advance. Mr Fowell Boston was a distinguished man, undoubtedly, but he was not a member of the Legislature and had never held any elective office in central or local government. He was never, therefore, subjected to the process of popular election and could not be regarded as the people's choice. On the contrary, as the proprietor and editor of his daily newspaper the *Daily Guardian*, he was an outspoken critic of the West African Youth League. He had opposed many

---

77 George Thomas was again tried with Willoughby in 1942 for an article critical of prison conditions. He was sentenced to a year's imprisonment and Willoughby to a fine of £5 or 1 month.

In November 1940, the respected editor of the *Daily Mail*, Mr T. J. Thompson, a barrister and one-time member of the pre-1924 Advisory Council and Mayor of Freetown was charged with libel and tried. He was acquitted. Public opinion regarded this prosecution as a farce.

demands for change and was widely regarded as a loyal supporter of the colonial government and an anti-nationalist. He had written scathingly about the rise of nationalist fervour generated by the activities of the West African Youth League and also, of Mr Sydney Boyle, who had been appointed to the Post-War Reconstruction Committee for the Rehabilitation of African Troops and Ratings by the government. On that occasion, he said:

> Government must be careful about the past records and associations of people whom it puts into committees .... and the subversive activities of traitors and fifth columnists in our midst.

The governor's nominee from the protectorate was Chief A. Caulker. He was a member of the Legislature and had held his seat by the grace of the government. There had still not been any question of elections in the protectorate and British policy had remained as it was in 1924, namely, that the people of the protectorate should be represented by their chiefs, nominated to serve by the government. Chief Caulker had not shown himself to be a nationalist. Nor had he contributed much, if any thing at all, to the debates of the Legislative Council. He was more or less, like all the other chiefs, a silent member of the legislature.

Comments on the Appointment of Africans to the Executive Council.
In 1943, executive authority was vested in the Crown as part of the exercise of the prerogative and this power was exercised by the governor on behalf of the Crown.[78] The governor had a wholly official Executive Council to assist him in his administration of the Colony and Protectorate of Sierra Leone. Asking Africans to share this authority was an important first step towards responsible government. The importance of this step was minimised by the manner in which it was taken. There was no consultation by the governor with the elected members of the Legislature from whose ranks one would have expected the first member of the Executive to be appointed. After all, this was a cardinal feature of the British system of Cabinet Government. In the United States, members of the cabinet are drawn from outside the legislature. Undoubtedly, there is a lot to be said for that system but the colonies were being grounded in the traditions of British democracy and so there was really no excuse for not selecting one of the elected members of the Legislative Council, except one concludes, inevitably, that this was a deliberate policy of the government to keep the Creoles out of government. For, it is submitted, that one of the basic assumptions of any attempted introduction of a form of responsible government in colonial territories is the participation by the people in the process of choice. Surely, it is not the governor who determines the eligibility of persons for political office, unless it can be argued that the governor was a better judge than the electorate of the interests of the governed and the persons appropriately suited to safeguard those interests — an absurd submission.[79]

78 See Halsbury: *Laws of England* 3rd Ed. Volume 6 p.318.

The war ended in 1945 and thereafter there was renewed agitation in West Africa, notably Nigeria and the Gold Coast for further political advance. Each of the four British West African possessions now began to work on its own for independence. In Sierra Leone, the leaders of the West African Youth League had been effectively eliminated from the political scene. Wallace-Johnson and George Thomas were ineffective. Boyle, decided to leave Sierra Leone for good and has never returned. So the organised opposition to the colonial regime which was initiated by the Youth League had petered out. However, the Ratepayers' Associations continued to be the only political force, and remained very active in local government. Later on the National Council of Sierra Leone was formed. All these parties were particularly colony oriented and they were designed to watch the interest of the colony. The National Council put forward Dr. G. C. E. Reffell as its candidate and in 1944, he spoke up in the Legislative Council for further constitutional advance and said that Britain should carry out her pledge of self-government in each of the West African countries under its rule.[80] Another member of the Legislative Council, Mr Otto During, then an urban elected member, said that the people of Sierra Leone should take a more effective part in the government of the country. He said that the Legislative Council should now consist of an unofficial majority. Interestingly enough, there was also a demand for further constitutional change from Paramount Chief A. George Caulker. The contributions of these three members of the legislature are short and can be briefly set out:

Paramount Chief Caulker said:[81]

I hope the Government of Sierra Leone has already drawn up plans to make this dependency what it should be after the war in the spirit of the Atlantic Charter.

Dr Reffell said:[82]

he hoped to see Britain's pledge carried out; that of self-government eventually in each territory.

Otto During moved the following motion:[83]

This council is of the opinion that the time has come when the people of Sierra Leone should take a more effective part in the government of the country and in order to harmonise with the principle of democratic government which is the prevailing policy

---

79 When the first African was to be appointed to the Advisory Council in 1863, the governor consulted the Mercantile Association. In Sierra Leone, apart from the West African Youth League, there were Ratepayers' Associations which put up candidates for election. These could have been consulted about an acceptable nominee. However, see the Governor's Address to the Legislative Council (1943 Leg. Co. Debates) explaining the Secretary of State's Despatch. Also press comments from the *African Standard*, the *Daily Mail* and the *Weekly News* for March, 1943.
80 See Debates of the Leg. Co. 1944.
81 See Debates of the Leg. Co. No. 1 of Session 1943. 43-4, p.65.
82 See Leg. Co. Debates 1944 No. 1 of Sess. 44-5, p.67.
83 See Leg. Co. Debates 1944 No. 1 of Sess. 44-5, p.118.

of His Majesty's Government respectfully requests . . . that the constitution of the Legislative Council be amended to provide for an unofficial majority.

The governor in response to the motion of the Hon. Otto During, said:[84]

Let me remind the council that over 90 per cent of the total population of Sierra Leone is in the protectorate and it cannot be denied that a vast majority of these people are in a backward state of political development . . . . Let us consider what would be the practical effect of changing the constitution of this council on the lines indicated by the Hon. the first urban member's motion. At present the representation of the colony in the Legislative Council is disproportionately high having regard to the enormously greater proportion of population in the protectorate, which incidentally is the main source of wealth of Sierra Leone. If the composition of the council were changed to provide for an official majority it would be essential to take this into account and to give the government a representation more in accordance with facts. It is my considered opinion that, pending the social development of the protectorate . . . . it would be clearly premature to consider the constitution of an unofficial majority in this council.

The pressure for change continued in West Africa generally. It reached its greatest intensity in the Gold Coast but the repercussions of the demands there were felt in all the other territories. The Sierra Leone Government responded by making some proposals which, at first, indicated that they were considering separate legislatures for the colony and the protectorate. They set up a Protectorate Assembly for the protectorate.

THE PROTECTORATE ASSEMBLY, 1946 TO 1955

BACKGROUND.
Following the appointment of Africans to the Executive Council in 1943, it became increasingly apparent that demands for the development of separate institutions for both colony and protectorate were being made with increasing intensity. The colony had at its disposal already well established forums and conduit pipes for putting forward its own demands for constitutional change. The Ratepayers' Associations[85] for example, were well organised and they filled the vacuum created by the absence of organised political parties. They pressed for advanced constitutional changes. In the protectorate, there was nothing similar to fulfil this role. In fact, there was nothing in existence remotely similar to a political party and there was no way in which public opinion could be

---

84 See Debates of the Legislative Council 1944 and the Despatch from the Governor, Sir George Beresford-Stooke to Sir Arthur Creech-Jones, dated 4th Jan. 1949.
85 The Ratepayers' Associations first developed for purely local matters and to put forward candidates for the municipal elections. Later they became the body putting forward candidates for national elections.

reflected. Nor did there appear to be any desire for one. The chiefs were autocratic and with 95 per cent illiteracy, there was no great demand from any quarter for the constitutional privilege of representation. The British Government were happy and recognised the chiefs as the spokesmen for their people. Later events proved that representation of protectorate interests by chiefs was not acceptable to the protectorate people in general, particulary the growing body of intellectuals who were now emerging on the political scene. The criticism and dissatisfaction of the new elite apart, it is a moot question whether in fact this kind of representation was in any way effective. The record of debates in the Sierra Leone Legislative Council shows that the chiefs were utterly impotent in the legislature. They rarely participated in debates and their silence on vocal and important issues was striking. On the other hand, they voted with sickening regularity with the Colonial Government and this tended to support the criticism that they were stooges of the administration who dared not depart from government policy. In this respect, it would be right to say that they represented no one but the Colonial Government which appointed them. Whenever they were bold enough to speak up and demonstrate some kind of independent thought, their contributions were ineffective and feeble. It is therefore not surprising that the new elite from the protectorate became quickly and wholly disillusioned with the representation which had been thrust upon them. They looked with envy at the colony politicians and the articulate manner in which they carried out their duties. They felt that having their own elected members would ensure the full projection of the needs and aspirations of the communities which they served.

The chiefs themselves became increasingly aware of their ineffectiveness in the legislature and began to hold Chiefs' Conferences. These conferences began in or about the year 1940 and by the year 1944 they were being regularly held in about ten of the twelve districts of the protectorate.[86] The chiefs found these conferences useful as they were able to discuss among themselves matters affecting the protectorate. They were free in their meetings from the presence and influence of the colony politicians whose interests were being put forward with consummate skill by well seasoned and intelligent politicians. The chiefs in their conferences began to formulate, for the consideration of the colonial government, common policies and approaches to problems of economic development. In the year 1945, the governor proposed that the conference, which had by now achieved some modicum of governmental recognition and support, should be replaced by formal meetings between the chiefs and district commissioners with the latter chairing the meetings as presidents. Paramount Chief Julius Gulama protested in the Legislative Council against this proposal on the ground that this would be a retrograde step since chiefs would not "be as free to speak their

---

[86] The first one was held in Moyamba. See Debates of the Legislative Council No. 1 of Sess. 1944-5 p.3.
Also Debates 1945-6. Nov. 30, 1945 at p.158.

minds in such meetings in the presence of the district commissioners as they had been in their conferences".[87]

At about the same time, a small band of protectorate professionals and intellectuals got together and formed the Sierra Leone Organisation Society. Their main objective was to get a body which would be able to represent protectorate interests as they alleged that the chiefs had not been able to do this.[88] After its formation, the Sierra Leone Organisation Society (SOS) claimed to be the authentic voice of the protectorate tribes instead of the chiefs. The birth of the SOS meant that there was in existence now two groups claiming to represent the protectorate, that is, the chiefs on the one hand and the new educated elite on the other. Strains were developing between the two groups and as the colony was increasing the tempo of its demands for a new constitution and it became painfully apparent that they could not be held back by the unfavourable climate for political change then existing in the protectorate, the Colonial Government then proposed the establishment of a new forum to meet the needs of the protectorate and to fill the vacuum created by an absence of a debating institution. The body designed to meet this contingency was called The Protectorate Assembly.

The Protectorate Assembly was set up as an advisory body to the government on protectorate affairs. This was the ostensible reason for its creation. It was however, an unconvincing one. To establish a representative assembly merely to tender advice to the governor and the British Government on protectorate matters, seemed a dubious and curious manner of securing advice. After all, the British Government had, for over fifty years, governed the protectorate and had been able to obtain all the advice it required through the chiefs as well as through the administrative machinery set up in the districts. It is therefore reasonable to speculate that there were other cogent and more compelling reasons for the establishment of the Protectorate Assembly. It is suggested that these were the factors which led to the creation of the assembly.

> FIRST: There had been persistent demands in the colony for further constitutional change. Progress was already being made in the other West African countries and Sierra Leone, which had been in the forefront of political and educational advance in West Africa, was being overtaken by events. The colony's progress was being held back by the backward state of things in the protectorate.
>
> SECOND: The tempo of constitutional change in Sierra Leone was much too rapid for the protectorate which was wholly unprepared for the whirlwind which was blowing across its borders. Practically the whole of the hinterland was terribly backward intellectually and educationally. The situation in both

---

[87] See Debates of the Leg. Co. 1945-6 at p.158.
[88] Those instrumental in forming the SOS as the group came to be called, were Dr John Karefa Smart; Mr Doyle Sumner; Mr R. B. Kowa; Mr Frank Anthony.
All of them subsequently became ministers of government.

the social and economic fields was much the same. There could not be a merger or the establishment of joint institutions for the colony and the protectorate without some desperate moves being made to up-grade the standards of life in every sector of governmental activity in the protectorate.

THIRD: There was no institution already developed or specifically set up for the protectorate which would identify possible leaders of public opinion other than the chiefs. Unlike the Municipal Council in Freetown, the district councils had not developed properly and did not have the expertise or skills of local government. Nor were its members particularly competent in dealing with the complex matters of modern government and administration. Representation at the district level was still indirect.

FOURTH: The new protectorate elite were largely professional or businessmen who did not reside in their home districts. They were all mainly in the colony which provided a base for them to launch their attacks on both the government and the colony politicians. They did not have a school to train them for democracy and entry to the legislature was closed to them as they were not chiefs.

FIFTH: In the face of the post war agitation which rapidly developed in the colony and the renewed demands for progress by the colony alone without tagging the protectorate behind, the Colonial Government could not keep the colony's progress at a standstill to await the protectorate.

SIXTH: The Colonial Government was a dilemma. It saw Sierra Leone's path to nationhood as best developed through the merger of the colony and the protectorate. The attempted merger had failed but separate development did not seem the right answer. Without admitting it, they realised that there was a need to find some way in which persons from the protectorate other than chiefs could participate in the political process. To do that required the establishment of a franchise and some method of selecting political representatives.

SEVENTH: The protectorate public had never been involved in the process of voting and they were ignorant of the elective process. There was thus a clear need to settle the problem of how to articulate public opinion about the whole process of national government and secure their support and co-operation.

EIGHTH: Tribal custom in the protectorate relegated women to an inferior position in the social stratification of the tribe. Some time was therefore needed to improve the educational facilities and to get the public to accept that women were part and parcel of the elective process.

In the light of these considerations, it is submitted that the Protectorate Assembly was designed (a) As a reserve legislature for the protectorate to take over the functions of the Legislative Council should demands for separate development reach such proportions that the government had to yield to them. (b) To serve as a training ground for protectorate members and to initiate the idea of political representation through publicly elected representatives instead of nominated chiefs. (c) To counter colony demands for self-government.

THE PROTECTORATE ASSEMBLY.

The Protectorate Assembly was inaugurated in 1946. It had a total of forty-two members, made up as follows:[89]

10 official members.[90]

6 nominated unofficial members of whom four were Africans.

26 other members, two each from the thirteen districts of the protectorate.[91]

The first meeting of the Protectorate Assembly was held at Bo from the 23rd to the 26th July 1946. Before long, it emerged that a major objective of the whole exercise was the unification of the various tribes of the protectorate. Later, this newly found unity and co-operation was used to exclude the colony Africans from holding any positions in government and substituting them in the Legislature by the protectorate members.

Paramount Chief Julius Gulama at the first meeting of the Protectorate Assembly, said inter alia:[92]

> Whoever thought that the Limba man, and the Kono man and all the tribes of the protectorate could meet like this today without exchanging swords? Whoever thought that all these tribes would meet together in one place and sit together in common?

The Protectorate Assembly held twelve meetings before it was dissolved in 1955. During the seventh meeting, the governor in a speech to the assembly, announced an increase in the representation of the chiefs to six.[93] The assembly continued to debate national issues, including constitutional matters and when eventually, the government was satisfied that further progress could be made on the colony/protectorate merger without any great danger or risk to life and property, the assembly was dissolved.

EVALUATION OF PROTECTORATE ASSEMBLY.

Legally, the Protectorate Assembly was the creation of statute. Further than that its legal power or authority in the Government of Sierra Leone was nil. It had no legislative powers and its influence on political developments was not very significant. Its resolutions were not binding on the government; they did not have the force or effect of law. Heads of departments sat in the assembly and their presence there together with the Chief Commissioner of the Protectorate gave it some semblance of

---

89 See: Laws of Sierra Leone 1946. Cap. 185 Sec. 7(2).
90 Sec. 7 of Ordinance No. 27 of 1945. These were one European: one Creole business member: one missionary and two protectorate educated Africans.
91 All of them chiefs.
92 See Proceedings of the Protectorate Assembly — 1st Meeting, 1946.
93 In the first four meetings, each of the elected members was a paramount chief. Thus the membership was heavily dominated by chiefs.

authority, but no more. Its debates were noted by the government and undoubtedly, must have been given some recognition and effect in the corridors of power. But, legally, they were of no effect whatsoever. The assembly did not exercise any powers of supervision over the officers administering the government of the protectorate. The district commissioners still exercised their powers and authorities subject only to the control of the governor and in so far as delegated thereto, by the Chief Commissioner of the Protectorate. The most that could happen to them was that their actions could be mentioned unfavourably in the debates of the Protectorate Assembly. But the record shows that this was hardly the case.

In the circumstances, the most that could be said for this unique institution is, that it was a glorified and prestigious debating club, designed to produce the legislators whom the protectorate so badly needed, before they could be elected into the Legislative Council in Freetown. Thus, the Protectorate Assembly proved to be a training ground for those inhabitants of the protectorate who were later to take their place in the Legislature of the colony.[94] The assembly duplicated as much as possible the rules and practices, and copied the style and procedure, of the Legislative Council. Had the colony's demands for independence been sustained to the point where the British Government would have had no alternative but to grant it, then, quite conceivably, the Protectorate Assembly would have ripened and developed into the Legislative Assembly of the protectorate.

The Protectorate Assembly was dissolved after it had been in existence for merely nine years. During that period of time, with demands for separate development of both parts of the country petering out, there was really no further justification for keeping the assembly in existence. By the time it was dissolved, the Constitution of 1951 had been bulldozed through and henceforth, the Legislative Council of the colony and the protectorate were one and the same. In substance and in fact, the demands of the protectorate for increased representation based on the preponderance of its population, had been conceded and the claims for separate development and separate legislatures, effectively put to rest.

*PROPOSALS FOR THE RECONSTITUTION OF
THE LEGISLATIVE COUNCIL.*

> Let it be always remembered that life is short; that knowledge is endless and that many doubts deserve not to be cleared.
>
> Dr Johnson — *The Idler*

---

94 The merger of the colony and protectorate, two separate dependencies, was the most complete example of multiple dependencies which attained a single legislative council. Sierra Leone was the first territory "where the governmental fusion became complete and the distinction between colony and protectorate lost its constitutional meaning". See Wright: *British Colonial Constitutions*, 1947. (O.U.P.) pp.83-5.

The crucial issue which faced the Sierra Leone Government between 1946 and 1951 when a new constitution was introduced was that of representation. The government had accepted as a matter of principle that there was no longer any necessity to have an official majority in the Legislative Council. The question of whether there should be one or two Legislative Councils for Sierra Leone had been resolved in favour of the merger between the colony and the protectorate. The issue now was the single question of how many representatives should there be from each sector. In the words of Lord Milner "the only justification for keeping an official majority in any colony is that we are convinced that we are better judges, for the time being, of the interests of the native population than they are themselves".[95] Both the colony and protectorate had now, apparently shown to the satisfaction of the Crown that they could determine their own interests, and the British Government was prepared to hand over the reins of government in a modified form.

There was a hot debate in the colony about the form of the proposed reconstituted Legislative Council. The colony politicians, quite naturally, sought to have an unofficial majority made up of a preponderance of elected members from the colony. The protectorate members on the other hand, saw this as a wonderful opportunity to take advantage of their superiority in numbers. The outstanding problem which stood in the way of the protectorate was the absence of a sufficiently large number of educated men and the absence of an articulate public in possession of the franchise.

The government put forward some proposals for the reconstitution of the Legislative Council in August 1947. Both the colony and the protectorate did not find these palatable and criticised them. In the colony, the old arguments about the merger of both sections of the country emerged, although there were very objective criticisms of the proposals as a whole in the interest of both sections of the country. For example, the *Weekly News* "suggested that the chiefs did not represent the popular will" and to have them in the new legislature "would amount to a conclave of feudal lords diluted by the elected municipal and rural members and the official membership".[96] It suggested, reflecting the strength of popular public opinion in the colony, that there should be a literacy qualification not only for entry into the Legislative Council but also among the voting public in the protectorate.

The Sierra Leone Organisation Society[97] put forward a memorandum dated 29th September 1947 on the subject and they also objected to the proposals. They claimed that "the common people .... are entitled to even more representation .... than the natural rulers" and that they would not get it since the district commissioners and the Protectorate Assembly "are merely composed of the natural rulers and the tribal

---

95 See TAYLOR: "*The Political Development of Tanganyika*" (1963).
96 See *Weekly News* of Sept. 13, 1947. "Critique of the Governor's Constitutional Proposals". The governor was Sir Hubert Stevenson.
97 The SOS was now the recognised articulate spokesman for the protectorate interests.

authorities and, therefore, are not democratic institutions from which an elected body can be formed for the people of the protectorate". As a result of these objections the proposals, known as "the Stevenson proposals", were sent to a Select Committee for consideration. The committee's membership was as follows:

    The Attorney-General.
    All unofficial members of the Legislative Council.
    The Chief Commissioner of the Protectorate.
    Three co-opted extraordinary members[98]
      Dr R. S. Easmon.
      Mr A. H. C. Barlatt and
      Dr N. A. Cox-George
    Four paramount chiefs

This committee met without the three co-opted members who resigned because they protested about the presence of the chief commissioner of the protectorate whose presence, they thought would be inimical to free and fair discussions between the chiefs and the colony representatives.[99]

Originally, Sir Hubert Stevenson had proposed that there should be an enlarged legislature whose total membership would be twenty three made up as follows:

    7 official members.
    2 unofficial members nominated by the governor to represent business.
    4 colony elected members.
    10 protectorate members 'elected' by the Protectorate Assembly.

The Select Committee finally recommended an increase in the colony representation to seven. The Protectorate Assembly had debated the matter and had refused a proposal that the colony representation should be increased from 4 to 5. The question of literacy was debated in the Select Committee which declined to make any recommendation on the matter on the ground that it was "too delicate".[100] The matter was taken to the Legislative Council which approved of the report of the Select Committee. The governor recommended that the question of literacy be left to the district councils, and this was agreed. A despatch was sent to the Secretary of State for the Colonies who accepted the revised proposals. The SOS sent a memorandum of protest to the Secretary of State for the Colonies and the colony politicians continued to oppose them.

The wrangling between the colony and the protectorate continued unabated throughout 1948 and the government sought to resolve the impasse it had created by getting the colony representatives to accept the

---

98 These members were elected at a combined meeting of the Freetown Ratepayers. It was a mammoth public meeting at which the proposals were discussed.

99 There were thus, seven chiefs in all in this committee. The opinion was widespread that they could not discuss freely in the presence of the chief commissioner or the district commissioners whose influence over them was complete and autocratic.

100 See Sessional Paper No. 7 of 1948, p.2 "Report of the Select Committee."

proposals. He did not succeed. On the 21st December 1948, the Hon. Otto I. E. During, moved in the Legislative Council, that in the light of the widespread opposition to the proposed constitutional changes, their implementation be deferred until they had been reconsidered.[101] One of the protectorate chiefs, Bai Koblo bitterly attacked the motion and demonstrated considerable animosity to the Creoles of the colony. The government said they did not propose to interfere in the matter and the motion was passed.[102]

Sir George Beresford-Stooke was appointed to replace Sir Hubert Stevenson who had lost the confidence of both sections of the country. On the 4th January 1949 Beresford-Stooke sent a Confidential Despatch to the Hon. A. Creech-Jones,[103] in which he expressed his preference for the admission of non-chiefs into the legislature from the protectorate. He said that "when framing a new constitution, particular attention should be had to the necessity of providing adequate opportunity for the expression of the opinion of the common people in general and the educated masses in particular . . . It would be a mistake to overlook the claims to representation put forward by the educated classes in the protectorate."

In May 1950, when there had still been no compromise between the colony and the protectorate, the governor recommended that the 1948 proposals of the Select Committee be implemented.[104] The governor recommended that literacy should be a requirement for membership in the new Legislative Council.[105]

In July, the Colonial Government took steps to prepare the necessary constitutional instruments to bring in the Stevenson proposals in a "slightly modified form". In August 1950, all the colony political groups joined together under the name and style of the National Council of Sierra Leone, except a group led by the Rev E. N. Jones, alias, Lamina Sankoh, known as the People's Party. The colony groups were urging that the reins of government should be handed to the articulate majority of Creoles in the colony. Lamina Sankoh's group sought closer co-operation with the protectorate and supported the joint institutions for the colony and the protectorate. Lamina Sankoh's People's Party had

---

101 See Leg. Co. Debates 25th Sess. No. 1 p.66 of Dec. 21 1948.
102 Ibid p.73. See, however, Sir Hubert Stevenson's ADDRESS in the Debate in the Leg. Co., Leg. Co. Debates No. 1 of Sess. 1944-5 at p.120 on the Unofficial majority. It was strange the government declined to intervene.
103 See Sierra Leone Archives — Despatch dated 4/1/49.
104 See Sessional Paper No. 2 of 1950, pp.1-2. Reconstruction of the Legislative Council of Sierra Leone.
105 The British Government through the governor, had expressed the view that "it would be unwise initially to exclude potentially useful members on the grounds of their inability to pass a literacy test in English". This was contrary to the 1924 proposals and it appeared they were playing ducks and drakes over this issue. The SOS in their memorandum to the Sec. of State in 1948, said that they "humbly pray that literacy qualifications be imposed". See also proceedings of the 3rd meeting of the Protectorate Assembly. By 1947, 20 per cent of the 200 chiefs were literate and 59 per cent of those who were in the Protectorate Assembly were also literate.

The 1924 Constitution

very little support in the colony.

In October 1950, the National Council petitioned the king in council proposing either[106]
  (a) the annexation of the protectorate and a declaration that all its inhabitants be British subjects, or
  (b) the separation of the colony from the protectorate and the granting to each section of its own legislature with full powers and that the colony in the meantime should proceed to full self-government.

As can be expected, neither proposal was accepted by the Colonial Office and the governor then proceeded to implement his proposals. In April 1951, Lamina Sankoh's People's Party, joined forces with the SOS and formed the Sierra Leone People's Party, eight months after the formation of the National Council in the Colony. The People's Party thus attracted a number of Creoles to its membership. In September 1950, Dr Margai, who had been elected President of the Sierra Leone People's Party, in a speech during the Seventh Session of the Protectorate Assembly attacked the colony elite. He said, inter alia:[107]

> We are very much unfortunate to have with us in this country, a handful of foreigners whose leaders, whatever one may do, can never bring themselves to wipe off the superiority complex, and they imagine themselves more like Europeans than Africans, which is indeed a very sad state of affairs and moreover, they have never impressed us as being sincere in their actions towards us ...

The governor then indicated that he intended to recommend that the new constitution be brought into effect "next year". Arrangements were made to streamline the district councils so that they could provide the 'elected' members for the new legislature. The stage was then set for the introduction of the Constitution of 1951.

---

106 See The *Weekly News* of Feb. 17, 1951.
107 Proceedings of the 7th Session of the Protectorate Assembly, pp.28-31.

CHAPTER VIII

CONSTITUTIONAL CHANGES 1951-56

The Constitution of 1951:
On the 19th November 1951, the British Government issued an order in council which was published in Sierra Leone as the Sierra Leone Legislative Council Order in Council, Public Notice No. 106 of 1951 which introduced the 1951 Constitution of Sierra Leone. This order revoked the 1924 Constitutional Instruments and brought into force a new constitution for the colony and protectorate of Sierra Leone. The constitution provided for a Legislative and an Executive Council and for an unofficial majority. It intended to introduce representative government, but as there was still no elective principle in the protectorate, this ideal was not achieved, since the members returned by the district councils were not truly elected representatives of the people.[1] Under the new constitution, the Legislative Council was composed of the following:

Official Members
The Governor (as President).
The Chief Commissioner of the Protectorate.
The Attorney-General.
The Financial Secretary.
The Director of Medical Services.
The Director of Agriculture.
The Director of Education.

Unofficial Members
Seven elected members from the colony.
Fourteen elected members from the protectorate, of whom one was to be nominated by the Governor and one nominated by the Protectorate Assembly
Two nominated members to represent trade and commerce

---

1 Under the District Councils Act at this period of time, members of the district councils were nominated thereto by the administration. A list was provided and drawn up by the district commissioner of members of the tribal authority and it was from this list that the nominees to the councils were drawn. The protectorate assembly 'elected' members from the district councils.

The Executive Council under the new constitution was to be made up of the following:
> *Four Ex-Officio members,* i.e.
> The Colonial Secretary.
> The Chief Commissioner of the Protectorate.
> The Financial Secretary.
> The Attorney General,
>   and
> *Six Unofficial Members.*

The constitution provided that there should be not less than four members of the Executive Council. The governor still presided over the Executive Council.

The instruments provided for the election of a Vice-President of the Legislative Council and Sir Ernest Samuel Beoku-Betts who had for many years served as an elected member of the Legislative Council.

There are certain features of this constitution which need pointing out. In doing so, one is reminded of the famous words of John Stuart Mill:[2]
> Political institutions are the work of men, they owe their origin and their whole existence to human will. Men did not wake up on a summer morning and find them sprung up. Neither do they resemble trees which, once planted, 'are aye growing', while men 'are sleeping'. In every stage of their existence they are made what they are by voluntary human agency.

The Governor.
The governor under the constitution retained his superiority over everybody in the country. He was superior even to the legislature in the sense that he still retained his powers of veto; he could reserve bills for the king's pleasure; he could introduce legislation for the consideration of the legislature; he had complete control of the executive and of the legislature. He was still firmly in control of the government of the country in spite of the "unofficial majority" in the Legislature. He controlled the judiciary and in every sense of the term he was very much a "Colonial Governor".

The Legislative Council.
The only matter which continued to bedevil the legislature, was its composition. Britain had created a merger between the colony and the protectorate when, on all accounts, the protectorate was ill prepared for this sudden change. Its repercussions were felt all over and there were unpleasant episodes between both parts of the country. It appeared that the British had taken sides with the protectorate already against the colony and this was not something new. Dr Eric Williams, writing in 1931, had commented that "strange as it may seem, the attitude of the British to the educated and westernized Creoles has been one of contempt and ridicule, somewhat analogous to their treatment of the

2 J. S. MILL: Representative Government. 1st Ed. (1861) p.4.

Indian intellectuals and bordering in many instances on outright rudeness". He continued:[3]

> Mr Churchill called it alarming and also nauseating to see Mr Gandhi, a seditious Middle Temple lawyer, now posing as a fakir of a type well known in the East, striding half-naked up the steps of the Viceregal Palace, while he is still organising and conducting a defiant campaign of civil disobedience, to parley on equal terms with the representative of the King-Emperor . . . .The Indian National Congress . . . . represent neither the numbers, the strength, nor the virtue of the Indian people. They merely represent those Indians who have acquired a veneer of Western civilization, and have read all those books about democracy which Europe is now beginning increasingly to discard.

As far as Sierra Leone was concerned, the colony had had a long history of democratic rule, in the sense that most of the traditional values of a democratic society had been introduced even if they had not been justly and fairly applied. For example, the colonial Africans had never been in control of government. The colonial power had always held the reins of government and had on no occasion permitted the Creoles to rule the country. Since the introduction of Crown Colony Government in 1808, this was the very first opportunity that had come their way for active participation in government and just when the apple was dangled before their eyes, the Colonial Government diverted it from the Creoles and pushed it firmly in the hands of the protectorate. The question therefore was what should be the relative strengths of the representation from both sectors? The colony argued that the larger number of seats should be allocated to it because it already had an electoral system in force and a large number of the people in the protectorate were unaccustomed to the western electoral process and did not understand it, nor was there any evidence that, even if they did, they wanted to have their own traditional system replaced by a foreign, complicated system. They reminded the British that their system of "Indirect Rule" was established on the basis of "a rule through the native chiefs, who are regarded as an integral part of the machinery of government, with well defined powers and functions recognised by government and by law, and not dependent on the caprice of an executive officer".[4] Consequently there was room only for token representation in the legislature from the protectorate and that the reins of government should be firmly in the hands of the colony which was a settled colony. On the other hand, the protectorate members argued with equal force that the size of the population was the only meaningful criterion that ought to be taken into account in determining representation of the protectorate in the Legislative Council. The British Government accepted the protectorate viewpoint and granted it greater representation in the legislature.

---

3 See ERIC WILLIAMS: *Documents illustrating the Development of Civilization*. (Harvard University, Washington, DC), Vol. III 1948, p.461.
4 See LORD LUGARD: *Political Memoranda* (1918) p.296.

Constitutional Changes 1951-1956

There was nothing unique about the Legislative Council of 1951. To become a member of the legislature one had to be literate in English; and be over the age of twenty-one years. He had to be either a British subject or a British protected person. Women were not excluded from membership of the legislature. There was a property qualification established.

The functions of the Legislative Council were to make laws for the peace, order and good government of Sierra Leone.

For the protectorate, the membership of the legislature was indirect. First, there were the native authorities called the Tribal Authorities then the District Councils, then the Protectorate Assembly and finally the Legislative Council. A man had to be eligible for membership of the first two, then obtain the support of the third before he graduated to the Legislative Council. So that, as far as the protectorate membership was concerned, the question of membership of the central legislature was one of selectivity, rather than electivity. The ordinary inhabitant had no part in the process of determining who was to be his MP. This was the set-up in 1951 when majority rule arrived in Sierra Leone.

The Executive Council.
The problem of membership of the Legislative Council bogged down the administration when it came to appointing members of the Executive Council. The constitution provided for not less than four members. The governor decided to appoint six Africans. He was himself the President of the Executive, so the constitution ensured that he had full control. He would, at his pleasure allocate portfolios. As he had to choose his executive from among the members of the Legislative Council some comment would be made on the first elections under the 1951 Constitution.

Elections in the Colony.
The only place where elections, properly so-called, could take place was in the colony. The National Council and the Sierra Leone People's Party put up candidates in all the wards excepting the rural area where the SLPP could not field a candidate. The National Council won five seats in the colony and lost to the SLPP in the east and to an independent candidate, A. G. Randle in the Sherbro urban district. So that on the basis of free and fair elections the National Council won the elections. Mr M. S. Mustapha was returned for the SLPP in the east, and A. G. Randle, the independent candidate in Bonthe, later on declared for the SLPP.

Elections in the Protectorate.
It would be legally inappropriate to describe what took place in the protectorate as "elections" in the strict sense of that word. However, the candidates were voted for, not by the people, but by the tribal authorities whose names were in the district council lists. The chiefs won eight of these seats and in the process defeated three of the candidates who were

solidly backed by the SLPP. Dr M. A. S. Margai was returned unopposed. The Protectorate Assembly chose Mr Albert Margai (later Sir Albert) and Mr Siaka P. Stevens as its representatives. The SLPP were suspicious that the British were working against the election of educated Africans.[5]

These results presented the governor with a dilemma and he suggested that there should be a coalition in the Executive Council. The reaction of Dr Margai was negative. He wanted all the seats and commented "We have had four years of this". On the 28th November 1951, in a speech in the Legislative Council the governor said that unofficial members would have to be persons who enjoyed the confidence of a majority of the elected members of the Legislative Council. He continued:[6]

> Where there is a well developed 'Party System' it is the practice for His Majesty the King or his representative to send for the leader of the party which commands a majority and invite him to form a government. Here in Sierra Leone today, I am not sure that the party system is yet quite sufficiently developed for me to introduce a procedure modelled mutatis mutandis on that which I have described.
>
> I propose therefore on this occasion to consult unofficial members at a private and informal meeting on the choice of those who are to be invited to form the government.

The private and informal meeting was held the next day in the Chamber of the Legislative Council and there were serious disagreements between the National Council members and the SLPP members. The governor asked, it is submitted illegally, all those who supported the SLPP to stand on one side and those supporting the National Council to stand on the other side. All the chiefs who had not been elected on the basis of the SLPP support, then joined the SLPP. The governor then concluded that the SLPP had a majority and proceeded to appoint members of the Executive from among them.[7] The leader of the SLPP, Dr Margai was then invited to be leader of government business and the Africans appointed to the Executive Council were granted "responsibility" for certain government Departments.[8] Dr H. C. Bankole-Bright and the other elected members of the National Council were incensed at the governor's action and claimed that they had been cheated and robbed of their legitimate success. At first, he declined to accept the title of 'Leader of the Opposition', but later accepted it. On the 29th July 1952, Dr Bankole-Bright moved a motion for independence for the colony alone, but this was defeated.

5 See Letter from H. E. B. John, Secretary of the SLPP dated Sept. 1951 to "*The Observer*" — a weekly newspaper, the organ of the SLPP.
6 Leg. Co. Debates Sess. 1951/2. Nov. 28, 1951, pp.8-9.
7 See Roy Lewis: Sierra Leone for a comment on this action of the governor.
8 See Leg. Co. Debates. Vol. 1 Sessions 1952/3 p.229. Also, pp.208/9. See also 9th Assembly proceedings of the Protectorate Assembly, 1952. The elections were held in 1952.

Constitutional Changes 1951-1956

The Validity of the Constitution is challenged.

The colony representatives were extremely annoyed and disappointed that the governor, had, so to speak, thrust down the Stevenson Constitution on the country and imposed a protectorate majority on the colony. This was anathema to the colony as a whole and steps were taken to test the constitutionality of the 1951 Constitution. Mr S. E. Balogun-Palmer who had been a member of the National Council and was in the forefront of the politics of the colony teamed up with others to sue the governor for a declaration that the Statutory Instruments under which the 1951 Constitution was made, were ultra vires and void. The plaintiffs contended inter alia that the constitution had been made and promulgated under and by virtue of the Foreign Jurisdiction Act 1890 *"and* of all other powers" enabling him (His Majesty) in that behalf. Since Sierra Leone was not a foreign possession of His Majesty, the plaintiffs contended that a constitution for the country, in so far as it was applicable to the colony could not be made under powers derived from a statute not applicable to it. Consequently, the constitution was void and inapplicable to the colony of Sierra Leone.

The Attorney-General appeared on behalf of the governor, the defendant in the suit,[9] and he took out a motion before the Supreme Court, under the rules, praying that the writ be struck out and the claim dismissed, on the ground that it was frivolous and vexatious and an abuse of the process of the court. The motion was heard by Chief Justice Sir Allan Chalmers Smith. He reduced the matter into a simple determination of whether or not the Statutory Instruments, No. 611, having been made under the Foreign Jurisdiction Act 1890 AND other powers, could apply to the colony. He answered the question in the affirmative. He said that the preamble to the instruments contained a recital to the effect that they had been made under and by virtue of a specific enactment and other powers. He said that the words "and of all other powers enabling him in that behalf" were intended to be a specific reference to the powers of the Crown under the British Settlements Acts, 1843 to 1945 through which the Crown derived authority to legislate for the colony of Sierra Leone. He declared that the intention of the Crown had clearly been to merge the colony and the protectorate into one single constitutional unit and that 'Sierra Leone' had been defined as meaning the colony and protectorate put together, and that there had been established only one Legislative Council in and for Sierra Leone, that is,

---

9 See PALMER-v-BERESFORD-STOOKE 1950-56 African Law Reports, (Sierra Leone Series) p.284.

the whole territory.[10] The learned Chief Justice further went on to say that the King-in-Council could legislate either expressly or impliedly for Sierra Leone and that there was no necessity for any express reference to the British Settlements Acts from which he derived his authority; that the words 'Foreign Jurisdiction Act, 1890' should not be construed eiusdem generis so as to restrict the authority of His Majesty in Council to the Foreign Jurisdiction Act, 1890.[11]

Without elaborating on the point, he based his judgment on the assumption that the governor of Sierra was in fact the government of Sierra Leone. Consequently he refused to deal with the following questions which had been raised squarely for determination in the action:
(a) Whether the governor was right in permitting the formation of political parties for the protectorate just prior to the allocation of portfolios when the elections in the protectorate had not been contested along party political lines and,
(b) Whether there was room for a government and opposition in the Legislative Council in the circumstances and whether, if so, the National Council ought not to form the government,
(c) Whether the governor was right in providing a special salary from public funds for the leader of the opposition.

An appeal was lodged against the decision of the Hon. Chief Justice to the West African Court of Appeal which upheld the lower court's decision.

It is submitted that the Supreme Court was wrong in law in upholding the Attorney-General's motion and dismissing the action without a hearing on its merits. The issues were of fundamental constitutional importance and were far from being frivolous and vexatious. Had it gone on to trial, no doubt the court would have found it necessary to pronounce against the validity of the statutory instruments because there had been an obvious mistake in promulgating the statutory instruments under the wrong statute. It is pretty obvious that the Crown could certainly not take powers under the Foreign Jurisdiction Act, 1890 to legislate for the colony as it had none. The judgment may have been

10 See 1950-56 A.L.R. 284. Note: Blyden, in considering the 1952 case of Palmer-v-Stooke is in error in assuming that the Gold Coast Protectorate was not annexed formally. He refers to the Ghana Act of Independence of 1957 which "was brought into being without any formal parliamentary act of annexation affecting the protectorate regions adjacent to the former Gold Coast Colony". It is submitted this is erroneous. Further formal annexation was not at all necessary since the territories had been annexed as early as 1901. See the Gold Coast Order in Council 1901, Sec. 3. This order annexed the protectorate territories and made them all an enlarged *colony* and a settlement. The Order in Council provided that all the protected territories should become part of the colony as from 1886 for all intents and purposes.

11 The Charter of Virginia first formulated the doctrine that British settlers carry the laws of England with them and the powers of the Crown under the common law cease. It was superseded by the British Settlements Act 1887 which empowered the Crown to establish non-representative legislatures in colonies. The first act was passed in 1843, extended in 1860, then in 1887 and finally 1890. Under the various acts the Crown had power to erect courts and to delegate its powers to a legislature of 3 or more persons.

sound on political grounds, but legally it was suspect.

Further developments, post 1952.
In 1953, the governor grouped the various government departments into five divisions and placed each division under an African 'Minister'. The sixth African member of the Executive was a chief who was designated Minister without Portfolio.[12] Later on, these ministers assumed policy making roles although they were still under the firm control of their secretaries who were civil servants. In spite of these developments, the governor remained firmly in the saddle. In essence he was still the only policy maker. He controlled finance, the judiciary, the civil service, defence and foreign affairs. The ministers were obliged to act in accordance with the advice tendered to them by their secretaries. The heads of the major government departments were still expatriate officials and they not only determined what government policy was, but were also dedicated and determined to see it scrupulously carried out. They controlled and "advised" the ministers. This necessarily had its strains and problems particularly as far as the more articulate or forceful of these ministers were concerned. The term 'Leader of the Opposition' was formally conferred by the governor on Dr H. C. Bankole-Bright.

During the 1953/4 Debates of the Legislative Council, Leader of the Opposition, Dr H. C. Bankole-Bright, moved a motion of censure on the governor for participating in politics and alleged that the governor's involvement in political matters was undesirable but even so, inconsistent with his role as the Queen's representative. Attorney-General Mr G. M. Paterson, put the constitutional position clearly and succinctly. He stated:[13]

> The honourable leader of the opposition seeks to apply to Sierra Leone certain rules of constitutional practice which are appropriate to a colony with a more advanced constitution.... The rules which are applicable to the Governor-General of a dominion, are not applicable to the governor of this colony.... The governor of this colony is both in form and in fact the Executive.... The governor may.... constitutionally reject the advice of the Executive Council. This is provided for in the (1951) Constitution.

The Role and Powers of the Ministers.
The 1951 Constitution brought ministerial government to Sierra Leone for the first time in its history. However, the governor was still the government of the territory. What then was the relationship between the ministers and the civil servants?

A cardinal principle of the British civil service is that it must serve faithfully whatever government is in power. It is doubtful whether the ministers of the Sierra Leone government under the 1951 Constitution

---
12 See: Assumption of Ministerial Portfolios, Sessional Paper No. 1 of 1953.
13 See Debates of the Leg. Co. 1953 p.229.

could properly be considered part and parcel of the colonial administration. They seemed to be in an ambivalent position. On the one hand they were keen and anxious to exhibit all the trappings of a national political force opposed to British administration and policy. On the other hand, they were working firmly within a colonial system and being trained for eventual self-government. Did they have any effective power? If they disagreed with the British colonial governor on any point, what would happen? Were the colonial servants expected to act on their instructions or on the instructions of the governor?

The ministers were supposed to have three kinds of powers, namely, discretionary; rule making and policy making. The discretionary powers were vested in the governor who delegated them to the heads of the various government departments. These were not as yet conferred on the ministers. The rule-making powers of government were retained by the governor himself and the policy making powers, he shared with his ministers. It is thus correct to say that whatever powers were available to the ministers were exercised subject to the control of the administration. The government officials did not always accord to the ministers the respect and attention they deserved and there were instances of serious clashes between Mr Albert Margai and the director of education and later on the financial secretary. Unfortunately, there was not much openness in the administration and the activities of government and of the ministers remained a mystery. This led to all sorts of allegations. Prof. Robson very aptly commented that "knowledge by the people about their government is indispensable if democracy is to succeed. The government cannot operate successfully if its activities are veiled in ignorance, misunderstanding and mystery. Public authorities must come into the market place and tell people simply and clearly what they are trying to do and why. They should explain and justify their methods. They should be frank about difficulties and shortcomings. Only by a deliberate effort of this kind can prejudice and ignorance or malevolent criticism be avoided and a discriminating body of public opinion built up".[14]

Unfortunately, there was not much frankness about what the ministers were supposed to be doing and so the criticisms soon began to build up. Typical of the concern felt by the population was the contribution of Mr Wallace-Johnson in the Legislative Council on the 5th November 1956 when he said that rumours were rife of corruption among the ministers, e.g. "that one minister since entering the Executive Council had built houses worth £9,000 and had £5,000 cash in various banks. Another had £6,000 worth of buildings, a transport company and one hundred acres of land; a third was supposed to be able to sign cheques of £30,000".[15] So the impression was created that while the ministers lacked effective power and authority in matters of government, they were nevertheless able to feather their nests by adopting an utterly corrupt posture.

14 W. A. Robson. The Governors and the Governed. (1964) pp.34-36.
15 See Leg. Co. Debates Sess. 1955/6 Vol. VIII, Nov. 5, 1956, pp.520-1.

Constitutional Changes 1951-1956

Further constitutional developments.

In 1954, the Keith-Lucas Commission on Universal Adult Suffrage was set up by government to examine the franchise and make recommendations thereon. The other members were Dr H. C. Bankole-Bright, Leader of the Opposition, Mr A. T. A. Beckley, Mr Y. D. Sesay, Mr Banja Tejan Sie and P. C. Kai Samba. They eventually recommended that universal adult suffrage should be achieved in two stages, first by granting the franchise to adult taxpayers who were males, in the protectorate and then substituting a full adult franchise in the colony in place of the existing income qualification. The recommendations were accepted by government.[16] In December 1954, Dr Margai called for proposals for further constitutional advance.[17] The various groups in the country responded and made their own proposals for further constitutional change. The Sierra Leone People's Party proposed a fifty-two seat legislature with one of three seats in each district to be reserved for a paramount chief. They suggested that all officials should be removed from the Executive Council and that the prime minister should advise the governor on portfolios. The district councils of the protectorate opposed any intended direct election of chiefs to the Legislature. They wanted the district councils or the chiefs themselves to be electoral colleges for returning chiefs to the Legislature. The National Council still argued in favour of the division of the country and said that the experience so far had proved that the proposed joint development of both parts of the country was a sad mistake. The UPP (The United Progressive Party) which had just been formed by a Freetown lawyer, Mr C. B. Rogers-Wright, proposed a forty-three seat legislature with fourteen seats for the colony and restricting chiefs to seven. They advocated a second chamber, a Council of State with limited powers which would accommodate chiefs and others who did not wish to be involved in the rough and tumble of politics but whose opinions could be helpful in national development.

Dr Margai, the leader of the SLPP tried unsuccessfully to convene an all-party conference. The opposition refused to be associated with it or to accept a government majority at such a conference. Finally, he invited those willing to attend and those who did approved the main suggestions which had been put forward by the SLPP. These proposals were submitted to government in October 1955.[18]

In February 1955, there were serious riots in Freetown, allegedly over the economic situation and particularly allegations of the hoarding of rice. A Commission of Inquiry was set up by government to investigate the causes of the disturbances. Three ministers of government, Mr Stevens, Mr Margai and Mr Mustapha alleged that their houses had been attacked.[19] Similar disturbances occurred in the protectorate and the Cox Commission

---

16 Report of the Keith Lucas Commission — Government Printer, Sierra Leone, 1954.
17 See Leg. Co. Debates, Sess. 1954-5 Vol. 1 Dec. 22, 1954, p.413.
18 See Collected Statements on Constitutional proposals — Sept. 1955. Govt. Printer.
19 See Shaw Report — Govt. Printer, 1955.

was set up. The commissioner, Sir Herbert Cox was assisted by Mr A. T. A. Beckley, A. J. Loveridge and Mr Justice S. P. J. Q. Thomas.[20] They reported that there was evidence of greed, extortion and widespread corruption on the part of chiefs. They concluded that these activities had a demoralizing effect on the people. The government did not accept all of the findings of the Cox Commission and put out a statement of its own.[21] In the following year, 1956, the conduct of fifteen chiefs was investigated by three special British commissioners, including two Chief Justices of other colonies. They found the conduct of eleven chiefs to have been subversive of good government. The government accepted their reports and deposed four chiefs. They had the humiliating experience of having to ask five, including the Minister without Portfolio and one who was a member of the Legislative Council to resign. They suspended two, but within four years, five of the chiefs had been reinstated. Not surprisingly, the chiefs formed the Sierra Leone National Association to preserve their sovereign rights "as provided by international law and so as to accord with the treaties and agreements made between various kings and the late Queen Victoria".

Finally, before passing on to the changes of 1956, 'the Leader of Government Business', as Dr Margai had been called, was, in 1954, designated 'Chief Minister'.

In 1956, the Sierra Leone People's Party held a meeting at which it emerged that serious differences had been brewing between Dr M. A. S. Margai, the Leader of the Party, and his brother Albert. This came into the open at a party caucus the following year. However, the government, that year published proposals for a new Legislature and these were approved by the Legislative Council. They were based on the proposals of the Sierra Leone People's Party accepted by the conference called by the prime minister. In spite of the family disagreement within the SLPP it was agreed that the elections should be held in 1957 and approaches were made to the colonial office which, on the 29th November 1956, issued the Sierra Leone House of Representatives Order in Council[22] making provision for a House of Representatives to replace the Legislative Council and establishing a new and enlarged franchise.

THE ELECTIONS OF 1957 AND CONSTITUTIONAL CHANGES FROM 1957 TO 1960

The legislature of 1951 should have been prorogued in 1956. Its life was prolonged to the 8th April 1957 on which date the Legislative Council and Executive Council set up under the 1951 Constitution were

20 Mr Beckley had been a member of the Keith-Lucas Commission. Mr Loveridge was an ex Gold Coast Civil Servant then in the Colonial Office and Mr Justice Thomas retired on the ground of ill-health. He returned to Nigeria and took no part in the final report.
21 See "Statement of the Sierra Leone Government on the Report of the Commission of Inquiry . . . ." page 190.
22 S. I. 1956 No. 1893. See also Sierra Leone Sessional papers Numbers 1 to 3 of 1956 and Debates of the Legislative Council for 1956.

dissolved. The Statutory Instruments of 1956 changed the title of the legislature from Legislative Council to House of Representatives. The membership of the house was fixed at fifty-seven. There was a speaker now who replaced the vice-president. The electoral provisions were not the same for the colony and the protectorate. In the colony, where the elective principle had been in existence since 1924, qualifications for voting were based on an income qualification of £60 per year, or alternatively, residence in a property whose annual assessed value was of the sum of at least £2 per year. Every voter had to be of the age of twenty-one years at least. The franchise was extended to men and women without discrimination.

In the protectorate where there had never been any franchise to vote granted to the ordinary men and women, the Statutory Instruments provided that men over the age of twenty-one years liable to pay head tax could vote. In the case of a woman she had to be over the age of twenty-one, be literate or must have in fact paid tax, or she must have been entitled in her own right to the use and enjoyment of land or of the rents and profits thereof. These electoral provisions were based on the recommendations of the Keith Lucas Commission.

The House of Representatives.
The new House of Representatives was the principal law making body and it replaced the Legislative Council. Its membership was made up of the following:
  Ex-Officio
  The Chief Secretary (the new name for the Colonial Secretary)
  The Attorney-General
  The Chief Commissioner of the Protectorate
  The Financial Secretary
  Elected
  14 from the colony
  25 from the protectorate
  12 chiefs from the protectorate
  Nominated
  2 nominated members
The governor withdrew from the Legislature and he was replaced by the speaker.

Elections.
In May 1957, the Sierra Leone People's Party held a party caucus at which Mr Albert Margai won the majority of votes as leader of the party. He defeated his elder brother, Sir Milton Margai by 22 to 21. Representations were made to him to step down on the ground that in customary law the younger brother did not supercede and take a superior position to the older brother. Eventually he agreed to step down in favour of his elder brother on condition that he was consulted and his

approval obtained before any ministerial appointments were made.[23]

In the elections of 1957, the principal political parties which contested were the National Council, the Sierra Leone Independence Movement;[24] the Kono Progressive Movement and the Sierra Leone People's Party. There were also a large number of independent candidates. The National Council did not win any of the seats. The UPP won nine, two from the colony and seven from the protectorate. The SLPP won eighteen and independents twelve. The chiefs and the independents swung to the SLPP and enabled it to form a government.

It would appear that after the elections Sir Milton Margai reneged on his undertaking with his brother and so there was a split in the ranks of the SLPP. Siaka Stevens resigned[25] and a few weeks later lost an election petition. Albert who had left with him stayed in parliament as a backbencher and attended the constitutional talks held in London with the British Government in December 1957 to arrange for a reconstitution of the Executive Council and to remove all official members therefrom with the exception of the governor. These proposals were approved by the British Government and the Sierra Leone Government then published "The Government's Proposals for Further Constitutional Change".[26]

Mr Wallace-Johnson who by now had fallen out with the National Council formed his own party called the Radical Democratic Party in 1958 but he was unable to attract much support. He gradually faded from the political scene and died in a road accident in Accra in 1965.[27]

Constitutional changes of 1958.

The Sierra Leone Constitution Order in Council 1958[28] introduced the changes which had been agreed upon between the Sierra Leone representatives and the British Government the previous year. These provided for the post of a deputy governor. The governor was named the President of the Executive Council from which all the official members now withdrew, that is to say, the chief secretary, the chief commissioner of the protectorate and the financial secretary. The Attorney-General remained there as chief legal adviser to the government and sat in the Executive "for the purpose of explaining legal technicalities and such like matters".[29] The offices of financial secretary and chief commissioner of the protectorate ceased to exist but the two nominated

---

23 On 4th July 1957, the Conciliation Committee of the SLPP reported success in reconciling both brothers and declared "Dr Margai retains the leadership of the party".
24 This movement was formed by Dr E. W. Blyden. It was eliminated at the elections and fell out of use afterwards. See: Scott: in Mackenzie and Robinson (ed). *Five Elections in Africa.* pp.229 et seq.
25 See *Daily Mail* of July 11, 1957.
26 Sessional Paper Nos. 1 and 2 of 1958.
27 He left the National Council in 1952, joined the UPP in 1954 and formed his own party after the elections.
28 Statutory Instrument No. 1259 of 1958.
29 As explained by Sir Milton Margai. See Debates of the Legislative Council, 1958.

members were retained.[30] Subject to his ultimate responsibility for the peace and good government of Sierra Leone, the governor was required to consult the Executive Council and act on its advice. The governor retained his control over external affairs, internal security, the police and the public service, which were specially reserved to him. Although the financial secretary withdrew from the Executive he remained in the civil service and had control of government finances and was responsible to the Governor and not to the Sierra Leone minister of finance to whom he was an adviser. This brought a cleavage between the SLPP and the government for the first time. It was generated by the young professionals and activists within the SLPP.

On the 14th August 1958, the premier as the chief minister was now designated, appointed Mr M. S. Mustapha, Minister of Finance. It had been widely expected that this position would go to his brother Albert who was excluded from the cabinet altogether. On the 2nd September 1958, Albert Margai and three others resigned from the SLPP[31] and formed the People's National Party (PNP). In January, Dr Margai was knighted by the Queen.

District elections took place in 1959 and the SLPP emerged with 219 candidates, Independents 59 and the PNP 29.

CONSTITUTIONAL CHANGES OF 1960.

On the 25th March 1960, Sir Milton Margai announced that a United Front had been formed. What had happened was, that he had invited all the political parties and interested groups to a round table conference in Freetown to form a "United Front" to approach the British Government with a request for independence for Sierra Leone. After all the preliminaries had been gone through the government proposed certain formal alterations in the constitution and then appointed a delegation of twenty-four, of whom seventeen were members of the House of Representatives to travel for the London talks. On the 23rd June 1960, Statutory Instruments were introduced providing for further constitutional change.[32] The Executive, under these new instruments, was now renamed the Cabinet. The premier, was re-designated the prime minister. The same number of members was retained in the Executive Council, thus, for the second time since the inception of the settlement of Sierra Leone and the first time in the country's history as a colonial territory, Sierra Leone had a wholly African Executive, now called the Cabinet. The instruments provided that the prime minister should "as far as possible" attend and preside at meetings of the cabinet. The reserved powers of the governor were retained but hardly ever applied. A new Public Service Commission and a Judicial Service Commission were created. Thus, Sierra Leone achieved for the first time

30 These were Mr E. D. Morgan (later Sir Ernest D. Morgan a businessman) and Mr McConnachie an expatriate manager.
31 S. T. Navo: A. J. Massally and H. I. Kamara. The first two later became judges. Maigore Kallon another SLPP stalwart resigned a few weeks later and joined the PNP.
32 S. I. No. 1056 of 1960.

since it became a Crown Colony and Protectorate of the British Crown, a somewhat representative Legislature and a full system of responsible government.

On the 1st November 1960, elections were held in the Freetown municipality. The newly formed All People's Congress[33] won two of the three seats and lost the third by a narrow margin.

Following a request made almost a year earlier by the Secretary of State for the Colonies, Sir Alan Lennox-Boyd, a conference was held in London from the 20th April, to the 4th May 1960 between the United Kingdom Government and the representatives from Sierra Leone. The latter delegation was described as an "All Party Delegation" and it went with the specific intention of asking for independence for Sierra Leone within the Commonwealth. The Sierra Leone delegation proposed that the date of independence should be the 7th December 1960, the birthday of Sir Milton Margai. This was not conceded by the British Government as they felt that time was too short for that. Instead, the date agreed upon by both sides was the 27th April 1961. On his return to Sierra Leone, the prime minister announced his intention of forming "a broad based government". He thereafter proceeded to enlarge his cabinet to include representatives of the various parties which had participated in the London conference and had come together at his invitation to form the United Front.

The Constitutional Conference went on very well. Independence was already conceded before the discussions started.[34] The agreement was signed by both sides, but one man, Mr Siaka Stevens, who had been a member of the SLPP Government and had held ministerial positions and who had subsequently broken away from the SLPP refused to sign the agreement with the UK Government. This was ironical in that he had been trained by the British as a trade unionist at Marampa Mines to deal with the industrial disputes which were then emerging. He broke away from the United Front and formed a movement which he called the "Elections before Independence Movement". He had disagreed that Sierra Leone should proceed to independence with the same parliament which was elected in 1957. He contended that the government should have a fresh mandate from the people to take the country into independence. He called for general elections. He was also quite unhappy with the defence arrangements which he thought were inconsistent with the new status of the country. By taking the independent line he did and refusing to go along with the crowd, he carved for himself a niche in the political and constitutional history of Sierra Leone as he later became prime minister and then president of the country. Some of the PNP delegation went along with Stevens in urging that a clear mandate was required from the people of Sierra Leone to

33 See p.195 infra for the story of the formation of the APC.
34 See Cmnd Paper No. 1029 for the speeches of Sir Milton Margai and Mr Iain Macleod. Also, See: Mansergh: *Documents and Speeches on Commonwealth Affairs 1963* (London), p.86.

take them on to independence and that the party winning the elections should do so. The government refused to concede to that.

In the meantime, the old sores were opening up again and an influential body of citizens in the colony started developing further pressures for the colony to be excluded from the independence arrangements being concluded by the Margai Government. They argued that the colony should retain its status for the time being and a petition to that effect was sent to Her Majesty the Queen. The British Government rejected the petition. In November 1960, the House of Representatives in Freetown passed a resolution asking the United Kingdom Government to introduce the necessary legislation to ensure that Sierra Leone became independent on the 27th April 1961.

In February 1961, as the date for independence drew near so the pressures for elections became intensified. The government alleged that the All People's Congress, the new name which the "Elections Before Independence Movement" had adopted, had devised plans to embark upon a campaign of violence and intimidation with the intention of disrupting the independence celebrations. The statement said that the prime minister was "concerned about the threats, intimidating words and malicious and false rumours which are being muttered by certain irresponsible members of the community . . . . The government will no longer tolerate such behaviour . . . ."[35] The government thereupon declared a state of emergency and proceeded to arrest the leaders of the APC on charges of incitement and criminal libel. They were detained as well under the emergency provisions.[36] Mr Siaka Stevens who was then in London was extradited to Sierra Leone. On his arrival, he promptly faced the same fate as his colleagues. He was charged with a criminal offence and tried and convicted, but his conviction was quashed. When he was finally released, he put out a statement calling on all members of his party to maintain the party policy line of (a) full respect for law and order and (b) constitutional and lawful procedures in all matters. "The APC has never stood, and will never stand, for violence sabotage or unconstitutional action" the statement concluded.[37]

In the House of Commons in London, the debate on the Sierra Leone Independence Bill took place on the 22nd March 1961. It was rushed through the house and was concluded within two hours. During the debate, Mr Norman Powell, decried the haste with which the bill was

---

35 See *Daily Mail* of February 20 1961.
36 M. O. Bash Taqui was sentenced to 1 year's imprisonment on the 19th February 1961. See *Daily Mail* of 6th May 1961. Charges were laid against Stevens, Kamara Taylor and Wallace-Johnson for publishing a seditious pamphlet. Wallace-Johnson was discharged at the preliminary investigations. Stevens and Kamara Taylor were convicted in the High Court and sentenced to six months imprisonment. Stevens' conviction was quashed by the Court of Appeal on 24/7/61. 18 leaders of the APC were detained. At independence the number was 43. All detainees were released on 15th May and the emergency revoked on 30th Aug. 1961.
37 See *Daily Mail* for May 29 1961.

being rushed through all its stages. He said inter alia:[38]

> I regret the delay in bringing this bill before the house . . . . Even more do I regret the haste with which the bill is being passed through all its stages. A colony with which we have had a connection for over 200 years is being, in a sense disposed of in a few hours. Whereas yesterday, we discussed for the whole day a matter of transitory and trivial importance — the salary of one man — today we are disposing of the destiny of two million people in less than half that time.

---

38 House of Commons Debates 22nd March 1961.

CHAPTER IX

FROM INDEPENDENCE TO REPUBLICANISM
1961 TO 1971

> Every constitution has to be a product of history. Even when it comes straight from the draftsman's pen; it is a product of the manner which the country concerned emerged as an independent state; of the conflicts which preceded that emergence and of the forces that have played upon it.
> SIR IVOR JENNINGS: *The Approach to Self-Government.* (1958) p.2.

On the 14th April, 1961, the Sierra Leone Constitution Order in Council was laid before parliament. The constitution of Sierra Leone was an appendix to the order. The order was, on this occasion, being made "by virtue and in exercise of the powers in that behalf by the Foreign Jurisdiction Act, 1890 *OR* otherwise in Her Majesty vested".[1] Obviously the ghost of Palmer-v-Stooke was still haunting the colonial office draftsman and he could not afford another spate of litigation on the same point.

Parliament passed "The Sierra Leone Independence Act" 1961[2] and so relinquished responsibility for the government of Sierra Leone, transferring its powers and authorities therein to the government and people of Sierra Leone. The constitution for the first time in the history of the country, contained a Bill of Rights. This was a peculiarity of the constitution and one of its outstanding features. Some of the provisions of the constitution, including the Bill of Rights were entrenched.

A correspondent of the *London Times*, writing to that paper made the following trite observation:[3]

---

1 Emphasis mine. In 1951 the word used in the Statutory Instruments was "and".
2 9 and 10 Eliz 2. c. 16.
3 See *The Times* of Jan. 23 1957 p.9. "Africa seeks her future. A continent in a hurry." By the Times colonial correspondent.

A colonial regime is authoritarian in essence, even though it may be acting as a school for democracy. The authoritarian sanctions are there in reserve and even occasonally used. The African Government taking over from such a regime has to govern a country where the electorate are immature, mostly illiterate and ridden by fear and witchcraft. They are deeply divided tribally, violence is endemic and the very boundaries of the country are recent and in some cases, purely artificial. Is it reasonable to suppose that any government will be able to control such a situation unless it is prepared to govern strongly?

When independence arrived in Sierra Leone, there were no fundamental unities binding the peoples of the country. The colony and the protectorate were torn apart and once again, litigation was commenced, this time in London, to challenge the constitutionality of the independence of Sierra Leone.[4] There was no great mass movement for independence as had happened in Ghana, for instance and so the legal framework for national unity was practically non-existent. The civil service was beginning to be politicised, there was considerable illiteracy and there was a deep tribal division. This was the kind of country which was taken over by the politicians of the Sierra Leone People's Party who had had just under a decade of experience in the running of a modern democracy. The provision of a Bill of Rights as an attachment to the constitution of Sierra Leone seemed a very necessary and desirable expedient.[5]

The features of the 1961 Constitution.
The independence constitution of Sierra Leone, embraced a number of basic concepts.

One of the most outstanding concepts of the independence constitution from the point of view of the legal history of Sierra Leone, was that of judicial review. For the first time, the Sierra Leone Constitution was doing away with the British constitutional principle of the sovereignty of parliament. Henceforth, any law passed by parliament which was not within the spirit and intendment of the constitution could be challenged in the courts.[6]

The constitution also made provision for the citizenship of Sierra Leone. Any person who on the 26th April 1961 was either a British subject, by reason on his having been born in the former colony of Sierra Leone, or a British protected person by reason of his having been born in the former protectorate of Sierra Leone, was on the 27th day of April 1961, a citizen of Sierra Leone.

Other features of the independence constitution were the principle of

---

4 The case of Buck-v-The Attorney-General will be discussed infra.
5 See W. S. Marcus Jones — *The Protection of Fundamental Rights and Liberties of the Individual in the Sierra Leone Independence Constitution,* 1961. (Unpublished Doctoral Dissertation, Yale University, 1965).
6 The case of Akar-v-the attorney-general will be discussed later.

responsible government with executive power being vested in the Governor-General, but exercised by him either directly or by and through the ministers of the government. There was full ministerial responsibility. Parliament was unicameral, consisting of the Governor-General and members of parliament, from whom the cabinet was drawn.

The Governor-General had the right to appoint as prime minister the person who appeared to him most likely to command a majority in the house. So the prerogatives of the British Monarch in respect of the appointment and dismissal of the prime minister and other ministers of government, were vested in him. He also had power to dissolve parliament and to make judicial appointments.

A Court of Judicature was set up by the constitution. This consisted of the Supreme Court, the Court of Appeal and the Privy Council to whom appeals lay from the Court of Appeal. The tenure of office of judges was entrenched.

The Governor-General.
Under the constitution, executive power in Sierra Leone was vested in him. From the constitutional point of view, the most interesting aspect of his function was that in relation to the prime minister. The relationship was squarely based on the British tradition of cabinet government. Conceived of as a position completely devoid of politics, it did not appear conceivable that there would be any problems arising out of the exercise by him of his powers to appoint a prime minister. Yet, within one year of independence problems had begun to emerge.

One of the constitutional fictions which was introduced by the independence constitution was the making of the Queen of Britain, Queen of Sierra Leone. Unfortunately, at the date of independence, the first Governor-General of Sierra Leone was Sir Maurice Dorman, the expatriate Governor of Sierra Leone at the time of the change of her status.[7] Consequently, it was hard for ordinary citizens to appreciate what independence was all about when, before their very eyes, were all the trappings of a colonial institution. The monarchy was in every respect foreign to the traditions and customs of Sierra Leone. That the Queen of England under the constitution of an independent state should also be Queen of Sierra Leone was not universally accepted.

Parliament.
The constitution established a parliament for the independent state of Sierra Leone. As has already been observed, there was no universal adult suffrage in existence consequently, parliament was composed of the Governor-General, the speaker and members of parliament elected in accordance with the provisions of the Electoral Provisions Act. The country was divided into single member constituencies, each of which returned one member to parliament. In addition, however,

---

[7] The first Sierra Leonean to be appointed Governor-General was Sir Henry Lightfoot-Boston who succeeded Sir Maurice Dorman in 1962.

constituencies in the twelve districts of the protectorate had additional members as there was one paramount chief member for each district. Qualifications for membership of parliament required, among others, that the person should be a citizen of Sierra Leone and be literate in English. The usual disqualifications were provided for, for example a person who was under sentence of death or had been sentenced to a term of imprisonment within the preceding five years, for a term of twelve months for an offence involving dishonesty; or if he was a lunatic; or being a professional person had been disqualified from following his profession.

The speaker could be appointed from among members of parliament, but in that event, he was required to vacate his seat. The office of speaker was not available to any public officer or minister and he was required to vacate his seat after a dissolution of parliament.

The High Court had jurisdiction to hear and determine questions about disputed elections to Parliament.

Parliament was constituted the supreme legislative authority for Sierra Leone. It had power to alter or amend the constitution but some of the clauses were entrenched. That meant that they could not be altered by the ordinary process of legislation. To alter the entrenched provisions required the passing of the proposed amendment by a two-thirds majority in one parliament, the dissolution of parliament and the passing of the same measure by a two-thirds majority in the first session of the new parliament. In so far as there was a substantial opposition in existence, this appeared to be a reasonable safeguard, but in the Sierra Leone situation, it ceased to be an effective one since the government always was in a position to muster a two-thirds majority in parliament anyway.

The legislative power of parliament was exercised by bills passed by parliament and signed by the Governor-General.

The Governor-General could dissolve parliament or refuse to do so and in the exercise of his judgment he was not bound to accept the advice of the prime minister. The death of the prime minister did not affect the government or parliament since the Governor-General could always call on someone else to perform the functions of that office. Thus, the Governor-General was not bound by the party's choice of a leader.

The Cabinet.
Executive power in the state rested with the Queen and it was exercised on her behalf by the Governor-General directly or through members of the cabinet or others to whom he could delegate these powers. The prime minister was appointed by the Governor-General during whose pleasure he held office. Other ministers were appointed by the Governor-General on the advice of the prime minister. The cabinet was collectively responsible for any advice given to the Governor-General or for the general execution of the duties of their office.

The Judicature.

The Chief Justice as head of the judiciary was appointed by the Governor-General on the recommendation of the prime minister. The other judges were appointed by the Governor-General on the recommendation of the Judicial Service Commission. Judges had to have been entitled to practice for ten years before holding any judicial appointment and they were required to vacate their office upon attaining the age of sixty-two years. The judges had security of tenure and could not be removed from office save on the grounds of misbehaviour or inability to perform the functions of their office.

Important Constitutional events.
Citizenship provisions. Akar-v-the Attorney-General.

In 1962, the Sierra Leone Parliament amended the citizenship provisions which were contained in the constitution to deprive any person "whose father and his father's father" were not persons of "Negro African descent". Such persons ceased to be citizens of Sierra Leone and the amendment was made retrospective to the 27th day of April 1961. One of the persons caught by this amendment was Mr John Akar. He contended that the provisions of the law were discriminatory; that they took away his vested rights as a Sierra Leone citizen, a status conferred upon him by the constitution since 27th April 1961 and rendered him stateless. He accordingly sued the Attorney-General for a declaration that the amendment was ultra vires the constitution and void.

The action was heard in the Supreme Court of Sierra Leone (as it then was)[8] before the Chief Justice Mr Justice Banja Tejan-Sie.[9] The learned Chief Justice held for the plaintiff striking down the enactment and holding that it was ultra vires and void. The government appealed to the Sierra Leone Court of Appeal. A strong court[10] reversed the Chief Justice and held, quite surprisingly, that the Sierra Leone Parliament was supreme and sovereign and that the court had no power to question acts of parliament or declare legislation passed by parliament, unconstitutional.

Akar appealed to Her Majesty in Council which restored the judgment of Banja Tejan-Sie, C. J. and reversed the Sierra Leone Court of Appeal.[11]

It was unfortunate that the newly independent state thought it fit in its first attempted amendment of the constitution, to introduce discriminatory legislation. Taking into account the history of the settlement and the high ideals on which it was founded, it was most unfortunate that such a blatant discriminatory law should find its place in the statue books. Undoubtedly, the intention was to prevent persons

8 Now the High Court.
9 Later Sir Banja Tejan-Sie. He was Governor-General and then sent on leave compulsorily in 1971.
10 Sir Samuel Bankole Jones, P. J. B. Marcus Jones J. A. and Dove Edwin J. A.
11 1964 2 All E.R. 668.

of Lebanese origin from entering the new Parliament of Sierra Leone. But was this a lawful and justifiable way of doing that? The influence of the Lebanese in the economy of the country was such and continues to be such that any attempt to exclude them from the socio-economic activities and of the political life of the country would be a futile and unrealistic exercise.

By the same token, the decision of the Court of Appeal was curious. It indicated quite clearly that the judges trained exclusively in the traditions of British jurisprudence had not bothered to look beyond Great Britain to other common law jurisdictions like the United States and India where the principle of judicial review is well settled. It took the Privy Council a non-resident court of great distinction and unquestioned impartiality, to help restore justice, not only to Akar, but to many others who had been caught in the web and who, through no fault of their own, were being put in the unenviable position where they were rendered stateless.

The Appointment of a new Prime Minister.
Sir Milton Margai, who had been Prime Minister of Sierra Leone at the date of independence, died in 1964 and the Governor-General, Sir Henry Lightfoot Boston had occasion to appoint a successor. Section 58(2) of the Constitution provided as follows:

> Whenever the Governor-General has occasion to appoint a prime minister, he shall appoint a member of the House of Representatives who appears to him likely to command the support of the majority of the members of the house.

He therefore had to act in his own deliberate judgment in making the appointment of a new prime minister.

In the party which formed the majority at that time, there were two possible contenders for the position, each with a substantial number of supporters within the party. They were, Mr Albert Margai, the younger brother of the deceased prime minister and Dr John Karefa Smart. The struggle within the party for leadership was intense and the Attorney-General of the day[12] in a confidential memorandum to the Governor-General advised that the constitution did not require any affirmative vote in parliament of the person seeking the leadership, nor the appointment of anyone by any political party as leader, before the appointment of such person by the Governor-General. He advised that the Governor-General should use his own deliberate judgement and choose whosoever appeared to him to command the majority in the house, without reference to any other source. It would appear that the Attorney-General himself was an unquestioned supporter of Mr Albert Margai. In the end, the Governor-General appointed Mr Margai as prime minister. Dr Karefa-Smart and some others refused to serve under Sir Albert (as he later was) and left the cabinet and parliament. He also left Sierra Leone for good.

Upon the appointment of Sir Albert Margai as Prime Minister of Sierra Leone, all the offices of minister became vacant under the

12 Mr Berthan Macaulay, Q.C. who has since left Sierra Leone and is in Jamaica.

provisions of Section 58(7) of the Constitution. This afforded the new prime minister a free hand to choose his team.

A similar problem arose in Nigeria in the case of Adegbenro-v-Akintola[13] where the Federal Supreme Court of Nigeria held that the Governor-General of the West required some objective criteria to help him determine who would be able to command a majority in the house and that he could only come to that conclusion after the nominee had gone to parliament and been able to secure a vote of confidence. The Privy Council reversed that decision and held that there was no necessity for a vote to be taken on the floor of the house before a new prime minister was appointed. The Western Region Assembly immediately thereafter reversed that decision.

It is submitted that the Privy Council decision is to be preferred to that of the Nigerian courts. It makes more sense since the intention of parliament was to put in the hands of an independent and responsible person the very important discretion of selecting an obvious leader in cases where there is a vacuum. A strong and courageous Governor-General who discreetly and wisely exercises that power can save the country from constitutional crises. The proper exercise of that discretion can also prevent the farcical situation which arose in the Congo with the president and the prime minister each attempting to dismiss the other.

Buck-v-the Attorney-General.[14]

In 1960, as the prime minister made it clear that he was proceeding with his demands for independence for Sierra Leone, the Settlers' Descendants Association actively challenged the government's proposals on the ground that independence for Sierra Leone would mean an indissoluble merger of the colony and the protectorate. They therefore commenced proceedings in the High Court in London against the Attorney-General of the United Kingdom, challenging the constitutionality of the Statutory Instruments of 1961. They appointed a delegation to travel to Great Britain to represent them in the High Court. The action which was commenced in the Chancery Division of the High Court, was intituled "Prince Buck and Others-v-The Attorney-General of the United Kingdom". It sought a declaration that the Statutory Instruments of 1961, in so far as they related to the colony of Sierra Leone, were ultra vires and void; that the colony was held in trust by the United Kingdom Government for the free community of settlers and their descendants; and that the Settlers' Descendants Association was entitled to set up for the colony, such constitution and government as the settlers themselves should think fit. It questioned for the first time in a British court, the constitutionality of creating a common legislature for a British colony and a protectorate which was in substance and in fact a foreign state.

The case took a long time to come on the list for hearing and was not disposed of until 1964 when it was heard and, ironically, dismissed by Mr

13 (1964) 1 All. E.R.
14 (1964) 2 All E.R. 668.

Justice Wilberforce, a descendant of the illustrious William Wilberforce, a descendant of the abolitionists. The action was dismissed on the 5th May 1964 on technical grounds.

The judgment was interesting. The learned judge said, inter alia, that the use by the Crown of the British Settlements Act, 1887 as amended to legislate for the colony of Sierra Leone was "clearly permissible" under the statutory instruments and fell within the ambit of the clause "or otherwise in Her Majesty vested", if, in fact, power existed and was available under the act. He said that far from destroying the settlement and handing it over to the Protectorate as the plaintiffs had alleged, the constitution for the independent state, set up joint institutions for the country. The process of integration began in 1924 and had been carried further; but it was still integration, not transfer. He further said that, although the action was being heard in 1964 and the proceedings had commenced in 1960, the claim was a far-reaching one in that the plaintiffs were asking for a declaration respecting the constitution and government of a foreign state in the absence of representatives of that state and against the Crown, although the Crown had since April 1961, ceased to have responsibility for Sierra Leone and no longer had any power of legislation or executive action over it.[15] Finally, he expressed the view that the colony of Sierra Leone ceased to exist as from April 27 1961, not by virtue of the statutory instruments, but by reason of the United Kingdom Statute, the Sierra Leone Independence Act, 1961. Consequently, the effect of the enactment was to transfer the administration of the colony from the British Government to the government of Sierra Leone and the court could not question the legality or wisdom of an act of parliament. In the circumstances the action was dismissed.[16]

LOCAL COURTS IN INDEPENDENT SIERRA LEONE.
The independent government of Sierra Leone was concerned to unify the system of justice throughout the country and one of the anomalies as it saw it, was the fact that the Creoles in the colony were not subject to the jurisdiction of the local courts. It therefore appointed the Brooks Commission to study the matter and report thereon. The Brooks Report on Local Courts highlighted a number of points. It illustrated that:
(a) There was a proliferation of litigation.
(b) Many law suits were frivolous and vexatious.
(c) A number of local courts depended on political rather than judicial considerations.
(d) Chiefs claimed political and judicial powers and got a share of the fees in litigious matters.
(e) There was dilatoriness in local court procedures.
(f) There were no qualifications for appointment to local courts.

15 See Hood Phillips. *Constitutional and Administrative Law,* 4th Ed. p.799.
16 On the U.K. Doctrine of the Supremacy of Parliament see Prescott-v-Birmingham (1955) Ch. 210. Padfield-v-Min. of Agriculture (1968) A.C. 997 Blackburn-v-A.G. (1970) A.C 853.

The report made many suggestions for a reform of the whole system of local courts and suggested that customary law should be clarified and developed and that the presidents of local courts should be African lawyers versed in customary law.[17] It also recommended a limitation on the powers of the executive over local courts since these were controlled by the minister.

The result of the Brooks Report was that the Local Courts Act No. 20 of 1963 was passed by the Sierra Leone Parliament, which, according to its long title, was designed to "consolidate and amend the law relating to the local courts, to provide for the extension of their jurisdiction and for the hearing of appeals from such courts and to make certain incidental and consequental provisions for the administration of justice in the provinces". An unwieldy and unsatisfactory attempt was made to define "customary law". The act empowers a court in Sierra Leone when determining matters arising in the provinces in its civil jurisdiction "to observe and enforce the observance of . . . . customary law". It excludes the jurisdiction of the High Court in respect of matters relating to title to land in the provinces and matters of family law governed by customary law.

The act extended the jurisdiction of local courts to all persons within its area. However, when one considers the extent of this jurisdiction, the matter becomes one of deep and anxious concern, particularly as the local courts also have competence in respect of matters arising under the general law.

One of the most essential characteristics of any legal system is that the law should be certain particularly if one is dealing with criminal justice. A man must know the offence he is alleged to have committed and it is of the utmost importance that persons who are required to obey and observe any law must know what that law is. The problem for Sierra Leone Customary law, like most customary systems, is that it is unwritten and varies from tribe to tribe.

It is now generally accepted as a good proposition of Sierra Leone Law that customary law is "foreign" in the sense that it has to be determined by evidence from experts what the particular rule or custom is. A court, in determining what is or is not customary law, may have to ascertain whether the alleged custom has existed from time immemorial and hallowed, or accepted, by long usage. The evidence in support of a custom as stated by a judge of the former Gold Coast colony,[18] "should be more than preponderating". When once a court has ruled that a particular matter is one of customary law, then it provides judicial precedent of what that custom is. The Judicial Committee of the Privy Council has recognised the need for courts to take judicial notice of customs which have become so notorious by frequent proof in the courts that further proof is no longer necessary.[19] Similarly, some rules of

17 This recommendation was made in the "Report of the Commission of Inquiry into Disturbances in the Gold Coast" p.72. Colonial Office No. 231 (1948).
18 Yerenchi-v-Akuffo 1905 Sarbah' Gold Coast Reports.
19 Angu-v-Attah (1915) Gold Coast Judgments 1874-1928 p.43.

customary practice, though never proved by evidence, are so commonplace and widely accepted, that the judge requires no further proof of their existence and accepts them without more. A good example of this type of customary practice is the absence of liability to account where the person concerned is either the chief or the head of the family. This was expressly recognised by the West African Court of Appeal in the case of Abude-v-Onano.[20]

Apart from formal court procedures, customary law recognises informal methods of settling disputes. Very often, a complaint is made to the chief or elder who then tries to settle the matter without recourse to formal litigation. One of the objectives of the Sierra Leone Local Courts Act was to transfer this jurisdiction from the chief to politically appointed court presidents. Another objective of the statute was to dispense with the duality of the system whereby customary law was administered exclusively in some kinds of cases and the general law in others. Thus an attempt was made to integrate the local courts into the general judicial system. Hence the provision in Section 13(2) of the Local Courts Act that the jurisdiction of the courts would extend to all persons and further that "where there is no provision of customary law, the general law shall apply".

Shortly after the passing of the act[21] the iniquity of making persons answerable for "offences" of which they were totally unaware became painfully apparent, albeit in a political setting. In one case, a defendant was sentenced to a fine and imprisonment for saying "Good Morning" in court. In another, a defendant was similarly incarcerated for wearing a turban in court, both cases being treated as contempt in customary law. Needless to say the defendants appealed and both sentences were quashed on appeal.[22]

Closely connected with the problem of determining what customary law is, is the question of its fair and impartial administration. Submitting matters of discipline and control to the administrative discretion of a minister of government may not be the best way of ensuring the independence and fairness of these tribunals. The presidents of these courts are appointed by the minister and answerable to him. No criteria are set out as to what the qualifications and experience of these 'Judges' should be. Lawyers are still not permitted to appear in local courts which administer a system of British law of which they are hopelessly ignorant. There is competing jurisdiction therefore between the local courts and the general courts which can only lead to uncertainty and injustice. In fact, it would be plainly unconstitutional for any defendant who is brought within the jurisdiction of a local court and who can have the same matter

---

20 (1946) 12 W.A.C.A. 102 at 104. See also Larinde-v-Afiko (1940) 6 W.A.C.A. 108 and Owiredu-v-Moshie (1952) 14 W.A.C.A. 11 which have held that it is wrong for a judge to decide a case and establish a rule as one of customary law merely on the basis of a single decided case on the point.
21 The Local Courts Act was brought into force in 1964.
22 I have been unable to locate the records of these cases in the High Court archives. Both cases were 'political' cases, defended by Mr T. S. Johnson.

tried in the general courts to be denied the right to counsel. For the constitution clearly establishes that as a man's constitutional right.

Four categories of cases are expressly excluded from the jurisdiction of local courts:
  (a) Cases relating to the civil status of any person.
  (b) The administration of estates under the general law.
  (c) Cases involving the government, a company or a public officer acting in his official capacity.
  (d) Libel, slander, false imprisonment, malicious prosecution, seduction and breach of promise.

There is thus an urgent need in independent Sierra Leone for a reform of the administration of justice in local courts. The position today has not changed significantly from what it was in 1926 when F. W. H. Migeod wrote as follows:[23]

> All natives like to have their cases heard by the district commissioner instead of by their chiefs. For one thing, it is cheaper. Justice is not obtained for nothing in a native court. The native always has the right of appeal to the district commissioner but few are such fools as to do so, for he is bound to be penalised afterwards by his own chief, who would not take such a flouting lying down, unless the complainant was a very big man with perhaps more power than his chief. In default, he would have to pay a big sum of money to the chief to make his peace.

THE SLPP PROPOSES A ONE PARTY STATE AND REPUBLICANISM FOR SIERRA LEONE.

On the 17th July 1966, the Sierra Leone Government issued a White Paper on the formation of a one party state for Sierra Leone. It invited comments and opinions on the one party issue. This proposal was severely criticised in the press and by various individuals and organisations. In spite of that, the government proceeded to appoint a committee to be chaired by the speaker of the house of representatives to look into the matter and report to government on the kind of one party constitution that Sierra Leone should have. An action was commenced in the High Court of Sierra Leone by Dr R. S. Easmon, Nancy Steele and others[24] to obtain an interim injunction against the Attorney-General and to prevent the committee from carrying out the work assigned to it on the ground that the activities of the One Party Committee would constitute an infringement of the fundamental rights provisions of the Sierra Leone constitution. The interim injunction was granted but the substantive application refused. The final judgment was delivered on the 3rd January 1967 by which date the government had decided to drop the one party issue altogether.

The SLPP Government, having failed in its bid to introduce a one party constitution into the country, now turned its attention to the issue of

23 Migeod: *A View of Sierra Leone* (London) 1926, at p.139.
24 See Steele & Ors.-v-Attorney-General, 1967-8 A.L.R. (Sierra Leone Series) p.1.

republicanism. At that time, elections to the Legislature were imminent, the last elections having been held in 1962. In 1965, parliament passed the Constitution (Consolidation of Amendments) Act, No. 52 of 1965 which provided that a bill to enact a new constitution could become law without the assent of the Governor-General if passed by a two-thirds majority in two successive sessions of parliament with a dissolution intervening. In 1967, the Republican Constitution Bill was published. It was introduced into parliament and passed. By the terms of the 1961 Constitution, before the proposed Republican Constitution could be brought into effect, there should be a dissolution of parliament and the bill passed in the first session of the new parliament by a two-thirds majority. The proposal was, again, subjected to severe criticism both in and out of parliament. The All People's Congress, which had a small number of parliamentarians in opposition thought that this was the final stage towards autocracy. The Bar Association took the unprecedented step of calling a public meeting to inform the public of the constitutional issues facing the country and to enlighten them about the proposals for a republic. There were notable contributions in the press and the atmosphere was highly politically charged.[25] The government then set the 17th February for the dissolution of parliament. It fixed the 17th March 1967 for the elections of ordinary members of parliament, the general elections, and the 21st March 1967 for the election of paramount chief members of parliament. Before the elections, a number of incidents took place which need to be recounted to put the picture in full perspective.

Background to the 1967 developments.
Following the death of Sir Milton Margai on the 28th April, 1964, a petition was signed by thirty-five members of parliament against Sir Albert asking that he should not be appointed prime minister of Sierra Leone. Shortly afterwards, the *We Yone* newspaper which was the official organ of the All People's Congress embarked on a campaign of criticism of various aspects of government policies. The reaction of the government was to institute several prosecutions for criminal libel against the editor and proprietors of the paper who were the political opponents of the government. In January 1965, one Michael Yanni, a staunch supporter of the APC commenced a private prosecution against a former Minister of Trade and Industry and Chairman of the Sierra Leone Produce Marketing Board for "conspiracy to conceal a crime". The Attorney-General entered a nolle prosequi and then published a

25 Examples of contributions in the press attacking the measures suggested by the government are contained in the following articles: Sarif Easmon — 'Breakers Ahead' in *"We Yone"* July 2 1966. The Record of Proceedings of the Fourah Bay College Departments of Law and Political Science on "The proposed Constitution for Sierra Leone" January 14 1967. An article by E. Livesey Luke (now Chief Justice) in the *Daily Mail* of Jan. 13 1967. Memo of the 1963 Committee of F.B.C. in *Unity*, January 1967: Also various editorials and comments by T. S. Johnson, proprietor of *'Think'* a mimeographed bi-weekly bulletin during the same period.

statement of his reasons for doing so in the *Daily Mail* of January 9 1965. Yanni then countered with an article in '*We Yone*' headed "My dialogue with the Prime Minister". This article was the subject of a prosecution by the state of the editor and reporter of the '*We Yone*' for sedition and defamatory libel. The judge found that the article was defamatory but the jury acquitted by a ten to two majority. The Prime Minister, Sir Albert Margai, described the verdict as "shameful".

In January 1965, the prime minister, when questioned about his intentions to introduce a one party state into Sierra Leone, replied "It might be". Two months later, in a speech at Bonthe, Sherbro, he threatened to shoot down all his opponents, and on the 30th March in a speech in parliament he told the APC parliamentarians that "the tide is ebbing fast" and that it would be easy "to liquidate" them. He said that he would seek an interpretation of the word "recognised" opposition as in reality there was only one party in the house.[26] On the 23rd March 1965, during a visit of President Sekou Toure to Sierra Leone, in an address to the Sierra Leone Parliament, the president made an appeal for a one party state for Sierra Leone[27] and on the 25th March, the Hon. Prince Williams, a Member of Parliament for Bo, said that Sierra Leone should have "one political flock and one shepherd".[28] Yet, in May 1965 at a Convention of the SLPP the prime minister said that rumours of a one party constitution were false. In June 1965, in London, the prime minister said that if Sierra Leone should become a one party state, it would come by agreement and not by compulsion. Eventually, the idea surfaced at a caucus of the SLPP held on the 5th October when it was passed.

On the 4th October 1965, President Kwame Nkrumah of Ghana paid a one day official visit to Sierra Leone and the Sierra Leone Prime Minister visited Ghana from the 19th to the 27th October, 1965. The prime minister during that visit said that "Government was not above the Party" and it was reported that Nkrumah had advised Sir Albert to sack his judges as there was a problem of how the one party state would be achieved with the present judiciary firmly installed. On the 30th October 1965, Sir Samuel Bankole Jones, the Chief Justice was removed from office and "promoted" to the Court of Appeal. The Bar Association interviewed the prime minister about the circumstances of the removal of the Chief Justice from office and were very abruptly received and dispatched.

Subsequently, various articles appeared in the *We Yone* making a number of allegations of improper conduct by the prime minister and various members of the government. The government reacted by embarking on a spate of prosecutions of which the following are

---

26 See Debates of the House of Representatives, 1965/6 Mar. 30, 1965 Col. 260: 261-2.
27 Ibid Cols. 24-5.
28 Ibid. Col. 93.

examples:[29]
    (a) R-v-Hollist and Taqui. Charged with libel in connection with an allegation that the Attorney-General had received a cheque for £20,000 from the Produce Marketing Board. The judge ruled that a case of justification had been made out. At that stage, the prosecution sought to enter a nolle prosequi. This was refused. The accused were acquitted and discharged.
    (b) R-v-Taqui. Charged with the same offences as in (a) two months later. Accused tendered a plea of autrefois acquit which was upheld.[30]
    (c) R-v-Hollist and Taqui. Charged with criminal libel arising out of an allegation that the prime minister with the aid of Afro-Lebanese diamond dealers, offered the Secretary General of the Kono Democratic People's Congress the sum of £15,000 to dissolve the party. The accused were found not guilty and acquitted and discharged.[31]
    (d) R-v-Hollist, charged with libel in connection with an allegation that the Acting Chief Justice, Mr Justice C. O. E. Cole was appointed to succeed Sir Samuel Bankole Jones, "on condition he co-operates with the ruling party". He was found guilty and sentenced to three months imprisonment.[32]
    (e) R-v-A. F. Thorlu-Bangura. Charged with Libel in connection with an allegation that the prime minister was behind the beating and imprisonment of eleven fishermen in Bullom. He was found guilty and sentenced to imprisonment for one year.[33]

In Port Loko, in November 1965, the prime minister made the first official statement on the one party issue.[34] On the 10th December 1965 at Kambia, at a large gathering of SLPP delegates, the one party issue was debated and approved. Later on in Port Loko, 3,500 women supporters of the government party at a rally held for the purpose, advocated the introduction of one party rule in Sierra Leone. Later on in parliament, paramount chief Bai Bairoh of Tonkolili tabled a private member's motion to the effect that:

    To ensure the solidarity and rapid development of this country, BE IT resolved that government give serious consideration to the introduction of a unitary (one party) system of government in this country.

The prime minister then sought the support of Mr Siaka Stevens, Leader of the Opposition, for the motion. Stevens said he would consult with his

---

[29] I was personally involved in the defence of a number of these actions in the High Court. In almost all of the prosecutions which were commenced by ex-officio informations signed by the attorney-general and tried by judge alone (without a jury) the accused were acquitted.
[30] See *Daily Mail* of April 25 1966 for the Judgment.
[31] See *Daily Mail* of Nov. 27 1965.
[32] See *Daily Mail* Nov. 20 1965.
[33] See *We Yone* of Nov. 20 1965.
[34] Ibid.

supporters and agreed he would abstain when the voting took place.[35] He did.

Apparently at this time, no formal policy had been decided upon by the APC on the one party issue. What their attitude appeared to be was to oppose its introduction in any event by the SLPP. Later, they concluded that the one party rule was inappropriate for Sierra Leone. The volatile nature of this matter is illustrated by the report that an APC member of the Bombali Chiefdom Council had praised the one party system. When this was disclosed, he wrote a letter denying that he had done so. He further went on to allege that the district officer had tried to get him to support the one party resolution but that he had refused. He was charged in the local court with "bringing the chiefdom councillors to ridicule and contempt" and sentenced to six months' imprisonment. He appealed to the Supreme Court which quashed the conviction on the 7th May 1966.

In January 1966, the APC decided on its policy with regard to the one party proposal. It decided to oppose it on the ground that it was a "violation of one of the entrenched clauses of the constitution which guarantees the right of freedom of association". It suggested that the matter should be settled by the "ballot box".

On the 24th February 1966, President Kwame Nkrumah was overthrown and on March 16, a mass meeting was called in Freetown by some distinguished citizens including the Bishop of Sierra Leone and the Head of the EUB Church.[36] This meeting decided to ask the government to suspend the one party proposals. The students of the university also opposed it. On the 21st March, the prime minister laid before parliament a White Paper "to collate and assess all views on the one party system both in and out of parliament and to make recommendations on the type of one party system suitable for Sierra Leone and the method by which it should be introduced". The proposed composition of the committee was as follows:

Mr Banja Tejan Sie (Speaker) — Chairman
3 ministers
4 other parliamentarians
2 representatives from the APC
    (which decided to boycott the committee)
1 non-paramount chief from each of the twelve districts
1 representative from the rural area
1 representative from the Freetown City Council
1 paramount chief from each province
2 representatives each from:
    The Federation of Labour
    The Teachers' Association
    The University

---

35 See Debates of the House of Representatives, December 20 and 21 1965.
36 Rev. Syl M. Renner.

1 representative each from:
   The Bar Association
   The Medical Practitioners' Union
   The United Christian Council
   The Roman Catholic Church
   The Muslim Congress
   The Youth Council

In May 1966, the Ag. Chief Justice granted an Interim Injunction to restrain the committee from meeting. The prime minister was so incensed that he ordered the committee to proceed with its work in defiance of the court injuction. The committee however adjourned sine die.[37]

The district elections held in 1966 did not augur well for the SLPP. They were held on the 27th May and in the North, the APC won seventy-two of the ninety-five seats contested. The SLPP, as later investigations proved, then did everything possible to ensure its return to power in the general elections to be held in 1967. In January 1967, it recalled Mr Gershon Collier, its ambassador in the United States, and a well-known supporter of the party, to be appointed Chief Justice of Sierra Leone. It then embarked on a number of changes in the laws of the country. It amended the Electoral Provisions Act to provide that two judges, instead of one, should sit to determine election petitions.[38] The deposit required from candidates standing elections was raised from two hundred, to five hundred Leones. The proportion of votes required to be gained before a candidate lost his deposit was raised from one-tenth to one fourth.[39] Candidates were required to attend between 9 a.m. and 5 p.m. at the office of the returning officer. The number of seats of ordinary members to be contested for was raised from sixty-two to sixty-six.

The Public Order Act of 1965 had been passed which gave a paramount chief an absolute discretion to allow or forbid meetings of twelve or more persons within his chiefdom.[40] This act was amended in 1966 to give the prime minister power to issue a proclamation of a state of emergency which would last for three months and under which the police would have a right to arrest without a warrant and disperse any meetings.[41]

On the 8th February, the prime minister announced that there had been a plot to assassinate him together with the Force Commander, Brigadier Lansana.[42] On the following day, seven army officers,

---

37 See *We Yone* of May 28 1966. Dr R. S. Easman wrote about this matter in the *We Yone* of July 2 1966 giving an account of what had transpired. The Attorney-General replied on the 9th July 1966 in the same paper.
   For an account of the dismissal of Sir Samuel Bankole Jones by the Bar Association, see *We Yone* of Nov. 27 1965.
38 See the Electoral Provisions (Amendment) Act, 1967, Section 1.
39 Ibid, Section 4.
40 Section 24 of the Public Order Act No. 46 of 1965.
41 Public Order (Amendment) Act, 1966 Sec. 2.
42 See *Daily Mail* of February 9 1967 for text of this announcement.

From Independence to Republicanism 1961-1971   213

including Brigadier Bangura[43] were detained. On the 8th February, the prime minister announced he had dropped the "democratic one-party system" proposals.

Comments on the Republic of Sierra Leone Bill.
The draft bill for the creation of a republic for Sierra Leone was published in the *Sierra Leone Gazette* on the 22nd December 1966.[44] The prime minister said that it preserved a considerable portion of the 1961 Constitution and made only formal changes to ensure the switch over from a monarchical to a republican form of government. The bill made the following significant alterations to the 1961 Constitution:
- (a) It replaced the Governor-General by a president.
- (b) The effective head of government remained the prime minister who controlled both the president and the Chief Justice.
- (c) It abolished appeals to the privy council and created the Supreme Court of Sierra Leone in its place.
- (d) It curtailed the protections contained in the fundamental rights provisions:
- (e) It provided for the appointment of the president by the cabinet, to hold office during the pleasure of the cabinet. In the absence of the president, the cabinet could appoint *any* person to act.
- (f) A naturalised or registered citizen could not contest an election for parliament until twenty-five years after his naturalisation or registration.
- (g) It precluded a public officer, a member of the armed forces of the Crown or the holder of any office or emolument under the Crown from seeking election to parliament within twelve months of his cessation of holding office.
- (h) The Chief Justice was made the head of the judiciary and the post of President of the Court of Appeal abolished.
- (i) The power of the president to withhold assent to bills was removed.
- (j) The provision for setting up a tribunal of at least three judges to hold an inquiry before the removal of a judge, was removed and replaced by a provision for parliament to debate the matter of a judges removal from office.

Contrary to the prime minister's assertions, the Republic Constitution Bill did make fundamental changes to the 1961 Constitution and greatly strengthened the position of the prime minister, conferring on him virtual autocratic powers.

---

43 Bangura became head of the military forces after Lansana had been deposed following the military intervention of 1967. This is discussed in the later pages.
44 No. XCVIII, 100 of Dec. 22 1966.

MILITARY RULE, 1967-8

Elections for the ordinary members of parliament were held on the 17th March 1967 and those for paramount chief members on the 21st March 1967. On the 21st March, after considerable delay in announcing the results of the elections by the Sierra Leone Broadcasting Service, Governor-General Sir Henry Lightfoot Boston, appointed Mr Siaka P. Stevens, Leader of the All People's Congress, Prime Minister of Sierra Leone. He administered the oath of office to him and as he, in turn, began to present the members of his cabinet to the Governor-General when the military burst into State House and halted the process. The Governor-General was arrested and detained and so were Siaka Stevens and some of his team. The head of the Sierra Leone Military Forces, Brigadier Lansana, declared 'Martial Law' and then put out a statement explaining why he had deemed it essential to interfere with the normal constitutional processes of government. He said:

> There is a widespread rumour, put out by the APC that the Governor-General has appointed Mr Siaka Stevens as prime minister. I want to assure the public that this rumour, if it is true, is unconstitutional, because the results have not all come in, and at this very moment I am speaking, the election of paramount chiefs is going on. No party has as yet got a sufficient number to form an over-all majority of the members of parliament. Only this morning, at about 10.30 a.m. the Governor-General assured me that he would not proceed with the appointment of a prime minister until he had consultations on Wednesday 22nd March. That is tomorrow. This rumour, being spread by the opposition, is an attempt to ignore the constitution and seize power by force. This, as I assured the Governor-General this morning, will lead to chaos and civil war. As custodian of state security, I have decided to protect the constitution and maintain law and order. Therefore, from now on, we are operating under 'Martial Law'. I repeat, we are operating under Martial Law. From now on, the army is in control, and will use all its power to see that the constitution is not violated. I appeal to you all to remain calm. You will be informed of further developments. In the meantime, I am advising you, those of you demonstrating in the streets, to disperse immediately. The last thing we want in this country is bloodshed. And if you disperse quickly, and go back about your lawful business, there will be no bloodshed. I sincerely hope to God that you will follow this advice. Thank you all very much.

On the 23rd March 1967, Major Blake made an announcement that the junior officers of the army had detained Brigadier Lansana together with Stevens and Margai and sent the Governor-General out of Sierra Leone on leave. On that date, the election of the paramount chief members had been announced and the Electoral commission had, on the 21st March, finally released the results for the elections of general members of parliament. They said that the APC had won 31 seats, the SLPP 32, and that two Independent candidates had been returned. The officers and junior ranks of the military forces then announced that they had set up the National Reformation Council (NRC) to govern Sierra Leone for the time being. The NRC was established by proclamation.[45] It was composed of senior officers of the military and the police forces. The NRC suspended the provisions of the 1961 Constitution inconsistent with the proclamation and the House of Representatives and all political parties were dissolved. The NRC announced the appointment of Lt. Col. Genda as chairman. He was then Second Secretary at the Sierra Leone Mission to the United Nations following his summary dismissal from the army. Without any explanation, his name was deleted from the Gazette Notice Extraordinary of the 27th March 1967 and Lt. Col. Juxon-Smith named as chairman. He also had been out of the country and was in Britain.[46] The NRC banned newspapers and issued a proclamation on the 26th March 1967 which said that all references to the Governor-General "shall be" references to the council or to persons appointed by the council. Same day, the NRC passed Law No. 7 which provided that no detention order made under the NRC proclamation could be questioned in any court. In effect, the NRC unsurped the governmental and constitutional powers of the government of Sierra Leone. They remained in office until they were overthrown by non commissioned members of the armed forces on the 18th April 1968. Before describing this episode in the constitutional and legal history of Sierra Leone, a few comments are pertinent about the legality of the NRC regime.

Was the NRC a Legal Government?
The National Reformation Council governed Sierra Leone effectively from the 23rd March 1967 to the 18th April 1968, just over a year. During that time they made appointments to the public service; appointed and received diplomats and foreign representatives; exercised full legislative powers by passing laws and detaining individuals; they imposed taxation and disbursed public funds. In fact they did everything a duly elected and properly constituted government could do.

The NRC contended that they did not take over the government of Sierra Leone from anybody but merely put down a military commander who had usurped the executive power of the state and wished to impose a military dictatorship on the country. But the facts are that it was the NRC who suspended the constitution. They suspended the Governor-General and sent him off to the United Kingdom where he subsequently died. They arrested Prime Minister Siaka Stevens who was already sworn in as head of government. They also arrested Albert Margai who should have been the leader of the opposition. Consequently, when the NRC

---

45 See "Administration of Sierra Leone" Proclamation No. 28 of 1967. Set out in Appendix VIII.
46 It is reported that the chairman was switched on the plane bringing both men to Sierra Leone. Genda was asked to return to the USA. He refused and was appointed ambassador to Liberia.

published their proclamation, there was in fact a duly constituted government in existence. Lansana never imposed any government on the country. It is submitted that when he spoke of "Martial Law" he did not understand what that phrase meant. The Governor-General had not called upon the military forces to assist the civilian authorities in a time of great emergency. The brigadier intervened of his own volition and, maliciously, to restore his friend and mentor Albert Margai to power against the wishes of the electorate. Under the 1961 Executive, power in the state was vested in Her Majesty and was exercised on her behalf by the Governor-General who was in the country and able and willing to perform the functions of his office when the NRC sent him off on leave out of the jurisdiction, without his approval or consent.

It is true that the courts will take judicial notice of laws passed by military regimes and that the court will not interfere when martial law exists.[47] But martial law, properly so called was not in force in Sierra Leone. The crucial question was why the NRC failed to hand over the authority of the state to the Governor-General and the prime minister when they put down Lansana's rebellion? Their assumption of office was plainly illegal and unconstitutional inspite of the promise given by Major Blake that they were soldiers "and wished to remain soldiers" and did not intend to impose a military regime on the country. They promised to restore the country to civilian rule as soon as the circumstances were propitious for that to be done. They never did.

Was there room for invoking the doctrine of "necessity" in this case, to justify the intervention of the military? It is submitted that unlike the cases of Nigeria or Cyprus, this was not a revolution created by necessity. The normal legislative and elective processes were going on smoothly and there would have been a change of government by and through the ballot-box had the army not intervened. The safety of the citizens was not imperilled. Lord Pearce in the case of Madzimbamuto-v-Lardner-Burke[48] said that "the principle of necessity or implied mandate is for the preservation of the citizen; for keeping law and order, rebus sic stantibus, regardless of whose fault it is that the crisis has been created or persists".

The Nigerian Supreme Court also had opportunity to comment on the legality of a military regime in the Lakanmi case.[49] The case arose out

---

47 See Marius-v-The General Officer Commanding and the Attorney-General. (1902) A.C 109.

48 (1969) 1 A.C. 645 at 647.

49 Lakanmi & Ola-v-the Attorney-General (West) 1970 S.C.58/69. The military in Nigeria legislated by edicts and decrees and claimed that the revolution was occasioned by necessity. They passed "decrees", which were described as laws "made under the legislative authority of the federal military government which authority shall be expressed through an instrument declaring itself a decree, which instrument shall require for its validity the signature of the head of the federal military government".

See also the case of Attorney-General for the republic-v-Mustapha Ibrahim of Kyrenia (1964) 3 Sup. Ct. of Cyprus 1: Also, Justice Willes in Phillips-v-Eyre (1871) 6 L.R. Q.B.1 and Uganda-v-commissioner of prisons 1966 E.A.L.R. 54. The prime minister abolished the constitution in the national assembly and substituted a new one which installed him as executive president. Also the Pakistan case of The State-v-Dosso.

of the military intervention in Nigeria and the court found that the military government had encroached on the judicial power. It pronounced the federal military government to be subordinate in authority to the 1963 Constitution except in matters of state necessity. In Sierra Leone, when the military took over the administration of the country, they required the judges to take their oaths of office again before them and to pledge allegiance to the military. Sir Samuel Bankole Jones the Chief Justice, hesitated at the time. He made a speech indicating his reluctance to do so, stating that he had not advised himself whether that was the proper thing to do. "These are not normal times" he said and so he signed the documents placed before him and took the oath of office. So did all the other judges.

The Military Government is overthrown.
On the 18th April 1968, the junior ranks of the Sierra Leone military forces, calling themselves the "Anti-Corruption Revoluntionary Movement" arrested the members of the NRC and forty senior army officers. They formed the NATIONAL INTERIM COUNCIL composed of four military and three police personnel with Warrant Officer Patrick Conteh at the head as chairman. An announcement was made by Sergeant Major Amadu Rogers that the NRC had been overthrown and that they intended to restore civilian rule to Sierra Leone without delay. The same day, they sent for Colonel Bangura from Washington and Lt. Col. Ambrose Genda from Liberia. They asked Bangura to head the council. On the 22nd April 1968, they appointed Mr Justice Banja Tejan-Sie as acting Governor-General of Sierra Leone and on the 26th April, they caused Mr Siaka Stevens to be sworn in again as Prime Minister, thereby restoring the normal constitutional process which had been interrupted by the military. Salia Jusu Sheriff, a former SLPP parliamentarian and minister was appointed to the government, but he resigned and returned to the opposition.

The civilian government of the APC was thus installed on the basis of the elections held in 1967 as confirmed by the Report of the Dove-Edwin Commission of Inquiry set up by the NRC. The government fixed the 26th November 1968 for the holding of by-elections in Bo and Kenema but these were suspended indefinitely because of a crisis which developed and which will form the subject of some comment in the next chapter.[50]

The Report of the Dove-Edwin Commission of Inquiry.
The NRC appointed a three-man Commission of Inquiry on the 22nd May 1967 with Mr Justice G. F. Dove-Edwin, Captain T. W. Caulker of the military forces and Supt. T. M. Kessebeh of the police,
> To enquire into the conduct of the last general elections held on the 17th and 21st days of March 1967, and in particular to inquire

---

50 See Chapter IX. Also see Public Notices Nos. 103 of 1968; 1 of 1969 and 23 of 1969.

into the following matters relating to the aforesaid general elections:
  (i) the compilation and operation of the register of voters
  (ii) the custody of ballot papers
  (iii) the conduct of political parties
  (iv) the results of the aforesaid general elections.

The commission sat on the 12th June 1967 for the first time and completed its task and reported to the NRC on the 23rd September 1967.[51] The commission found inter alia:

  (a) That the APC had won the general elections by having won 32 contested seats, none of them unopposed;

  (b) That the SLPP won 22 contested seats and had 6 unopposed, which were subject to appeal;

  (c) That Independents won 6 seats and did not declare for the SLPP as had been previously announced.

  (d) That eleven paramount chiefs were elected and one was returned unopposed.

The commission also found that there had been grave irregularities in the conduct of the elections and that the SLPP Government employed "corrupt means" in order to win the elections. They had convened a seminar for administrative officers in July 1966 to get returning officers to use improper means to ensure the return to power of the SLPP.

With regard to the intervention of Brigadier Lansana, the commission concluded that he had seized power from a duly constituted government and that the Governor-General was constitutionally right when he decided to appoint Mr Stevens as prime minister.

The NRC issued a White Paper setting out its own views on the report. They agreed, inter alia, that:
  (a) That there were anomalies in the compilation and operation of the register of voters.
  (b) A lot of ballot papers went into unauthorised hands and that the elections were rigged.
  (c) That both political parties were culpable for the disturbances which took place and that the difference between them was only a matter of degree.
  (d) That the electoral commission failed to announce the true position of the parties and this created suspicion in the minds of the public.
  (e) The false announcement that certain Independents had declared for the SLPP was "a final and desperate effort on the part of the returning officers concerned to assist the Sierra Leone People's Party Government to be returned to power".

The NRC expressed the view that there was nothing in the constitution preventing the Governor-General from appointing a paramount chief as

---

51 See Report of the Dove-Edwin Commission of Inquiry and the Government Statement thereon — Govt. Printer Freetown. Also: Govt. Notice No. 647 published in the Gazette No. XCVIII No. 47 of 23rd May 1967.

prime minister and that by appointing a prime minister before the results of the paramount chief members had been declared the Governor-General "Inadvertently deprived" the paramount chief members of their rights to have one of their members elected as prime minister. This was a spurious argument as paramount chiefs have never headed a political party nor are they constitutionally geared to be heads of government. Such a role would be inconsistent as his role as a chief places certain tribal obligations upon him which would not make it possible for him to desert his tribe for the more austere position as head of government. The chiefs traditionally, have also never been intimately involved in politics.

The NRC also commented that the chairman of the commission had been one of the persons present at State House at the time a number of influential people "thronged the State House and pressurised the Governor-General to appoint Mr Siaka Stevens as prime minister". They described the intervention of the soldiers on the 23rd March as a "rescue operation" which was not intended permanently to impose a military government on the people. They repeated an extract from the broadcast of Major Charles Blake on the 23rd March 1967 when he said, inter alia:

> I want to remind you, my dear people, that we are soldiers and want to remain soldiers and politics is not our ambition. We will hand over to the politicians as soon as the situation becomes favourable.

The NRC later on set up a Civilian Rule Committee to advise it on the method and procedure for handing over to a civilian government.[52]

THE NRC AS A DE FACTO/DE JURE GOVERNMENT.

The case of Thomas-v-Johnson[53] provided an opportunity for the Sierra Leone Court of Appeal to pronounce on the nature and validity of the NRC Government. The NRC had passed a "Prohibition of Transfer of Assets Decree" which precluded former ministers from transferring their assets without the approval of the NRC. A former minister made an oral agreement to sell a house to X as soon as such approval was obtained but then offered it to Y at a higher price. The approval of the NRC was not obtained before the deed of sale was executed. Tambiah J. A. exhaustively considered the legal position of the NRC "a military government which was not elected under the constitution of Sierra Leone". He did not consider it necessary to deal with the questions whether all the laws passed by the NRC were valid as the Madzimbamuto case had thrown light on the effect of laws enacted by a rebel government. Nor did he think it necessary to consider "whether the majority view in that case is relevant to determine the question whether the prohibition of transfer of assets decree was valid". He found that the principles which allow de facto governments to make laws for the subjects in these circumstances are based "either on the implied mandate of the sovereign .... or on the doctrine of necessity". Finding that the

---

52 See page 221 infra for composition and terms of reference.
53 See 1968-9 A.L.R. (Sierra Leone Series) pp.380-395.

Parliament of Sierra Leone "appears to have recognised the validity of some NRC decrees", he held that the purported sale was null and void.

Before closing the chapter on military rule in Sierra Leone, a couple of important matters deserve some comment as they are of some importance in the legal and constitutional history of Sierra Leone. These are, firstly, the Commissions of Inquiry set up by the National Reformation Council in 1967 and, secondly, the treason trials of the military, the police and some civilians, immediately after the overthrow of the NRC.

The Commissions of Inquiry.
In what was widely interpreted as an obvious response to popular opinion, the National Reformation Council mounted certain Commissions of Inquiry covering the period January 1961 to March 1967, under the provisions of the Commissions of Inquiry Act, Chapter 54 of the Laws of Sierra Leone, 1960. They covered a wide range of subjects from the assets of ex-ministers and civil servants to trade unions. Those of some importance were:
   (a) The Forster Commission of Inquiry into the Assets of ex-Ministers, ex-Deputy Ministers and Civil Servants:
   (b) The Dove-Edwin Commission of Inquiry into the conduct of the 1967 General Elections.
   (c) The Beoku-Betts Commission of Inquiry[54] into the Sierra Leone Produce Marketing Board.
   (d) The Fashole-Luke Commission of Inquiry[55] into the Conduct of the Immigration Quota Committee.
   (e) The Percy Davies Commission of Inquiry into the Activities of the Freetown City Council.
   (f) The Browne-Marke Commission of Inquiry into the Activities and the Finances of the United Mineworkers' Union.

The FORSTER Commission:
Mr Justice Samuel J. Forster headed this commission of three, the other two members being Major Samuel H. King of the military forces and Superintendent Elkanah E. Coker of the Sierra Leone police force. The terms of reference were simple. They were to investigate the assets of ex-ministers, ex-deputy ministers and senior civil servants during the six-year period from the 1st January 1961 to the 23rd March 1967 with a view to discovering whether there was any evidence of undue enrichment or improperly obtained assets. The commission reported in March 1968 and the opening paragraphs of the report indicate, in substance, the findings of the commission. It said:

---

54 Mr Justice Ronald Beoku-Betts died on the 6th January 1968, and Justice Percy-Davies was appointed in his place.
55 Sir Emile Fashole-Luke declined the appointment, and Mr Wales was appointed in his place. See p.222.

The history of the sixties of this century will record one of the most turbulent epochs of the African continent. Sierra Leone was no exception and the political leaders who brought a politically rich above average country of this continent to a standstill and returned her well nigh to jungle-law times, were inexcusably guilty of grave moral lapses.

The Commission found that corruption was widespread among the former politicians and some civil servants and recommended that the ill-gotten gains should be refunded to the state.

The DOVE-EDWIN Commission.

The only comment pertinent to this commission's activities which have been discussed before[56] relates to the NRC's commitment to return the country to civilian rule. In paragraph 48 of its comments on the report, the NRC reiterated that it "appreciates the earnestness of local aspirations for a return to civilian rule at the earliest possible time. Not only does the council agree in principle to handing over to a civilian government at the shortest possible time, but it is cognisant of the promise which it has consistently held out to the nation from the time of its assumption of power on the 23rd day of March 1967 . . . .[57] Therefore, the National Reformation Council has decided to institute a Civilian Rule Committee comprising of representatives of paramount chiefs, local government authorities, religious bodies, the banned All People's Congress, the banned Sierra Leone People's Party with the exception of Sir Albert Margai, Trade Unions, the National Advisory Council, the Medical Association, the Bar Association, the Chamber of Commerce, and the six independent successful candidates in the last general elections".

The Civilian Rule Committee was set up with Dr Raymond S. Easmon as chairman and Mr M. S. Mustapha as deputy chairman. The secretary was a civil servant, Mr V. O. Young. Its terms of reference were as follows:

> To advise the National Reformation Council on the necessity for fresh general elections before a return to civilian rule.
> If the committee decides on "no elections" the methods of forming a national government in order to ensure a peaceful return to civilian rule.
> If the committee decides that there should be another general election, the stages by which the handing over should be effected.
> Any other action which the committee considers necessary to effect a peaceful hand over.

On the 21st February 1968, they were addressed by the Chairman of the NRC Col. Juxon-Smith,[58] and on the 21st March, they handed over their report to the NRC. No steps had been taken towards implementing the report before the NRC Government was overthrown.

56 See infra pp.217-219.
57 Paragraph 51 page 5 of the report.
58 See the Newspaper, '*UNITY*' of March 22 1968.

The BEOKU-BETTS Commission.

Mr Justice Ronald Beoku-Betts, a Judge of the Supreme Court (as it then was) was appointed to head this Commission of Inquiry. Four reports were presented to government[59] by this commission. They dealt respectively, with:
  (a) The Coffee Deal
  (b) The sale of palm-oil, rice and coffee haulers, nut-cracking machine and the industrialisation programme.
  (c) The Price Maintenance Fund, and
  (d) The Canteen Accounts.

The most important, and from the public point of view, the most sensational, was the 'Coffee Deal'. The commission's report on this transaction was submitted on the 4th August 1967 and the NRC accepted its recommendations ordering the persons found involved to pay monies to government. In some cases, real estate belonging to the affected parties was confiscated.[60]

Following the death of Mr Justice Beoku-Betts in January 1968, Mr Justice Percy R. Davies was appointed to continue the work of the commission and he submitted the last two reports.[61]

The FASHOLE-LUKE/WALES Commission.

Sir Emile Fashole-Luke was appointed sole commissioner to investigate the affairs of the Immigration Quota Committee. He declined and Mr J. G. Wales a retired police officer was appointed in his place. The terms of reference were as follows:
  (a) To inquire into the conduct of the Immigration Quota Committee from 1st January 1961 to 23rd March 1967, and in particular to inquire:
    (i) whether or not any malpractice or irregularity was committed by any member of the Immigration Quota Committee with respect to the granting of immigration quotas during the aforesaid period:
    (ii) the nature of such malpractices and irregularities if any; and
    (iii) the identities of the persons involved in such malpractices and irregularities.
  (b) To make recommendation for a better and more effective system of granting of immigration quotas.

---

59 The chairman and the other two commissioners, Messrs O. J. C. Williams (police) and Major Sheku Tarawalli (army) signed the first report. The second report was compiled from notes made by the chairman before he died.
60 See '*Unity*' Nov. 2 1967.
61 Mr O. J. C. Williams was the sole commissioner to sign the Price Maintenance Fund Inquiry Report as the place of Major Tarawalli had been taken by Major Noah after the overthrow of the NRC. Noah also, was facing a criminal charge at the time the report was submitted. In the case of the Canteen Accounts, Mr Justice Percy Davies was reappointed by the civilian government as sole commissioner.

From Independence to Republicanism 1961-1971 223

This commission, like all other commissions set up under the NRC was suspended by the Anti-Corruption Revolutionary Movement when it overthrew the National Reformation Council in April 1968. The Wales Commission was reappointed by the civilian government in May 1968 and reported to the prime minister on the 28th October 1968. The government put out a statement on the 17th December 1968,[62] approving some of the recommendations of the report and, in particular, accepting that a Business Immigration Quota Committee should be set up with the following membership and terms of reference:

> The Minister of Trade and Industry (Chairman)
> The Minister of External Affairs
> The Minister of Development
> A representative of the S. L. Chamber of Commerce
> Two citizens to be appointed by the Prime Minister
> The Principal Immigration Officer, (Secretary)

The functions of the committee were to include:
(a) receiving applications for quotas and considering all the facts of the case prescribed on the application form:
(b) Compilation of an up-to-date list of all expatriates in the country.

The PERCY DAVIES Commission.
This commission was set up by the NRC on the 6th June 1967 with Mr Justice Percy R. Davies as chairman and Messrs E. J. Davies and J. C. O. Hamilton as members to:

> Inquire into and report on all activities of the Freetown City Council from 1st January 1964, and, without prejudice to any criminal prosecutions which may be pending, to make recommendations with a view to a more efficient and effective system of administration in the Freetown municipality.

The commission reported to the NRC on the 7th October 1967, which accepted the recommendations in substance and issued a White Paper thereon. The NRC requested a number of individuals to repay the total sum of twenty-two thousand nine hundred and seventy-eight Leones forty-six cents found to have been acquired illegally.

The BROWNE-MARKE Commission.
This was set up to look into the administration and finance of the United Mineworkers' Union, but as this body was not of any constitutional or historical importance in Sierra Leone, no further discussion of this inquiry will be made.

EVALUATION.
The Commissions of Inquiry set up by the NRC are of interest and importance to the constitutional or legal historian purely from the perspective of their legality. They were all set up under the provisions of the laws of Sierra Leone and, with the solitary exception of the Wales

62 See The Wales Report (Govt. Printer, Freetown) 1968.

Commission, were all chaired by judges. In the course of their activities, they summoned witnesses, exercised powers of contempt and made orders against private citizens. The NRC itself confiscated private property under the provisions of the Forfeiture of Assests Decree.

It is submitted that the status of these commissions is tied up with the status of the NRC itself. After the return to civilian rule, the government took the view that the NRC was an illegal government and replaced most of its laws. They did the same with the commissions. They reappointed the commissioners with the same terms of reference and allowed them to continue their work. An indemnity act was passed which purported to cure all the defects of the administration under the NRC. Since the NRC during its tenure of office had itself passed a decree prohibiting the challenging of any of its orders in a court of law, it was not open to anyone to challenge the validity of the commissions set up by the NRC. They were, however, very popular in any event as they exposed a great deal of the corrupt practices of the outgoing civilian administration of Sir Albert Margai.

The TREASON TRIALS.
The civilian government of Mr Siaka Stevens conducted two treason trials, following the restoration of civilian rule. The first, popularly described in Sierra Leone as the First Treason Trial, was that of The State against David Lansana and:

    Leslie William Leigh (Commissioner of Police)
    Augustine Charles Blake (Military — NRC)
    Bockarie I. Kai Samba (Military — NRC)
    Samuel Hinga Norman (Military)
    Kande Bureh (SLPP — ex-Minister)
    George Sulaiman Panda (ex-Civil Servant)
    Thomas Decker (ex-Civil Servant)
    Ella Koblo Gulama (Paramount Chief — SLPP)
    John Kallon (ex-Civil Servant)
    S. B. Daramy (ex-Civil Servant — Financial Secy.)
    Berthan Macaulay, QC (Attorney-General)
    Abu A. Koroma (Lawyer, later Attorney-General)
    Momoh G. Foh (Civil Servant — Elections Office)
    Sam Margai (Politician)
    A. B. Paila (Politician — Mende Tribal Headman)

Originally, they were charged on an indictment containing twelve counts of treason, treason felony and misprision of treason. A number of the counts were struck out and the indictment amended by order of the Hon. Chief Justice who was the trial judge, on the 7th February and 1st July 1969. The treason charge was brought under the provisions of the Treason and State Offences Act, 1963 of the laws of Sierra Leone. Various overt acts of treason were alleged. For example, it was alleged that the accused had agreed:

    (a) To imprison the Governor-General Sir Henry Lightfoot Boston and Mr Siaka P. Stevens who had been appointed prime minister.

(b) To seize control of the State House in Freetown, the seat of the executive head.
(c) To seize and take control of the Sierra Leone Broadcasting Service transmitting stations in Freetown.
(d) To suppress the publication and announcement of the appointment of Mr Siaka Stevens as prime minister.
(e) To declare martial law in Sierra Leone and take over the government of Sierra Leone.
(f) To impose and enforce a curfew.
(g) To assemble members of parliament.[63]
(h) To delay and suppress the publication of the results of the 1967 general elections.
(i) To falsify the results of the 1967 general elections.

At the end of the case for the prosecution, various submissions of no case were made to the court, but these were, on the 1st July 1969, dismissed by the Acting Chief Justice.[64] The trial continued and at the end, on Saturday the 18th April 1970, three were acquitted and discharged, that is, Abu Koroma, Samuel M. Margai and Abu B. Paila; two were sentenced to seven years' imprisonment each, that is, John Kallon and S. B. Daramy and the rest were sentenced to death.[65]

The convicted persons appealed to the Sierra Leone Court of Appeal[66] which held that the trial was a nullity. It quashed the convictions of all the accused. The government put out a statement that the accused would be retried but this retrial never took place.[67]

Although the judgment of the Court of Appeal was quite a lengthy one, the conclusion was based on a narrow point. The indictment had charged the accused with "endeavouring or preparing" to overthrow the government of Sierra Leone by unlawful means. The court found the charge duplicitous as they concluded that "endeavouring" was a separate offence from "preparing" to overthrow, under the provisions of the Treason and State Offences Act, 1963. In the result, the accused were all discharged.[68]

THE SECOND TREASON TRIAL — R-v-JUXON-SMITH & ORS.

The second Treason Trial was fixed for hearing in the Supreme Court on Tuesday the 19th May 1970. Standing trial for treason were the following:—

Ex-Brigadier A. T. W. Juxon-Smith
Ex-Commissioner of Police Leslie William Leigh.

---

63 Lansana the head of the military, after declaring 'Martial Law' had made a public announcement summoning members of parliament to meet.
64 See R-v-Lansana, 1968-69 African Law Reports, S.L.Series at p.250.
65 See *'Unity'* April 20 1970.
66 Presiding was Mr Justice Tambiah, a retired judge from Ceylon who was serving in Sierra Leone: Mr Justice Philip R. Bridges, Chief Justice of the Gambia and Mr Justice S. Beccles Davies, from Sierra Leone.
67 See *Daily Mail* of May 12 1971.
68 See R-v-Lansana & Ors. 1970 A.L.R. (S.L. Series).

Col. Augustine Charles Blake
Col. Bockarie I. Kai Samba
M. M. Koroma
Berthan Macaulay QC
Sahr James Foyah
Sam M'Boma

There were two counts in the indictment charging the accused with preparing or endeavouring to carry out by force an enterprise which usurped the executive power of the state. Several overt acts of treason were alleged, including the announcement of a complete take over of the country by the army and the police, the formation of the National Reformation Council, the suspension of the constitution; the placing of the Governor-General under house arrest; the putting of the prime minister under protective custody and the publishing of decrees and other enactments purporting to be for the administration of Sierra Leone in violation of the country's constitution.

Juxon-Smith refused to plead and contended inter alia:
>That judges of both the Court of Appeal and the Supreme Court had taken oaths of office before the NRC.
>That the court recognised the validity of the NRC Government and gave effect to its decrees, citing the case of R-v-Bob-Jones.
>That the government of Sierra Leone as then constituted, recognised and gave effect to the policies of the NRC, the prime minister having been sworn in by Mr Justice Banja Tejan-Sie, then Ag. Governor-General who was himself appointed to that office by the NRC.

In spite of Juxon-Smith's attitude and the legal objections he raised to being tried by the court, he was tried and convicted and sentenced to death. He appealed to the Sierra Leone Court of Appeal along with the others and his conviction was quashed.[69]

As in the Lansana case, the Court of Appeal held that under the Treason and State Offences Act, "prepares" and "endeavours" were separate offences which should be charged separately, and an indictment which joins them will be bad for duplicity. "A person can prepare to do an act without endeavouring to do it or endeavour to do it without preparing at the same time to do it."[70]

---

69 There was yet another treason trial — that of Paramount Chief Madam Ella Koblo Gulama of the Moyamba District who was charged with Mr Robert Combey Kajue, MP and army officers Henry H. Swarray, Joseph B. Buanie, Benedict W. M. Gbondo and Sahr James Foyah. The trial was terminated by the Prime Minister Mr S. P. Stevens on account of the illness of Mr C. B. Rogers-Wright who had been instructed to conduct the prosecution on behalf of the Crown.
70 See Juxon-Smith-v-The State 1970-71 A.L.R. (Sierra Leone Series) 361 at p.367.

CHAPTER X

THE REPUBLICAN CONSTITUTION, 1971

Introductory
Ever since Sierra Leone achieved its independence in 1961, the question of republican status had been a live issue. The conservative politicians felt that a monarchy was best as it would remove from the politicians the ever present incentive to be authoritarian and corrupt. They saw the existence within the hierachy of government, of a Governor-General who was the Queen's representative as a valuable possible check against the tempestuous desires and wishes of a prime minister craving for power. On the other hand, the more vocal nationalists saw the existence of a monarchy as infra dignitatem, embarrassing and undesirable. They wanted to have a president and were prepared to accommodate their opponents by having a formal president rather than an executive president.

In 1967, the Albert Margai regime precipitately brought forward the issue of republicanism and in the process caused genuine fears among the population that he intended to use this form of government as a means of establishing autocratic rule, silencing his opponents and entrenching himself in power and suppressing free speech and fundamental liberties in Sierra Leone. The manner in which the constitution was sought to be amended in 1967 by rushing through a hurriedly drafted bill for republican rule, with all the important arms of government, including the judiciary, under the control of the prime minister, merely served to increase the suspicion and uneasiness generally felt that republicanism, in any shape or form, was a bad thing.

After the overthrow of the military regime, there were attempted coups and threats of coups and a proliferation of arrests of numerous persons including leaders of the defeated Sierra Leone People's Party. Thus, following election petitions which were heard in 1968 as a result of which a number of elected members lost their seats because of election irregularities,[1] the civilian government of Mr Stevens, fixed dates for

---

1 There were several election petitions against the SLPP candidates. A large number of these were successful. This was understandable especially as the Dove-Edwin Report had shown extensive malpractices by the outgoing government.

holding these by-elections.[2] They were suspended indefinitely. On the 22nd November 1968, the Sierra Leone Parliament passed a resolution approving the Declaration of a State of Emergency and two opposition newspapers, the *"People"* and the *"Express"* were banned.

The motion for declaring a State of Emergency was moved by Mr M. O. Bash-Taqui, Minister of the Interior on the 22nd September 1968. It was passed the same day by a majority of fifty-two to two, the two voting against being F. M. Jabati and F. M. Minah.[3] Subsequently, some of the former SLPP parliamentarians and others were arrested on various charges of riotous conduct, incitement and unlawful assembly.[4] A number of detentions were effected under the emergency provisions. The State of Emergency was revoked on the 26th February 1969, but, as will become apparent later on, was restored on the 14th September 1970.

In April 1969, the government announced its intention of setting up a committee to sound public opinion on the desirability of introducing a republican form of government for Sierra Leone. In June 1969, the committee was invited to meet. It held its inaugural meeting at the Parliament Building on Monday the 23rd June 1969. This committee had wide representation. The only notable absentee was the Sierra Leone People's Party which, when invited, declined to participate. It was composed of representatives of the following organisations:—

    The Sierra Leone Bar Association
    The Medical and Dental Association
    The United Christian Council
    The Roman Catholic Mission
    The Sierra Leone Muslim Congress
    The University of Sierra Leone
    The All People's Congress
    The Committee of Management of the Rural Area Council
    The Labour Congress
    The District Councils
    Representatives of the Paramount Chiefs

Curiously, this committee was convened without being given any terms of reference. The secretariat however, drew up rules of procedure for the committee to settle. One of the proposals made by its chairman immediately after the commission had been addressed by the prime minister, was that certain clauses of the 1961 Constitution were to be amended and that a recommendation to that effect should go to parliament. As some members felt that this would be unconstitutional since Section 43 of the 1961 Constitution prescribed the manner for amendment of the constitution, the proposal was not accepted and the work of the commission was hampered.

    Late in 1969 and early in 1970, the Sierra Leone Parliament debated the question of republicanism and the inevitable delegations from all

---

2 See page 217 infra.
3 See House of Representatives Debates, Session 1968-9. Vol. II. No. 24.
4 See the case of The State-v-Jusu Sheriff & fifteen others.

over the country began to descend on the capital Freetown in support of a republican form of government for Sierra Leone. On Friday the 23rd January 1970, after a three-day debate, parliament passed a resolution that "it is now overdue for our country to improve its constitutional status". The motion was passed by a large majority in the house. The prime minister then tabled a government motion which read as follows:[5]

> BE IT ALSO RESOLVED that a commission be set up to sound public opinion throughout the country as to the type of constitution by means of which Sierra Leone could achieve its desired objectives, and as to any other matters ancillary thereto and make recommendations as it may deem fit.

Apparently, this was in keeping with an undertaking given by the prime minister some months earlier that the abortive Republican Constitution Committee which had been dissolved, would be replaced by "a Commission which would sound public opinion throughout the country."[6]

The motion was passed and on the 10th June 1970, Government Notice No. 611 was published in the *Sierra Leone Gazette* announcing that under the provisions of the Commissions of Inquiry Act, Cap. 27 of the Laws of Sierra Leone, 1960, a Commission of Inquiry had been set up by the Governor-General to review the present constitution and to inquire into and determine the desire or otherwise of the mass of the people of Sierra Leone to change the present constitution in such a manner as to introduce a republican form of government. On the 17th June 1970, this new Constitutional Review Commission, chaired by Sir Emile Fashole Luke, Speaker of the Sierra Leone Parliament, held its first meeting. This time, the commission was given terms of reference. These included the following:

(a) To study and review the present constitution of the state of Sierra Leone.

(b) To enquire into and determine the desire or otherwise of the people of Sierra Leone to change the present constitution in such a manner as to introduce a republican form of government.

(c) In the event that the commission finds that a change to republican status is desired, to ascertain what kind of republican constitution the nation should adopt.

(d) To examine the status, role, duties and mode of appointment of a president.

(e) To look into the constitution of the courts with particular reference to the possibility of appeals from the Supreme Court and the relationship with the Judicial Committee of the Privy Council.

---

5 See House of Representatives' Debates Second Session 1969/70.
6 In its 1967 general election manifesto, the APC had said that "as a very first step, an APC government would consult the people whether or not they want a change to a republican form of government and if the answer is that they want a change to republican status, what type of republic they would want".

(f) To look into the composition of parliament, citizenship and literacy qualifications, the position of paramount chiefs and the question of a second chamber.

(g) To examine the public services in order to ensure that any changes in the form of government will not disrupt their efficiency.

(h) To look into the role of the auditor-general in respect of the submission of his report on the accounts of Sierra Leone to a parliamentary committee three months before the budget each year.

The commission was also charged with defining such things as "the principle of separation of powers, the Rule of Law, the Independence of the Judiciary, the preservation of human rights and freedoms and the law of nations". It held several meetings both in the capital Freetown, and in the provinces, but before it could make a report on its activities, the security situation in the country had deteriorated so badly that this was not possible.

THE BIRTH OF A NEW OPPOSITION.

> For Forms of Government let fools contest:
> What'er is best administered is best.
> *Alexander Pope*

From the date of its assumption of the reins of government in 1968, many people had become suspicious of the APC government and distrustful of its motives in trying to establish a republican form of government in Sierra Leone.[7] On the 10th June 1970, a new party, the National Democratic Party was formed to provide a viable opposition to the government. This followed the wave of arrests of SLPP members in April, 1970.[8] On the 22nd July, a motion was introduced into the house by S. A. T. Koroma,[9] MP for Port Loko West, asking for a re-delimitation of parliamentary constituencies. This motion was adopted by parliament. On the 12th September, two senior ministers of the government, Dr M. S. Forna and Mr M. O. Bash-Taqui who held the portfolios of finance and works respectively, tendered their resignations from the government following serious disagreement with the prime minister over the party's moves to introduce a republican form of government with the prime minister as Executive President. Dr Forna's letter of resignation was long and detailed and was an attack on the prime minister and his policies. On the other hand, Bash-Taqui's was short as he did "not wish to enumerate here, the several issues over which we have disagreed".[10]

---

7 See, for example, Dr R. S. Easmon's article "Fears over Constitutional Change" in the *Daily Mail* of Saturday May 16 1970.

8 This included the leader, Mr S. Jusu-Sheriff and other supporters such as Regina James of Kono and paramount chief Ella Koblo Gulama.

9 He was a strong APC supporter and activist.

10 See *'Probe'* Special Edition — The Folly of S. Stevens.

On the 11th September 1970, the following resolution was issued under the hand of the Secretary General of the APC, Mr C. A. Kamara-Taylor:
It is hereby resolved at this meeting of the central committee held at H. S. 56, Hill Station, Freetown, and by a resolution tabled by "Comrade" J. Barthes Wilson and seconded by "Comrade" S. I. Koroma, it was unanimously resolved that the following should be expelled from the All People's Congress (APC) as from today, Friday, 11th September 1970.
1. Hon. Mohamed O. Bash-Taqui
2. Mr Abu Lakkoh
3. Mr Ibrahim Ortole Kargbo
4 Hon. Ibrahim Bash-Taqui
5. Hon. Dr Mohamed Forna

On the 14th September 1970, the prime minister broadcast to the nation, alleging that some people were trying to gain power by unlawful means. He then declared a state of emergency. This followed the expulsion of five members from the central committee of the party and a notice from the Ministry of Information and Broadcasting suspending all public meetings.[11]

The ban notwithstanding, a meeting was held at a public place[12] on Sunday the 13th September 1970 by a "Committee of Citizens" under the chairmanship of Dr R. S. Easmon. It was addressed by three erstwhile supporters of the APC, Dr John Karefa Smart, Dr M. S. Forna and Mr Ibrahim Taqui among others.[13] On the 21st September 1970, a new party was formed called the United Democratic Party. It was a merger of the National Democratic Party and the Committee of Citizens.

On the 28th September 1970, after acting in that office for two years, Sir Banja Tejan-Sie was confirmed as Governor-General of Sierra Leone. On the 8th October, the UDP was declared illegal and all its leaders arrested. On the 19th October 1970, parliament passed a government motion ratifying the state of emergency.[14] Thereafter, parliament passed an indemnity act precluding the institution of any legal proceedings in any court in respect of anything done during the period 13th September when the state of emergency was declared and 19th October when parliament ratified the declaration. Applications for writs

---

11 The notice, under the hand of the minister, K. A. Daramy, said: "In view of the confusion and political threats to law and order that have been created by recent political meetings, the undertone of subversion and the active attempts by ill-disposed persons to create serious discord in the security forces the conclusion has been forced upon government that further public meetings in existing circumstances and conditions are not in the public interest. The holding of all public meetings throughout the country is therefore suspended until further notice . . . .
12 The Queen Elizabeth the 2nd Playing Field.
13 See *Probe* Special Edition — "The Folly of Siaka Stevens" op. cit. at pp.10 and 12. Also the *Daily Express* of Sept. 14, 1970, Vol. 4, No. 83.
14 See Parliamentary Debates Vol. II Sess. 1970/71. No. 29. Speech of the PM on Govt. Motion of the State of Public Emergency. The record relating to the Indemnity is at p.5.

of Habeas Corpus were made for the release of politicians detained under the emergency. These were granted by the Acting Chief Justice.[15] The Act of Indemnity covered acts done in good faith and in the execution of duty or in the public interest.

The Secretary of the Constitutional Review Commission, Mr J. B. Jenkins-Johnston, died on the 4th September 1970. The commission then, "in order to conduct their work more expeditiously" appointed a seven-member sub-committee to "study and review in closer detail the present constitution . . . . and to report back its findings to the commission." The commission also designed a questionnaire to the public and set up a standing committee of seven members, namely: P. C. Foday Kai, Mrs Cassandra Garber, Dr W. H. Fitzjohn, Dr R. E. Mondeh, Dr W. S. Marcus Jones and Messrs H. D. Charles and J. S. Funna. The terms of reference of the standing committee, were as follows:

(i) Primarily, to vet important releases to the press and the public, on behalf of the commission and to determine suitable publicity material and arrangements, in collaboration with the Ministry of Information and Broadcasting:

(ii) To aim partly at obviating the sort of difficulty connected with the determination of the last questionnaire which was issued out to the public, and generally at making the press and publicity aspect of the commission's work, expeditious effective and workable, as this aspect is vital to the success of the commission:

(iii) To be reporting back periodically to plenary sessions of the commission.

There were five other sub-committees formed "to enquire into and determine the desire or otherwise of the mass of the people of Sierra Leone to change the present constitution in such a manner as to introduce a republican form of government". These sub-committees toured the country, collecting evidence and sounding public opinion.[16]

The courts were kept busy between October and December 1960. Rev Paul Dumbar, a Kono District former SLPP Parliamentarian, and five others were charged with malicious damage to the APC office in Koidu: Two army officers were dismissed and nine others detained, including Morlai Kamara whom, it was widely believed, had been instrumental in leading the revolt against the NRC. It was alleged that a quantity of ammunition was missing. Jonathan Lengar a lecturer at Milton Margai

15 Among the people detained were Dr R. S. Easmon, Dr Karefa-Smart, Dr M. S. Forma and Mr M. O. Bash-Taqui, the last two, being the ministers who had resigned from the government. In the case of Kamara and Others-v-the Director of Prisons 1972-3, A. L. R. (S.L. Series) at p.162 the detainees, all of whom had been detained under the emergency regulations applied for Habeas Corpus. The court upheld the solicitor general's contention that the court could not inquire into the grounds on which the president had exercised his jurisdiction to issue the detention orders. He was the proper person to sign them. When once a return had been made to the writ, the applicants should refute the averments contained therein.

16 See Govt. Notice No. 1219 in the S. L. Gazette Vol. CI of Thursday, 19th November 1970 at p.1244.

Teachers' College and Councillor Mohammed Kanu a former APC supporter, were detained. Alhaji Monrovia and Suyllay Conteh were charged with various offences including assault, at Lunsar: Mr Mohammed Bash-Taqui, the former Minister of Development was charged with fifteen others, with riotous behaviour in the Port Loko district.

The prime minister's office announced in November that eleven army detainees were to be tried[17] by court martial while eighteen civilian detainees had already been put on trial leaving only seventeen more in detention. The statement denied allegations that Mr Stevens wanted to be the executive president of a republican Sierra Leone and said he had never expressed such a wish. It commented that the government could not introduce a republic in Sierra Leone under the existing constitution without first dissolving parliament and then holding fresh general elections.

On the 8th December 1970, a government motion to increase the number of members of parliament from 66 to 85 was passed. At a press conference held at the prime minister's office on the 15th December, the prime minister said that, since the invasion of Guinea and the subsequent meeting of the Organisation of African Unity in Lagos, it had been decided to group regionally for defence and other purposes. In this regard, Sierra Leone was taking the initiative to create a sub regional grouping with her immediate neighbours, Guinea and Liberia. The prime minister announced that parliament would be recalled as a matter of "great urgency" to debate the defence arrangements. On the 22nd December, parliament debated the motion on the subject, introduced by the Minister of External Affairs, Mr C. P. Foray which read as follows:

> BE IT RESOLVED that in view of the vital need for common defence arrangements among the newly emerging states of Africa so as to protect not only their individual interests but their common interests as a whole and in view of the desperate need for such action against the threat of foreign invasion as shown in the recent invasion of the Republic of Guinea:
>
> BE IT RESOLVED that the Government of Sierra Leone, for a start, shall enter into immediate negotiations with the Government of the Republic of Guinea and the Republic of Liberia, its next door neighbours, with a view to concluding mutual defence arrangements within the context of an all African Defence Organisation under an African High Command.

After a stormy debate the measure was passed.

On the 23rd December, the prime minister released from detention the widely respected and admired Dr Raymond S. Easmon.[18] A new court martial presided over by Mr Justice S. C. E. Warne was convened to try

---

17 The trial began of Warrant Officer Class II, Alex Conteh and others. The Judge Advocate, Mr Justice S. Beccles Davies said the whole proceedings were a nullity and ordered a retrial of the soldiers. He said that the court martial had no jurisdiction.

18 See *Unity* for Thursday, Dec. 24, 1970.

Warrant Officer Class II, Alex Conteh and Others. The Constitutional Review Commission continued its work. On the 6th January 1971, Mr Freddie Short was sworn in as a member by the Governor-General. At that date, there were three vacancies to be filled. Dr R. S. Easmon, who was detained and released just before Christmas and who did not return to the commission: Mr E. Livesey Luke who had by then been appointed a judge and Mr C. B. Rogers-Wright who died in January 1971. On the 10th January 1971, at an APC Convention held at Cape Sierra Hotel, a motion calling for the introduction of a republic was passed unanimously. At the same convention, the delegates moved another motion calling for the postponement of general elections in the country "until the full term of the present government expires".

On the 4th February 1971, the Attorney-General, James E. Mahoney Esq., entered a nolle prosequi in respect of prosecutions which had been instituted against two former SLPP ministers, M. S. Mistapha and Doyle Sumner. On the 6th February, a Government delegation went to the Republic of Guinea to discuss defence arrangements.[19] On the 18th February, Karefa Smart and other UDP members were released from detention. A prominent barrister, Mr Cyrus Rogers-Wright, who had been in detention, was released on the 25th January.

While these developments were taking place in Sierra Leone, the students in London were engaged in their own form of protest against the developments at home. On the 21st January 1971, they seized the Sierra Leone High Commission in London, held all the staff of the commission hostage and then telephoned to the Prime Minister in Freetown that they had appointed their own high commissioner. The London police intervened. They were subsequently arrested on a charge of conspiracy. They were tried in the High Court and convicted. They appealed unsuccessfully all the way up to the House of Lords.[20]

On the 2nd March 1971, the Court of Appeal, consisting of Sir Samuel Bankole Jones, Mr Justice Dove-Edwin and Mr Justice J. B. Marcus Jones, quashed the conviction and sentence passed on Warrant Officer Class II Alex Conteh by the Army Court Martial, of the offence of incitement to mutiny. He had been sentenced to death. On the 10th March 1971, the President of the Court of Appeal, Sir Samuel Bankole Jones was hurriedly sent on leave by the government. Mr Justice C. O. E. Cole was sworn in as Acting President of the Court of Appeal on the 17th March 1971. On the 20th March the prime minister's office put out a statement explaining the circumstances leading to the leave granted to Sir Samuel. The statement read as follows:

> It is announced from the prime minister's office that on the strength of authoritative reports recently received in connection

---

19 The delegation consisted of: Brewah, Minister of Health: S. I. Koroma, Min/Agriculture and Natural Resources: C. A. Kamara-Taylor, Min/Lands Mines and Labour: Shears: Min/Works: Kargbo: Min/Transport. Dan Decker, Perm Sec. Min/Defence. M. M'Bayo, Sen. Asst. Sec. Min/External Affairs; Kawusu-Conteh, Min/Southern Province A. B. S. Janneh, Dep. Min/Finance.

20 See D. P. P.-v-Kamara and Others (1973) 2 All.E.R. 1242: (1974) A. C. 104.

with certain incidents at the Sierra Leone High Commission in London on January 21 this year, when a group of students seized the High Commission, held the commission's staff as hostages, declared one of themselves as newly appointed commissioner, the government has reviewed the general position and matters directly connected with it.

Following this review, Sir Samuel Bankole Jones, President of the Court of Appeal (who returned from his last vacation in 1967) has been invited by the government to take his full entitlement of 409 days vacation leave.

Sir Samuel duly proceeded on leave with effect from March 15 1971, on which date Justice C. O. E. Cole the substantive Chief Justice, took up office as Acting President of the Court of Appeal.

On the 22nd March 1971, the government denied that it had taken a decision on republicanism for Sierra Leone.[21] The next day, March 23rd, during the early hours of the morning, an attempted coup was staged by sections of the armed forces. They tried to assassinate the prime minister by going to his residence and shooting wildly at his residence. He escaped but later on during the day the soldiers made another attempt, this time at the prime minister's office. This time also, he escaped unhurt. The head of the Sierra Leone military forces, Brigadier Bangura, made a broadcast over the government controlled Sierra Leone broadcasting service that he had taken over the government of the country. Shortly, following an exchange of gunfire it was announced by a senior military officer, Colonel Sam King, that the army recognised only the government of Mr Siaka Stevens and had put down the rebellion of the brigadier. Subsequently, the brigadier and others were arrested. On the 24th March, Dr Karefa Smart left the country, and on the 25th March, the tour of the western area by the Fifth Working Group of the Constitutional Review Commission was suspended. On the 26th March, five senior army officers were arrested.[22] In the meantime, the prime minister left Sierra Leone unannounced and went to the Republic of Guinea where he signed a defence agreement, pursuant to the resolution of parliament passed on the 22nd December 1970, to enter into tripartite negotiations with Liberia and Guinea within the context of an African high command. Following the signing of this treaty, the Republic of Guinea stationed troops in Sierra Leone.

On the 28th March, the prime minister broadcast to the nation announcing the signing of the agreement and giving reasons therefore.[23] On the 29th March, the Governor-General, Sir Banja Tejan-Sie was relieved of his post and the Chief Justice, Mr Justice C. O. E. Cole,

---
21 See *Daily Mail* of March 23, 1971.
22 The officers were: Major Abu Noah: Major S. E. Momoh: Cap. L. F. Sesay: Lt. Bull and Lt. Eric Mansaray.
23 See *Daily Mail* of March 29 1971.

appointed to act in his place. On the 31st March, the Governor-General left Sierra Leone for London. The same day, Brigadier Bangura and twelve others were put in detention.[24] On the 7th April 1971, parliament ratified the defence agreement with Guinea signed by the prime minister on the 26th March. On the 15th April, Sierra Leone Military Forces (Amendment) Act was passed which denied the right of appeal to anyone found guilty by a court martial.

THE REPUBLICAN CONSTITUTION.

> A constitution is but a means to an end; and the end is good government. The quality of government depends upon the people who exercise it not upon the constitution.
>
> *Sir Ivor Jennings.*

On the 15th April 1971, by a majority of 51 to 5, the Sierra Leone Parliament amended Section 51 of the 1961 Constitution retrospectively to the 27th April 1961, to provide that a bill enacting a new constitution could be passed by the House of Representatives in two successive parliaments, (as opposed to two successive sessions), without the concurrence of the Governor-General, there having been a dissolution between the first and second of those parliaments.[25] On the 19th April 1971, parliament approved by a majority of 53 to 10, a bill establishing a republican form of government for Sierra Leone. The bill so passed, was identical with that passed by the Albert Margai Government in 1967. Mr Justice C. O. E. Cole was then sworn in as the First President of Sierra Leone under the new republican constitution. Same day, Prime Minister, Dr Siaka Stevens[26] assured the people of Sierra Leone that the government would revise the constitution to reflect more fully the views, aspirations and desires of the Sierra Leone peoples when the results of the Luke Commission of Inquiry were known. He said the government would not take advantage of the undesirable provisions of the republican constitution prepared and passed by the previous government in June 1967.

On the 20th April 1971, the president swore in the new judiciary under the republican constitution. On the following day, that is, the 21st April 1971, the constitution was further amended to establish the office of executive president and to create the office of vice-president. The prime minister was then unanimously elected President of the Republic of Sierra Leone following a resolution of the house to that effect. Dr Siaka Probyn Stevens thus replaced Mr Justice C. O. E. Cole as the Second President of the Republic of Sierra Leone, who, after holding office for

---

24 The prime minister on the 31st march 1971, in a speech in parliament said that "man is a brute and it is only brute force that he understands". He was speaking on the attempts on his life. See Report of Emergency Session: Also *Daily Mail* 1/4/71.
25 This paved the way for the passing of the Sierra Leone Republic Bill which had received its first affirmative two-thirds vote in 1967.
26 He had by then been granted an Honorary Degree by the University of Sierra Leone.

two days, reverted to his substantive position as Chief Justice. On the 23rd April, seventeen cabinet ministers were appointed and five deputy ministers and on the next day, Mr Sorie Ibrahim Koroma was sworn in as the First Vice-President of the Republic of Sierra Leone. On the 19th May 1971, three new ministers and two deputy ministers were appointed.

Brigadier Bangura Tried and Executed.
Brigadier Bangura and others were charged with incitement to mutiny before a court martial and convicted. It is sufficient to reproduce the government statement from the president's office on the matter:

> It is announced from the office of the president that in accordance with the provisions of the law, the cabinet has now studied the conclusions reached by the recent court martial at which Brigadier John A. Bangura and 8 other officers were on trial for incitement to mutiny with violence contrary to Section 37(1) (a) of the Sierra Leone Military Forces Act, No. 34 of 1961 as amended.
>
> The cabinet has noted that, in accordance with the Army Act, 1955, and the Sierra Leone Military Forces Act No. 34 of 1961 the finding and sentence of the said court martial have been confirmed and promulgated.
>
> The cabinet accepts unreservedly the finding and sentence and order of the court martial in respect of the individual officers as follows:
>
> SENTENCED TO DEATH
> 1st Accd. Brig. J. A. Bangura (SL/2)
> 3rd Accd. Major S. E. Momoh (SL/48)
> 4th Accd. Major F. L. M. Jawara (SL/36)
> 7th Accd. Lt. J. B. S. Kolugbonda (SL/89)
> SENTENCED TO DEATH WITH RECOMMENDATION FOR MERCY
> 2nd Accd. Major D. D. K. Vandi (SL/17)
> 5th Accd. Lt. F. L. Sesay (SL/132)
> SENTENCED TO FIFTEEN YEARS' IMPRISONMENT
> 9th Accd. Lt. H. Bull (SL/133)
> SENTENCED TO FIVE YEARS' IMPRISONMENT
> 6th Accd. Lt. E. B. S. Mansaray (SL/60)
> HONOURABLY ACQUITTED AND DISCHARGED
> 8th Accd. Lt. M. M. Kosia (SL/90)
> It is announced for the information of the public that the 1st, 3rd, 4th and 7th accused, Brigadier J. A. Bangura, Major S. E. Momoh, Major F. L. M. Jawara and Lt. J. B. S. Kolugbonda were all duly executed at the Central Prisons, Pademba Road, during the early hours of Tuesday June 29 1971 . . . .

The Provisions of the Republican Constitution.
The Republican Constitution of 1971 was identical with that passed in 1967 as the Republic of Sierra Leone Bill. The Government of Sir Albert Margai was at pains to declare that the proposed republic would be a

"democratic" one. This assurance was also given by the Government of Dr Siaka Stevens. As understood in institutions which have been derived from or have adopted the practices of the British Parliament, the word "Democracy" has two meanings. First, it connotes what is commonly described in the words of Abraham Lincoln, as government of the people, by the people and for the people. In other words, inherent in any democratic parliamentary institution is the implication of the right of the people and their absolute entitlement to participate through their accredited representatives, in the administration of the country. Second, democracy in the Greek connotation of the concept, simply means a government by the majority. Unfortunately, in most African countries there has been too much of a tendency to adhere to the second view. In either sense of the term, it is open to serious question whether the Republican Constitution of Sierra Leone as passed by the Sierra Leone Parliament can qualify for description as democratic.

The constitution made provision for a number of important matters, including a Bill of Rights, the presidency; parliament; legislative and parliamentary procedure; the exercise of executive authority; the judiciary; public finance and the public service. Equally, there were significant omissions as well as certain phenomena which gave the mistaken impression of democratic liberalism, for example, the absence of preventive detention.

Fundamental Rights Provisions.
The Fundamental Rights Provisions substantially reproduced those of the 1961 Constitution and were set out in the opening paragraphs of the Republican Constitution in Sections 1 to 14. The constitution was declared to be enacted by "the freely elected representatives of the people of Sierra Leone". A disturbing and unsatisfactory feature of the declaration of the rights and freedoms of the individual, was the extensive exclusionary clauses they contanined.[27] Apart from being of a general nature, some of them were so extensive as to render the guarantees themselves utterly useless and meaningless.

Although the constitution itself did not contain any explicit declaration of its supremacy over ordinary legislation, this fact was not only implicit in some of the provisions relating, for example, to amendments, but also could be derived from the privy council decision in the case of Akar-v-the Attorney-General. Most of the sections required that laws passed by the Sierra Leone Parliament should conform to what is reasonably required in the "interest of defence, public safety, public order, public morality or public health" and be shown to be "reasonably justifiable in a democratic society."[28] The government, in drafting the republican constitution took pains to revise the privy council decision on

---

27 See W. S. Marcus Jones — Unpublished dissertation on "The Fundamental Rights and Liberties of the Individual in the Sierra Leone Constitution, 1961" (Yale University, 1965) op. cit. where this matter is discussed in great detail.
28 See S. A. de Smith: Fundamental Rights in the British Commonwealth (1964).

citizenship in the Akar case and reversed it by providing in Section 13(4) (g), the protection from discrimination, the following:
Subsection (1) shall not apply to any law so far as that law makes provision:

*** *** ***

(g) for the limitation of citizenship to persons of negro African descent and for any restriction which may be placed upon certain classes of persons by the law relating to citizenship.

The Constitution in Section 14 gave power to the High Court in the exercise of its original jurisdiction to hear and determine any application made by any person who alleged that his fundamental rights and freedoms had been contravened. Any constitutional question arising in any court other than the High Court, the Court of Appeal or the Supreme Court, relating to the fundamental rights of any individual could, by Section 14(3) be referred to the High Court for determination.

The Presidency.
The constitution by its Section 16, made provision for a President of Sierra Leone to be Head of State and Commander in Chief of the Armed Forces. He was to be appointed by the cabinet,[29] and hold office during the pleasure of the cabinet. A significant omission was the absence of any provisions relating to his qualifications for office. The lacuna in the independence constitution as to the manner of his selection was filled. Apart from the fact that he was required by Section 17 to take and subscribe the oath of office, nothing was provided in respect of his role in the processes of government. Under the constitutional convention derived from Britain whereby the prime minister has weekly audiences with the Queen when she is kept informed of the activities of the government, the prime minister in Sierra Leone should have been required, as a constitutional obligation, to keep the governor-general, and now the president, fully informed of the general conduct of government and furnished with such information as he may require.

In the Congo, one of the major problems was the failure of the constitution to delineate the respective jurisdiction of the president and the prime minister and the tragedy of the situation which developed when each purported to dismiss the other is well known. The Sierra Leone Constitution, similarly left this important, and highly explosive potential, entirely unprovided for. There was nothing about what would happen if the prime minister refused to resign or dissolve the house. In short, there was an obvious need to incorporate in the constitution some constitutional conventions in this, as well as other areas.

In making this submission, one is not unaware of the problems of codification but the president, in any country, and particulary so in the developing countries has a tremendous duty to preserve impartiality in

---

[29] The discussion here is limited to the constitution as passed by parliament, and not to the subsequent amendments which will be discussed later.

the administration. He has a general duty to ensure the continuity of the state and the government. He must therefore be in a position to intervene to resolve a deadlock and to secure a return to normality as quickly as possible if and when the circumstances demand it. He is the ultimate guardian of the constitution and his powers and functions ought to have been better clarified.

PARLIAMENT.

The republican constitution provided for a unicameral parliament. It preserved the privileged seats given to paramount chiefs, thus, again perpetuating the disparity in the electoral provisions whereby electors in the provinces had the right to two representatives, namely the ordinary members of parliament and chiefs' members of parliament, whereas those in the western area, the former colony, had only one. Qualifications for election to parliament were set out in Section 21 and the age limit to qualify for membership was 25. It was a requirement of the constitution that a person, to be elected to parliament, should have sufficient proficiency in English "to enable him to take any active part in the proceedings of Parliament". Thus, one can assume that there was an express desire that those who claimed the right to legislate for the country should take an enlightened self-interest in the parliamentary process and in their ability to contribute to its deliberations. In modern democracies, membership of a legislature provides a forum for an intellectual and intelligent debate of issues. Sierra Leone has never been deficient in its supply of enlightened legislators, but the party political structure has tended to create a mood of frustration and disillusionment among those who could make excellent legislators and parliamentarians. Further, the constitution made no provision for ensuring that the party machinery coud bring in only its ablest and best members forward to occupy the exalted position of "Honourable" member of the Sierra Leone Republican Parliament.

With regard to the elective process, the constitution prescribed the manner in which laws were to be passed. Section 47 empowered the president to summon meetings of parliament. That apart, there were no other provisions for prescribing the frequency of parliamentary meetings.

The High Court was empowered to determine questions as to membership of parliament.

In the exercise of his powers to prorogue or dissolve parliament, the president was required to act on the advice of the prime minister. He could, however, refuse to dissolve parliament if he thought that such dissolution would not be in the best interests of Sierra Leone.[30] The question of a vacancy in the office of a prime minister, for example, by death, was settled by the third proviso to Section 46(4) which provided that if the president in such circumstances considers that there is no prospect of his being able to appoint a person who can command the

30 See Proviso to Section 46(4) (a).

support of the members of parliament within a reasonable time, then he may dissolve parliament.

Executive Powers.
Executive power in Sierra Leone was vested by Section 49(1) in the president who could exercise such power directly or through the cabinet, ministers, deputy ministers or public officers while there was established the positions of prime minister, members of cabinet, the Attorney-General, permanent-secretaries and the like. The constitution did not take account of the opposition. In the Jamaican Constitution, for example the Governor-General is directed to appoint as leader of the opposition, the member of the house of representatives who in his judgment, is best able to command the support of a majority of those members who do not support the government. He is empowered to revoke that appointment at any time.[31] The absence of any recognition of an opposition and its leader is at least strong evidence that the framers of the Republican Constitution were uneasy about the continued existence of an opposition in Sierra Leone. The government, in countries where the opposition is granted respectable status, would consult with the leader of the opposition on various matters, such as electoral matters[32] and all matters where the head of state is required to act on the recommendation of the prime minister. There could, conceivably, be matters such as the appointment of Chief Justice and other judges of the various courts, the public service commission chairman, the auditor general, the electoral commissioner, the speaker and other offices where a strictly non partisan approach would be desirable and healthy for the country.

With regard to the removal of the prime minister, it was a striking omission of the Constitution that the governor was not given a personal discretion to remove the prime minister. This is a most important and desirable constitutional safeguard in a democracy. Similarly, with regard to the appointment of a prime minister, it would have been eminently more desirable for power to be given to the president to appoint the person who, in his judgment is "best able" rather than "likely" to command the support of the majority of the members of the house.[33]

The power of the president was being exercised by and through his ministers and civil servants. At the date of independence, the vast majority of top civil servants were expatriates. There was inevitable

---

31 Sec. 60(1) (4) (5). The leader of the opposition in Jamaica has the right to advise and recommend 8 persons to fill the Senate of 21, to the Governor-General.
32 In Uganda before the military rebellion, the constitution required the prime minister to consult the leader of the opposition before tendering advice on the appointment of members to the electoral commission. In Jamaica also, the leader of the opposition appoints 3 members to the standing committee on the delimitation of boundaries.
33 See Sec. 50(2) of the Constitution of Sierra Leone Act. No. 6 of 1951.

conflict between the ministers and these officials.[34] The Sierra Leonisation of the service did not minimise these conflicts. On the contrary, so long as the party system was in existence, it tended to exacerbate them. There were many complaints of civil servants trying to frustrate the policies of the ministers because they belonged to a different party. However, the formal presidency in Sierra Leone did not last for more than two days before an executive presidency was introduced. It would have been quite interesting to observe and analyse the factors of political power in a situation where the functionary exercising the powers of the president was not a politician but a non-party and independent individual as was the case when Sir Henry Lightfoot Boston was governor-general.

The JUDICATURE.
The provisions of the republican constitution relating to the judicature, were most disturbing. They raised serious questions of whether the constitutional provisions in England relating to the independence of the judiciary, could be applied in Sierra Leone.[35] The constitution abolished appeals to the Judicial Committee of the Privy Council and substituted, for the Privy Council, the Supreme Court of Sierra Leone. Three superior courts were established, the High Court, the Court of Appeal and the Supreme Court. The Chief Justice was designated head of the judiciary and the person responsible for the administration of the courts. All the judges of the High Court and the justices of the Court of Appeal and the Supreme Court were to be appointed by the president acting on the advice of the prime minister. To qualify for appointment as a justice of the Supreme Court or of the Court of Appeal, a person was required to be entitled to practise as an advocate or solicitor in a court having unlimited jurisdiction in civil and criminal matters in some part of the Commonwealth or in a court having jurisdiction in appeals from any such court and had been so entitled for not less than ten years. With the exception that the length of time, in a case of judges of the High Court was seven years, the qualifying provisions were the same.

With regard to tenure, all the judges and justices were required to vacate their offices on attaining the age of sixty-two years. They could all be removed for inability to perform the functions of their offices, (whether arising from infirmity of mind or body or any other cause) or for misbehaviour. They could be removed if a resolution supported by a two-thirds majority of all members of parliament, recommended such a removal. Before the resolution is put to the vote, the "person whose inability or misbehaviour in question shall be given an adequate

---

34 See Adu, A.L. *The Civil Service in New African States* (Allen & Unwin) London, 1965 p.167. Also the report of the W.A. Survey Mission on the training of Civil Servants in Nigeria (Central Government) Federal Govt. Printers, Lagos, 1954. The Imrie & Lee Report.

35 See S. A. de Smith — Judicial Independence in the Commonwealth. *The Listener,* Jan. 15 1959 p.94. Also, E. McWhinney, *Judicial Review in the English Speaking World* 2nd ed. Toronto 1960 p.182.

opportunity of appearing and making representations either in person or through a representative of his own choice".

These provisions were regarded throughout the country as iniquitous and infra dignitatem and not providing any safeguard for the judiciary against the excesses of political power.

SUMMARY.

> The theory that the constitution is a written document is a legal fiction. The idea that it can be understood by a study of its language and the history of its past development is equally mythical. It is what the government and the people who count in public affairs recognise and respect as such, what they think it is. More than this. It is not merely what it has been, or what it is today. It is always becoming something else and those who criticise it and the acts done under it, as well as those who praise, help to make it what it will be tomorrow.
> CHARLES A. BEARD and WILLIAM BEARD *"The American Leviathen"* p.39.

The Republican Constitution which the APC Government thought it desirable to bring into effect in 1971, was designed and produced by the SLPP to entrench its position in Sierra Leone as the dominant party and to prevent any other party from having a chance to exercise effective power. It was totalitarian in every respect, subversive of the judiciary which it sought to bring firmly under the control of the prime minister and restrictive of fundamental rights and liberties. The judges had already been shown to be painfully at the mercy of the politicians. First, the manner of the appointment of Mr Gershon Collier as Chief Justice in 1967, had demonstrated with incredible ease and clarity that the position of Chief Justice was not as impregnable as Sierra Leoneans had at first imagined. It was effected with remarkable ease and the ostensible intention of the prime minister was suspected to be to get his trusted friend and colleague to deal satisfactorily with the election petitions which would have had the effect of exposing election malpractices and defeating a large number of SLPP candidates who had "won" the elections.

Second, the treatment of Sir Samuel Bankole Jones, first, by the Albert Margai regime and then by the APC government, showed also that the government's sensitivity about the activities of the courts was something of importance in the political and social life of the country.

The republican constitution incorporated chiefs into the representative legislature along with others and made it difficult for unity to be maintained. The inequity of the electoral process rankled badly with the Creoles in the former colony and it did nothing to assist the governmental processes. A number of chiefs found themselves at loggerheads with the government when one inquiry after another terminated with a recommendation for the deposition of the chief. The republican constitution did not improve the atmosphere in this regard.

Sierra Leone had an opportunity to choose between a monarchical and a presidential system of government. It chose the latter on the crucial issue of whether the president should be executive or merely formal, there was a concession to strong public feeling and so the constitution provided for a largely ceremonial president with effective power in the hands of the prime minister. The relationship between the head of state and the prime minister was patterned after the fashion of the British system of cabinet government. It did not solve the problem of two executives bent on competing for supremacy or even parity within the one constitutional system. The appointment of Mr Stevens in 1967 by the governor-general indicates that the constitutional provisions were difficult in a practical situation as it is apparent that there would have been a good deal of trouble and dissatisfaction whichever way the Governor-General had exercised his discretion.

One important matter which the republican constitution failed to provide for, in spite of the experience of 1967, was the succession to the leadership of the government. Twice the same problem affected Sierra Leone. In the case of Sir Albert in 1964, he virtually walked into a problem of inadequate provisions for party succession. Subsequently, he tried to strengthen his position within the party in the manner of the PDG in Guinea (the Party Democratique de Guinee). He was singularly unsuccessful.

The republican constitution indirectly continued the politicisation of the civil service. Section 60 provided that where any minister has been charged with responsibility for any department of government, "he shall exercise general direction and control over that department; and subject to such direction and control, the department shall be under the supervision of a permanent secretary, whose office shall be a public office." Thus, the civil servants became largely answerable to politicians and under their general direction and control. The ministerial system was different from the colonial system which provided the specimen and ideal for the independent governments of the former colonial territories to follow. The colonial system was effectively one-party, with the nationals of the dependent territory forming the "opposition" to the government. Hence, the civil service changed its character from being the mainstay of British colonial policy to the mainstay of the political power in the former colony. In Sierra Leone, the Dove-Edwin Commission found out that the civil service was deeply implicated in the electoral process and the irregularities which were exposed. The republican constitution unfortunately did nothing to remedy this situation.

Initial amendments to the Republican Constitution.
In keeping with its undertaking not to enforce the objectionable provisions of the Albert Margai Republican Constitution, the government took an early opportunity to amend some of the provisions of the constitution. These were effected by Act. No. 7 of the same year, (1971). Significantly, the provisions relating to the judiciary were not altered. The following represent, in summary, the principal amendments.

The Republican Constitution 1971

The Office of President. Sections 16-18.
The amendments here were quite extensive. The president was no longer to be appointed by the cabinet but by the members of parliament. The procedure for his election was set out with the Chief Justice as returning officer. The opportunity was taken to prescribe qualifications. He was to be a citizen of Sierra Leone who has attained the age of 45 years and not disqualified for election as a member of parliament. His incidents of office were specified and his immunities and privileges as well.

Parliament.
Originally, the members of the electoral commission were to be appointed by the president acting on the advice of the prime minister. This was altered so that they could be appointed by the president alone. The electoral commission was now required to report its activities to the president from time to time.

Executive Powers.
Section 49(2) was amended too, providing that in the exercise of any function under the constitution or any other law, the president would act in his own deliberate judgment, instead of on the advice of the cabinet, unless otherwise provided for; and he "shall not be obliged to follow the advice tendered by any other person or authority".

In place of the prime minister, the office of vice-president was created who was designated the principal assistant to the president. The attorney-general, ministers and deputy ministers were now to be appointed exclusively by the president. All references to prime minister, were changed to vice-president. Section 57 required the vice-president and the cabinet to keep the president informed of the general conduct of the government of Sierra Leone. The secretary to the cabinet was brought under the direct control of the president. Finally, the president was made responsible for the appointment of deputy ministers without acting on the advice of the vice-president.

CHAPTER XI

A BRIEF HISTORY OF THE LEGAL PROFESSION IN SIERRA LEONE

When the settlement of Sierra Leone was established in 1787, one of the institutions of government set up by the settlers was a system of courts. There is no evidence that there were any trained lawyers among the settlers, but judicial functions were exercised by the governor and other subordinate officials. Certainly, Governor Richard Weaver, had no legal training. Nor did any of the lay justices who sat from time to time to adjudicate over disputes. So it can confidently be asserted that the settlement began without any formal legal training requirement for lawyers. There was no legal profession and no specialist training for a legal career. At the beginning therefore, the settlement was spared the technicalities and the specialist character of an English court of law. This had distinct advantages as well as its drawbacks. On the positive side, the technical rules of evidence had not been developed and could not be readily applied. So there was common sense justice for all. The disadvantages, however were numerous. One striking difficulty, was that the law was not universally known and one could not tell with certainty what offence or offences he was committing. The process of legislation was slow, and English law which it was agreed should form the basis of the legal system was embedded in the breasts of British lawyers who were not readily available in Sierra Leone. Another disadvantage of equal proportions, was that the administrators of the law were merchants and laymen and the justice which they meted out to the ordinary people was too much influenced by the executive and was rather rough justice. The Administrators of the system had no idea of the complexities of English law. The justice therefore, had perforce to be largely discretionary, depending to a very large extent on the particular individual's notions of what were justice and fair play.

This situation did not last, however, for very long. There soon developed a practice whereby the courts would allow interested persons who had been frequent visitors to the courts, or any nominees of either accused persons or litigants to "speak" up for them. These persons were greatly assisted by the company's marshalls and by the year 1795 the marshalls had been recognised as persons who had some experience of both legal and police duties and who could greatly assist the court since they had acquired legal expertise through their long association with the courts.

Representation by unqualified persons continued in Sierra Leone throughout the mid seventeen-nineties. By the turn of the century, professsional lawyers from England had appeared on the scene. First they came as company's servants and the company set up a register of advocates and notaries. The company reserved to itself the right to admit persons to practise as such advocates and notaries and did not limit their discretion to only legally qualified persons. It was the practice for the applicant to write and petition the company who would place the matter before the council and consider it. If the resolution was passed in council that the applicant be admitted, he was thus enrolled to practise. Apart from those with legal qualifications, there were a lot of advocates who were self-taught and many in this category were retired persons from the service of the company or who had held positions such as sheriff, marshall or member of council.

The Crown took over the Sierra Leone Company in 1808 and started to administer Sierra Leone as a crown colony. They continued the practice of enrolling both legally trained persons and also those who were experienced, but had no formal legal qualifications.[1] They did not limit the right of entry into the legal profession to those resident in the territory. There are records of persons who arrived for particular cases. However, by the second decade of the eighteenth century, the idea of informal representation by untrained lawyers was beginning to crumble and this gave way to the more formal patterns of British legal jurisprudence. This was largely due to the personality and superior qualifications of the first Chief Justice under the Crown, Sir Robert Thorpe. He had a dispute with Governor Maxwell which he took to the courts in Britain. Nevertheless, he did a great deal to promote the establishment of a highly qualified and competent bar for Sierra Leone. He initiated action in the Sierra Leone courts against Alexander Smith who eventually secured the service of a lawyer Michael Hamilton through whom he filed his petition praying for relief against the claims of Thorpe.

Although the minutes of the council show that lawyers were being admitted before the year 1800 it was only in the early eighteen-hundreds that the first legally qualified person became enrolled in Sierra Leone. The country thus became the first in British-speaking Africa to have a system of formalised registration of lawyers, although no special qualifications were prescribed. The Roll of Court which was eventually established was started in 1823 since when there is a permanent record in the law courts of all lawyers admitted to practise in Sierra Leone.

---

1 See C.O. 270: 13 at p.11 for example where it is recorded on the 19th July 1811 that Messrs Francis Hopkins and Darl Molley Hamilton were admitted to practice as Barristers and Attorneys at the Law Courts and Advocates and Proctors of the Court of Vice Admiralty. They took the oaths required by law.

248 Legal Development And Constitutional Change In Sierra Leone

Existing Legislation — 1971.

Although Sierra Leone has had university education since 1827 when Fourah Bay College was founded, there has never been any provision for legal education in the country. Historically and traditionally, all professionals have been trained in England or elsewhere, at the expense of their parents. Only since the twentieth century, around the year 1943, has there been government grants for professional studies at government's expense. In 1965, the Sierre Leone Government set up a commission to look into the establishment of legal training in Sierra Leone. The commission recommended the setting up of a law faculty and a law school in Sierra Leone, but this has not been achieved.

The Sierra Leone legislation governing the admission of legal practitioners to practice in Sierra Leone, is the Legal Practitioners Act, Cap. 11 of the laws of Sierra Leone, 1960. It was first passed as Ordinance No. 9 of 1945. It defines a "Barrister and Solicitor" as a person enrolled as a barrister and solicitor on the roll of the High Court under Section 7.

The act requires the master and registrar to keep a roll of court in which shall be enrolled the name of every person admitted to practice as a barrister and solicitor of the court. The right of admission is vested in the Chief Justice who, in accordance with the provisions of Section 3 may approve, admit and enrol to practice anyone who meets certain qualifications. To entitle anyone to so practice, he must be entitled to practice as a barrister in England, Northern Ireland or the Republic of Ireland, or as an advocate in Scotland and who produces testimonials sufficient to satisfy the Chief Justice that he is a person of good character and has read in the chambers of a practising barrister in the country in which he is called to the bar for one year or has practised in the country of his call for two years or read in the chambers of a barrister and solicitor in the western area of Sierra Leone of ten years standing at least, for two years subsequent to his call or admission.

Notwithstanding that a person fulfils the qualifications required by the act, the Chief Justice still has a discretion to refuse him admission "upon good cause shown." A person whom the Chief Justice has decided to admit is required, before admission, to take and subscribe the oath, or declaration and affirmation of allegiance prescribed by the Act.

These provisions, cumulatively, restrict the right to practice in Sierra Leone to persons who have obtained their qualifications in the United Kingdom. Although this provision has been severely criticised, it is understandable, since English law is substantially what is practised in Sierra Leone and not any other legal system. However, there is certainly a strong case for admitting persons who have obtained their qualifications from other common law jurisdictions.

GENERAL.
The bar in Sierra Leone has over the years distinguished itself as an independent and fearless bar. It has championed unpopular causes and generally sought to maintain the high traditions of the profession. There have been occasions, however, when some members of the bar have been disciplined. Happily, those occasions are few and far between.

Likewise, the Sierra Leone Bar Association is the oldest on the continent, having been in existence since 1827.

BIBLIOGRAPHY

Reports of the Directors of the Sierra Leone Company Public Records Office:
- C.O. 267 Series: Governors' despatches to the S. of S: Letters to the Colonial Office from Government Departments: public bodies; individuals.
- C.O. 268 Series: Entry Books of Commissions Instructions, Charters, Warrants, Letters etc.
- C.O. 270 Series: Minutes of Council — Leg. Co. and Ex. Co.
- C.O. 271 Series: Government Gazettes.
- C.O. 272 Series: Annual Blue Books of Statistics.

Sierra Leone Archives at Fourah Bay College, Freetown.
Adderley, C.B. Review of the Colonial Policy of Lord J. Russell's administration and of subsequent Colonial History, London, 1861.
Adegbite: L.O. The concepts of the Rule of law in African Societies. Ph.D. Thesis (London) 1966.
Andrews: The Royal Disallowance.
Blyden, Edward E. III — Sierra Leone. The pattern of Constitutional Change 1924-1951. Ph.D. Thesis, Harvard.
Burge's Colonial and Foreign Law, Vol. 1, 1907.
Anderson, J.N.D. — The Adaptation of Muslim Law in Sub-Saharan Africa.
Allott: Judicial and Legal Systems in Africa London, 1970.
Clark, Cumberland, The Crown Colonies and their history. London. The Mitre Press, 1939.
Crooks: History of the Colony of Sierra Leone, 1903.
Dike — Trade and Politics.
Dicey A.V. — The Law of the Constitution 10th Ed. Debates of the S.L. Legislative Council. 1863 to 1971.
Elias, T.O. Nature of African Customary Law.
Elias, T.O. The Evolution of Law and Government in Modern Africa.
Elias, T. O. Constitution and Laws of the Commonwealth (Sierra Leone and Ghana).
Elias, T. O. Nigerian Legal System.

Bibliography

Evans — An Early Constitution for Sierra Leone (Sierra Leone Studies, 1932).
Fyfe, C. A History of Sierra Leone, Oxford, 1963.
Fyfe, C. The Sierra Leone Inheritance, Oxford.
George, Claude — The Rise of British West Africa, London, 1903.
Grieves Averill Mackenzie — The Last years of the English Slave Trade.
Hoare: Memoirs of Granville Sharpe.
Hargreaves, J. D. Prelude to the Partition;
Harrell-Bond, Howard and Skinner: Community Leadership and the transformation of Freetown 1801-1976.
Harlow and Marsden — British Colonial Developments 1774-1834, Oxford, 1953.
Hargreaves, J. D. The Establishment of the Sierra Leone Protectorate, 1956 12 Camb. Hist. Jo.56.
Hertslet — British and Foreign State papers.
Habtesselassig B. The Executive in African Governments. A comparative Study (London) Ph.D. 1967.
Jones-Kime — History and Administration of East India Company.
Goddard — A Handbook of Sierra Leone, 1925.
House of Representatives Debates.
Jones, W. S. Marcus — The Protection of Fundamental Rights and Liberties of the Individual in the Sierra Leone Constitution 1961. Unpublished J.S.D. dissertation, Yale University, 1965.
Kedsings Comparative Archives.
Kilson, M. Political Change in a West African State.
Kimble — Political History of the Gold Coast.
Kup, A. P. History of Sierra Leone 1462-1787.
Laski, R. Liberty in the Modern State.
Levi, J. L. Memorandum on the Evolution of the Legislative Council.
Lindley: The Acquisition of Backward Territories.
Little, Kenneth: West African Urbanisation.
Lucas, C. P. Historical Geography of the Br. Colonies 1900.
Lugard, Lord: Indirect Rule.
Mathieson, Gilbert: A short review of the Reports of the African Institution, London, 1816.
Manning, H. British Colonial Governments after the American Revolution, Yale, USA, 1933.
Martin — British West African Settlements, 1750-1821 London, 1927.
Mellor, C. R. British Policy in relation to Sierra Leone 1808-52. M. A. Thesis, Lond. 1935.
M. McCulloch — People of the Sierra Leone Protectorate.
Migeod: A view of Sierra Leone.
Newbury C. W. British Policy Towards Africa.
Padmore: George — The Gold Coast Revolution.
Porter: A. T.: Creoledom.
Page, J. P. An introduction to the History of West Africa.
Peterson J. — Province of Freedom.

Perham, Margery: Native Administration.
Parry, C. H. — British Nationality.
Hood Phillips, O. — Constitutional and Administrative Law.
Robson, W. A. The Governors and the Governed.
Shuyler, K. L. Parliament and the British Empire.
Scott: The Sierra Leone Elections, 1957 in Mackenzie ed. Five Elections in Africa OUP, 1960.
Sibthorpe — History of Sierra Leone.
Simon: Slavery.
Spitzger, Leo — The Creoles of Sierra Leone.
Sawyer & Marcus Jones: The Constitutions of the World Sierra Leone — Oceana.
Stephen Paul B. — Sierra Leone Protectorate. Unpublished dissertation.
Taylor: The Political change of Tanganyika.
Thorpe, Robert — Letter to Wm. Wilberforce Esq., MP, London, 1815.
Wadstrom: An Essay on Colonisation 1794.
Sir Kenneth Roberts-Wray — British Colonial Law. Commonwealth and Colonial Law.
Wight, M. The Development of the Legislative Council.
Wight M. The Gold Coast Legislative Council.
Williams — Bibliography of Sierra Leone 1925-1967.
Williams — Civilization.
The Edinburgh Review XXI 70-71.
House of Commons Sessional Papers.

Sierra Leone Papers — *Daily Mail: Unity: Express: Weekly News: The African Standard: The Daily Guardian: Probe: Think.*

INDEX OF STATUTES

Imperial Legislation
The Sierra Leone Company Act, 1791 31 Geo. III c. 55
Abolition of Slave Trade Act, 1807, 47 Geo. III c. 36
Sierra Leone Company Act, 1807 47 Geo. III Sess. 2 c. 44
Mixed Court of Justice Act, 1819 58 Geo. III c. 36 and 35
West Africa Act, 1821 1 & 2 Geo. IV c. 28
Abolition of Slavery Act, 1833 3 & 4 Will. IV c. 73
British Settlements Act, 1843 6 & 7 Vic. c. 13
Foreign Jurisdiction Act, 1843 6 & 7 Vic. c. 94
Appeals to the Judicial Committee of the Privy Council Act, 1844 7 & 8 Vict. c. 69
Status of Liberated Africans Act, 1852/3 16 & 17 Vict. c. 86
British Law Ascertainment Act, 1859 22 & 23 Vict. c. 63
Administration of Justice Act, 1860 23 & 24 Vict. c. 121
Trial of Offences committed within 500 miles of the Colony of Sierra Leone Act, 1861 24 & 25 Vict. c. 31
Colonial Laws Validity Act, 1865 28 & 29 Vict. c. 63
Trial of Offences committed within 20 miles of the Colony Act, 1871 34 Vict. c. 8
Extradition Act, 1873 36 & 37 Vict. c. 60
Courts (Colonial) Jurisdiction Act, 1874 37 & 38 Vict. c. 27
Fugitive Offenders Act, 1881 44 & 45 Vict. c. 69
Colonial Courts of Admiralty Act, 1890 53 & 54 Vict. c. ee
British Settlements Act, 1887 50 and 51 Vict. c. 54
Foreign Jurisdiction Act, 1890 53 & 54 Vict. c. 37
Foreign Jurisdiction Act, 1913 3 & 4 Geo. V c. 16
The Statute of Westminister, 1931 22 & 23 Geo. V c. 4
Emergency Powers (Defence) Act, 1939 2 & 3 Geo. VI c. 62
British Nationality Act, 1948 11 & 12 Geo. VI c. 56
Sierra Leone Independence Act, 1961 9 & 10 El. II c. 16

ORDERS-IN-COUNCIL.
Declaration of Sovereignty over Quiah and Sherbro — 26th April, 1862
Royal Instructions — 30th May, 1863
Charter of Justice — 27/5/1863

254 Legal Development And Constitutional Change In Sierra Leone

Regulations for Appeals from the Supreme Court of the Gambia Colony to the Supreme Court of the Colony of Sierra Leone — 24th Nov. 1891
Rules Amending the same, made by the Chief Justice of the Supreme Court of Sierra Leone — 3rd February, 1893
Regulations under the Foreign Jurisdiction Act — 1890 — 24th Aug. 1895
Regulations for Appeals from the Supreme Court and Circuit Court of Sierra Leone to H. M. in Council — 15th February 1909
Letters Patent dated 28th January 1924
S.L. Leg. Co. Order in Council 1924
Instructions under the Royal Sign Manual & Signet, 28th Jan. 1924
S.L. Leg. Co. (Amendment) Order in Council 1939
S.L. Leg. Co. Order in Council 1951
S.L. House of Representatives Order in Council, S.I. 1956 No. 1893. 29th Nov. 1956
Statutory Instruments 1958 No. 1259 of July 30, 1958
Statutory Instruments 1960 No. of 23rd June, 1960

LOCAL ORDINANCES.
- 1/1811   Absconding Debtors, non-resident in Colony. Attachment of personal property.
- 5/1825   Small Debts.
- 7/1829   Real Estate Subject to sale for Debt.
- 14/1838 Pardons — Formalities on granting
- 16/1838 Small Debts
- 19/1839 Commissioners in Court of Requests
- 28/1847 C.J. to be Judge of Court of Ordinary (Court of Probate)
- 32/1849 Court of Recorder — Jurisdiction and Practice
- 50/1853 C.J. to be Vice-Chancellor of Sierra Leone
- 59/1853 Juries
- 66/1854 Juries
- 72/1855 Indemnification of Gov. S. J. Hill & Others
- 91/1857 Vice-Admiralty Court Practice
- 93/1857 Land Commission
- 96/1857 English Laws up to 1857 to be in force
- 100/1857 Power of Governor and Council to punish for contempt
- 94/1857 Registration
- 10/1858 Administration of Justice
- 8/1859   Administration of Justice
- 13/1859 Small Debts
- 3/1862   English Laws to 1862 extended to Colony
- 1/1863   C.J. to have powers of Vice-Chancellor
- 5/1864   Administration of Justice
- 8/1864   Sittings of the Court
- 9/1864   Consolidate Laws relative to Jurors and Juries
- 12/1864 Managers of Districts and to amend law relative to small debts
- 15/1864 Jury
- 16/1864 Appeals to the Privy Council

Index of Statutes

—/1865 Court of Requests, Small Debts, District Courts
4/1866 Supreme Court
5/1866 Summary Court, Court of Requests
4/1867 County Court Acts in Force in England to apply to Sierra Leone
5/1867 Judge of Summary Court to have powers of Commissioner of Land
6/1867 Court of Requests, Sherbro and Bulama
3/1869 Appeals to Governor in Council abolished
7/1869 To remove doubts as to the Verdicts of Juries
4/1871 Power to appoint Deputy Judge of Summary Court
7/1875 Married Women's property
4/1877 Appeals from Magistrates
1/1880 C.J. West African Settlements to be C.J. Sierra Leone
9/1881 Supreme Court
17/1883 Define term "Governor-in-Council"
4/1885 Women not to be whipped
14/1886 Aliens empowered to hold land
4/1893 District Commissioners
6/1893 Incorporation of Freetown
8/1894 Court of Requests
8/1895 Trial by Assessors
20/1896 Protectorate
12/1897 Protectorate Jurisdiction delimitation
6/1903 Protectorate Courts Jurisdiction
14/1904 Supreme Court
29/1905 Magistrates Court
11, 27 and 47/1924 Protectorate Jurisdiction
9/1929 West African Court of Appeal (Civil Cases)
10/1929 West African Court of Appeal (Criminal Cases)
7/1945 Courts
18/1960 Courts (Appeals)
20/1963 Local Courts

APPENDIX I

PLAN

OF A

SETTLEMENT

TO BE MADE NEAR

SIERRA LEONA

ON THE

GRAIN COAST

OF

AFRICA

Intended more particularly for the fervice and happy eftablifment of Blacks and People of Colour, to be fhipped as freemen under the direction of the Committee for Relieving the Black Poor, and under the protection of the Britifh Government.

BY HENRY SMEATHMAN, ESQ.
Who refided in that Country near Four Years.

LONDON

Sold by T. STOCKDALE in Piccadilly — G. KEARSLEY.

A LIST of the COMMITTEE for relieving the BLACK POOR.
JONAS HANWAY, Efq. Red Lion fquare, CHAIRMAN.
MONTAGU BURGOYNE, Efq. Harley Street.
B. JOHNSON, Efq., Liffon Green.

Appendix I

SIR JOSEPH ANDREWS, Bart. Knightsfortage.
GEORGE PETERS, Efq., Old Bethlem.
JOHN OSBORNE, Efq., New Norfolk Street.
JOHN JULIUS ANGERSTEIN, Albemarle Street.
JAMES PETER ANDREWS, Efq., Brompton.
SAMUEL HOARE, Efq., Lombard Street.
GEORGE DRAKE, Efq., Bedford Square.
F. MATHEWS, Efq., Bridge Street, Weftminfter.
WILLIAM WARD, Efq., Fenchurch Street.
RICHARD SHAW, Efq., London Bridge.
JOHN CORNWALL, Efq., Duchefs Street, Portland Place.
S. THORNTON, Efq., M. P. King's Arms Yard.
H. THORNTON, Efq., M. P. Bartholomew Lane.
THOMAS BODDINGTON, Efq., Mark Lane.
GENERAL Melville, Brewer Street.

HANDBILL ATTACHED TO DR SMEATHMAN'S PLAN

BLACK POOR

It having been very maturely and humanely considered, by what means a support might be given to the Blacks, who seek the protection of this Govt; it is found that no place is so fit and proper, as the grain coast of Africa; where the necessaries of the day be supplied by the force of industry and moderate Labour, and life rendered very comfortable. It has been meditated to send Blacks to Nova Scotia but this plan is laid aside, as that country is unfit and improper for the said Blacks.

The Committee for the Black Poor accordingly recommended Henry Smeathman Esq., who is acquainted with this part of the Coast of Africa, to take charge of the said persons, who are desirous of going with him; and to give them all fit and proper encouragment, agreeably to the humanity of the British Govt.

Batson's Coffee House,
7th May, 1786

By desire of the Committee
JOHN HANWAY,
Chairman

Those who are desirous of profiting by this opportunity, of settling in one of the most pleasant and fertile countries in the known world, may apply for further information to Mr Smeathman, the Author of the Plan, and Agent for the Settlement at the Office of free Africans, No. 14, Canon Street.

PLAN OF A SETTLEMENT, &c.

** ** **

ANY person defirous of a permanent and comfortable eftablifment, in a moft pleafant fertile climate, near SIERRA LEONA, where land be purchafed at a fmall expence, may have an opportunity of doing it on the following advantageous conditions.

They will be carried out at five Guineas each perfon, and fupplied during the voyage, with an ample and falutary allowance of provifions per week, viz:

  6 lb. of Bread.
  1 ditto Beef.
  3 ditto Pork.
  ¾ ditto Melaffes.
  1½ ditto Flour.
  1 ditto Pot Barley.
  ½ ditto Suet.
  ½ ditto Raifins.
  1 pinto of Oatmeal.
  1½ ditto of Peas.
  2 dittos of Rum for Grog.

With a proper quantity of Spices, as Pimento, Ginger, &c.

They will alfo be fupplied with the fame allowance, for three months after their arrival on the coaft, which is as long a time as will be neceffary for their fafe eftablifment; the fame will coft at the rate of 3 l. 15s. each perfon.

Thofe who have money, and can afford to go as fteerage, ftewardroom, or cabin paffengers will be accomodated accordingly.

As foon as poffible after their arrival on the coaft, a certain diftrict of land will be purchafed for the Community of Settlers, to be their joint property; the moft convenient that can be found for procuring the feveral advantages for which the fettlement is intended.

When the land is purchafed, which may be done within a few days after their arrival, a townfhip will be marked out; and houfes run up by the joint labour of the whole, for immediate fhelter: This may eafily be effected in that country, the climate not requiring either compact not durable houfes: a flight but is a fufficient fhelter for the fevereft feafon of the year; and the materials for building are fo near at hand, that a company of ten or twelve men may erect very comfortable habitations for themfelves and their families in a few days.

Each person will be allowed, by common confent, to poffefs as much land as it may be judged he or fhe can cultivate, to which they will always be at liberty to add as much more as their neceffity, or convenience may require; and of which they may enjoy the poffeffion and produce, in fecurity and freedom.

Appendix I

It is propofed to take out proper artificers among the fettlers, for erecting the neceffary buildings, for carrying on the works propofed, as well as to lay out the regular divifions and lots of land.

Befide the advantages which individuals may obtain from their own fpots of land, by moderate labour, they will have other eafy means of fupplying themfelves, not only with the neceffaries, but alfo the conveniencies and comforts of life. Such provifons as fowls, hogs, goats and fheep, are very cheap, being propagated with a rapidity unknown in thefe colder climates; and great quantities of fifh may be caught with the utmost facility: the forefts abound with venifon, wild fowl, and other game.

The productions of this country are Rice, and a fpecies of Indigo fuperior to any other, Cotton and Tobacco equal to thofe produced in the Brafils, and purchafed of the Portuguefe, Dying Woods of various kinds, Ivory, Wax, Tortoife Shell, Gold, and other merchandife. Add to this, the woods and plains produce fpontaneoufly great quantities of the moft pleafant fruits and fpices, from which may be made oils, marmalades, wines, perfumes, and other valuable articles, to fupply the markets of Great Britain and Ireland.

Such are the mildnefs and fertility of the climate and country, that a man poffeffed of a change of cloathing, a wood axe, a hoe, and a pocket knife, may foon place himfelf in an eafy and comfortable fituation. All the cloathing wanted is what decency requires: and it is not neceffary to turn up the earth more, than from the depth of two or three inches, with a flight hoe, in order to cultivate any kind of grain.

Thefe favourable circumftances, combined with the peaceable temper of the natives, promife the fafeft and moft permanent eftablifment of commerce; the numerous advantages refulting from the quiet cultivation of the earth, and the exportation of its valuable productions, which may be exchanged to great advantage for the manufactures of this country.

In all probablitiy this fettlement will in due time invite a number of adventurers, as has happened in other countries formerly in a more rude and uncultivated ftate. The Africans in the neighbourhood of Sierra Leona, are fagacious and political, much beyond what is vulgarly imagined.

The climate is very healthy to thofe who live on the productions of the country. The caufe why it has been fatal to many white people, is that they have led the moft intemperate lives; have fubfifted chiefly on dried, falted, rancid, and other unwholesome provifions; and have indulged themfelves beyond all bounds, in the ufe of ardent fpirits; they have been alfo cooped up in fhips, fmall craft, or factories, ftationed for the advantage of trade in clofe rivers or creeks, not choofing healthy fpots, as by the propofal before us is to be done. Add to this that the furgeons of fhips trading thither have hitherto been generally ignorant of the proper mode of treating difeafes in that climate; or they have not been fufficiently fupplied with medicines. Many perfons have perifhed for want of good diet or nurfing, and not a few from the total neglect of that mutual affiftance, which the fettlement propofed will furnifh.

The adventurer on this new eftablfment will be under the care of a Phyfician, who has had four years practice on the coaft of Africa, and as many in the West Indies. He is qualified, from his knowledge of the country, and of the difforders, that generally prevail there, to afford them much valuable information; and being well provided, and accompanied by fkilful affiftants, in Surgery, Midwifry, Chemiftry and other medical arts; and by feveral prudent and experienced women, they will enjoy every neceffary affiftance.

It is alfo intended that the adventurers fhall be accompanied by a Clergyman, in order to promote Chriftian Knowledge; likewife a Schoolmafter and Miftrefs, that thofe who have children may have them infructed. This is propofed to be done at the expence of the whole community.

Such will be the fituation of thofe adventurers, who occupy themfelves on their plantations for their own advantage: but as many of the fettlers, inftead of working wholly for themfelves, may choofe occafionally to ferve the Agent, and Conductor of the Settlement, or any other individual among the Settlers, for hire: fome will employ their money in cultivation and trade: in that cafe the labourers will be fupplied with provifions, and paid for their daily labour in the currency of the country.

Only eight hours of fair labour each day will be required, in Summer or Winter: and on Saturday's only fix hours. Sunday, being the Sabbath, will, as among all chriftian nations, be fet apart as a day of reft, inftruction, and devotion.

Thofe who ferve the Agent of the Settlement, or other gentlemen on the above terms, will of courfe have much leifure on their hands, from the limitation of the time of labour, which leifure time they may employ, in the cultivation of their own freehold plantations and gardens.

By this means they will have the advantage of raifing Corn, Rice, Livestock, and other produce, to a confiderable amount annually. For the produce of fuch induftry and ingenuity they will find a ready market, and receive the manufacturers and other neceffaries imported from Great Britain in exchange. On the fame principles a lucrative trade may be carried on with the natives, in the neighbouring ports and rivers.

The Settlers being under the protection of the Britifh Government, will confequently enjoy both civil and religious liberty, as in Great-Britain.

With refpect to difputes relative to property, or offences committed among themfelves, thefe will be fettled by the laws, which are judged of by their own peers, that is, by a Town Meeting, according to the cuftom of the country, which is invariably fair and equitable.

In regard to offenders against the natives, in neighbouring diftricts, they will be amenable to the laws of the country, unlefs the Agent of the Settlement, under whofe immediate protection they refide, fhall be able to compound for the penalty.

In addition to thofe perfons who are able to pay for their paffage, it is intended to conduct this enterprife upon the moft humane principles: it will be extended to others who have not money, on condition of agreements for their refpective hire, to be calculated according to the ages and abilities of the parties, fo that every one may be fure of having a comfortable provifion made, after a fhort period, on the reafonable terms of moderate labour.

And whereas many black perfons, and people of Colour, Refugees from America, difbanded from his Majesty's Service by fea or land, or otherwise diftinguished objects of Britifh humanity, are at this time in the greatift diftricts, they are invited to avail themfelves of the advantages of the plan propofed.

The Committee, appointed for the relief of the Black Poor, having reprefented their unhappy fituation to the Right Hon. the Lords Commiffioners of the Treafury, Government has agreed to furnifh them, not only with a paffage and provifion, but alfo with cloathing, provifions for three months after their landing, together with all forts of tools and implements of hufbandry, neceffary for the eftablifment of a new fettlement, according to the fchedules annexed.

Such perfons will be also entitled to the neceffary allotment of a quantity of land, and other benefits, in as great a latitude as will render their lives eafy.

An opportunity fo advantageous may perhaps never be offered to them again; for they and their profterity may enjoy perfect freedom Settled in a country congenial to their conftitutions, and having the means, by moderate labour, of the moft comfortable livelihood, they will find a certain and fecure retreat from their former fufferings.

HENRY SMEATHMAN.

APPENDIX II

A SHORT SKETCH OF TEMPORARY REGULATIONS, &c.

FRANKPLEDGE

The most certain and effectual mode of securing peace, right, and mutual protection, for any community, is the old English system of mutual Frankpledge, or free suretyship, given by all the householders, for themselves and each other, in exact numerical divisions of tens and hundreds; which, in the English law-books, is called "Maxima securitas" — "the greatest security," though it is now unhappily neglected, and consequently crimes abound and increase; so that, notwithstanding the horrible increase also of bloody laws to intimidate offenders, yet there is no effectual security from violence and robbery, either in our streets or roads, or even in our chambers; since the houses of the rich and great, nay of the first officers of the state, are not exempted from the nocturnal intrusion of house-breakers, insomuch that even the Lord Chancellor and Honourable Speaker of the House of Commons have lately experienced the common danger, and the deplorable want of the antient "Maxima securitas." That fundamental system of English polity is so little known among us at present, that many well-meaning persons are induced, by their fears, to wish for security, on a much less eligible plan, formed on the model of the arbitrary system of government in France, commonly called police, the introduction of which would be an utter perversion of the first principles of legal government in England. The inhabitants even of the most distant settlements under the crown of Great Britain must not adopt any polity that is essentially inconsistent with the Maxima securitas, ordained and required by the common law of England.

The community of free African settlers, however, have already adopted (as I am informed) a small variation from the old English model of numerical divisions, by forming themselves into divisions of dozens, instead of tithings or tens; but as this little change is by no means inconsistent with the true principles and intention of our legal English frankpledge, I am at liberty to acknowledge a most hearty approbation of it, as being an arrangement far more convenient and effectual for securing perfect subordination, peace, and good government, even than the antient legal divisions into tens or decenaries, because each dozen will have one chief or headborough, and one assistant headborough, to govern and lead a compleat complement of ten deciners; so that the division may still with propriety retain the old legal name of a tithing or decenary; and the hundred division may be rendered literally and strictly an hundred families, by appointing one hundredor, two chiefs of fifties, and one town clerk (or clerk of the hundred) over every eight dozens; whereby the legal hundred, in its civil capacity (for the maintenance of peace, justice, and common right, according to the first principles of our constitutional polity, the most effectual for all the purposes of good government) will consist of:—

1	Hundredor, or centurion,[1]—
2	Chiefs of fifties — superior constables, and presiding justices in the weekly Tithing-courts[2];
1	Town-clerk, or Clerk of the hundred,[3]
8	Headboroughs being constables in ordinary.
8	Assistant Headboroughs being constables in extraordinary.
80	Deciners — masters of families or householders,[4] viz.

100 Householders in all, who must equally contribute to support all the burthens of the state, and of course must be entitled to an equal voice in the "common council", or parliament, of their settlement; which on the African coast is called Palaaver; and if the whole body of householders should hereafter, by God's blessing, become too numerous for a personal attendance in their common council they will be all equally entitled to elect a proper number of deputies from their respective divisions to represent them in the supreme council; and that, in a due and equal proportion to their numbers; for otherwise their representation would be rendered most banefully delusive and corrupt!

And in a military capacity the same hundred householders will form a corps of militia consisting of

1	Captain
2	Lieutenants
1	Muster master and commissary
8	Serjeants
8	Corporals
80	Milites or men of arms

Amounting altogether to 100 (free militia men or armed deciners.

1 Who in the common law is a high constable and "justiciarius," or justice of the peace.
2 Or rather, in the courts or four tithings, or dozens, collected together.
3 With a proper salary, to register all judgments and debts, and to be allowed two or more assistants, if necessary, from the best qualified of the deciners, with suitable salaries also for their trouble.
4 Who, jointly with the chiefs of their several divisions, pledge each other, and their respective families or dependants for the publick peace and common right, and are termed in law, boni et legales homines, "Good and true men."

To these must also be added the sons, apprentices, and identured servants of the deciners, viz. all the males of 16 years of age and upwards, who by the common law are required to be armed, and of course to be disciplined in the use of arms. The average of males above 16 years of age may be stated, I believe, at three to each family, including all the persons above described: so that in a few years, if the settlement succeeds, there may probably be added to the 100 armed deciners at least } 200 Privates or rank and file

In all 300 militia men in each hundred division, a corps that may be rendered sufficiently effectual to support the executive justice of a free, legal government, within any extent of land which an hundred families can fairly occupy, and amply sufficient to supply a roster or rotation of very easy service in the necessary watch and ward of the settlement.

N.B. This average number of males would be rather too large, were not apprentices and indentured servants included; but in a new settlement, where ordinary labour is chiefly wanted, there is a great probability that the indentured servants will far exceed the number I have estimated.

WATCH AND WARD.

> Rotation — Exercise — Discipline preserved by Fines of Labour — Watch Duty of Indentured. Servants to be allowed and deducted from the Term of their Indentures.

The hundred deciners should serve, three at a time at least, with fix privates, in due rotation, as the nightly guard of the hundred division; which guard being divided into three parties of one deciner and two privates each, one party may patrole, whilst the other two are stationed at the gate-house, or watch-tower, alternately watching and resting every four hours; but the patrolling and watching party must relieve each other every two hours, until it is their turn to rest four hours in the inner guard room; by this means the watch duty may be rendered very easy and equal to all ranks of persons in the hundred; and even if the captain and four of the oldest deciners, together with eight of the youngest privates be excused the nightly duty, the rotation of this easy service to each individual will be only once in thirt-two nights, viz. less than twelve nights in a year, which cannot interfere with their ordinary employments: but for the sake of keeping up proper discipline, triple the number ought to assemble in rotation, every evening and morning, to set and to discharge the guard after the performance of a short military exercise all together, under the inspection of the captain, or one of the lieutenants, (being previously trained or drilled in small squads under the inspection of their espective serjeants) and this attendance may be rendered perfectly equal and regular to all ranks, by a proper roster of service, duly distinguishing the courses of Watch and Ward from the rotation of attendance for mere exercise.

Want of punctuality in musters, or absence, should be punished in proportion to the time left, by equal fines on all ranks of men, estimated at so many days or hours labour (as hereafter explained) towards the support of the public Exchequer.

Disobedience of orders on service, and inattention or carelessness in exercise, and all such other misdemeanors, should be likewise punished by fines of labour for publick profit.

The watch duty of an indentured servant should be rewarded by a deduction of one day's service from his indentures for each night that he attends on military duty, which will encourage his vigilance, and win his attention to the interests of the settlement; and by his being entered on the same roster with the whole body of deciners, and by serving in due rotation with them, he will soon perceive the facility and happiness of becoming a deciner himself, by proper diligence in fulfilling his contract of labour; especially as the regulations, hereafter to be mentioned, will insure him from the imposition of more service than is due, and from the fraud or oppression of an unjust master; and he will acquire still further security by being known, and by becoming acquainted with other deciners (besides his master) in the militia service.

FREE LABOUR

> Free Labour to be the Standard or Medium or Traffick instead of Cash — Times of Labour (publick or hired) to be general and uniform — Evening Prayer and the Advantages of it — Limitation of Labour per Day to eight Hours — Six Hours on Saturdays — That the People may attend the Courts and Folkmotes to improve their Decernment of Good and Evil.

Human Labour is more essential and valuable than any other article in new settlements, which chiefly depend on the cultivation and produce of the earth for their subsistence and commercial profit. On this account, though the price of provisions is generally lower in new settlements than in communities of long standing, yet the price of Free Labour is always much higher; and higher still, or rather infinitely more expensive (however slaveholders may reckon) is the labour of slaves, besides the abominable injustice, the corruption of manners, the danger, and other curses, which always attend the toleration of slavery! Free labour, therefore, in all new settlements, ought to be made the standard, or medium, whereby to rate the value of all the necessaries of life, as well as of all articles of commerce in the settlement: a cow, sheep, or hog, or a bushel of corn, should each be valued at a proportionable number of day's labour, estimated at eight hours actual labour per day; and a pig, rabbit, or fowl, at so many hours labour, according to their respective sizes; and for the fractional estimation of smaller articles, the hours may be reduced to minutes, and thereby afford an excellent substitute for money as a medium of traffic and exchange, whereon a paper currency may be established, which will always bear an intrinsic value, without diminution, as hereafter explained under the head of Publick Revenue.

The daily commencement of publick labour and of hired labour, and all the necessary cessations from labour for rest and refreshment, should be limited to stated periods of time, rendered uniform and general, throughout the settlement, by the periodical summons of a publick bell, as in our dock yards and great manufactories, for the more effectual prevention of imposition by the employer or employed.

By the limitation of labour to eight hours per day, the rateable or legal days work (instead of continuing from six in the morning to six in the evening, as with us) will end at four in the afternoon, including two whole hours for necessary refreshment and rest; unless it should be thought more convenient in general to begin at five in the morning, and to work three hours till eight, and then, after resting half an hour at breakfast, to work three hours and a half more till noon, when a moderate and temperate meal, suitable to the heat of the climate, may be rendered more refreshing and healthful to the labourer by a general sestoo, or sleeping time, during the meridean heat till half past one; which rest of one hour and an half, at one time, will be amply sufficient to recruit them for the remaining burthen of the rateable labour, or legal day's work, viz. one hour and a half more, ending at three o'clock in the afternoon, when the evening of the antients commenced, and the appointed hour of evening sacrifice in the patriarchal times. If, therefore, the new society would agree to assemble at that hour, in whatever place they shall afterwards appropriate to religious worship, and there join together in a very short general form of prayer and evening sacrifice of thanks (in which, to remove all objections about the value of time, they need not be detained much longer than about five minutes, to express all that may be absolutely necessary for every good purpose of prayer and thanksgiving, at least as a daily service) they will soon be convinced that no human measure is so well calculated to add real dignity to the ordinary labourer, as well with respect to his own internal improvement, as in the outward esteem and consideration which it will necessarily insure to him from others, by continually reminding the rich and higher ranks of men that the daily labourer is their brother and their equal in the fight of God, and that all men ought to be equally servants to the same Lord! I could wish that a short daily morning prayer might also be adopted at nine o'clock, after breakfast, but I propose with diffidence, lest publick prayers even only once a day should be obtained with difficulty.

As some of the out lots will be distant about two miles from the centre of the township, it may perhaps be more expedient to commence the rateable daily labour even half an hour sooner still, than I have last proposed, viz. at half past four in the cool of the morning, whereby all publick labour will end at half past two in the afternoon, which will allow time for labourers in the distant lots to repair to the general assembly of the township, at evening prayer. And an officer from every dozen may be ordered to be prepared, by a previous examination, at the publick bank of all the indents in course for each day's labour; that after being discharged in the publick books, they may be cancelled, and most expeditiously returned to those who have fulfilled them; all which, by the happy system of Frankpledge, may be most easily effected with very little loss of time; so that the labourers may return from the centre of the township to their own private lots, and have near five hours of leisure to themselves to cultivate their own land, even if they work no later than eight at night, which will allow them ample time for rest, especially as the mid-day sesta too will render less sleep necessary at night.

A seventh part of the year shall be appropriated more particularly to God's service, and shall be duly observed and kept holy, on the penalty of seven weeks, or forty-two days labour in the publick lots for every breach of this universal law of God, either in buying, selling, or working for pecuniary profit; or for travelling, unless a very urgent necessity can be proved: and this penalty to be doubled on a repetition or continuance of the offence.	52	(Sundays or days (of our Lord.
Two more days shall be appropriated to a religious commemoration of our Lord's birth and expiatory death, at the usual seasons; and a third day to the great annual view of Frankpledge, to be appointed at some convenient season, after the greatest and most general harvest of the year, the remembrance of which shall also be solemnized on that day by religious thanksgiving both at the opening and conclusion of the view of Frankpledge:— so that the 365 days of the year will be further reduced by the deduction also of	3	Holidays
The abovementioned Sundays and holidays, amounting to fifty-five days, being deducted from the year, there will remain only	310	Days of labour.
	365	

The days of labour shall be rated throughout the new settlement only at eight hours actual labour each day, in all agreements or contracts for labour, as well of apprentices and indentured servants, as of those who are hired by the day; that all labourers may have some leisure hours every day to cultivate their own private lots of land. And only six hours labour are to be required by law on Saturdays, without any deduction from the labourer's profit for the deficiency, because it is for the publick benefit that the people should have leisure to attend the courts and folkmotes (to be held on Saturdays) in order that they may gradually improve that natural faculty of reason or knowledge which is inherited by all men from our first parents, and may "have their understandings exercised by habit to discern both good and evil."

FREEDOM AND PROTECTION TO STRANGERS

> Limitation of Indentured Service — An injured Indentured Servant to be turned over to the Publick Exchequer — Fugitive Slaves to be protected, and allowed to purchase Land by Labour, and after due Time of Probation to be admitted to the Rank of Deciners.

As soon as a slave shall set his foot within the bounds of the new settlement, he shall be deemed a free man, and be equally entitled with the rest of the inhabitants to the protection of the laws, and to all the natural rights of humanity. And the service even of indentured servants shall be strictly limited, viz. no person to be bound for a longer term than five years after the age of twenty-one, or of seven years if bound after the age of fourteen years, or of ten years if bound after the age of eleven years. And if any indentured servant shall have just cause to complain of his master's behaviour to him, he shall be turned over to the care of the general asylum for males; and his labour, for the limited term of his indentures, shall be turned over to the publick Exchequer, which shall purchase of the master all the remaining term of service. If any slave shall escape from his master in any part of the neighbouring country where the abominable traffic in human beings is tolerated, and shall apply at any township within the free settlements for an asylum, he shall be received and protected in the publick asylum; for this is required by an indispensable moral law of God, and, of course, by the laws of England — "Thou shalt not deliver unto his master the servant" (or slave, for all slaves are servants) "which is escaped from his master unto thee; he shall dwell with thee, even among you, in that place which he shall choose, in one of thy gates, where it liketh him best: Thou shalt not oppress him," Deut. xxiii. 15, 16. The stranger, however, shall be required to promise obedience to the laws of the settlement, and due legal submission to the chiefs of the division, wherein he is admitted and pledged; and also to enter himself on the publick roster of equal service in Watch and Ward, when of proper age. And in order to obtain his livelyhood, independently of individuals, he shall, if he is above twenty years of age, be allowed to purchase, of the publick Exchequer, one quarter of a lot of land, for one year's service, consisting of 310 days service of eight hours each, (and a proportionable addition to the term, if under that age) for which quarter of a lot, he shall be taxed only one quarter part of a deciner's contribution to parochial and publick exigences and expences; which proportionable contribution of labour for taxes shall commence from the time he receives the land; but the Exchequer shall give him credit for the labour of purchase until the second year after he receives the land; in the course of which only half of the labour, viz. 155 days, may be demanded, and the remainder in the course of the third year, whereby the stranger will have spare days of labour to enable him (by giving indents for it) to purchase necessaries for his farm: And he shall be allowed a separate chamber in the publick asylum or inn, until he is able to build an house or cottage upon his own lot. After he has faithfully discharged his debt of service according to his first contract with the Exchequer, and also his other contract debts with private individuals (for all such private debts should be entered in the publick Exchequer, in order to give intrinsic value to the indentures for labour, as the state of every man's credit and circumstances will then appear on the publick books) he shall be allowed another quarter of a lot on the same terms, and so on till he has acquired a compleat lot; when, if he has by his good and faithful behaviour proved himself worthy of the rank and trust of a deciner, he shall be admitted to all the privileges and civil rights of the community as a free member and equal proprietor of the whole settlement.

REDEMPTION FROM SLAVERY

> Redemption from Slavery — Price to be repaid by a short limited Service to the Publick Exchequer — Profit by Redemption infinitely superior to the Profits of the Slave Trade.

Though it is a fundamental principle of the settlement, that all slaves be deemed free as soon as they enter it, so that no person can retain, or sell, or employ, a slave within the bounds of the settlement, yet there can be no impropriety in providing a means of repaying the expense of redeeming slaves, on the condition of a short limited service, as an apprentice or indentured servant, provided that the actual prices given for redemption can be sufficiently authenticated, that no more may be repaid, except, perhaps, a limited profit, not exceeding ten per cent by way of interest, for advancing the price; and provided also that the said limited service of the contract be not claimable by any individual, but by the publick Exchequer only, after the redeemed person has consented to work out the price; whereby all possibility of domestic slavery, or private oppression, will be excluded; and the Exchequer will give an ample equivalent to the redeemed person, to insure his voluntary consent to a contract for a limited time of labour, not only by the protection it will afford him, but also by putting him in possession of a portion of land, equal to the quarter part of a deciner's lot, to be increased as he discharges his debt of labour; and by finding him provisions until he shall be able to raise provisions from his own land. The publick Exchequer will be enabled, by the consent of a majority of the settlers, thus to dispose of land, because all the unoccupied land in the settlement is to be deemed as common, in which the whole body of settlers, sent out from England, if above sixteen years of age, whether indentured or not, shall be entitled to an equal share, and therefore no land must be appropriated, but by common consent. Suppose the redemption of a man should cost ten pounds (which I believe is about the average price on the coast) and suppose the labour of such a stranger be estimated only at sixpence sterling per day (though it is certainly worth much more, perhaps three or four times as much) a limited service, by the redeemed person, of five years to the publick Exchequer, as an equivalent for the purchase of a full lot of protected land, with a gradual introduction to all the privileges of a free English settlement, will amount, at 310 working days per annum (fifty-two sundays and three holidays being deducted for the reasons already mentioned under the head of Free Labour) will amount, I say, to 38 l. 15s. out of which, after paying 10 l. the price of redemption, and 10 per cent for the advance of money, viz. 1 l. more, there will remain in the publick Exchequer (towards supplying food and necessaries to the labourer, till he can provide for himself, and for risque of loss by sickness or death) the sum of 27 l. 15s. the surplus of which, if the redeemed person lives and does well, becomes the property of the publick, in which he himself enjoys an equal share of profit; so that the purchase of a slave, under so equitable a regulation, will be really and truly a Redemption from Slavery to a state of freedom and protection. And if the voluntary labour of a man should really be worth three times what I have estimated (as I really believe it is) the profit for redemption, for 11 l. disbursed, will amount to 105 l. 5s. which is 956 $9/_{11}$ l. per cent in favour of the publick Exchequer! Nay, the profit may be fairly estimated at a much higher rate! for if the free labour, which the redeemed person pays for his lot of land, be employed by the elected trustees of the Exchequer in the publick lots of land, they may expect to receive at least the ordinary production of land, for the labour bestowed upon it; which even in our northern climate may be rated at a triple amount (and much more may certainly be expected in the fertile and productive climate of Africa) so that the ordinary profit may fairly be stated at 315 l. 15s. for 11 l. disbursed, which is at the rate of 2870 $5/_{11}$ l. per cent in favour of the publick Exchequer in which the redeemed person himself would have an equal property with the rest of the community. Let the advocates for slavery show, if they can, that involuntary servitude is equally profitable. The intolerable expense of all kinds of labour wherever slavery is permitted, when compared with the price of labour in free countries, will sufficiently confute them. But more shall be said of the great profits of Free Labour, under the head of **Publick Revenue, &c.**

AGRARIAN LAW

Money for purchasing Land, to be invested in Presents for the African Chiefs — Chiefs to be previously acquainted with some necessary Conditions — All the Settlers to be restrained from purchasing Land for private Property, until the Bargains for the Publick Land are concluded— The Presents to be deemed Publick Stock. — All the Settlers above sixteen years of age to be equally entitled to the Land — Precautions for fixing on the Spot for the first Township — Settlers to be obedient to the Agent and how long — Reverse of Land — Limitation of Land — Limitation of landed Possession — Manner of laying out a tenth Lot for the Conductor — Also two more Lots for Publick Uses — Likewise ten other Publick Lots for every hundred private Lots — How to be appropriated. General Asylum for Males and Females, and for married Persons — Hospital for Sick — Penitentiary Lot — Glebe Land — No layman to have Benefit from the Glebe — Limitation of the Cure of Souls — Lot for Parish Clerks and Beadles — Under Beadles or Trumpeters — Lot for a Town Clerk — Lot for two Assistant Clerks of the Hundred — One reserved Lot to make good Deficiencies — Allowance of Land to Apprentices and indentured Servants — Sons of Settlers how to purchase Land — Indentured Servants allowed to redeem the Terms of Service and how — And to purchase Land by Labour.

The money which has been paid into the hands of the trustees to procure land for the settlement shall be vested in such articles of merchandize, as are deemed most proper for presents to the petty chiefs or Cabo-sieurs, on the African coast, and shall be disposed of among them to the best advantage, to engage their peaceable consent to admit the new settlers, and to give up to them a sufficient tract of uninhabited land, bordering on the sea, or on some navigable river or creek where fresh water also may be procured, with every other natural accommodation suitable and necessary for the proper settlement. But in treating for the land, the Cabo-sieurs or chiefs shall be informed, as a necessary part of the agreement, that the land which they are requested to give up to the new settlers, is intended to be dignified with the title and privileges of a land of freedom, like England, where no man can be a slave; for as soon as a slave sets foot on English ground, he immediately becomes free, provided he conforms himself to the laws of the state. And therefore, if any slave who has escaped from his master, (in the neighbouring country, where slavery is allowed,) should fairly get within the boundary of the new settlement, he is afterwards to be considered as a free man. And no man must pursue him to take him away by force, nor be offended with the new settlers for refusing to deliver him up: because they are indispensably required by the laws of God, and of England, to protect the slave that has escaped from his master. (See this further explained under the head of freedom). This previous declaration is absolutely necessary to be made, as one means of avoiding future disputes with the neighbouring inhabitants. And in order that as much land as possible may be procured for the new settlement by the abovementioned presents, the agent or agents, for the settlers, and every individual among them, shall be restrained from purchasing or making any agreement whatever for separate private property in land (on pain of forfeiting all right to a share in the profits of the settlement) until an agreement is made and concluded for the whole common flock of land: and until the bounds of it are actually marked out and made known to the whole body of settlers. An invoice shall be made of all the articles for presents, in which the money intended for the purchase of land was invested; so that if any articles remain more than are necessary for the purpose, they shall be deemed a part of the common stock, and shall be registered accordingly. The whole body of original settlers that go together from England above the age of sixteen years, whether male or female, apprentice, or indentured servant, shall be equally entitled to all the land within the bounds of the settlement; subject, however, to the rules hereafter expressed for the appropriation of it, from time to time when wanted: and all unappropriated land shall be deemed common. No land shall be appropriated but by the free consent of a majority of the settlers, after a full discussion of the reasons on the common council, or folkmote.

When the agent-conductor shall have carefully viewed and considered the tract of country thus vested in the community of settlers, he shall recommend to them a proper situation for the first encampment and principal township, as nearly in the center of their territory as the necessary accommodations of a constant supply of fresh water, and a navigable communication with the sea will permit: and he shall lay before the community his reasons for the choice, and if any other person or persons should propose different situations of equal propriety, the elected heads of dozens, or a sufficient deputation from them must carefully examine all the proposed situations; and after duely weighing the reasons assigned for each proposal, they shall make their report to the common council; and the opinion of the majority shall decide the question; for it is absolutely necessary that the majority of the settlers should be well satisfied and contented with the situation of their principal township, whether it be better or worse than was first proposed. But in all other points they must be obedient to the advice of the agent-conductor, and follow his directions in clearing the ground, marking out and entrenching the first encampment, building temporary barracks, and store-houses, for the accommodation of the whole community, and in digging, sowing, and planting, in the publick grounds, for the common support of the whole body of settlers; and no man shall separate himself to work for private emolument, until a small portion of land for a town lot, and a larger portion for an out lot agreeable to a plan annexed (No. 2) shall be marked out, and sufficiently cleared by publick labour for every settler; nor until the said portions of land are equally and indifferently appropriated to each person by lot, to avoid disputes, and shall be duly registered with the names of the respective proprietors. Whether or not the separate private houses should be built by joint and publick labour, may be afterwards discussed and determined in the common council. Land shall be reserved in the township for such new settlers as may afterwards arrive, which may in the mean time be cultivated for public benefit, but it shall not be appropriated until it is really wanted for such additional settlers as may afterwards join themselves to the community: for no man ought to be the proprietor of more than one town lot, with its proportional out lot, according to the limitation hereafter mentioned. And therefore if any additional land, either of town lots or out lots, or both, should be acquired by marriage or by inheritance, or legacy, or by any other lawful means, the inheritor shall be allowed three years to dispose of them: but in any other cafe, if it should be found out, that one individual possesses more than one town lot, or more land in out lots, than is declared in the following table, such land and lots shall be forfeited to the community.

EXCEPTION

N.B. The agent or first conductor of the settlement is excepted in the above regulation, because he is to be allowed every tenth lot that is laid out for private property, on account of his extraordinary care and trouble in agreeing for the land, and for laying out the lots.* And also such publick officers are to be excepted who hold publick lots, hereafter mentioned, in right of their respective offices, as the chaplain, clerk of the hundred, two assistant clerks of the hundred, and the three beadles, each of whom may be allowed to possess one separate lot, in their private capacity, besides their official publick lots.

If any man should be dissatisfied with the situation of the first township, and can find eleven other deciners of the same opinion, they may afterwards dispose of their registered lots, and agree with the community (to whom all the unoccupied land within the bounds of the settlement doth jointly and equally belong) for sufficient land to form a proportional township in some distant part, as proposed in the general scheme of the settlement (plate No. 2) according to the following limitation.

LIMITATION OF LANDED POSSESSIONS

NO person shall possess in his or her own right, more land (exclusive of the Town lot where the person dwells) than the number of acres

---

*Memorandum. Mr Smeathman the agent, and first proposer of the settlement, having unfortunately caught a putrid fever of which he died, July 1, 1786, the gentlemen of the committee must now determine whether this exception ought to be made in favour of any other agent; or whether this tenth lot ought not rather to be reserved for such publick purposes as the committee may hereafter think proper to direct. As more money than what is allowed by government will probably be wanted, the reserved tenth lots may enable the settlers to repay whatever money may be necessary for them to borrow for the first exigencies of their little community.

expressed against the following descriptions of places, viz.

	Acres.
Within 3 miles of the principal town	20
Within 3 miles of the sea, navigable river, creek, or haven in any other part of the settlement	not more than 40
Within 7 miles of Do.	100
Within 12 miles of Do.	200

Whenever nine lots are laid out, a tenth of equal size, shall be laid out closely adjoining to them, which shall be numbered and registered as the property of the conductor; or for a reserve to pay publick debts (the first conductor to whom the promise of every tenth lot was made, having lately died the committee are at liberty to dispose of this reserved land, as they shall think most just and right) and an account shall be kept of whatever odd number of lots are laid out at the same time, more than the ten last appropriated, and less than the amount of another nine; that as other new lots are demanded, the conductor may have a tenth lot of equal size close adjoining to any of the last appropriated lots which he shall chuse: but, for every ten lots thus marked out for private property, two lots of equal size, shall be also marked out adjoining to them, for publick uses, to be registered as such, which under the care of an elected committee, in every district, controlled by the common council of the state, shall be cultivated by publick labour (hereafter more fully explained) and the produce be appropriated to a publick fund for religious instruction, schools, poor, hospitals, salaries of publick officers, and all such just and reasonable expenses besides as ought to be defrayed by a publick exchequer. And also to every hundred lots laid out for PRIVATE property ten additional publick lots* shall be laid out closely adjoining: viz. One lot for a general asylum for poor males, under the care and direction of the oldest and most prudent deciners in the hundred, elected as a committee, expressly for that truth.

Secondly, One lot for a general asylum of poor families, under the care of the elderly widows, or of such other prudent matrons as shall be elected to the charge.

Thirdly, One lot for a general asylum of poor families, of both sexes together, that the branches of a family may not be separated through misfortunes or poverty; but that each family may be allowed a distinct and separate habitation to themselves at the publick expence, until they can be otherwise provided, and more comfortably established, under the care and patronage of the committee of elder deciners above mentioned. Spare chambers shall also be prepared to accommodate

---

*N.B. The publick lots are not to be reckoned with those that are tithed in favour of the conductor, but only the lots which are laid up for private property.

strangers and travellers, as at an inn, but separately in the said three lots, according to their respective descriptions of male, female, or family.

Fourthly, One lot for the support of an hospital for the sick and hurt, divided into separate wards, for males and females, subject respectively to the visitation and direction of the two separate trusts abovementioned.

And Fifthly, One penitentiary lot to be strongly fenced (with palisades, ditch, and parapet, having all the defences reversed or facing inwards) for the secure confinement of all felonious offenders, and to be divided into three distinct compartments; two for the separation of the two sexes; and a third for the married persons of either sex, that they may not be separated from their spouses, or families, in case they should desire to attend them. And

Sixthly, One lot to be registered as glebe land; and to be reserved for the chaplain of the hundred, whenever a clergyman duly qualified shall be elected by the majority of the deciners or householders in the hundred; but no layman, during the vacancy, may receive any profit from the glebe, though he may officiate gratis, as far as a layman may lawfully be allowed to interfere in the sacred office. And no chaplain shall be inducted to a legal charge or cure of souls over more than one hundred families of deciners and their dependants, at one time; with due exception, however, to clergymen of episcopal authority, in case God's blessing on the settlement should hereafter render the appointment of bishops necessary.

Seventhly, One lot, half of which to be appropriated to the use of a parish clerk, who shall also act as a head beadle in all assemblies of the hundred; and the other half in equal parts to two inferior beadles, for his assistants; who, as soon as they can be taught, shall have an additional salary as trumpeters, to summon the people to the courts of justice, and to assemble the militia at the head quarters in case of publick danger.

Eighthly, One lot for a town clerk, or recorder of the hundred, who shall keep an exact register of all the appropriations of land in his division, the rosters of service, both civil an military, the judgments of the courts for fines of labour; and the due registering of all private contracts for labour, in which duty he shall be subject to the control and accompt of the publick Exchequer in the principal township.

Ninethly, One lot for two assistant clerks of the hundred to be elected from the body of deciners, the most prudent and best qualified to acquire a general knowledge of the principles and maxims of the common law, as well as of the regulations of the settlement, that they may be able to advise the headboroughs on all occasions. And

Tenthly, One publick lot reserved to make good the deficiencies of any of the rest, or to be applied to any other publick use that the Hundred Court shall think proper to direct. And if any of these publick lots, or any parts thereof, remain uncultivated, the directors of the nearest bank, with the consent of the Hundred Court, may cause the superflous land to be cleared and cultivated for the increase of the publick stock, and revenue.

Every apprentice, or indentured male, above the age of sixteen years, that shall afterwards be introduced into the settlement from Europe, and every male bred in the settlement, as they arrive at that age, shall be allowed by the publick as many acres of land to himself, adjoining to the out lot of his parent, or of his master, as will amount to an eighth part of a lot, in order that he may employ his leisure hours to his own profit; and as soon as he is twenty-one years of age, he shall have an addition from the publick of one-eighth more, amounting in all to one quarter of a lot, gratis: and the son of a settler, when arrived at that age, shall be allowed to purchase three-fourths of a lot more, to compleat his proportion for a deciner, at the rate of half a year's service for each fourth part — that is in all for 465 days labour to the publick: half of which to be demanded before the end of the second year, and the remainder gradually before the end of the third year. But with respect to an indentured servant or apprentice, if he shall be able, even before he is of age, to purchase out his indentures, either by the produce of his private portion of land, or by entering himself at the town bank, for such a proportion of his extra hours, or evening's labour, as shall be deemed equal to his strength, without injury to the labour due to his master, but not exceeding two hours (making ten hours labour in all per day:) the master must consent to the redemption, and the late indentured person, even though he is not of age, shall be allowed to purchase one quarter of a lot in whatever township he shall chuse, for one year's service (viz. 310 days labour paid by installments as above) to the Exchequer of the township; but on condition however that if he does not chuse to settle in the township of his late master, he shall give up the land which he there held, on being allowed the value of it, by the Exchequer; and that he shall previously apply to the headborough or chief of the division wherein his desired lot is situated, in order to obtain the assent of the inhabitants to his admission among them; which being granted, he shall make a publick declaration in open court of his sincere intention to comply with the laws of the settlement, and to behave himself consistently with the necessary peace and good order of a civilized society. And after he has approved himself to the vicinage of his new settlement by good behaviour, and by a faithful discharge of the stipulated service or price, he shall be admitted (if he is twenty-one years of age, or as soon as he attains that age) to all the civil rights of the community, provided that he solemnly renews the said declaration at the next publick court or folkmote of the district which he inhabits; and he shall then be allowed to purchase at the publick Exchequer as much more land as will amount to a compleat lot. And every indentured European, above the age of twenty-one, shall be allowed gratis, half a lot of land adjoining to his master's out lot; and as soon as the limited demand of labour, due to his master, shall be faithfully discharged, either by service or by redemption, he shall be allowed to purchase half a lot more for two years service (with reasonable credit or allowance of time to perform it in) to the Exchequer or publick bank and shall be admitted to all the civil rights of a deciner, as soon as the stipulated service is faithfully discharged: or sooner, if the Hundred Court shall be satisfied that he is worthy.

PUBLICK REVENUE AND PAPER CURRENCY OF INTRINSIC VALUE

Tax on Day's work required from all Males above eighteen Years of Age — Number of Indentures to be given by every Male — Indentures how to be certified — Every Man to have an Accompt of Labour open at the Exchequer, certified by the proper Officers of his Division — Apprentices and Indentured Servants to be registered — Publick Labour to be deducted from the Terms of all Indentured Servants — Accompts of Labour how to be settled and discharged — Estimation of Labour — Additional Tax on the Rich, and on those who have more profitable Employments than ordinary Labour — The Payment of Tithes of Property always grievous and inconvenient — Tax on Pride and Indolence. The Advantages of making Ordinary Labour the Medium of Traffic — That poor Men will never want Employment, nor lose Time in searching for it — Will obtain Credit for Necessaries, and for the Assistance of Articifers — Indentures how to be certified, entered, and put in Circulation — Indentures will be ready Cash to the Merchant, Tradesman, or Articifer, and will enable them to redeem their own more valuable Labour, and to draw back on the Bank for Paper Cash to circulate, or for Labour to accommodate Planters, who will repay in Produce; that the Indentures will be really as intrinsically valuable as ready Cash — The Author's Doubts — A few Objections removed Debts of Labour to be demanded only by the publick Banks — Applications either for Labourers or Labour to be made at the publick Banks — Planters to pay a small Commission per Cent. to the Bank for supplying Labourers — Labourers to be summoned in due Rotation some every Day, with due previous Notice, according to the Dates of their Indentures not balanced — Guard against Bankruptcy, and against Oppression of indentured Labourers — In case of Death, Debts of Labour due to the Exchequer to be made good out of the real and personal Estate of the Debtor — The System of Frankpledge the chief Security of this Revenue — Publick Fines and Forfeitures — The peculiar Improvement which even Frankpledge will obtain by Fines of Labour — Even Neglect of publick Labour may be turned to the publick Advantage — the Revenue of Fines reserved to make up all Deficiencies in this Calculation as it would probably amount to a Third of what is already reckoned, and the Profits of the Sale of Land probably even more than the Fines — The Savings by this Arrangement would be almost as extraordinary as the Gains.

In order to establish an efficient publick revenue, and at the same time to render industry and honest daily labour honourable, or at least creditable by being general — All contributions to the state, and all publick fines, (except those laid on persons convicted of felony within the settlement, which are to be worked out in the penitentiary lots, (before described) shall be levied in day labour, estimated (whatever a man's calling, art, or ability may be) at the rate of eight hours work per day of an ordinary labourer; so that persons who have money, or more valuable employments, may compound, or find a sufficient substitute accustomed to ordinary labour; but the substitute must be a free man; because no slave, nor even an apprentice or indentured servant, if bound for a longer term than what is limited under the general head of freedom, shall be permitted to work within the bounds of the settlement, lest any discredit should thereby be thrown on honest labour. And for the same reason the fines of days work laid on persons convicted of felony, within the settlement, shall not be entered on the same books of the Exchequer which contain the names of the rest of the community, but shall be registered in a distinct book, as a separate branch of the revenue, and shall be worked out in the penitentiary lots.

All written contracts or indentures for labour, publick or private, shall be entered in the books of the Publick Exchequer, to which shall be made compleat indexes of reference, that the state of every man's engagements may easily be known, whereby no man will have it in his power to dispose of indentures for more labour than such a reasonable proportion of his leisure as he may be supposed capable of fulfilling and discharging in due time.

	Days
A tenth part of the 310 days of labour shall be appropriated to the support of Religious instruction, schools, widows, poor, and other parochial exigencies.	31
And also another tenth for other general expenses of the community or state.	31
This publick contribution of two-tenths, or one-fifth of the work-days in a year, shall be equally required of all males above the age of eighteen years, and shall be estimated at the value only of ordinary labour in cultivating the earth, amounting for each person, per annum, to sixty-two days of ordinary labour	62

For which every male of the above description shall anually sign indentures for the undermentioned portions of his labour, viz.

			Days Work
1 Indenture for	20 Days Work		20
1 Do.	10 Do.		10
1 Do.	5 Do.		5
4 Indentures for	2 Do.		8
10 Do.	1 Do.		10
10 Do.	4 Hours work or ½ a day each		5
8 Do.	2 Do.	or ¼ do.	2
16 Do.	1 Do.	or ⅛ do.	2
--			--
51 Indentures.	Days work of ordinary labour		62
--			--

The small portions of time are necessary to form a rateable medium for the prices of all kinds of small articles in traffick, and to afford a convenient exchange when the indentures are circulated like bills in lieu of cash; and for such articles as may require a still smaller fraction to express any gradual rising or fall of price, the proper fraction of an hour into sixty minutes, will be sufficiently small for all purposes; and if any species of so small a value as one minute (or even as five or fifteen minutes) should be thought necessary, small pieces of copper or other cheap metals, amber, or particular kinds of shells or beads, may be substituted for it. But if indentures, (for the sake of uniformity in the currency) should be preferred an indenture for ten minutes, the sixth part of an hour, will amount exactly to one farthing, at the lowest price of ordinary labour, i.e. one shilling per day.

In the indentures must be expressed the name of the township, or of the hundred, and the number, or other denomination of the tithing or dozen, wherein the signer lives; and when the indenture is cut at the figured tally, the signer of it shall keep the cheque in his own possession, but shall deliver the full number and value of his signed indentures into the Exchequer, in the presence of the chief of the dozen to which he belongs. If he himself is an headborough, or chief of a dozen, he shall deliver his indentures in the presence of his hundredor, or of three other headboroughs, of the same hundred, and the hundredor himself in the presence of four headboroughs of his own division.

The entry or counter checque in the publick treasury of every man's accompt of indentures, for which he is a debtor to the publick, shall be carefully examined and certified by the Hundredors, or their assistants, or at least by four of the Headboroughs, of the particular division to which each debtor respectively belongs, which will be very little trouble to each chief, as the highest will certify only for 100 families; and the regularity of the frankpledge, and the certain knowledge of each individual in a division, which every chief obtains by it, will effectually secure every individual from forgeries; so that no man will be liable to answer any demands for labour, but what may be amply proved and authenticated by comparing the checques in his own hands with the certified entry in the Exchequer.

Masters of apprentices, and also of indentured strangers, brought by them into the settlement, shall be obliged to register the said indentured persons in the publick Exchequer of the township where he lives, together with the terms of their indentures, on the penalty of 310 days labour for every wilful failure herein; and he shall be obliged to deduct from the limited time of indentured service, all the time that the apprentices or servants have worked for the publick benefit.

When a man has worked out, or otherwise redeemed any of the paper money, for which he is nominally responsible, and shall have received back the indenture, after the service, he may produce it at the Exchequer, together with its corresponding checque, that it may be cancelled in the publick accompt; whereby the discharge of publick debts may be as regularly proved and authenticated as the just demands abovementioned; and the state of a man's publick debt may always be known at the publick Exchequer by the balance of indentures in his accompt; and thereby all frauds and impositions may be easily traced and detected.

As Labour in all new settlements where land is cheap, is, of course, much higher and more valuable than in old established states, the intrinsic value of the labour, in the proposed new settlement, might fairly be estimated at double the price of labour in England; but at present I will rate it only at one shilling per day, on account of the limitation of eight hours instead of ten, commonly required in England. About 300 males have already entered their names; which number multiplied by sixty-two the tax of days work due from each per annum, by this regulation, will produce 18,600 days of labour in the year, due to the publick; which, estimated at the low average rate of only 1s. per day, will amount to 930 l. per annum. And as the value or expence of labour, when applied to land, (at the ordinary estimation of increase by the products of the earth in return for labour and care) is expected to produce at least triple the amount of the disbursement, even in our northern climates, so the value of 930 l. bestowed in labour on the publick lots of land in the fertile and productive climate of Africa, where very little labour is necessary, might certainly be estimated much higher: but even at the ordinary rate it will amount to 2790 l. per annum, which is a very great publick revenue, if it be remembered that it is calculated on the very small number of 300 males, reckoning rich and poor together, which are only the ordinary average number of males in an hundred division, or 100 families of a well established settlement, at the rate of three males to a family!

The general contribution, which I have proposed, is equally laid on the poor as on the rich, the former being equally capable of paying it, and that certainly with more ease to themselves, by being accustomed to ordinary labour. Nevertheless the rich (it may be said) ought to contribute more than the poor, on account of the superior advantages which accrue to them by their association with the poor in one well regulated political body. The superior advantages I speak of are — 1st, The personal ease or exemption from labour, which their riches may always procure to them in such a society — and secondly the effectual security of their property, or wealth, procured in Frankpledge, or "Maxima securitas," by the equal exertion of persons, who have no property, and by an equal risque, also of their lives, in case of actual danger. So that it seems clearly reasonable and just, that the rich and higher ranks of citizens should contribute more to the publick revenue, than the poor; — but in what proportion is rather difficult to determine; though it may be readily answered, that the quantity of riches should, in due proportion, determine the quantity of contribution; yet this cannot be done without a general tax on property, which, as experience teaches us, is liable to many inconveniencies; so that even the antient and ordinary tax of tithes to the clergy is deemed grievously inconvenient, on account of the difficulties, disputes, quarrels, and vexations, which too frequently happen, as well in compounding for them as in the collection of them in kind. The only expedient, therefore, which I am able to devise, at present, for procuring a larger contribution from the rich, is a tax on pride and indolence; a tax which, though it will not produce in exact proportion to the property of the wealthy, will nevertheless most certainly obtain from the wealthy and luxurious a contribution exactly proportionate to whatever pride and idolence may be occasioned by the superfluous wealth of the community; and in aid to this tax on superfluous wealth, the affluence likewise of the more useful members of society, whose employments procure them a more profitable reward than they could obtain by ordinary labour, might be made to yield a reasonable addition to the revenue in consideration of their superior abilities to contribute, which men of this respectable class certainly have.

TAX on PRIDE and INDOLENCE, and on Persons who have superior Emoluments above the ordinary Class of Labourers.

Though labour is the common lot of man, according to the divine sentence, or penal judgment, denounced against our first male parent — "In the sweat of thy face shalt thou eat bread, till thou return into the ground," &c. Gen. iii. 19. and though an apostle also has declared, that "if any would not work neither should he eat," yet many persons there are, in every community, who by some means or other seem to be exempted from the necessity of personal labour, the ordinary condition of human life! How this may be accounted for, and reconciled with the divine decree, is stated more at large in my tract on the Law of Nature, and Principles of Action in Man, p.21-30. Nothing, therefore, according to natural religion, can be more reasonable and just, or more consistent also, according to the second foundation of law, with the revealed will of God in the holy scriptures, than that all persons who have wealth sufficient to purchase an exemption from this ordinary lot of man, should be required to contribute in a larger proportion to the exigencies of the community, than persons who depend on their daily labour for their daily bread. And this additional contribution may very easily be levied, without making any other additional object of taxation than what I have already proposed to be the single article of general contribution, viz. the two-tenths of ordinary labour; let a redemption of the general tax of sixty-two days' contribution, viz. two-tenths of ordinary labour be required at the rate of a double, or, if necessary, of a triple value of the service, from all persons who, having no real bodily infirmity or incapacity, shall decline a personal attendance for the general contribution, either through pride, by setting themselves up above their brethren in their own estimation, as superior to the common lot of ordinary labour, or else by having a better and more reasonable motive, that of a more profitable occupation for the employment of their time, which will equally render them capable of paying, without any actual hardship, the additional tax for the safe, indulgence, and superior profit, which they enjoy by the purchase.

Suppose there be ten men in an hundred, or thirty males in one hundred families, whose pride, or wealth, or indolence, would induce them to decline personal labour: such men ought surely to redeem their exemption at a triple value, which cannot amount to any real hardship or oppression; as the alternative, and only hardship to those who may love too well their wealth, and deem the tax too heavy, is to submit to the ordinary lot of their brethren, in complying with a short limited service for the publick benefit, in which they themselves have an equal profit. And suppose there be also double that number of persons in an hundred division, who have useful arts and more profitable trades and occupations to induce their redemption of personal service:— The produce of the tax will be as follows — the first class of thirty gentlemen, or idle men, taxed at triple the value of the sixty-two days of ordinary labour, will pay all together the sum of 279 l. but as the sixty-two days of labour from each is already included in the former general calculation, one-third must be deducted from the estimated value of this additional tax, whereby it is reduced to:

                                                      l.   s. d.

                                                     186 0 0

    The second class of 60 merchants, tradesmen, or useful artificers, who will be induced by more profitable occupations to redeem their personal labour, will each pay a double tax, viz. the value of 124 days ordinary labour at 1s. per day which all together is only 6 l. 4s. per ann. to each man; but as they are already charged half that sum, in the general estimate of contributions, the other half alone must here be reckoned, viz. 3 l. 2s. which multiplied by 60 amounts to   186 0 0

Total additional tax on the 2 classes abovementioned in one hundred families   372 0 0

Which addition, if laid out on the cultivation of land in the publick lots, would produce three times that value, according to the ordinary increase of land, for the labour bestowed on it. The risque, indeed, of a misapplication of the labour, or of a defalcation of the increase, may reasonably be objected, according to the ordinary misconduct of persons intrusted with the care of farms, at present in this country; but the same objection will not hold where Frankpledge is duly established, because the eye of every neighbour would be a watchful guard against fraud, all being equally interested in the publick profit. I will therefore multiply this additional tax by 3, the ordinary rate of increase to be expected from the land which is cultivated by it   3 0 0

                                  1116 0 0

To which add the general contribution before estimated at   2790 0 0

The total amount of revenue for one single division of an hundred families   3906 0 0

Thus an ample source is opened not only of publick credit but also of private security, or trust, in traffick, by the same easy means; whereby poor labouring men may be enabled to obtain all the necessary articles of merchandize, though they have no ready money to advance. For, as ordinary labour is rendered the medium of traffic, instead of cash, the first advantage to a poor industrious man, accustomed only to ordinary labour, is, that he will, at all times, have it in his power to obtain employment; in the search of which, with us, many honest men, in all the three kingdoms, are obliged to leave their native country. And the second material advantage to him is, that he can always obtain an immediate credit, proportionable to the value of his unengaged time, for any articles of trade that he may want, by giving the merchant, or tradesman, in return for them, an indenture for as many days labour as the purchase is worth; and he is also enabled to employ a blacksmith, carpenter, or other useful articifer (in case he should want their assistance on his own lot) by giving them, in like manner, an indenture, for as many days of ordinary labour, as will amount to the value of the work. These indentures (as before proposed for the indentures of general contribution) should express the names of the hundred, and of the dozen in which the signer is associated, and should be previously carried by him to be entered at the public Exchequer, or bank, of the hundred, and be there properly certified, as before proposed; after which the labourer may cut off the indentures from his checques, at the printed tally, and pay them to the merchant or tradesman, for the article purchased; or to the articifer for his job, retaining the checques in his own custody, that he may always know the amount of his debt of labour. On the other hand, the merchant, tradesman, or articifer, who receives such an indenture from a poor labourer, can immediately realize the value of it in his own favour, by paying it into the public Exchequer, or bank of the township; where, of course, it will be posted to the credit of his accompt of labour, and will enable him to redeem a part of his own indentures, without his own personal labour, which, of course, is much more valuable than ordinary labour; and in like manner he will proceed with all other indentures for ordinary labour, that he has procured by his traffic, or more valuable occupation, always paying them to the credit of his account at the bank, until the amount exceeds his own debt for public service: when, from the balance of labour in his favour, according to the amount of it, he will always be at liberty to draw on the bank for indentures of days work, either for circulation, as ready cash, or for labourers, to cultivate his own lot of land, or else occasionally to accommodate planters who want labourers, and are willing to pay the value of them, in produce, &c. whereby private credit (as well as public credit, already provided for) will be amply supported: and the indentures for labour, by which this most essential public and private service is effected, will be, in fact, A PAPER CURRENCY OF INTRINSIC VALUE, answering all the purposes of ready cash, as a medium of traffic, as well as all the necessary purposes of negociable bills, to support public and private credit; and yet they cannot be, at all, liable to depreciation!

The advantages appear to me so great and extraordinary, that I can hardly give credit, as I proceed, to my own estimation of them; and am inclined to suspect that I am, in some way or other, enormously mistaken; but as I cannot yet find out my error, I must leave by censure to some more able head. A few obvious objections, however, I am prepared to remove by a timely proposal of adequate remedies. As for instance — Whatever might be deemed troublesome, or disagreeable, in exacting the payment of these debts of labour, may be effectually withdrawn from individuals, by investing the public bank of each township with the sole authority of demanding the labour for the indentures, that have been respectively entered and certified therein. And that the several banks may be enabled to realize the value of these indentures, all applications either for labourers, or labour, shall be made at the several town banks; where planters may be sure of a supply of labourers, and the labourer equally sure of a constant supply of work, without danger of oppression, or non payment of wages, being secured from both by the mediation of the bank, which employs him, and disposes of his service. And both parties, or at least, the planters, ought to pay some small allowance per cent to the bank, by way of commission, or profit for the negociation. And each bank should regularly summon, (with due previous notice for every day) a sufficient number of the indentured labourers that are entered on their books, not only to cultivate the public lots of land under their care, but also to supply the current daily demand of labour that may be wanted by planters and other private individuals; but all persons summoned to labour, shall work on the public lots, until such demands are made, by which means the labourers will lose no time in waiting for work. The daily summonses to labour, issued from the bank, should be made in due rotation, according to the dates of the indentures entered on the books, and according to the quantity of debt which each individual has to work out. And, that no man may run deeper in debt, by disposing of his labour to a greater amount than he may be able to discharge in due time, all indentures whatsoever for the labour either of apprentices or servants, should be entered at the bank of the township, where the parties reside, whereby not only the state of every labourer's debt may be always known, and, of course, likewise his ability to discharge it, but also, on the other hand, the labourers, apprentices, and servants themselves, will be thereby more easily protected from the oppression of such avaritious masters, as might otherwise be inclined to exact more service than is due by the terms of their contract.

If any person should die before his indentured service is discharged to the public bank, his land, stock, and effects shall be answerable to the amount of his deficiency to the publick, in preference to all other debts: whereby the paper currency, will preserve a standard value; and, at the same time, afford a most convenient medium for traffic and exchange. If any further difficulties, more than I have foreseen and guarded against, should still be objected, I flatter myself that the salutary establishment of Frankpledge will be sufficient to obviate them all. For this maxima securitas, renders every individual completely responsible for all debts or demands that can justly be made upon him, and for all charges against him whatever, because the residence of the meanest member of society can be most expeditiously known by the public books; so that he may be immediately traced at any time to his very chamber, and no individual in Frankpledge can resist the united power of a free people — for if any one should neglect or despise the summons of the public bank, his tithing or dozen may be compelled (on the penalty of a heavy fine for neglect) to produce him: and should the tithing or dozen neglect, the hundred is summoned to enforce satisfaction, and so on with respect to higher divisions, until the strength of the whole community is united, as one man, to render executive justice, to fine, or otherwise punish all contumacious delinquents against common sense, and to enforce obedience to the determined justice of the majority. This occasional mention of misdemeanors and fines, reminds me that I have omitted to add to the amount of my calculation of Revenue, the profit of the public fines and forfeitures, which must always be very considerable where Frankpledge is established; not only, because the regularity and order of the system renders the levying of fines and forfeitures extremely easy, expeditious, and free from expence, but also, because the penalties of fines and forfeitures are, in Frankpledge, extended to the minutest immoralities, and negligences, in order to render the peace and regularity of society as perfect as possible. Add to this a very particular advantage, which the ancient mode of punishing by fines and forfeitures, will acquire by the application of my proposal of universal calculation by days labour — an advantage which could never before be obtained; viz. that the poorest man has, thereby, something to forfeit, even sometimes very considerable, because his personal labour is equally valuable, and probably more so, than the labour of a man of superior rank; so that even the happy system of Frankpledge itself is very materially improved, and rendered much more effectual, as well as more profitable, by the proposed addition.

All contempts of legal summonses to labour, would, of course, be sinable; as also apparent sloth, or remissness in working; both of which would thereby be made effectual to increase the value of the paper currency, instead of diminishing it, as might be expected. Likewise all contempts of court, neglects of summons to attend juries; want of punctuality in attending the duties of Watch and Ward, in the rotation of the public roster; and all inattention or disobedience while on duty; all breaches of the sabbath, swearing, drunkeness, and immodesty, as well as fornication and adultery (both of which should be very strictly, and very severely mulcted, for the more effectual promotion of honourable marriage) giving or accepting a challenge to fight, even though no mischief should ensue; all unneccessary wrangling, fighting, or striking, and even every wilful provocation by word or gesture, and every other misbehaviour that is inconsistent with the peace, order, and quiet of a happy society, would be punished by a suitable fine of day's work, in proportion to the offence, by which altogether this essential article of fines and forfeitures (which, in England, through neglect of Frankpledge, are hardly an object of consideration) would necessarily occasion a much larger addition to the public revenue than I can venture, at present, to estimate; and, therefore, I must beg leave to reserve this valuable article of fines, to make up any deficiencies, which, perhaps, may be afterwards discovered in my other calculations; to which must also be added, as a further reserve, the profits arising from the sale of land for day labour, not yet estimated, though it would probably amount even to more than the fines.

I have already, without these profitable articles, carried my estimation of the public revenue nearly to the amount of 4000 l. per annum, for every 100 families, including equally both rich and poor, which far exceeds the proportionable revenue, I believe, of any kingdom on earth; for indeed, the same means are not practicable in any country or nation, unless the most excellent system of Frankpledge be previously established which I must frequently repeat. But, for the sake of comparison, let us apply this scheme to the computed average number of taxable houses or families in England and Wales. The one million families (as they are commonly estimated) would raise, by merely taking on themselves the very moderate and equal burthen of only a 5th part of their most ordinary labour, estimated at the low rate of one shilling per day, together with the additional tax on pride, and the easy levy on profitable occupations, with the due increase of the whole profit, when applied to the cultivation of public land, would raise (I say) at the rate of 3906 l. for every hundred families, before calculated, the amazing revenue of 39 millions, and 60 thousands of pounds sterling, per annum. If I am questioned on the possibility of raising a sum so enormously great, that it far exceeds the whole annual produce of all our accumulated taxes, customs, and other means of revenue, I must confess, that I am at a loss how even to satisfy my own doubts about it; and that I know not what reasons to assign for such an incredible accumulation of wealth, arising from so trifling a burthen laid upon the people, unless it may be attributed to the effectual employment of all the labouring poor; and of others capable of labour, and also to the effectual means of which the proposition seems to promise of rendering that general employment of ordinary labour profitable, not only in the circulation of the indentures as bills and cash; but also in the increase which may be naturally expected from the actual labour, when applied to the earth. But there are other advantages attending the proposal, which are not yet reckoned.

The previous re-establishment of frankpledge, without which the raising of such an increased revenue could not be practicable, would, at the same time, render absolutely unnecessary the greatest part of our most expensive establishments both civil and military.

So that, upon the whole the gain might fairly be estimated at nearly triple the effective, or neat amount of all the other deviseable "Ways and Means, &c. &c." — That this is not an exaggerated statement of our publick burthens, will be allowed, I believe, by all parties. I wish they were equally agreed in opinion about the necessary remedy!

GRANVILLE SHARPE.

Old Jewry, 3rd July, 1786.

APPENDIX III

SHARP'S ADDITIONAL REGULATIONS

As it will be expedient for the welfare of the new settlement, that at least 4 persons of liberal education, should be employed in each hundred families, to register estates as well as judicial determinations, and keep an exact account of all public debts, receipts and expenditures, in the books of each hundred: being also such persons as may be capable of readily acquiring by study some general knowledge of the Common Law of England, that they may be prepared on all occasions, to give proper information and advice to the hundredors, headboroughs and others who probably may not have had the opportunity of acquiring that kind of knowledge.

It is proposed that sufficient salaries by paid to all persons so employed in the public service: and that they may not hold these offices of profit in a precarious or base tenure, it is also proposed that they shall be elected to hold their respective offices on the same terms, as law officers in England, viz: "quandiu se bene gesserint". "As long as they shall behave themselves well": that is, until they are actually convicted by "due process of the law" of same notorious malversation or dishonesty, whereby they incur a legal incapacity for their offices by ceasing to be "good and true men" — And yet, as it might be dangerous to the new settlement to permit men to hold offices of considerable profit without annual re-election, if they were permitted at the same time to obtain and hold offices of power — it is, therefore proposed (from the example of the Common Law of England) that the officers of magisterial powers and command over the militia, as sheriffs, heads of thousands, hundredors or headboroughs and their respective deputies or assistants, shall not be allowed any salaries: nor be elected into any offices to which salaries are annexed, unless they shall consent to give up their offices of power and command . . .

* * *

That all these ministers with salaries shall be amenable to their own Hundred Court, according to the due process of the law, for all such charges as are cognizable by the court, when duly preferred against them: but lesser differences or disputes may be discussed amongst themselves in their own half-tithing (wherein they pledge each other): and may be submitted to the opinion of the majority of them: subject, however, to an appeal, if required, to the weekly Court of 4 Tithings, or to the monthly Hundred Court, and still higher, if the business or complaint cannot otherwise be settled.

* * *

That in the weekly Courts of 4 Tithings, the hundredor, or one of the assistant hundredors shall preside in the court of the first 4 Tithings of the hundred: . . . .

* * *

That the Common Council of the settlement be assembled according to the ancient established rules of County Courts, viz: "twice every year" and "more often if need be".

APPENDIX IV

C.O. 267/25
Enclosed in Gov. Thompson's
dispatch No. 6 of 11/2/1809.

KNOW ALL MEN BY THESE PRESENTS, that I King Tom, Chief of Sierra Leone on the Grain Coast of Africa, by and with the consent of the other Kings, Chiefs and Potentates subscribing hereto, in consideration of these presents, as by a list annexed, now made me by Captain Bouldon Thompson of His Britannic Majesty's ship Nautilus, Joseph Irwin Esqre and the Revd. Patrick Frazer on and behalf of and for the sole benefit of the free community of settlers their heirs and successors now lately arrived from England and under the protection of the British government, have granted and by these presents do grant, and for ever quit claim to a certain district of land for the settling of the said free community to be theirs, their Heirs and successors for ever, that is to say, All the land, wood and water which is contained from the Bay commonly called Frenchman's Bay but by these presents changed to that of St. George's Bay, coastways up the River Sierra Leone to Gambia Island and southerly or inland twenty miles. And further be it known to all men, that I King Tom do faithfully promise and swear, for my chiefs, gentlemen, and people, likewise my heirs and successors, that I will bear true allegiance to His Most Gracious Majesty King George the Third, King of Great Britain, France and Ireland etc. etc. and protect the said free settlers his subjects to the utmost of my power against the insyrrections and attacks of all nations and people whatever. And I do hereby bind myself, my Heirs and Successors, to grant the said free Settlers a continuance of a quiet and peaceable possession of the Lands granted their Heirs and Successors for ever.

IN WITNESS WHEREOF I and my Chiefs have set our hands and seals the eleventh day of June 1787.

Witness to the executing the above and the presents made:
Thomas Bouldon Thompson
Joseph Irvin
Patrick Frazer A.M.

The mark of King Tom
X
Chief Pabongee
X
Queen Yammacouba

Eight muskets
1 barrel gunpowder
2 bags of lead balls 1 cwt.
3 doz. of hangers with red scabbards
24 laced hats
5 small niconees
4 cotton Romals
1 cask of rum containing 10 gallons
34lb of tobacco manufactured
25 iron bars
10 yards of scarlet cloth
117 bunches of beads
13 pieces of Britannias
1 puncheon of rum containing 120 gallons.

See: Fyfe *S. L. Inheritance* pp.112-13.

APPENDIX V

No. 1 SIERRA LEONE. Aug. 22 1788.

KNOWN ALL MEN BY THESE PRESENTS that I, King Nambaner, Chief of Sierra Leone, on the Grain Coast of Africa, by and with the consent of the other Kings, Princes, Chiefs, and Potentates, subscribing hereto. In consideration of the presents, as by a list annexed, now made me by Captain John Taylor, of His Britannic Majesty's brig *"Miro"* in behalf of and for the sole benefit of the free community of settlers, their heirs and successors, lately arrived from England and under the protection of the British Government, have granted, and by these presents do grant and for ever quit claim to a certain district of land for the settling of the said free community to be theirs, their heirs and successors, for ever, that is to say:— All the land, wood, water, &c. &c. which are now contained from the bay, commonly called Frenchman's Bay, but by these presents changed to that of St. George's Bay, coastwise up the River Sierra Leone to Gambia Island, and southerly, or inland from the river side 20 miles. And further be it known unto all men that I, King Nambaner, do faithfully promise and swear for my Chiefs, gentlemen, and people, likewise my heirs and successors, that I will bear true allegiance to His Most Gracious Majesty George the Third, King of Great Britain, France, and Ireland, &c., &c., &c., and protect the said free settlers, his subjects, to the utmost of my power against the insurrections and attacks of all nations or people whatever. And I do hereby bind myself, my heirs and successors, to grant the said free settlers a continuance of a quiet and peaceable possession of the land granted, their heirs and successors for ever. In witness whereof I and my Chiefs have set our hands and seals this 22nd day of August 1788.

And it is also further agreed by the aforesaid Contracting Parties, that the customs payable by vessels anchoring in St. George's Bay shall pay ten bars to the free settlers and subjects of His Britannic Majesty, and the customs paid for watering to be paid to King Nambaner, his representatives or successors, that is to say, 15 bars as customary, and if to anchor and not to water, the customs as above to be paid to the free settlers of St. George's Bay as aforesaid.

In witness whereof to this additional part of these presents and all others contained herein, we have made our marks and signed our names with our seals affixed this 22nd day of August 1788.

    (Signed)   JOHN TAYLOR
        "   RICHARD WEAVER
        "   THOMAS PEALL
        "   BENJAMIN ELLET
                their
        "   KING X NAMBANER
        "   JAMES X DOWDER
                marks
        "   PABONGEE
        "   DICK ROBBIN
        "   ABRAM ELLIOT GRIFFITH
                Secretary to the King.

A LIST of the PRESENTS given in consideration for COMPLETING the PURCHASE OF LAND, &c., hereunder annexed, viz:—
One embroidered bersode coat, waistcoat, and breeches.
A crimson satin embroidered waistcoat.
A lead coloured satin coat, waistcoat, and breeches.
A mock diamond ring.
Two pairs of pistols.
One telescope.
Two pairs of gold earrings with necklaces and drops.
Eight dozen bottles of wine.
One puncheon of rum.
A tierce or three hundredweight of pork.
One box of smoking pipes.
Seven muskets.
Twenty pounds of tobacco.
One piece of fine white cotton or calico.
Ten pounds of beads in lots.
Two cheeses weighing twenty-eight pounds.
Two hundred gun flints.
One dozen bottles of red port wine.

This is to certify to all to whom these presents may come, that we whose names are hereunto subscribed maketh oath that the purchase of the land, &c., made by Captain Thompson was not (to our certain knowledge) valid; it having been purchased from people who had no authority to sell the same.

APPENDIX VI

THE SIERRA LEONE COMPANY after its incorporation agreed to accept into the Colony all free blacks who were willing to migrate to Sierra Leone.

The S. L. Company, willing to receive into their Colony such free blacks as are able to produce to their Agents Lt. Clarkson of His Majesty's Navy and Mr Lawrence Hartshorn of Halifax or either of them, satisfactory testimonials of their character (more particularly as to honesty, sobriety and industry) think it proper to notify in an explicit manner upon what terms they will receive at S.L. those who bring with them written certificates of approbation from either of the said Agents, which certificates they are hereby respectively authorised to grant or withhold at discretion.

It is therefore declared by the company that every free black upon producing such a certificate shall have a grant of not less than twenty acres of land for himself, ten for his wife, and five for every child, upon such terms and subject to such charges and obligations with a view to the general prosperity of the Company as shall hereafter be settled by the Company in respect to the grants of land to be made by them to all settlers and whether black or white.

That for all stores and provisions etc. supplied from the Company's warehouses, the Company shall receive and equitable compensation, according to fixed rates, extending to blacks and whites indiscriminately.

That the civil, military, personal and commercial rights and duties of blacks and whites shall be the same and secured in the same manner.

And for the full assurance of personal protection from slavery to all such black settlers, the company have subjoined a clause contained in the Act of Parliament whereby they are incoporated, viz.

PROVIDED also and be it further enacted, that it shall not be lawful for the said company either directly or indirectly, by itself or themselves, or by the agents or servants of the said company, or otherwise, howsoever, to deal or traffick in the buying or selling of slaves, or in any manner whatsoever to have, hold, appropriate or employ any person or persons in a state of slavery in the service of the said company.

Given under our hands, London the Second day of August, 1791.

Henry Thornton — Chairman	Samuel Parker
Philip Sansom — D. Chairman	Joseph Hardcastle
Charles Middleton	Thomas Clarkson
William Wilberforce	Vickeris Taylor
Granville Sharpe	William Sanford
John Kingston	Thomas Eldred
	George Wolff

APPENDIX VII

SIERRA LEONE — Manuscript Orders and Regulations from the Directors of the Sierra Leone Company to the Superintendent and Council for the Settlement (John Clarkson, Alex. Falconbridge, James Cocks, Dr. John Bell, John Wakerell, Richard Pepys, James Watt and Charles Taylor), for the Trade, Cultivation, Civilization, Defence, Government and General Welfare of the Settlement, neatly written on 69 pages, folio, circa 1791. £8.

From the Melville collection of State Papers.
Gives a general outline of the views and principles of the Company. The duty of Exports and Imports is never to be higher that 2½ per cent. The Company, by its own wishes, is prohibited by Act of Parliament, from selling slaves. A Fort, Church and schools are to be built. The money medium is to be the Spanish Dollar, valued for the sake of uniformity at 5s. Dealing with the towns that are to be built . . . .
"You are to name the first town Free Town."

To
John Clarkson, Esquire
Mr Alex. Falconbridge (Surgeon, died 1792)
Mr James Cocks
Dr John Bell
Mr John Wakerell
Mr Richard Pepys
Mr James Watt
Mr Charles Taylor

OUR SUPERINTENDENT AND COUNCIL AT SIERRA LEONE.
1. Having in consequence of the power vested in us as Directors of the Sierra Leone Company, lately established by authority of Parliament, appointed you to be the Superintendent and Council for the Settlements and affairs of the said Company on the Peninsula of Sierra Leone: We

now proceed to give you such Rules and Instructions for your conduct, as appear to us to be necessary or material at the commencement and in the early progress of the undertaking in which you are engaged.

In the great multiplicity of objects which the establishment of a new Colony presents, those only which are of first importance can be immediately attended to; but in the course of carrying on this work, and as occasions arise, we shall supply you with what ever further directions may appear to be wanting.

Object of the Institution.
2. The object for which the Sierra Leone Company is instituted is the establishment of a Trade with Africa on the true principles of Commerce, carrying out British Manufacturers and other articles of Traffick and bringing back African Produce in exchange.

Trade.
3. The Proprietors of the present Company are fully persuaded that if proper means are taken and prosecuted with diligence and perseverance, the Continent of Africa will furnish Commodities for the support of an extensive and increasing commerce, without resorting to the miserable expedient of selling the inhabitants as slaves in order to furnish a return, a Traffic which in the case of the Sierra Leone Company the Act of Parliament incorporating them has in compliance with their own wishes for ever expressly prohibited. Several means have occurred to the Directors for the presecution of this great end.

4. An internal Trade by light Vessels sailing up the rivers, or by communications with Caravans that may be drawn from the interior country is one great and obvious resource.

5. A trade along the coast, by means of which a large quantity of scattered produce may be collected in their stores, is also undoubtedly to be attempted, and the cargoes which are now sent out are furnished in part for these purposes.

Cultivation.
6. It has however clearly appeared to the Directors that an increase of the exportable African produce is the basis on which the extension of Trade, proposed by the Act of Parliament, must ultimately rest; and since the Africans have been both directly and indirectly discouraged and even prevented by the Slave Trade from availing themselves of the natural advantage of their soil and climate, it must be the leading object of the Company to turn their views to cultivation.

7. The most effectual means of doing this is for the Company to set them an example by a spirited cultivation in their own district, and on their own account; and as there is reason to think the Company will every way benefit in proportion to the Agricultural improvements which they

shall be able to bring about in Sierra Leone, so if such cultivation should become general on the African Coast, the trade to Great Britain will proportionately be increased, its manufactures extended, and its interest as well as those of Africa promoted on the sound principles of a fair and reciprocal commerce.

8. Both on the public ground therefore of advantage to Great Britain, and also that of profit to the Company, the introduction of a system of spirited cultivation in Africa is most highly desirable.

Civilization.
9. Cultivation however naturally implies the civilization of those among whom it is to be introduced, for without this no great degree of effective industry is to be expected.

10. Civilization is therefore even in this commercial view a fundamental point; but the Directors would be extremely insensible to the principles by which they know the Proprietors are actuated, if they were to fail in observing to you that it is a spirit of benevolence and a zeal for the extension of light and knowledge in a Continent which has been kept in misery by the Slave Trade, that have chiefly prompted them to the present undertaking; and though the establishment of an advantageous trade by means of an increasing produce is one leading object, yet you are to remember also that the introduction of Christianity and civilization is a point, which in compliance with the wishes of the Proprietors, and in hearty conformity to our own, we enjoin our Council to have in view; and for the promotion of which, in conjunction with an honourable Trade, you are to consider yourselves as sent out.

11. To those whom agreeable to the instructions you will receive from us, you may receive under your jurisdiction, you are to afford the Asylum of an equal and good Government; you are to instruct and assist them on the one hand, you are to avail yourselves on fair terms of their labour on the other, and to endeavour by the most prudent management to turn it to good account.

12. We trust also that by teaching the Africans the advantage to be derived from free labour, and by securing to every man personal protection and the enjoyment of the fruits of his own industry, the abolition of the Slave Trade will be assisted, which the Proprietors in general have exceedingly at heart.

13. Such, we wish to have it understood by every individual in our service, are the general views and principles of the Sierra Leone Company, and these it will be the duty of each in his particular station to regard: and we charge you as our Council to take care that none living under our patronage and protection shall be suffered in any wise to counteract them.

14. In attempting to establish a Colony and to set up a system of Commerce new to that country, we are sensible that considerable difficulties must arise; and that to effect all the objects had in view by the Company, requires a more than ordinary zeal; but we trust that this zeal will not be wanting on your part, since it has been one general principle with us in the choice of our servants to select such persons as we believed to entertain a predilection to the service.

15. The preservation of general harmony being of the first importance to the attainment of every object of the institution: We not only recommend it to you in the strongest terms, but think it right to declare that we shall deem the disposition to promote it one of the chief criterions of zeal for the public services. But if misunderstandings should at any time unfortunately arise among you, we expect and require that instead of proceeding to open ruptures or quarrels (which we would in all cases interdict) or to the interruption in any shape of the duties of your several functions a reference for redress be made to the Director, who when such instances occur, will impartially consider them with the attention they may seem to deserve, and afford the requisite relief. It is our order that any person in our employ giving or accepting a challenge shall be immediately suspended from our service. We think it necessary to add, that settlers of every description being dissatisfied with the decision of the Council upon any reference before them may appeal to the Court of Directors.

Constitution of the Government of Sierra Leone.
16. In the appointments given to you as well as the address of this letter, you will understand what we now more formally notify, that the Government of the Peninsular of Sierra Leone is to be vested in a Superintendent and a Council. We proceed now to describe the nature and the exercise of your powers; but shall first particularize the Order in which you are respectively to rank.
 1. John Clarkson, Esq. (Superintendent)
 2. Mr Alexander Falconbridge
 3. Mr James Cocks
 4. Dr John Bell
 5. Mr John Wakerell
 6. Mr Richard Pepys
 7. Mr James Watt
 8. Mr Charles Taylor.

General Powers of Superintendent and Council.
17. As our Superintendent and Council you are hereby invested with the Government of the Peninsula of Sierra Leone in all matters, civil, military, political and commercial, to hold the same under the authority which we ourselves possess, until a new Constitution shall be fixed, and to conduct them agreeably to our Orders. And when you have not specific orders from us, you are, looking to the general principles already

explained to you and the scope of our general instructions, to act with the same power as we ourselves might do in such case, being responsible to us for the exercise of this discretion. All Acts and Orders of your Board are to run in the name of the Superintendent and Council of Sierra Leone, even though the Superintendent may not have been present or may have been out-voted.

18. Our servants at Sierra Leone are to be under obedience to your authority. They are to receive from you their Orders and Instructions as well those which we ourselves may think proper to give as those originating in your Council. They are also to report their proceedings to you (all which reports are to be recorded on your Consultations) to recieve their salaries from you, and to be liable to your suspension. In conformity to this arrangement, the specific instructions which we think should be given to each of them respectively at the commencement of their several employments, will be transmitted to you that they may be issued through the channel of your Board: and we hereby require that each and all of them, whether Members of the Council or otherwise pay a prompt and implicit obedience to your Resolutions when signified in due form; for on the subordination of all our servants to the supreme power at Sierra Leone, the peace and well-being of the Colony essentially depend.

19. Mr Falconbridge having been dispatched before the formation of the Council was completed, we were obliged to give him some separate instructions of which we now furnished a copy for your information.

Duties of the Superintendent and Council.
20. The principal duties of the Superintendent and Council will be the forming of General Regulations for the good order and prosperity of the Colony, the providing of general means of defence, the chief administration of justice, the prevention and correction of abuses of every kind, and also the general charge of all pecuniary interests of the Company, and the chief care and control of trade, cultivation, building and all other concerns, etc., conformably to the Orders which by this and any further Letters they receive from the Court of Directors.

Powers and Duties of Superintendent.
21. The Superintendent is in every respect to have the precedence in the Colony; he is to be our Representative with the native chiefs; he is to head the Military, to command the Fort, and is to take the chair in the Council, where he is to have a casting vote, that is to say where the numbers including himself are on each side equal, he is to have another vote to decide the question. He is to introduce such questions for discussion as he thinks proper, which shall be disposed of, before any questions introduced by any other member of Council shall be discussed, so that he does not put off the proposed motion of any member longer than two meetings. He may correspond with the Court of Directors, if he

pleases, without communicating his letters to the council, which no other member of Council is officially to do. He is always to be concluded by the resolutions of the majority, and to see that the determinations of the Council are executed. It will be his business also to summon the Council who are to meet twice a week at least, which if he should fail in doing, you are to meet of your own accord at the Council House giving him notice of it. But you are to observe, that neither the Superintendent nor any of the Council is to issue money, make appointments, or act in any other matters of his own authority without the sanction of the Government on the spot.

22. In the case of the death or resignation of the Superintendent, the senior Councillor on the spot is in all respect to stand in his place, until a Superintendent is appointed by the Court of Directors; and in case of his absence from the Council on service or on account of sickness, the next member of the Council in rank is to preside there.

23. All the proceedings, resolutions, Orders and correspondence of the Council shall be entered in a book to be kept for that purpose wherein their reasons at large are to be stated; and in case of any differences in opinion these differences with their reasons, if required by the person dissenting shall be minuted also, and copies of all the proceedings in Council shall be sent home for our inspection. The Resolutions of one council shall have no force until confirmed by a succeeding one, except when the immediate execution of it may appear necessary for the preservation of the Colony or of some important interest of the Company.

24. You are to maintain a constant correspondence with us sending us duplicates of all your despatches, and your letters (numbered in paragraphs as this is) which are to be agreed to and signed in Council; and if any one or more members of the Council shall wish to make any communications to us contrary to the sense of the majority, he or they may make a minute of them which shall be entered in your consultations, of which a copy must without delay be transmitted. All public letters or Orders, however must be signed by the whole body of the Council or their Secretary for them; and in your answers to our letters you will please to be specific, that is to reply to each paragraph distinctly, quoting the paragraph by its number on the one side and noting the answer to it on the other.

Appointment of Servants.
25. In case any places should become vacant, except the seats in Council, you are to make temporary appointments to them, we give you as already mentioned the power of suspending any of our servants, but you are to understand that this power is to be exercised only after a servant is charged and found guilty by the Government of an offence meriting this punishment. If however there should be a strong appearance of guilt, the

party may be immediately and during the time of his trial (which should be carried on without delay) suspended from the exercise of any office he may hold in our service; if he is fully acquitted he is to be restored to the exercise of his office; but if ground of suspicion remains, he may be removed from such office until the Court of Directors finally determines on his conduct. Your proceedings in all such cases are to be fully stated to us.

26. In case the creation of any new office should appear to you necessary, we give you liberty to make a temporary appointment stating at large in your consultations the circumstances which constituted such necessity, in order that we may have full materials for forming a correct judgment.

27. The following persons we have admitted into the line of our service under the name of preferable servants at salaries at present of £30 per annum each; and in order that from among these you may select any one that appears the most proper for filling either any vacant place, or any office to be created. They are not to consider any advance made in their salary to be permanent until on your representation of the duties of the office it shall have been so fixed by the Directors; and the order in which their names are placed here, is not at all to determine the order in which you are to employ them, which we leave to your judgment:

Mr John Beckett — now at Madeira
Mr Peppard
Mr Jefferson
Mr Jones,

to whom two or three more may at a future time be added by us.

We trust that the power now lodged with you of creating new places will need to be but very rarely exercised. We propose only to lodge it with you during the infancy of our establishment and in the case of all appointments or suspensions we shall hold you strictly responsible.

28. We have appointed Mr Strand to be Secretary to the Superintendent and Council.

Committee.
29. We submit to your consideration that in consequence of the variety of business to be transacted by the Council, it may be convenient to form yourselves into distinct committees who may report their opinions on particular points to the Council for their ultimate decision.

30. Every member of the Council and every servant of the Company unless especially excepted by us is to be restricted from trading, from purchasing or holding land either in the Company's district or from the native Princes and from taking presents.

Principle of Internal Legislation.
31. The Directors consider it as a fundamental principle on which the Company ought at all times to proceed, and as a point in the highest degree essential to the welfare and comfort of the resident members of the Settlement, to ensure to them a due share in its internal Legislation; and they trust that they shall e'er long be able to institute a plan for that purpose adapted to the infant state of the Colony, and capable of being extended by degrees in proportion to its growing population and prosperity. At present however they deem it advisable to abstain from doing more than thus recognising and recording the principle itself, and they avail themselves of this occasion to observe that they have thought it most conducive to the effectual accomplishment of their views in establishing the Colony to take experience for their guide, and to proceed gradually and circumspectly both with respect to the practical application of general principles and especially with regard to sending out Settlers from this country, a measure in which peculiar caution has in every view been thought absolutely necessary.

Administration of Justice.
32. In order to provide for the present administration of Justice in the Colony, each member of the Council is to possess the powers and exercise the function of a Justice of the Peace, and if any member of the coummunity shall violate any Law of England (such law being of a class not inapplicable to the state of the Colony) he shall be apprehended and detained on the Warrant of a Justice. If his case is one of that inferior sort which is subject by the Law of England to the decision of one or more Justices of the Peace, it shall be so decided without delay. If it is one not subject to such decision he shall be committed for trial by the Justices by whose Warrant he was apprehended and tried if it be practicable, within fourteen days, by a jury that shall be summoned for that purpose, and the trial shall proceed according to the Law of England. In case the prisoner be a black man or person of colour, at least one-half of the persons empanelled for the jury shall be blacks or people of colour, and if a white man, at least one-half shall be white men, with the usual right of challenge. The Council shall summon the jury and shall sit as judges. You are in no case however to proceed to Capital punishment, but shall substitute for Capital offences some punishment short of death, and of a kind that is recognized by the Laws of England substituting fines for coporal punishment as much as possible; and a majority of the Council shall in all cases have a power to be exercised impartially and on weighty grounds according to the equity of the case to mitigate the punishment, or grant a free pardon, recording their proceedings in every such instance, and the reasons on which they act. In cases of conviction as above for murder, the Council are at liberty either to punish the criminal on the spot or to send him to England for trial, provided such witnesses as will be sufficient to substantiate the charge, are willing also to come over being indemnified for their expense and loss of time by the Company.

33. Civil suits shall be tried also by a jury according to the Laws of England and full costs of suit may be imposed on the parties who are cast according to a tariff to be published by the Council.

Debts.
34. We cannot at present lay down any permanent system respecting debts; but in the meantime you will act agreeably to the following Regulations:

Cases of debt under £2 shall be determined by a Justice of the Peace who if satisfactory proof is brought of the debt, shall issue a Warrant of Distress on the personal property of the debtor.

If the debt be above £2, a Warrant of Distress shall in like manner be issued, but the goods shall not be sold until the debt is proved by a jury, before one or more of the members of the Council nor shall the property be sold for three months, provided security sufficient in the opinion of the Council is offered by the debtor. In case the personal property is insufficient the whole or part of the Debtor's real property may be sold in like manner.

If from the sale of the real and personal property a sum sufficient to discharge the debts should not be produced, the Creditor shall be at liberty at any future time to apply to the Council for a fresh Warrant of Distress, pointing out to them the former determination in his favour and an entry on the judicial record that the sum before raised was insufficient, and then a fresh Warrant of Distress or sale as above shall be granted him; and so toties quoties.

In all cases where the debt shall amount to more than £10 and there shall be no property of the debtor found within the Colony to answer the debt, the Creditor shall be at liberty to take the person of the debtor in execution, and he shall be detained in prison thereon for three years, or until satisfaction of the debt; but a discretionary power shall be vested in the Council on his delivering up all his real and personal estate upon oath for the equal benefit of all his Creditors to liberate his person, but not to discharge his future effects, nor shall such future effects be discharged, even after three years imprisonment, until full payment of the debts.

The members of the Council shall not in any case be imprisoned for debt, but their effects and salaries shall be liable to attachment and distress in the same manner as those of other debtors.

Election of Peace Officers.
35. The settlers may select from among themselves Twenty Housekeepers out of every hundred, and out of every twenty so chosen the Council may choose ten for Constables.

Miscellaneous Instructions.
36. Having stated to you the several permanent duties of the Council, we now subjoin a variety of particular instructions of which we request your attentive observation.

Attention to Engagements.

37. You are punctually to attend to whatever is enjoined us by the Act of Parliament, and to fulfil all contracts and engagements which we have in anywise entered into according to the true spirit of them, and for these purposes we annex the following documents: viz. —

    Copy of the Act of Incorporation.
    Copy of the Declaration of the Sierra Leone Company to the Native Kings and Chiefs of Africa.
    Copy of the Terms offered to the American Settlers.
    Copy of the Terms of such Settlers as shall sail from England within three months from the date thereof, dated the 3rd of November, 1791.
    Copy of the Declaration to Artificers.
    Copy of the Agreement with the several Artificers whom we send out.
    Copy of all Appointments to all such Servants as we send out to Sierra Leone.
    Copy of Grants of Land from King Nambaina and King Jammy, etc.
    Copy of sailing Orders, and a Note of all Payments and Advances made to any Servants of the Company.

An Account of all the Salaries to be paid at Sierra Leone to any of our Servants, which you are to pay either in Dollars at Sierra Leone at the rate of 5/- per Dollar or in goods from the Company's Stores at their current price, or by means of Bills which each Servant may draw on us in London, which we shall pay on your countersigning the same; and you will be particularly careful in examining before you countersign such Drafts that the amount on them is due to such servants respectively.

Estimate of Expences already incurred.

38. We send you for your general government a rough estimate of the probable expences of our establishment at home and abroad up to Christmas, 1792; as well as a rough estimate of the probable charges of our whole establishment here and abroad, which though unable to render accurate, we have been desirous of furnishing you with for the sake of assisting your general judgment of affairs of the Company.

General Attention to Economy.

39. We thus put you in possession of the same information that we have ourselves, in order that you may carefully co-operate with us in conforming the scale of your expenditure to the General Circumstances of the Company and may strive in the same manner as we have done ourselves to confine each department to its due proportion of expence.

    It must be obvious to you that with a capital of £150,000 of which it appears that not less than £30,000 is likely to be sunk the first year in outfit, an establishment of £7,000 per annum is sufficiently considerable and that your utmost vigilance must be exerted to keep down all expences in the Civil and still more in the Military Line which are not absolutely necessary.

40. The extension of our cultivation or commerce will naturally occasion an extension of our commercial charges which it is reasonable to hope that the profits of trade will pay and wishing as we do to prosecute with spirit these objects. We prescribe no particular limit to the charges attending either of them. Observing only that we trust our servants in general will feel the duty we are under of making all the salaries very moderate; that they will observe a general simplicity in the manner of living and in their expences and will consider themselves as thus adding credit to the Institution, remembering that on the Public opinion of their conduct, will depend in a great measure any future extension of the capital and enlargement of the undertaking. Besides the great sum which will be sunk to the Company the first year or two a greater uncertainty than is commonly incidental to trade attends the whole undertaking. It is true that a more than common profit on the other hand is by no means to be considered as improbable; but it behoves every one under these circumstances to moderate his own private expectations until the Council shall make it appear that a profit is arising to the proprietors sufficient to support their establishment and to redeem in process of time their first disbursements for without growing pecuniary advantages it is obvious that the purposes even of benevolence cannot long be answered and that subscriptions afforded on this principle must be soon exhausted.

41. The zeal of the Council therefore must be exerted in every way to promote the Colony's prosperity, and the servants from the highest to the lowest must be taught to consider their own private interest as embarked in the same bottom with that of the Company and may be assured that in proportion as they advance the interest of the Company they will themselves eventually partake in its success. They must consider the difference between the present case and that of large Companies assisted by great landed revenues or that of long established colonies supported by the purse of Government. They must remember that it is the spirit of individuals which has originated and must maintain the present undertaking, and that this spirit will undoubtedly cease if after the experience of a few years the Company's affairs abroad should be found to yield little mercantile emoluments or if a suspicion should arise of any careless or profuse application of their property; on the other hand the Directors are not afraid of assuring you that they are disposed to spare no expence that appears absolutely necessary, and they will not be deterred by such little discouragements as are incident to every new Colony from giving you the opportunity of making a fair experiment.

Regularity in Accounts.
42. It is of importance to the right management of our concerns that clear comprehensive and methodical accounts of the whole affairs of the Settlement should be kept be punctually brought up and come at stated times under your observation. For this purpose each considerable department under you as that of the Commercial Agent, Storekeeper, Manager, etc., should have a subsidiary set of Books and there should be

a general set to comprehend all these and every other branch of our affairs. The instructions to our Accountant which are to be sent by another opportunity will speak more particularly to these heads but we think it necessary to point out here the general object of accounts as a material part of your duty; and we have further to remark as of present importance on this subject that as it will be requisite for you to have from time to time distinct views of the actual state of every branch of our affairs, so it would be proper that the Commercial Agent, the Storekeeper, the Manager and every other officer in considerable charge under you should furnish monthly an account of his receipts and disbursements for the month past with an estimate of his wants for the current month and on occasion of every dispatch of a ship to England, they should lay before you for transmission to us an estimate of their respective wants for a year to come, you are to take care that no unnecessary delay shall be suffered in the entering or balancing of the accounts and you are to send half-yearly to us a clear statement of all expences incurred in the preceeding half-year; under the heads of Civil charges, Military expences, Commercial charges and Miscellaneous, distinguishing such as are likely to be annual from such as are incidental. You will also transmit an account of all rents received and of any other receipts of Sierra Leone, which may be set against the charges of your establishment nor shall we be backward on our part to furnish our servants with an account of our profits resulting from Commerce and Cultivation, that being fully informed what degree of success attends our affairs, and having the same facts to judge from, they may enter more entirely into all our views.

Estimates required.
43. We also require you to furnish us with such estimates as you are able to form of the total probable expenditure of the Company at Sierra Leone for the year coming under the same heads of Civil, Military, Commercial and Miscellaneous Charges, and also with an estimate of the total sums likely to be laid out in buildings, cultivation and commerce, as well as an estimate of the Goods both from Cultivation and Trade, which you expect to send us in return; in order that we may the better be able to form a judgment of the quantity of articles that there will be occasion to send out and of the capital wanted by the Company for the conduct of all its affairs.

Inventories of Goods for the African Market.
44. You are also to transmit to us from time to time, Inventories of such goods as are likely to suit the African market with particular instructions as to the quality; all which it will be peculiarly the duty of our Commercial Agent to prepare.

We shall on our part send you patterns of many articles as yet new to the African market.

Register of Grants of Land.
45. It will be of the utmost importance that an exact Register shall be kept of all lands granted away by the Company, with the names and descriptions of the persons to whom they are granted as the Register will be the legal evidence of their title and that you should devise effectual means of registering the name of the new proprietor in case of alienation. The Secretary at present may act as Registrar.

Register of Births, etc.
46. You are to take care also that a Register shall be kept of all births, deaths and marriages either of settlers or others, and that a Bill of martality be made up with as much exactness as possible, and transmitted to us once a year at least, and still oftener at the first.

Declaration from Settlers.
47. We think it necessary to desire that you call upon every person whatever, who may now, or shall hereafter be resident in the territory of Sierra Leone, to sign without delay the following declaration:
"The Sierra Leone Company having engaged to establish a Government and laws in their territory as similar to those of England as circumstances shall appear to them to admit, we do hereby engage in consideration thereof to submit to the Government, laws that are or shall be established here" — each individual member of the Council and all the servants of the Company on their first landing should set the example of signing it.

48. You are also to interchange with every Settler a printed Instrument (a number of which we shall send you) to be signed by you as our Council on the one part and by each of them on the other, conveying to them their respective Lots of Land and expressing the terms on which the land is to be held.

Delivery up of Offenders.
49. It may be desirable to form some mutual agreement between the Sierra Leone Company and King Naimbainna, and also any other neighbouring Chief for mutually delivering up offenders who may have fled from one territory to the other, you taking care to stipulate however that no person delivered up by you shall be sentenced to be sold for a slave as his punishment. You are also to take care that the offence be clearly proved before the Person is given up.

Slaves.
50. We wish you in adherance to the great principle of our institution not to surrender up any persons who are claimed merely as being slaves and on the same principle we wish you not to permit any one to continue to be a slave on our district; but your own prudence must dictate on the spot the time and the mode of asserting these principles in perfect consistency with the safety of the Colony; and if you find that a

peaceable acquiescence on the part of the Natives can be brought about at a small or moderate expence, we permit you to incur it. You will therefore inform the native traders in slaves of the principles and views of the Sierra Leone Company in this respect.

51. As it may probably be very desirable to King Naimbainna and other native chiefs to obtain for their children and other near relations the advantages of European education, we have no objection to gratify them in this circumstance.

Duty on Imports and Exports.
52. You are to inform the Settlers from Nova Scotia and elsewhere of the determination of the Company in case they should ever lay a duty on Imports and Exports, never to carry it higher than the sum of 2½ per cent on the Imports, and 2½ per cent on the Exports.

As no case of this sort is likely to be brought for your determination immediately, the present ships carrying out no goods except furniture, and goods on account of the Company, any other directions on this subject are reserved by us for further consideration.

Behaviour towards Blacks.
53. We are persuaded it would be unnecessary to say anything on this subject, were you yourselves only concerned. We cannot suffer ourselves to doubt but that by the general liberality of your minds, no less than from a regard to the very first principles of our design, you will be disposed on all occasions to conduct yourselves towards Black and White men not only with the same impartial justice in your public capacities but with the same condescension and familiarity in all the intercourse of private life. It is possible however, that among some of the inferior and less informed members of the Colony there may exist prejudices on this head; these therefore you will watch against and if they should appear will make it your business to discountenance and repress them. Nothing could be more injurious either to the interests of the Company or the harmony and welfare of the Colony than these invidious distinctions: Every trace of them therefore should be carefully eradicated. In this view, we recommend it to you to employ in your service, so far as you are able, black and white men indiscriminately, and when you discern in any of the former, talents which might render them useful in any way, to endeavour to call these talents into action and afford them all possible means of cultivation and encouragement.

Money Medium.
54. We are of opinion that the institution of a money medium in Sierra Leone would tend considerably to promote our views of Commerce, Cultivation and civilization there. The present rude methods of bartering commodities or making a sort of standard of iron bars of no determinate quality or weight must greatly obstruct the currency of transactions, and the free circulation of commerce, as well as leave many openings for

fraud and imposition in dealings and for uncertainty and difficulty in calculations and accounts; neither do we see how a community can be established in regular habits of Industry and traffic without an exact and profitable medium of value to which all nations have recourse in the progress of improvement, and since the finer metals have universally been found best to answer this purpose, we wish to introduce the use of silver and perhaps of copper coin in Sierra Leone. Spanish Dollars, we think, will best serve for this design, and we therefore mean to consign to you of this currency to some amount valuing the Dollar for the sake of uniformity at 5/-, which will be near the cost in Sierra Leone reckoning the risk and expense of transportation. We wish labour and commodities to be rated in this specie and you will of course learn how to adjust the specie to those things of which it is to be the measure, by its relative value to whatever was before the most common medium of exchange. In respect to accounts, however, we are of opinion that on the whole it may perhaps be found most expedient to keep them and the Books of the settlement especially in pounds sterling.

Cultivation on the Company's Account.
55. Our conviction of the utility of cultivation to all our views in Africa both respecting the Natives and the Company, and the apparent necessity of setting and encouraging example in this way, having determined us according to what we have already intimated to undertake an extensive plantation for this purpose, Mr Watt whom we have nominated to a seat in Council is engaged. He is to be the Conductor of the first attempt to be made and for the present will generally superintend the cultivation undertaken for the Company. We expect that a considerable experiment will soon be made on the sugar-cane. Mr Watt is to choose the ground for it and to be left at liberty to act in all other matters relating to the work in which he is engaged according to his own judgment and skill, of which in business of this kind we have had a testimonial. He is to receive from you the funds necessary to pay his labourers (whom you are to assist him in procuring) and defray the other expences of the plantation; the accounts of which he is to render regularly to you according to the general Rule already prescribed. We do not as above intimated make him liable to your interference in the management or details of his own department, but we note this without meaning to exempt him from that superintendence which as a collective body you are to exercise over every individual member of the settlement. What further relates to this head will be found in the separate instructions to Mr Watt himself, and we shall only add here, that we are on reflection strongly disposed to the utmost extension of cultivation on behalf of the Company which may consist with our engagements to the settlers, being persuaded that this is one of the best methods of reimbursing the great expence of establishing the Colony and answering its benevolent designs. On this and other grounds it will be desirable that you should procure as many labourers as possible to which end perhaps liberal encouragement should be held out to them, and in this view we think it will be expedient to promise small

lots of land to such labourers as behave industriously and satisfactorily after they have worked for one year. If the sugar-cane of Sierra Leone should not be found of a good sort it may be advised to dispatch a small vessel to Brazil in order to obtain the excellent species of cane there, as also the cotton plant of Ternamburg, the Plantain Tree and whatever else it may be expedient to take the advantage of such an occasion of procuring.

Premiums.
52. With a view to produce a proper spirit of emulation in the Colony it is recommended to you to propose certain moderate Premiums both for any remarkable diligence in the cultivation and Improvement of the Soil, and for any eminent instances of good conduct in private or in family life.

Measures to be taken on First Arrival.
57. We now add the following directions as to the measures which you are to take on your first arrival at Sierra Leone.

King Nambainna.
58. Having proceeded thither with as little delay as possible, you are to send notice to King Nambainna of your arrival with a view of pursuing the objects mentioned to him in a letter already sent to him by Mr Falconbridge in the Amy, a copy of which is annexed (and to the general tenor of which you will of course conform) in order to be delivered to him in case the Amy should not yet be arrived. You are to repeat to him that our intentions are peaceable, and to advertise him that a number of free Black Settlers are expected from America with the same peaceable views in a short time conducted by Lieutenant Clarkson of His Majesty's Navy, whom we have appointed to be our Superintendent. You are to endeavour to obtain free labourers to work for us through his assistance; and you are to make some present to King Nambainna on this occasion, a further present being given him by Lieutenant Clarkson on his arrival. And you are to apply in like manner to the other neighbouring Chiefs, giving them also some small presents.

Choice of Situation for a Town.
59. You are then to proceed with as much dispatch as possible, taking the help of the best Guides to examine such parts of the country as appear to you most suitable for the building of our chief Town.

You are to consider concerning this first and principally the healthiness of situation, wherein regard is to be had to the purity of the air, distance from swamps, etc., secondly, its safety from attacks; and you will naturally prefer the higher ground for these reasons, thirdly, its convenience with a view to commerce, fourthly, the conveniences of good running water, of adjacent Port, etc.

Clearing Ground for Town.
60. Having determined the spot which you as our Council are to do, the greatest dispatch is to be used in clearing the ground for building so as not to hurt or endanger the health of the labourers.

Plans of Houses.
61. We give you annexed Plans of Houses of different sizes to which we think it will be desirable that you should conform; but we are too little informed what may be the materials which you will find at Sierra Leone for building, to lay down any positive instructions on these points; only it is obvious that the buildings of the town must be your first work. We fear it will be impossible to raise houses for all the Black Settlers before the rains; and in that case would recommend that a large building of the cheapest materials should be erected for their temporary accommodation on such a plan as to serve afterwards for some public purpose. It may be proper to remark that in forming the town, due regard should be paid to the cleanliness of it, by directing, if possible, channels of water into it, and by disposing in the most suitable manner whatever belonging to it might have a tendency to prove noxious to the inhabitants.

A Church must also be erected and we think the plan herewith sent may be found convenient; but until this work is performed, which may require some time (though as little delay as possible should be made) you will provide a temporary place which may afterwards be applied to some other service for the regular performance of Divine Worship. One or more School houses will also be necessary, and should be erected as soon as possible, and the temporary building erected for Divine Service may be applied to this purpose.

Another point relative to this subject to which we must require your attention is the cost of the Buildings. The cost of each house should be ascertained with so much accuracy as to serve for a standard in fixing the demand of the Company for its rent or its sale.

Fort.
62. You will build a Fort capable of holding eight to twelve or sixteen guns, making a secure place for our Stores within it.

If when all those works first necessary are completed, you judge that a hospital, and a prison will also be wanted, you may proceed to erect them on the most frugal terms, providing the means, however, of solitary confinement. But we may expect to hear from you before you are so far advanced and in the meantime we conceive the ships will serve for those purposes.

Victualling the Colony.
63. You are to pay early and strict attention to the means of victualling the Colony; both by sowing and planting immediately for this purpose and also by collecting articles of provision around you as well as live stock for food and for breeding, and we request you to be very accurate in your calculations on these subjects as you will have to transmit to us the

most distinct and full information of the extent to which you are likely to supply yourselves from your own district and neighbourhood in order that we may not go to any needless expence in sending a supply from hence. And as it is of the utmost importance to the health of the Colony that sufficient supplies of fresh provisions be procured, you will pay the utmost attention to this subject. With regard to the daily allowance of provision to be dispensed from your stores to our Servants and the Settlers, you will find among the papers annexed, two tables of rates which we furnish for your information. We do not wish these allowances to be at all inadequate but you will see the necessity of establishing a proper standard in this matter and of adhering regularly to it. We leave it to you to determine according to circumstances for what number of days provisions may be issued at one time, and we on our part shall endeavour to provided, that you may never have less than six weeks full supply of English provisions in store exclusive of what you may raise or procure.

64. We have already suggested to you the expediency of sending to the nearest convenient station for provisions in case you should not be able to procure sufficient supplies in the Peninsula of Sierra Leone or in the adjacent districts. Concerning the mode of paying for supplies they obtained from Teneriffe or any other place, we think it now necessary to add, that it would be most agreeable to us to pay for them in the goods consigned to you for sale, if they could be bartered at a reasonable rate, and for this purpose the Ship sent for provision might carry a suitable assortment of them. If our goods cannot be exchanged in this manner, we know of no alternative for the payment of provisions but that of Dollars or drawing Bills upon us. This last is a method to which we are unwilling to have recourse, and we never wish to make use of it but in case of real necessity. When such a necessity, however, occurs, you will give authority in writing to the person whom you depute for supplies to pass bills upon us, limiting and defining the amount, and transmitting to us by the first opportunity advice of this transaction with a copy of the instructions given by you on the occasion. From the person sent on this service you will be careful also to receive the fullest account of all his proceedings.

65. To facilitate your obtaining of supplies of provisions at Teneriffe we shall take the precaution of informing Messrs Pastey and Co. of the possibility of application on your part there. The supply of provisions during the Infancy of the Colony and the payment of the salaries of our servants in the mode already prescribed, are the only occasion on which as far as we can foresee you will have to recur to the expedient of drawing Bills upon us, and expedient which we must repeat we wish to be adopted as seldom and as moderately as possible, and the use of which we shall watch over with jealous attention.

Future Supplies of Provisions.
66. In case it should appear that towards the end of six months no

adequate means are likely to be found by the Settlers themselves for obtaining provisions, you are to take care to procure an effectual supply which you will either sell to them at a fair price or furnish in part of payment for their labour. We trust that in a point of such serious importance as that of victualling the infant Colony, your diligent and accurate attention will not be wanting; but this is by no means to be understood as if the Colony were to derive its permanent subsistence from without, for on the contrary, we are fully persuaded it can never flourish or even be secured in the abundance that would be desirable; until it produces within itself provisions sufficient for its own sustenance.

67. Meanwhile we think it necessary that a certain quantity of provision ground for the use of the Settlers should be cultivated on the Company's account and that this ground should be selected from the reserve made for the Company. From examining the nature of the soil and considering the number of Settlers and other circumstances of a local nature, you will have a better opportunity of judging what appropriation of Land should be made for this purpose.

Working of Artificers etc.
68. With a view to health also, we wish you not to oblige any European to work out in the sun, and that you allow the Artificers a sufficient time to rest in the heat of the day.

Causes of Death and Sickness to be specified.
69. You are to desire that in every case of death or material sickness, at the first the causes of disorder shall be reported to you, that they may be notified to us.

Free Blacks from America.
70. We annex extracts from the letters of Lieutenant Clarkson by which you will find that a very considerable number of Free Blacks perhaps a 1,000 or 1,200 may be extricated to arrive at Sierra Leone in a short time and we are becoming anxious for your speedy arrival on their account.

71. You are to apply your upmost attention and care to the accommodation of this body of Settlers. You are to give three months allowance of provisions, and three months half-allowance to them in the same manner as is promised to the Settlers sailing from hence. But we conclude that such provisions as remained on board the Transport unconsumed and were supplied for their use, will either be divided among themselves, or be entrusted to our care on their account; and these provisions will undoubtedly go in part of the allowance. We were not bound by the terms held out to them in America to furnish any provisions gratuitously to these Settlers, but we have determined for the sake of attaching their minds to us, and encouraging them on their arrival to put this advantage into their hands and we hope you will make them sensible, that while in all other respects we fulfil the whole of our

engagements, we have determined in this particular to exceed it. You are to give the same allowance of provisions according to the table annexed to all the Company's servants also.

Sketch of Town.
72. We annex the sketch of a town,* which allowing about a quarter of an Acre for every two houses, will accommodate about 250 Housekeepers. These we conceive to be as many persons as are likely to remain permanently in one town, since supposing only 150 of these to be Proprietors of Land the lots appropriated to them will probably extend to a distance of near a mile and-a-half from the town. You will observe from the sketch that a single acre lot is given to each house; and that as many of them as convenience would admit, are immediately annexed. We imagine that those whose lots are situated at a distance of more than a mile and-a-half will rather choose to live nearer to them in a second town that will be hereafter built; and we therefore submit to you, that it may be desirable to form the plan of your allotments with this view, reserving a ground about three miles distance from the first town for a new town and for single acre lots according to the before-mentioned system; and forming the distant allotments in such a manner as to surround this reserved space.

Allotting Lands.
73. Concerning the allotments to be first made of land, we think the following method of procedure will be proper, and recommend the adoption of it accordingly as soon as all the American Blacks shall be arrived, first to assign the site of the houses to the acre lots and Settlers lots of land only reserving the houses for the Europeans and Artificers; next to mark out perhaps twenty or more houses, acre lots and lots of lands, and having done this to let all the Settlers draw lot (blanks being prepared except for 20 numbers) whereby these houses and the lots so drawn being disposed of, you may then proceed to mark out a further number of twenty houses, etc., and to draw again in the same manner and so again until as many sites of houses are appropriated as the space allotted for the town will contain. It may then perhaps be desirable to suspend drawing any more, until the second town is begun. But this last order is given only on a supposition that the Free Blacks will consent to

---

* Since our preparing these Instructions the Directors have received a plan of a larger town which they also annex, leaving it to your discretion to adopt the whole or such part of either of these plans as may appear most suitable to the circumstances of the place when you are on the spot. You are to observe however that we by no means wish you to make so large a reservation of land for the town or to employ the Settlers so long against their inclination in clearing it as to delay materially the appropriation of their allotments in which we could wish a beginning to be made within a few weeks after the Americans arrive. The importance of realising as soon as possible their expectations of having lots of their own to cultivate we are persuaded you will see as strongly as ourselves, and will adapt your whole plan to this object.

If a great number of native labourers can be procured the site of the reserved land for the town may be in some measure proportionate.

such suspension and if they do, you will take care that no unnecessary delay shall be made (for the sake of advantage of the first town from the application of labour in its vicinity) in the marking out of the second town and the allotment of the land belonging to it.

74. We desire that no land immediately adjoining the river shall be granted to Settlers till further directions are received from us.

75. We do not imagine it will be desirable or even practicable, for you to proceed systematically to the building of a second town until after Xmas, 1792; but if any of the settlers should wish to take immediate possession of their distant lots, and build themselves habitations in their neighbourhood, you may allow them so to do, on condition that they build on the site of the second town, observing the lines that have been previously marked out for streets, and complying with such directions as you may think proper to give with a view to health and security. But we rather hope they will many of them be glad to work 'till that time on hire for the Company, being supplied by us with provisions and having a reasonable pay added, which you will therefore offer, assuring them that in this arrangement we have an eye to the health and welfare of the Colony. We must however leave the particular determination of the size, as well as the manner of building the town, in a good manner to your own discretion.

You are to name the first town Freetown.

76. You are to require of every settler, that he shall furnish his proportion of labour for the clearing of the ground, for the town, and Fort and a few acres for the Cattle as being matters of common concern, and as we suppose the town to cover a space of about thirty-six acres we should imagine that the whole may probably be cleared in two or three weeks, by about 250 labourers. The acre lots for the Company's servants, are to be cleared at the Company's expence.

Military Defence.
77. We have already engaged and now send out in the Harpy, fourteen English Soldiers, two Sergeants, a Drummer and fifer.

We are willing, if you should see the expediency of it, to add to those twenty Black Soldiers on the same terms (which terms are noted in the appendix) and authorize you to propose to them accordingly. And you are to require of all the Settlers, black or white, that they shall do duty as Militia men occasionally, having their provisions allowed them. We think that fifty Settlers might be called out to do militia duty one morning in the week by rotation, and we recommend that Saturday, or some week day shall be the day appointed for it. We must however strongly enjoin you to beware of embarking us without evident necessity, in any Military expence, which a general observation of the statements now furnished you must demonstrate, would render our charges quite disproportionate to the scale of our Capital and destructive of all idea of pecuniary success to the Company without a corresponding retrenchment in our civil or commerical establishment.

Morals, etc.
78. You will give your best attention both as members of the Council, as Administrators of Justice and as private individuals, also to the general maintenance of good morals in the Colony. You will be particularly careful to prohibit all open immorality cognizable by the laws of England, by a due execution of them; and you will apply such restraints as you may judge most prudent, and at the same time the most effectual to this end. The general licentiousness which commonly prevails where polygamy and also where slavery exists, will receive, we trust, a great and immediate check by the examples which all our servants will set, for it is to their example we must chiefly trust for the effecting of a considerable change in the general morals of the District. We have already given pointed instructions to the Captains of our ships on this subject being anxious that they should use every means of promoting order among the Sailors by maintaining Public Worship, by repressing vice and profaneness, and preventing licentiousness of every kind.

We are persuaded the zealous labours of the Clergymen whom we send out will not be wanting in this great cause of promoting morals as the result of Christian principles; and it will be your part to strengthen their hands, and assist their labours by discountenancing every vicious practice. You will be able, we trust, to repress excessive drinking by a careful regulation of any house or houses for retailing liquors, which you may find it necessary to licence as such; we should trust, however, that no such necessity may soon exist.

You will take every proper means of discouraging Polygamy where it has been already engaged in, the toleration of it seems unavoidably, but new engagements of this sort among those who settle in our lands, we think ought by no means to be permitted. The common arguments for it appear to us quite ill founded, and the practice subversive of domestic peace as well as good order and morals.

In the case of adultery, damages must be granted as in England, by a civil suit and in the case of natural children, the father when sworn to be such by credible testimony must be compelled to take the charge of their maintenance. It may be proper to have a quarterly or half-yearly inquest jury whose province it shall be to inquire and make regular presentments to the Council of all immoralities, nuisances and other offences against the public; it is our purpose to provide as far as possible for the general instruction of the Colony, by appointing Schoolmasters to be sent from home, and we wish you to encourage and assist natives in general, and particularly those in your service or under your influence to learn to read and write.

You are carefully to maintain due obedience to the English Laws in being for the observance of the Sabbath in every part of the settlement, both by preventing, buying, selling and labouring also, except in case of absolute necessity.

You are likewise to observe that no person is to be prevented from perfoming or attending Religious Worship, in whatever place, time or manner he thinks fit, or from peaceably inculcating his own religious opinions.

80. It appears to us important that we should be apprized as early as possible of your state and circumstances after landing and commencing your operations; and we think you may dispatch one of the ships to England by the 21st March or sooner if the American Blacks are arrived, or if you see particular occasion, you may probably also be able to notify your arrival by means of letters conveyed by Teneriffe or other islands, by vessels which you send thither for provisions and you will take care to give us whatever general information you can furnish us with by every such channel.

The points on each of which we especially wish to have distinct intelligence, by the first regular communication, and on which you will not fail to write to us, are the following, and we beg you to quote each query on one side and to place your answer opposite it:

1. Health.
2. Progress in clearing buildings and cultivating actual and probable particularly what prospect there is of providing a healthful and comfortable new made town for all the settlers against the next rainy season.
3. Opportunities of victualling and prospect of Colonies supplying itself from within or from the neighbouring Country.
4. Situation of the town and face of the adjacent country and nature of its soil.
5. What running streams and whether saw mill, sugar mills, etc. can be worked by them, purposes to which different woods may be applied and whether they are capable of being sawn.
6. What additional lands are purchased where situated and whether more may be obtained.
7. What number and description of labourers and at what pay.
8. What materials used in or wanted for buildings, and what the expence of sawing and preparing timber there, that we may know whether it will not be equally or more reasonable to send if from hence.
9. What articles are likely to proceed in cultivation and what lands in what situations are reserved in the town district or are particularly desirable to be reserved in other parts for cultivation on the Company's account.
10. What towns and what number of inhabitants in them or in villages are within our districts, and what are their occupations and descriptions severally.
11. What arrangements for the conveyance of letters either to or from Sierra Leone through any adjacent Islands can be made so as to save the necessity of sending a vessel on purpose.
12. When we may expect to hear from you either by indirect

communications or by your sending a second ship.
13. What articles and what quantity of them are wanted from England for the purchase of African commodities or for the use of the settlement; particularly what seeds are wanted and seem to thrive best.
14. Whether a supply of any particular description of Artificers is materially wanted.
15. Whether any and what articles already sent out have been found unserviceable or unsuitable.
16. Any information you may be capable of giving us as to the nature and qualities of the first returns.
17. What are the disposition of any neighbouring chieftains towards the Colony and what expectation of obtaining free labourers from them, and what is the general population.
18. Whether any credible information has been obtained respecting the interior country.
19. Extent to which the Slave Trade is carried on in the neighbourhood and any incidents leading to throw light on that subject.

Bristol Ship.
81. We expect that a vessel from Bristol will sail in three weeks from this time, freighted with articles of which a note is annexed carrying about eighteen or twenty Artificers. We hope one or more light vessels each of them bringing out a small quantity of provisions will be procured here in time to preceed to Sierra Leone very soon afterwards which will be serviceable in procuring live stock, provisions and articles of trade.

Instructions to Servants.
82. The specific instructions which we propose to give to each of our members appointed to separate offices of trust you will herewith receive so far as they are yet prepared, you are to transmit them to those officers respectively through the channel of your Board, keeping copies of them, and you will please to observe that by this mode of conveyance the double purpose is intended of establishing the authority of the Council over every individual and of communicating to you the general rules and principles according to which you are to exercise that authority over the officers in question.

83. Mr Falconbridge having been so long detained at Falmouth, he will probably have no opportunity of acting upon the separate instructions given to him on leaving London, and we therefore enclose another letter to him directing him to fall into his station under the general arrangements now made and to act in subordination to the voices of the Superintendent and Council.

84. As a safe regular mode of conveying letters between this country and Sierra Leone is a matter interesting to all parties connected with the Colony, the following regulation is to be observed concerning it. When

the Superintendent and Council have determined on dispatching a ship to England, either directly or circuitously they are to give a few days' notice of such intention to the settlement (a locked Box of which the Secretary is to keep the key) having an aperture at the top, is to be placed in the Secretary's office, and therein all individuals are to deposit their letters for England.

When the ship is to be dispatched these letters are to be taken out by the Secretary and put into another Box, which shall be nailed up. Marked Private Letters, and directed to the Court of Directors of the Sierra Leone Company. On the arrival of such box in London, the Secretary of the Court of Directors shall forward the letters according to their addresses.

The packet of the Superintendent and Council for the Court of Directors is to be put up separately; marked Company's Packet and addressed to them in London, the same order both with respect to private letters and the Company's dispatches for Sierra Leone will be observed by the Secretary of the Company here. You will receive by the first opportunity a seal of the Sierra Leone Company which is to be used in all your Public Acts and despatches.

85. You will received herewith, Invoices of the Goods and Provisions consigned to you by the ship Harpy, Captain Wilson, amounting to £.

You will observe that credit is to be given to the Company in the general Books of the Sierra Leone Settlement for these and all other consignments made or that shall be made to you.

Conclusion.
86. Such Gentlemen, are the principal Topics which the Directors think proper to recommend to your especial attention. They comprehend you will observe the chief objects which belong to the formation of a Colony in a country, already peopled but at present in a rude and uncivilized state. Such are — its interior government the preservation of Peace and Good Order within and the defence against attacks from without; the means of supply and the precautions to be observed, with a view to health, in fine the laying of a sure foundation of a continually increasing commerce the creation and diffusion of a general spirit of cultivation and a steady adherence to such a system and conduct towards the natives as may convince them, you are come not to enslave and oppress them, but to protect and improve them, not to enrich yourselves at their expence but to make them participate in your prosperity. On your integrity, public spirit, fortitude and discretion on your diligence and attention to the preservation of general harmony, the success of this undertaking must in fact depend.

In the execution of every plan of this nature, many difficulties must be expected to arise, many obstacles to be surmounted and many dangers to be encountered.

But you will be prepared for every exercise of courage of activity and perseverance, by retaining in Steady Contemplation the immense importance of the task in which you are engaged. You cannot indeed be too deeply impressed with its extreme magnitude: This is not merely a mercantile speculation; it is not merely the Profits of a Trading Company that are at stake, or even the commercial interests of a great Kingdom, tho' these surely are deeply concerned in the present undertaking, it would be greatly to degrade the project to consider it only in this view! And on you is devolved the Honourable Office of introducing to a Vast Country long detained in Barbarism the Blessings of Industry and Civilization. Should this experiment fail, it may be long if ever, before a similar one may be again attempted; whereas its success may call forth a spirit of benevolent attention towards this long neglected or much injured country. Millions yet unborn may have reason to look up to you as being under heaven the instruments of rescuing them from a State of darkness, oppression and disorder, and of imparting to them the light of Religious Truth and the security and comforts of Civilized Society.

APPENDIX VIII

270 5 p.90.
Copy Paper of Laws stuck at Abraham Smith's house by the Hundredors and Tythingmen, September 3, 1800.

If anyone shall deny the settlers of anything that is to be exposed of in the colony, and after that shall be found carrying it out of the colony to sell to anyone else shall be fined 20 pounds or else leave the colony and for palm oil, one shilling quart, whosoever is found selling for more than one shilling quart is fined twenty shillings; salt beef, sixpence; anyone selling for more, shall pay the fine of forty shillings and salt pork, nine pence, shall pay the fine of forty shillings; and for rice, 50 cents to a dollar, 5 shillings, and whosoever is found selling for less than for a dollar shall pay the fine of 10 pounds; and rum is to be 5 shillings to the gallon at the wholesale and anyone that sells for more than 5 shillings shall pay the fine of 3 pounds and the retailers is not to sell for more than 6 and 3 by the gallon and to sell as low as the gill at 6 and 3 gallon as low as single glass as three cents and if anyone should sell for more than that shall pay the fine of 3 pounds; soap at 15 pence and whosoever shall sell for more than 15 pence shall pay the fine of 20 shillings; salt butter, 15 pence and if any more than 15 pence, shall pay the fine of 20 shillings; and if anyone found keeping a bad house is fined 20 shillings; and for abuse, 1 pound; for trespass, 10 shillings; for stealing shall pay for time, the value for stealing; a blow, 5 pounds; for removing his neighbour's landmark shall pay 5 pounds; for cutting timber or wattles on any person's land without their leave shall pay 5 pounds. For drawing a weapon or any edge tool shall pay 5 pounds and for threatening shall pay 2 pounds 10 and for lying or scandalizing without proof shall pay 2 pounds 10. For Sabbath breaking, shall pay the fine of 10 shillings. Cheese to be sold, 1 shilling and if more than 1 shilling, shall pay the fine of 20 shillings; sugar, 15 pence and whosoever is found selling for more than 15 pence is fined of 20 and if any man shall serve his summons or warrant or execution without orders from the hundredors and

Tythingmen must pay the fine of 20 pounds and if any person shall kill a goat or a sheep, or cause her to slink her young shall pay the fine of 5 pounds, or shall kill cow, or horse, shall pay the fine of 5 pounds; and if a man's fence is not lawful, he cannot recover any damage. And if a man that has a wife shall leave her and go to another woman shall pay the fine of 10 pounds; and if a women leave her husband and take up with another man, she shall pay 10 pounds and if children shall misbehave, they shall pay a fine of 10 shillings or otherwwise be severely corrected by their parents.

And this is to give notice by the Hundredors and Tythingmen that the laws they have made that if the settlers shall owe a debt to the company, they shall come to the Hundredors and Tythingmen and prove their account and swear to it and swear to every article agreeable to the proclamation, they they shall take the produce for their goods and not for their goods pay any cent on it and all that come from Nova Scotia shall be under this law or quit the place. The Governor and Council shall not have anything to do with the colony no further than the Company's affairs, and if any man shall side with the Governor and against this law shall pay 20 pounds.

This is to give notice that the law is signed by the Hundredors and Tythingmen and Chairman. They approve it to be Just before God and Man.

Given under our hands this 3rd September 1800, James Robertson, Hundredor; Ansel Zizer, Hundredor; Isaac Anderson, Hundredor and Nathaniel Wansey, Chairman, signed this as a law in Sierra Leone.

APPENDIX IX

PROCLAMATION

By His Excellency Lt. Col. Arden Lowndes Bayley, Officer Commanding the troops on the West Coast of Africa, Administrator of the Government of the Colony of Sierra Leone, etc.
A. L. Bayley,
Administrator.

WHEREAS HER MAJESTY has been advised that it is best for the interest of the people in the territories adjacent to the Colony of Sierra Leone and on the British side of the Boundary between the British and French possessions to the North and East of the Colony aforesaid fixed by an agreement dated the 21st day of January in the year One Thousand Eight Hundred and Ninety-five and made between Great Britain and France, that Her Majesty should assume the Protectorate over the said territories.

AND WHEREAS it is Her Majesty's pleasure that the said territories should come under the Protectorate of Her Majesty.

AND WHEREAS HER MAJESTY has authorised me to take necessary steps for giving effect to Her pleasure in the matter.

NOW THEREFORE I do hereby proclaim declare and make known that the territories adjacent to the Colony of Sierra Leone and on the British side of the boundary between the British and French possessions to the North and East of the Colony aforesaid fixed by the agreement dated the twenty-first day of January in the year One Thousand Eight Hundred and Ninety-five and made between Great Britain and France are now under the protection of Her Majesty.

GIVEN under my hand and the Public Seal of the Colony of Sierra Leone at Government House, Fort Thornton, in the City of Freetown in the Colony aforesaid this Thirty-first day of August, in the year of our Lord, One Thousand Eight Hundred and Ninety-six, and of Her Majesty's reign the sixtieth.

By His Excellency's Command
W. J. P. Elliott,
Ag. Colonial Secretary.

GOD SAVE THE QUEEN

APPENDIX X

PUBLIC NOTICE

Supplement to the Sierra Leone Gazette Extraordinary Vol. XCVIII No. 29 dated 25th March, 1967

PUBLIC NOTICE NO. 28 OF 1967
Published 25th March, 1967.

PROCLAMATION
ADMINISTRATION OF SIERRA LEONE
(NATIONAL REFORMATIONAL COUNCIL) PROCLAMATION, 1967

PROCLAMATION FOR THE INTERIM ADMINISTRATION OF SIERRA LEONE BY A NATIONAL REFORMATION COUNCIL; ITS ESTABLISHMENT AND CONSTITUTION, AND FOR OTHER MATTERS CONNECTED THEREWITH

WHEREAS it is a funamental duty of the Sierra Leone Military Forces and the Sierra Leone Police Force to maintain and secure public safety and public order;

AND WHEREAS the actions and utterances of the political parties and their leaders have resulted in tribal factions and brought about a situation which has led to an almost total breakdown of law and order, bloodshed and imminent tribal war;

AND WHEREAS it is expedient in the situation aforesaid that due provision should be made for the maintenance of law and order in Sierra Leone, and the proper administration, by law of the State of Sierra Leone;

NOW, THEREFORE, we the members of the Sierra Leone Military Forces and the Sierra Leone Police Force in co-operation with the people of Sierra Leone, in order to ensure the maintenance of law and order, ensure domestic tranquility, the future enjoyment of the blessings of liberty to citizens of Sierra Leone and all persons living therein and their posterity, do hereby proclaim as follows:—

1. (1) There is hereby established a Council to be known as the "National Reformation Council".

(Constitution of National Reformation Council)

* (2) The Council shall be constituted as follows:—
   (a) Chairman;
   (b) Deputy Chairman;
   (c) other members, not exceeding six in number;

(3) Subject to the immediately preceding sub-paragraph the Council may by a majority vote at any meeting appoint members or terminate the appointment of any member.

(4) There shall be a Secretary-General who shall be appointed by the Council and shall perform such functions and duties as the Council may direct.

2. (1) All the provisions of the Constitution of Sierra Leone 1961, which came into operation on the 27th of April, 1961, which are inconsistent or in conflict with this proclamation or any law made hereunder shall be deemed to have been suspended with effect from the 23rd day of March, 1967.

(P.N. 78 of 1961. Suspension of certain provisions of the Constitution.)

(2) In addition to and without derogation from the generality of the foregoing sub-paragraph —
   (a) the House of Representatives elected under the said Constitution of Sierra Leone is dissolved; and
   (b) all political parties are dissolved and membership of political parties is prohibited with effect from the 23rd day of March, 1967.

3. (1) The National Reformation Council shall have power for such purposes as it may think fit and in the national interest to make and issue laws.

(Council to legislate by law.)

(2) Any law made and issued by the National Reformation Council may be amended or revoked or suspended by another law made and issued by the Council.

(3) Every law made and issued by the National Reformation Council shall be deemed to be an Act as defined in section 2 of the Interpretation Act 1965.

(Act No. 7 of 1965.)

*The names of the members of the National Reformation Council have been published as Government Notice No. 452 in the Sierra Leone Gazette Extraordinary issue dated 25th March, 1967 Vol. XCVIII No. 29.

(4) Any law made and issued by the National Reformation Council shall be signed by the Chairman or (in the absence of the Chairman) the Deputy Chairman of the Council.

(5) Subject to any law made and issued by the National Reformation Council, all enactments in force in Sierra Leone immediately before the 23rd day of March, 1967, shall continue in force:

Provided that any provisions of the enactments in force in Sierra Leone immediately before the 23rd day of March, 1967, which are inconsistent or in conflict with any provision of this Proclamation or any such law shall be deemed to have been suspended as from the said 23rd day of March, 1967.

4. Subject to any law that may be made and issued by the National Reformation Council the Public Service of Sierra Leone as it existed immediately before the 23rd day of March, 1967, shall continue in existence as it existed before that date and any person holding or acting in any office in the public service immediately before the said date shall continue in office subject to any laws in force after that date.

(Public Service to continue.)

5. Subject to any law that may be made and issued by the National Reformation Council and reference to Governor-General, Prime Minister, Minister or Cabinet in the Constitution of Sierra Leone which shall come into operation on the 27th day of April, 1961, or in any enactment continued in existence by virtue of this Proclamation shall, on and after the 23rd day of March, 1967, be construed as a reference to the National Reformation Council or to such person as the Council may by Order appoint.

(Adaption of references to Governor-General, Minister, etc. P.N. No. 78 of 1961.)

6. (1) The National Reformation Council may make an order against any person directing that he be detained, where it considers it necessary in the interest of public safety or public order so to do.

(Detention of persons.)

(2) The provisions of the immediately preceding paragraph shall be deemed to have come into operation as from the 23rd day of March, 1967.

7. The National Reformation Council shall have full power and authority to amend, revoke or suspend this proclamation or any provision thereof.

(Power to amend Proclamation, etc.)

MADE at Freetown this 25th day of March, 1967.

L. W. LEIGH, M.V.O.,
Commissioner of Police.
For and on behalf of the Sierra Leone
Military Forces and the Sierra Leone
Police Force.

APPENDIX XI

THE CONSTITUTION OF SIERRA LEONE
ARRANGEMENT OF SECTIONS

PROTECTION OF THE FUNDAMENTAL RIGHTS AND FREEDOMS OF THE INDIVIDUAL

Section No.
1. Fundamental rights and freedoms of the individual.
2. Protection of right of life.
3. Protection from arbitrary arrest or detention.
4. Protection of freedom of movement.
5. Protection from slavery and forced labour.
6. Protection from inhuman treatment.
7. Protection from deprivation of property and compensation for loss suffered in the public interest.
8. Protection for privacy of home and other property.
9. Provisions to secure protection of law.
10. Protection of freedom of conscience.
11. Protection of freedom of expression.
12. Protection of freedom of assembly and association.
13. Protection from discrimination.
14. Enforcement of Protective Provisions.
15. Interpretation of Chapter 1.

Chapter II
THE PRESIDENT
16. Office of President.
17. Oath to be taken by the President.
18. Discharge of President's functions during vacancy.

Chapter III
PARLIAMENT
PART I — COMPOSITION OF PARLIAMENT

19. Establishment of Parliament.
20. Members of Parliament.
21. Qualifications for membership of Parliament.
22. Disqualifications for membership of Parliament.
23. The Speaker.
24. Deputy Speaker.
25. Voting at elections of Speaker and Deputy Speaker.
26. Tenure of seats of members of Parliament.
27. Electoral Commission.
28. Constituencies and elections.
29. Filling of vacancies.
30. Determination of questions as to membership of Parliament.
31. Clerk of Parliament and Staff.
32. Interpretation.